CIVIC REPUBLICANISM AND
THE PROPERTIES OF DEMOCRACY

CIVIC REPUBLICANISM AND THE PROPERTIES OF DEMOCRACY

A Case Study of Post-Socialist Political Theory

Erik J. Olsen

LEXINGTON BOOKS

A Division of
ROWMAN & LITTLEFIELD PUBLISHERS, INC.
Lanham • Boulder • New York • Toronto • Plymouth, UK

LEXINGTON BOOKS

A division of Rowman & Littlefield Publishers, Inc.
A wholly owned subsidary of The Rowman & Littlefield Publishing Group, Inc.
4501 Forbes Boulevard, Suite 200
Lanham, MD 20706

Estover Road
Plymouth PL6 7PY
United Kingdom

British Library Cataloguing in Publication Information Available

Library of Congress Cataloging-in-Publication Data

Olsen, Erik J., 1953–
  Civic republicanism and the properties of democracy : a case study of post-socialist
political theory / Erik J. Olsen.
    p. cm.
  Includes bibliographical references and index.
  ISBN-13: 978-0-7391-0890-1 (cloth : alk. paper)
  ISBN-10: 0-7391-0890-5 (cloth : alk. paper)
  ISBN-10: 978-0-7391-1309-7 (pbk. : alk. paper)
  ISBN-10: 0-7391-1309-7 (pbk. : alk. paper)
  1. Common good. 2. Civics. 3. Property. 4. Materialism. 5. Democracy. 6. Republicanism.
I. Title.
JC330.15.O58 2005
321.8'6—dc22   2005021549

Printed in the United States of America

♾ ™ The paper used in this publication meets the minimum requirements of American
National Standard for Information Sciences—Permanence of Paper for Printed Library
Materials, ANSI/NISO Z39.48–1992.

To the memory of J. K.,

father, mentor, kindred political spirit, and friend

Contents

The idea of property is rather like an iceberg. It is more complicated than it looks, and much of its significance is submerged.

Kenneth R. Minogue

Acknowledgments

THIS BOOK WAS MANY YEARS IN THE MAKING, and many people have helped along the way. I have an enormous debt to the teachers and advisers who worked with me when I was a graduate student at the University of Wisconsin, Madison, in the late 1980s. Booth Fowler sparked my interest in the subjects of civic republicanism and communitarianism, and guided me through the initial formulation of my arguments in my dissertation. Jim Farr opened my mind to the importance of history, not just in relation to the exploration of civic republicanism, but also in relation to political theory in general. Dirk Hartog was instrumental in getting me to investigate the historical connections between civic republicanism, property, and authority. And to Patrick Riley I owe much of my desire to approach political theory from a philosophical point of view. After graduate school, my thinking about civic republicanism and property began to move in different directions. My wife, Saroja Reddy, helped to make this transition less difficult through her patience and support, and by providing critical assistance in the clarification and refinement of my ideas and arguments. I am also greatly indebted to Dan Dombrowski of Seattle University for his encouragement, his willingness to read and comment on various drafts of things, and for countless conversations about liberalism and political theory. Ken Hoover of Western Washington University read portions of the manuscript, and as he has done for many years, provided invaluable feedback, advice, and assistance. I also owe special thanks to Eric Gorham of Loyola University New Orleans for all his help and encouragement through the years, and for his careful and insightful reading of the manuscript. The steadfast support of my editor, Robert Carley, made it possible to turn this project into a book. Josh Petersen helped me to work through issues of republican theory and historiography. Dean Peterson of Seattle University tried to educate me about matters of economics and helped me to see connections between my own work and economic history. Lara-Anne Jordan was a thoughtful reader of early drafts of several chapters. And Joey Cheatle provided assistance with some of the research.

I would be remiss if I did not mention all the friends and colleagues who, while not contributing directly to this book, provided the kind of supportive intellectual environment that is so important to scholarly inquiry. Thanks also to my students at Seattle University for making teaching such an enjoyable learning experience.

More than anyone else, my parents made this book possible. They gave me a loving family environment as well as a love of learning. I am profoundly grateful for having had a father who took the time to read and study my manuscript when his vision was failing, and when he was fighting a constant battle against discomfort and exhaustion. Last, and certainly not least, thanks to my daughter, Rekha. She cannot possibly imagine what joy she has brought to my life.

1

Introduction

THIS BOOK EXAMINES THE RELATIONSHIP BETWEEN PROPERTY, civic virtue, and democracy in post-socialist political thought. It is prompted by, and is a response to, a curious confluence of developments in contemporary political theory. As civic virtue has moved from the periphery to the center of theoretical discussions of democracy, property has gone in just the opposite direction.

The increased attention to the relationship between civic virtue and democracy is largely the result of the growth and influence of the episode of political theory that is variously described as "republicanism," "neorepublicanism," "communitarian republicanism," or (as I prefer) "civic republicanism." Civic republicanism is one of several theoretical visions of virtue and community that came to the fore in the 1980s. These visions were informed by a sweeping critique of liberal political thought. "Liberalism," in this context, refers not simply to left-leaning "welfare liberalism," but rather to the long and broad tradition of political philosophy that places the rights, interests, and choices of the individual at the center of theories of justice, obligation, and legitimate government authority. The "communitarian" critique of this tradition that emerged in the 1980s focused on what was said to be liberalism's deeply flawed conception of moral personality. By now, it is a very familiar argument in academic theoretical circles: The liberal self is a "socially disembodied" and "radically unencumbered" being who lacks meaningful communal attachments.[1]

Taking their theoretical bearings (and their name) from the classical tradition of civic humanist republicanism, civic republicans put forward a version of the communitarian critique of the liberal self that emphasized the threat to the public liberty of self-governing citizens. Liberalism, on the civic republican view, is marked by a pronounced tendency to view politics and public life as mere instruments for the furtherance of self-interest. Such a vision impoverishes and ultimately threatens democracy by validating forms of identity in which individuals have few (if any) civic attachments and lack norms of responsible civic engagement. In order to address and correct the corruptive influence of liberalism, civic republicans developed a wide-ranging project of civic recovery and renewal. In one form or another, and allowing for some changes over time, this project is one of revitalizing democracy in liberal capitalist societies such as the United States through the recovery of an ethos of public spirit and responsible citizenship.[2]

Perhaps the most striking feature of the "republican revival" is simply its sudden rise to theoretical prominence. In the first half of the 1970s—not that long ago when viewed from the longer perspective of the history of political theory—the idea of renewing liberal capitalist democracies through the recovery of a republican ethos of civic virtue would have been viewed by many, and probably most, political theorists and analysts as a somewhat peculiar project, and certainly as a project well outside of the theoretical and scholarly mainstream. Although some historians were in the process of tracing classical Greek and Roman idioms of virtue and corruption into the early modern era, these idioms were apt to sound archaic and more than slightly antiquarian to most political theorists. This was about to change, for after the publication of J. G. A. Pocock's *The Machiavellian Moment* in 1975, the republican revision in historiography hit full stride, and it became increasingly difficult for historians and political theorists alike to exclude classical republicanism from their narratives of the history of Western political thought. Where previous interpretations of classical republicanism focused on local episodes such as the American Revolution, Pocock claimed to have discovered a larger historical and theoretical "moment"—a moment of Renaissance civic humanism—which, on the one hand, looked back to and drew on ancient ideals of active citizenship and public service, and on the other hand, informed the great republican revolutions of the early modern era. In what Pocock saw as its paradigmatic Machiavellian formulation, this moment was associated with a theoretical structure in which a broadly Aristotelian view of civic virtue as an excellence and end of human development is recast as a capacity to master those historical circumstances which, if unmastered, would lead to the corruption and ultimately the collapse of republican liberty.[3]

It is no coincidence that the current revival of civic republicanism began to take shape a few years after the publication of *The Machiavellian Moment*. Indeed, few (if any) works of historical synthesis have exercised as much influence on political theory. But in the early 1970s, this "moment" of cross-fertilization between republican historiography and political theory had not yet arrived. As a term of theoretical discourse, "republicanism" was usually employed only in connection with very general notions of limited government and popular rule. A handful of political theorists had developed arguments around classical republican themes, the foremost example being Hannah Arendt. But while those familiar with Arendt's work often expressed admiration for her intellectual and theoretical abilities, this was seldom accompanied by an interest in exploring her republican theoretical agenda. Republican virtue, whether in Arendt's distinctive sense of excelling in a public realm of action or in the more usual sense of patriotic commitment to the common good, simply was not a high priority for most political theorists and analysts.[4] If discussed at all, the project of recovering any kind of republican politics of civic virtue was likely to be portrayed as the idiosyncratic and nostalgic project of thinkers possessed of an inordinately high regard for the political thought of Western antiquity.

There continue to be skeptics and critics, of course. However, what has changed, and dramatically so, is the amount of attention given to the project itself. In the hands of a new, and considerably larger group of political theorists and analysts, it has moved to the center of theoretical inquiry and intellectual debate and discussion. Civic republicanism is now a well-established theoretical perspective. Its imprint is seen in numerous areas, including the following: the emergence of virtue-centered forms of liberal theory, the rediscovery of civil society, the effort to outline and defend a deliberative form of democracy, the ongoing reexamination of Arendt's thought, the philosophical debate over the question of whether "teleological" conceptions of the human good or "deontological" conceptions of the right should have priority, the recovery of civic virtue as a norm of American constitutional law, and the reinvigoration of the project inaugurated by Leo Strauss of grounding Western liberal democracy in the Socratic quest for wisdom about the good life.[5] The influence of civic republican theory and historiography is even seen in the neoMarxian critique of globalization that is developed by Antonio Negri and Michael Hardt in their controversial book, *Empire*.[6]

What Robert Booth Fowler said about the republican revival back in 1991 is still true: "Ours is a time of vigorous health for the republican vision."[7] On the other hand, ours is a time of declining health for theoretical visions that focus on property. Recently, there have been some slight indications of renewed theoretical interest in property.[8] But looked at in relation to the entire field of political theory, the indications seem ever so slight. It is difficult to escape the conclusion that the primary interests of most political theorists lie elsewhere. It matters little whether the issues at stake involve the various developments associated with communitarianism and civic republicanism, postmodern deconstructions of "essentialist" and "foundationalist" thinking, explorations of cultural diversity and the politics of identity, the crisis of Western modernity, globalization, or even debates over distributive justice—in these areas and others, questions and issues of property are usually given scant and fleeting attention.

Though curious, this confluence of developments is hardly coincidental. To the contrary, the relationship between them is close to being an inverse one. Civic republicans and their allies often make their case for virtuous civic engagement at least partly by showing the bankruptcy of those theoretical and ideological perspectives that are mired in issues and concerns pertaining to property. It seems at times that the displacement of property in contemporary political theory is a matter of elevating communal virtue as property's replacement in the theoretical universe. We shall see that things are more complicated than this. Still, there is a pronounced tendency among civic republicans and other theorists of virtue, community, and civic engagement to be both morally and theoretically dismissive of property. As Ronald Terchek points out, one of the distinguishing features of civic republicanism and other forms of contemporary communitarianism is the "general neglect of property ownership." "Today," he writes, "most communitarians pass over the economic well-being of citizens and write as if a robust, coherent community is unrelated to the security of its citizens. When they look at private property, they see individualism, acquisitiveness, and materialism."[9] With respect to civic republicanism, the suggestion that there is no interest in the "security of its citizens" is overdrawn. There are also some important exceptions with regard to civic republican discussions of property that receive little or no attention in Terchek's account.[10] But his basic point is valid: Civic republicans and communitarians seldom discuss property, and when it is discussed it is almost always in connection with the corruptive forces and tendencies said to be at work in liberal capitalism.

The Contours of My Response

My response to these theoretical developments has three components, each of which is associated with a major thesis. First, there is a critical component involving the possibilities and problems of a civic republican vision of democracy. Property and the "general neglect" of it by civic republicans are at the heart of my critique. In this regard, the first and central thesis of this inquiry is that issues of property are more deeply, more complexly, and more problematically implicated in the sources and conditions of democracy than has been recognized to this point by civic republicans and like-minded theorists of civic engagement. This is partly a matter of arguing that any theory of democracy (or for that matter, justice, freedom, and equality) that seeks to be both comprehensive and practical needs to address issues of property in a systematic manner. But in the context of the present inquiry, it is also, more specifically, a matter of highlighting the question of how property and civic virtue are to be related to each other in a democratic republic, and challenging civic republicans to consider this question more thoroughly and critically than they have to this point. This means going beyond the issues associated with acquisitiveness and possessive individualism to consider the broader question of how property is to be understood, established, and arranged in a civic republican democracy. I hope to show that civic republicans have failed to provide a convincing and cohesive answer to this question, and furthermore, that this failure is indicative of substantial and serious problems in their project of recovery and renewal. Hence, the following corollary of my central thesis: Property is more deeply, more complexly, and more problematically implicated in the civic republicans' project of recovery and renewal than they have recognized.

It is not my intention to reverse the theoretical priorities of civic republicans so that property is once again privileged over civic virtue. While property is an important part of democratic theory, and while I believe that it is incumbent upon democratic theorists to show how and where property fits in, it is nonetheless only one part of a very rich and variegated field of inquiry and debate. Nor therefore do I wish to suggest that what civic republicans have said about civic virtue and democracy has theoretical value only when viewed through the lens of property issues. Qn the other hand, I *do* wish to suggest that there is something both significant and troubling about the confluence of the republican revival and the displacement of property in contemporary political theory.

This brings us to the second part of my response, which has to with the development of an interpretive framework within which to make some historical and theoretical sense of the relationship between the rise of civic republicanism and the displacement of property. I believe that part of the significance of this relationship has to do with the decline and delegitimation of the kinds of issues and issue frameworks that dominated political theory during the period of intense debate and conflict over socialism. Property issues were central to this debate and conflict, and in this respect, the displacement of property in contemporary political theory is a matter of property being dislodged from the central position it had when the socialist critique of capitalism was at the forefront of democratic theory. By the same token, the movement away from property can be seen as part of a historical movement away from socialism, at least with respect to its more conventional, collectivist forms and expressions. How far this movement away from socialism will go, whether conventional forms of socialist collectivism will ever make a comeback, and the extent to which socialism will be redefined in terms of new issue frameworks such as environmentalism—these are questions that are unlikely to be answered definitively in the foreseeable future, and about which I am not going to hazard any predictions. But what we can say with a fair degree of certainty is that the movement away from socialism in the last several decades has been accompanied by the emergence of new ways of thinking about politics. One of these new ways of thinking is what I am calling "post-socialist" political theory. I have in mind the emergence of virtue-centered forms of political theory that continue in the socialist tradition of being strongly critical of liberal capitalism while at the same time being strongly critical of the materialist vision of progressive liberation that has informed most modern expressions of socialist thought.

Post-socialists are not the only contemporary theorists who have moved away from property issues. The displacement of property is a broader phenomenon having to do with moral and philosophical opposition to materialism. However, post-socialism represents a kind of ideal-typical form of this broader reaction against modern materialism. For one thing, the post-socialist redescription of the problems of liberal capitalism in the idiom of virtue and corruption provides an especially telling example of this broader reaction. For civic republicans and other post-socialist thinkers, the primary goal is not to overcome economic exploitation and alienation through collective ownership and control of property, but rather to renew moral and civic life by overcoming the corruptive influence of materialism. In addition, post-socialist thinkers generally go farther in their opposition to materialism, and they are generally more systematic in their critique. For post-socialists, the issues at stake with both materialism and property are nothing less than the issues associated with modern Western (i.e., European and Euro-American) ideals of historical progress and progressive emancipation from suffering and oppression. Post-socialists are deeply skeptical of these ideals in both their liberal and leftist forms, and it is this skepticism about progressive modernity that informs and structures their generally dismissive, post-materialist perspective on property. I hasten to add that these ideals of progress and progressive emancipation are not completely absent from post-socialist theory. Indeed, I hope to show over the course of this inquiry that civic republicans and other post-socialists are more indebted to them than they imagine. Still, even moderate post-socialists see themselves as critics of the dominant assumptions and beliefs of progressive modernity. And from the post-socialist point of view, the philosophy and culture of materialism are deeply implicated in these assumptions and beliefs.

In sum, I wish to explore the juxtaposition of the "vigorous health" of civic virtue and the declining health of property in the larger context of the emergence and influence of the post-socialist critique of materialism. There is a post-socialist "logic" at work in this juxtaposition—a flawed logic in key respects, I am arguing, but a logic nevertheless. Property-based political theory is said to reflect a misguided and narrow materialism which, on the one hand, debases democracy, justice, and freedom by tying them too closely to improvements in the material conditions of life and, on the other hand, validates the pursuit of economic interests at the expense of moral and civic virtues.

This critique of modern materialism has been a hallmark of the republican revival from the outset. In what can now be recognized as the first full elaboration of the contemporary civic republican project of recovery and renewal, William Sullivan developed the case against "philosophic liberalism" along the following post-socialist lines: "Promoting freedom, that is, security and prosperity through economic calculation, promised to provide a safer basis for public peace and order than the dangerous passions of aristocratic honor, religious enthusiasm, or civic virtue. Yet the [liberal] pursuit of prosperity, the augmentation of what is one's own, not only dampens the dangerous ardor for glory; it also threatens the sinews of self-restraint and moral virtue."[11] According to Sullivan, the fundamental problem is that liberal views of morality and human nature are rooted in an "image of the individual working on nature" apart from social relationships and bonds. "From this first postulate comes the liberal emphasis upon freedom understood as security of possession. This security becomes possible, in the absence of interhuman ties, only on the basis of the control of material conditions . . . " "Civic republicanism," on the other hand, "denies the liberal notion that individuality exists outside of or prior to social relationships. Instead, the republican tradition has taught that there is an ineluctably participatory aspect to political understanding that develops only through the moral maturation of mutual responsibility." But to recover this civic republican vision, it is necessary to break free of the modern ideal of progress, for in both its liberal and its socialist expressions, this ideal is built around "the primacy of [economic] growth over justice, of the material over the spiritual."[12]

Here we see the post-materialist arguments and assumptions that give rise to the civic republicans' dismissive stance on property. The implication of Sullivan's argument is clear: Property is by its very nature an ever-present threat to virtue, community, and justice because it is the object of progressive modernity's relentless and corruptive pursuit of economic growth and material mastery. To put this in the Aristotelian idiom of the revival, to focus on property is to focus on merely instrumentally valuable "external goods" at the expense of those intrinsically valuable "goods of the soul" that require the cultivation of moral and civic excellences of character.[13]

Thus, my central thesis regarding the importance of property for democratic theory is directed at the civic republicans' post-materialist philosophical orientation. But we can also think of this in terms of a second critical thesis that considers civic republicanism as an example of post-socialist political theory. This second thesis goes like this: Civic republicans and other post-socialists have overreacted to the corruptive influence of modern materialism, and this has left them with inadequate theoretical accounts of both the perennial problem of oppressive economic power and the new problem of creating post-socialist institutions of property and political economy.

Of course, it is the civic republicans' overreaction to materialist excesses that most interests me, and it is their failure to address issues of democratic theory pertaining to property and political economy that will occupy most of my attention in this inquiry. It is my hope that my critique of civic republicanism will shed light on the possibilities and problems of post-socialist thought in general. But I say this fully aware of the need for caution in extending the conclusions I reach about civic republicanism to the broader category of post-socialist political theory.

The third and final component is one of theoretical construction and reconstruction in the areas of property and its relationship to democracy. The first two parts of my response revolve around issues of property and political economy that are either unaddressed or inadequately addressed by civic republicans and other post-socialist political theorists. But this last part is about building on what civic republicans have said about the background conditions of democratic citizenship. Although I hope to show that the introduction of property as a mediating term of analysis between civic virtue and democracy has unsettling implications for the civic republican project of cultivating the habits and dispositions of virtuous citizenship, I also hope to show that there is much to be learned about the properties of democracy by looking at the relationship between property and this "formative project."[14] Hence, the third major thesis of this inquiry: Civic republicanism provides conceptual tools with which to see aspects of property and its relationship to democracy that have been obscured or mystified in much modern political thought.

This thesis is not developed in isolation from the other two; rather, it is part of an inquiry into democracy that proceeds by moving dialectically between civic republicanism and property. Or what amounts to the same thing, my approach is one of "imminent" or "internal" criticism that seeks to illuminate the properties of both democracy and property by working within, and through, the terms of the contemporary civic republican project of recovery and renewal.

Obviously, I would not proceed in this manner if I did not think highly of the contributions that civic republicans have made to our understanding of democracy. Adapting a description of the republican tradition put forward by the civic republican legal theorist Frank Michelman, this study is undertaken in the belief that contemporary civic republicanism has considerable heuristic value as a "semantic field for normative debate and constructive imagination."[15] This is true even with respect to property, for while civic republicans generally have neglected issues pertaining to property, much of their theoretical perspective on democracy and civic identity is relevant to my own approach to property. For one thing, civic republican criticisms of acquisitiveness and possessive individualism open up the possibility for a reexamination of a traditional problem of republican theory having to do with the question of how to sustain the public liberty of self-governing citizens in the face of the corruptive power of commerce. I am calling this "the problem of a commercial republic." In addition, the civic republican understanding of the self as a "situated" being is at the very heart of my approach to property. By recasting the "situated self" as a concept pertaining to the relationship of the self to property arrangements, I shall attempt to illuminate a "locational" dimension of property alongside the more familiar dimension of rightful possession and ownership of things. To introduce terms of art that I will be using throughout this inquiry, a dimension of "placeness" is revealed alongside the more familiar dimension of "thingness." Property, on this reconceptualization, is (or can be) part of the ethical and civic situation of the self, and this placeness of property provides a theoretical framework within which to recover and reformulate connections between property, moral personality, and democratic citizenship.[16]

As sympathetic as I am to civic republicanism, and as much as I wish to build on their arguments and ideas, I am nonetheless a critic, and a liberal critic at that. As a liberal critic of civic republicanism, I believe that there are substantial gaps and blind spots in the "semantic field" established by contemporary republicans, and furthermore, that these gaps and blind spots are indicative of serious problems within their civic project. And it is in relation to these gaps and blind spots that property takes on importance in my critique of the civic republicans' post-socialist vision of democracy.

Some of the gaps and blind spots pertaining to property have to do with neglect of the role of liberalism in challenging property and wealth as bases of legitimate political authority. Nor is this just about liberalism. Rather, I hope to show that this is one of the ways that liberalism has fed into other traditions of modern Western political thought such as socialism. And this, I believe, is true not only of modern left-leaning reform liberalism, but also of classical liberalism of the type represented by John Locke. In fact, Locke emerges (or reemerges) in the pages that follow as something of a foundational figure in the development of modern progressive thinking about property and authority.

Equally important are the gaps and blind spots pertaining to traditional republican views of property. One problem is that most of today's republican
theorists have overstated the anti-commercialism of their own tradition.[17] But
aside from this, and more important to my critique, civic republicans have
been extremely reluctant to confront those traditional republican ideas of
property and civic virtue that run counter to modern democratic sensibilities
and commitments. Much traditional republican thinking about both property
and the problem of a commercial republic revolved around a vision of virtuous propertied independence in which the capacity for civic virtue was seen
as a function of being the independent master of a household estate.[18] The
roots of this "masters' vision of civic virtue" (as I am calling it) can be found
in the republics of ancient Greece and Rome, and because of this it evokes ancient slave economies. But as is detailed in chapter 5, the influence of this vision reached well past antiquity, and its modern—or more precisely, early
modern—reformulations were frequently accompanied by arguments against
slavery. It is, in fact, the reformulations that were accompanied by opposition
to slavery that I am most interested in, not, of course, because the link between
republicanism and slavery is insignificant, but because it is important to see
that the masters' vision of civic virtue is an example of a problem in republican thought that includes but also extends beyond the problem of slavery.
This broader problem is one in which civic capacity is developed through the
rule and guardianship of those adults deemed to be incapable of civic independence. I am calling this "the problem of republican paternalism."

The paternalistic aspects of the republican tradition are sometimes difficult
to see in the midst of rhetorical affirmations of political equality and popular
rule. This is one more reason for focusing on property, for property is associated with the kinds of background conditions and contexts within which paternalism lurks. However, the problem of republican paternalism is not confined to beliefs and arrangements pertaining to property. It is a larger
theoretical problem having to do with the potentially undemocratic consequences and conditions of the project of cultivating a capacity for civic virtue.
I hope to show that it is also an enduring problem for thinkers in the republican tradition, and especially for those such as contemporary civic republicans who seek to integrate republican ideals of virtuous independence into
modern democratic norms of equal citizenship.

If I am right about the persistence of the problem of republican paternalism, then there are good reasons to think that liberal critics of the republican
revival have been right to question whether civic republicanism is a worthy alternative to liberalism.[19] There would also be good reasons to doubt the argument that has been pressed recently (by Maurizio Viroli in particular) that the
reappropriation of early modern classical republicanism provides a way of re-

solving and overcoming the tensions and contradictions between liberalism and democratic theory.[20] For example, even if classical republicanism provides a way to bring together liberal commitments to the rule of law and limited government and democratic ideas of popular rule, there would still be the challenge of making sure that the paternalistic tendencies of republicanism do not undermine equal citizenship in either its liberal or its democratic forms.

Does the persistence of the problem of republican paternalism mean that the project of cultivating an ethos of responsible citizenship is antithetical to democracy? Not at all. It is both unnecessary and unwise to throw out the ideal of public spirit along with exclusionary and hierarchical forms of civic engagement. But the persistence of this problem *does* point to a vision of democracy and its properties that is both more pluralistic and more tragic than that put forward by civic republicans. It is more pluralistic in that it places greater emphasis on multiple forms and modes of civic identity and agency. It is more tragic in that it recognizes that the same conditions of civic virtue and pluralism that sustain democracy also threaten it, in no small part because they threaten each other. However, civic republicans also give us reasons to be cautiously hopeful, not just by reminding us that self-government has a nobility of purpose, but also by providing tools with which to open up new spaces and locations of citizenship, thereby creating spaces and locations with which to counter an increasingly hegemonic commercialism. This is the promise that is held out by the placeness of property.

Let me summarize the aims of this inquiry. By working within and through the terms of the contemporary civic republican project of civic recovery and renewal, I hope to be able to shed light on the background of conditions and understandings through which democratic practices are sustained. In particular, I hope to be able to shed light on those properties of democracy pertaining to property itself. Property, I believe, is deserving of far more attention than it has received in recent theoretical discussions and debates pertaining to civic virtue and democracy. In addition, issues of property provide a framework within which to explore and evaluate the growth of post-materialist and post-socialist forms of political thought. Finally, I wish to outline a democratic theory of property around the relationship between property's placeness and its thingness.

Changing the Terms of Discussion and Debate

The content, scope, and influence of the republican revival are (I trust) signs of a flourishing field of inquiry and debate. It is as a contribution to this field that this book is intended. However, I enter this field as someone who is not only a critic of civic republicanism, but also a critic of many of the terms in which civic republicanism has been debated. My emphasis on property is the chief example of this. I will have more to say about the role of property in my challenge to the prevailing terms of debate shortly. But before doing so, I want to call attention to two other areas where I am challenging these terms.

From Communitarianism to Post-Socialism

First, by developing my critique of civic republicanism as a case study of post-socialist thought, I am challenging the tendency to treat the debate over civic republicanism simply as an episode within the debate between communitarians and liberals. This does not mean that I am rejecting the "communitarianism versus liberalism" framework in its entirety. It has been a remarkably fecund theoretical "imaginary," and I will be drawing on it at numerous points, most especially in relation to questions involving the communal sources and contexts of moral and civic identity. Nevertheless, "communitarianism" is simultaneously too broad and too narrow as a descriptive rubric for civic republicanism, too broad in that it glosses over important differences between civic republicans and communitarians and too narrow in that it fails to capture the broader themes and tendencies of post-socialist thought and theory.

On my reading, civic republicanism is a distinctive episode that needs to be understood on its own terms. Civic republicanism and communitarianism are closely but often also uneasily related to one another. For one thing, civic republicans tend to be more moderate in their opposition to the liberal tradition than more purely communitarian theorists of virtue. True, there are some civic republicans who come across as unrelenting critics of liberalism (Michael Sandel and Ronald Beiner are cases in point), and liberalism is viewed by almost all civic republicans as a tradition that puts too much of a damper on democratic aspirations. Still, the goal for most civic republicans is not to supplant liberalism entirely, but to move beyond a narrow liberal individualism in order to redeem the democratic promise of liberal democracy. In addition, civic republicans are less interested in community for its own sake than in the renewal of a democratic community. To be sure, most expressions of civic republicanism posit a strong sense of community as an important condition and end of democratic politics. But even in these more purely communitarian forms of civic republicanism the critical focus is on the danger that liberal individualism poses to the communal conditions and contexts of public liberty and democratic citizenship. No wonder, then, that several leading figures in the revival have made a point of distancing their approach from communitarianism.[21]

But if we were to leave things here, we would not be able to account for what civic republicans and communitarians share at the level of broader themes and developments in social and political theory. What they share at this level is not just a general interest in community, but also a perspective— a post-socialist perspective—on liberal capitalism and the modern Western vision of progressive emancipation. Elaborating on what I said earlier, this perspective is informed, first, by the hope for moral and civic recovery in the face of the corruptive power of liberal capitalism, and second, by disillusionment with socialism and other modern visions of progressive emancipation. This combination of post-socialist hope and disillusionment is characteristic of several contemporary theoretical perspectives besides civic republicanism and communitarianism, including, among others, "neopopulism" of the type represented by Christopher Lasch, certain expressions of the "third way" alternative to collectivism and neoliberalism, the politics of caregiving within so-called "maternalist feminism," Cornel West's vision of a trans-racial "politics of conversion" in which downtrodden and marginalized groups are empowered through a "love ethic," several contemporary reformulations of participatory democracy, and some forms of "bioregionalist" environmentalism.[22]

All of these episodes are marked by disillusionment with conventional forms of socialism and leftist politics. However, it cannot be emphasized too much that these episodes also share a certain continuity with earlier socialist and leftist critiques of liberal capitalism. This continuity, I wish to suggest, is as important to post-socialist thought and politics as the emergence of new idioms and issue frameworks pertaining to virtue, community, and moral recovery. In this respect, my definition of "post-socialism" refers not to the end of leftist and left-leaning "progressive" impulses regarding the reform or transcendence of capitalism, but to their transformation and partial submergence in an era when socialism and related ideologies are in a state of decline and when the modern, Western ideals of progress and progressive emancipation have lost much of their luster for a substantial sector of the intellectual community.

New Issues of Democratic Theory

My challenge to the terms of discussion and debate also involves some changes of orientation in matters of democratic theory. For civic republicans, the central issues of democratic theory revolve around the habits and dispositions of responsible citizenship that sustain practices of public liberty and collective self-government. These issues are important to me as well. But by emphasizing the problem of republican paternalism as an ongoing problem within a politics of civic virtue, I wish to argue that civic republicans have not succeeded in explicating the conditions under which the shared practice of self-government becomes democratic as well as republican. That democracy involves collective self-government seems indisputable. This is one of the few constants in the conceptual universe of democratic theory. So civic republicans are right to talk about democratic renewal in terms of strengthening shared practices and norms of citizen self-rule. The problem is that the idea of collective self-government also has a long history of being associated with forms of popular governance that are republican, but not democratic in any meaningful sense of the word. The difference, at least as it has come to be understood in the modern era, has to do with what Robert Dahl calls the "problem of inclusion," by which he means the problem of determining which "persons have a rightful claim to be included in the demos."[23] For all the diversity of modern democratic beliefs and practices, there is nevertheless a well-established norm of equal inclusion that says that collective self-government does not and cannot reach the level of democracy unless all or nearly all adult members of the political community are included on roughly equal terms in the community's practices of collective decision-making. Unless and until some such norm of equal inclusion is part of the political culture of a self-governing community, we cannot be sure that democracy will result from renewed attention to shared beliefs and practices, the reappropriation of idioms of civic virtue and public-spirited participation, or the adoption of a more deliberative mode of collective decision-making. Such things may sometimes promote democratic terms of equal inclusion; they may even be necessary conditions for the achievement of a robust democracy. But the history of republican political theory provides ample evidence that they are not sufficient conditions for even a minimally democratic form of collective self-government. By the same token, it is easy to imagine a form of collective self-government that does not satisfy modern democratic standards for inclusion even while it approaches a robust democracy in other respects. This possibility is as old as ancient Athenian democracy.[24]

Thus, issues of political equality and inclusion are central to my critique of civic republicanism. In making these issues a priority, I do not mean to suggest that civic republicans have failed to affirm the principle of equal and inclusive citizenship. On the contrary, civic republicans have made their commitment to equality quite clear. What is not clear is how they expect to ensure that their politics of virtuous civic liberty will have equal and inclusive terms of citizenship.

If we qualify "community" as a "formative civic community," what Fowler has said about contemporary communitarian views of equality in general could be said of civic republican views in particular: "Community is often taken to imply equality without question." Like Fowler, I believe that the "pervasive and usually uncontested premise" of equality "demands more argument than it gets."[25] Yet it is not just civic republicans and their communitarian allies who have been cursory and superficial in their treatment of the issues associated with equal and inclusive citizenship. Such issues have received surprisingly little attention from the critics of civic republicanism. For the most part, critics have been content to conduct the debate on the terms established by the civic republicans themselves. As a result, there has been a considerable amount of arguing back and forth about liberty and democracy, particularly with respect to the theories of moral personality and practical reason that are associated with different conceptions of liberty. True, there also has been some debate over the compatibility of a politics of civic virtue with democratic understandings of equal citizenship. However, this debate usually has lacked the depth and sophistication of the debate over liberty, often amounting to little more than an exchange between critics who cite the exclusionary and hierarchical features of traditional republican thought and civic republicans who proceed to acknowledge this darker side of their tradition while also affirming their own commitment to modern democratic norms of equal and inclusive citizenship. Naturally, I think that the critics are right to be concerned, but there is much more to be said about the matter as a theoretical problem.

There is also much more to be said about another area of democratic theory. This is the area of authority. Much of the motivation for my interest in authority has to do with its long historical association with property. This is seen, for example, in the complicated relationship between ownership and jurisdiction in Western history. But authority is also deserving of attention apart from its relationship to property. As a concept concerning normative claims about the propriety or impropriety of relations of ruling and being ruled, "authority" provides a crucial link between perennial issues of power and the civic republican project of cultivating a capacity for virtuous self-government. Despite this, issues of authority have been treated even more superficially than the issues of equal and inclusive citizenship.[26]

To be sure, both civic republicans and their critics have evoked traditional themes and issues pertaining to the perennial controversy concerning the degree to which democracy is undermined by forms of concentrated power. These traditional themes and issues are also at stake in my own exploration of democracy and authority. To this extent, my emphasis on authority is simply a variation of traditional issues of democratic theory relating to the distribution of power. The relationship between authority and power also connects this inquiry to the early modern republican understanding of "dominion" as a form of potentially dominating control and rule.[27] Nevertheless, there are good reasons to focus on authority along with dominion and power. The capacity for virtuous self-rule is not completely reducible to abilities to control, influence, or dominate other people (though the fostering of such abilities *is* one of the key issues at stake in my critique). Rather, we are also dealing with the capacity (or purported capacity) of citizens to govern themselves in ways that are both morally and politically authoritative. Some such notion of a capacity for authoritative self-rule is found in expressions of contemporary civic republicanism. And in all cases, we are confronted with the questions of whether and how the cultivation of a ₁capacity for authoritative self-rule is related to the "formative" experience of ruling over non-citizens and second-class citizens.

The Priority of Property

In effect, this inquiry represents an attempt to provide a systematic theoretical explanation of the tensions between the civic republicans' post-socialist vision of politics and democratic norms and understandings of liberty, equality, and authority. But in all of these areas, we always come back to property, for it is with a very definite focus on property that I am investigating these tensions. That is to say, I am recasting the relationship between civic virtue and the properties of democracy as a question having to do with property itself. While civic republicanism is the subject matter and the critical focus of my case study, property is the conceptual and theoretical thread that connects the different parts of this inquiry together. This does not mean that the developments which prompt this inquiry are simply points of departure for a disquisition on property. Property is one of several destinations in this journey; or more precisely, property is both a destination and a point of departure for other destinations. It is a destination in that one of my aims is to move towards a democratic theory of property based on the relationship between thingness and placeness. It is a point of departure in two respects: first, because my analysis of property and its displacement in contemporary political theory sets my critique of the civic republicans' post-socialist project of civic recovery and renewal in motion; and second, because the relationship between property and civic virtue provides the framework within which I am investigating the properties of democracy.

It is, then, in relation to property that my departure from the prevailing terms for discussing and debating civic republicanism is greatest. This is due in large part to the fact that my perspective on thingness and placeness is at odds with the more conventional understandings of property that are held by both civic republicans and their critics. But in the first instance, it is simply a matter of giving property far more attention than it has received in the debates and discussions revolving around civic republicanism.

Civic Republicanism, Liberalism, and the Neglect of Property

It cannot be emphasized too much that inattention to issues of property is characteristic of both civic republicans and their critics. Recall Terchek's observation about the "general neglect of property ownership" by civic republicans and communitarians. In truth, Terchek could just as easily have called attention to "the general neglect of property ownership" by the theorists and analysts who have engaged civic republicans in debate. Most striking in this regard is the degree to which property has been marginalized by the very same non-libertarian, left-leaning reform liberals who have been the object of so much civic republican and communitarian criticism. (I make a point of limiting this to non-libertarian reform liberals because the defense of private property is of course the hallmark of the libertarian, free-market capitalist branch of liberalism.) Terchek himself is something of an exception. He is one of the very few theorists participating in the debate to discuss classical republican views of property. He also makes a point (with good reason, in my view) of criticizing contemporary republicans for failing to follow the lead of many of their classical republican predecessors in seeking to give citizens stakes in society. But even Terchek abandons property in the end, concluding that it has little relevance to the theory and practice of democracy in a "postindustrial world."[28]

When left liberals have engaged civic republicans on issues of property, it often has been in response to civic republican charges about the role of liberalism in unleashing and validating corruptive forms of self-interested acquisitiveness and commercialism. Liberals are apt to complain that civic republicans have exaggerated the importance and influence of such property-related beliefs and values in the liberal tradition. For example, Thomas Spragens has complained that the "near-exclusive focus" of civic republicans on "the question of the relationship between private commerce and public good" has led them to exaggerate the differences between the republican and liberal traditions.[29] As a matter of historical interpretation, I think that Spragens has a point. In the meantime, however, both civic republicans and liberals have begged the question of how property is implicated in the other issues that have preoccupied them, namely, issues pertaining to the sources of moral identity and agency, the nature of practical reason, the relationship between the right and the good, and the "proceduralist" ideal of a morally neutral state. It is precisely in relation to issues such as these that I am arguing that property is more deeply, more complexly, and more problematically implicated in democracy than has been recognized by civic republicans. And we can now amend this in the form of another corollary to my central thesis: Property, I am arguing, is more deeply, more complexly, and more problematically implicated in the debate over civic republicanism than either civic republicans or their critics have recognized.

It is tempting to explain the increasingly marginal role of property in contemporary left liberalism in terms of the fact that liberals have turned their attention from issues of property to the issues that have been raised by civic republicans and communitarians. This perhaps is one reason that Terchek did not extend his argument beyond communitarianism to liberalism. But while the influence of communitarianism and civic republicanism is undoubtedly an important part of the explanation, it cannot be all of it if for no other reason than that the decline of liberal interest in property issues preceded the civic republican and communitarian revivals. Both of these revivals took shape in the early 1980s, and certainly no earlier than the end of the 1970s. But there were clear signs in the early 1970s (and probably earlier) that property issues were being relegated to the margins of liberal theory.

Rawls's reformulation of liberal social contract theory in *A Theory of Justice* is an instructive case in point. First published in 1971, no work of contemporary liberal theory has provided more grist for the mills of civic republican and communitarian criticism of liberal "individualism, acquisitiveness, and materialism" than has *A Theory of Justice*. Because of this, because of the importance of property in the tradition of liberal social contract theory, and especially because *A Theory of Justice* is centrally concerned with questions of distributive justice, someone reading it for the first time would naturally expect to find a substantial amount of analysis of issues of property. What she would find, however, is that while issues of property are often evoked, they are rarely discussed directly and explicitly, let alone systematically. As Thomas Grey pointed out several years ago in relation to *A Theory of Justice*, "The concept of property rights plays only the most minor role in that monumental treatise."[30] Nor is *A Theory of Justice* an exception in terms of the development of Rawls's work. If anything, for example, property has an even smaller role in *Political Liberalism*.

We are led to the irony that civic republicans and contemporary left liberals such as Rawls are more alike than unalike in their approaches to property. Often echoing and evoking C. B. Macpherson's classic critique of liberalism as a tradition of "possessive individualism," civic republicans (and post-socialists in general) seek to draw a sharp contrast between their own perspective and what one civic republican refers to as "the liberal theme of 'pursuit of property.'"[31] But while contemporary left liberals tend to be more accepting of private property rights than their civic republican critics, they are also apt to evince the same kind of theoretically detached and morally dismissive attitude towards property.

The Enduring Importance of Property: A Radical Perspective

I can imagine some readers scratching their heads and wondering why any of this matters. Why does it matter whether property has played a marginal role in the debate over civic republicanism? Why is property such an important subject of democratic theory? I can also imagine this perplexity being put more pointedly in the form of a question about the relevance of property at a time when the leading alternatives to capitalist property arrangements have been revealed as either morally and politically bankrupt (as with statist collectivism) or as inadequate to the task of social and political transformation in the era of global capitalism (as with cooperative economic arrangements). These are apt questions, but also questions that I cannot even begin to answer adequately until I have developed my critique of civic republicanism and the accompanying analysis and argumentation pertaining to the constellation of relationships between property, civic virtue, and democracy. But what I can do is explain the reasons why I think that property remains an important subject for democratic theorists.

There are three reasons for making property a theoretical priority. The first one is simply that it makes good theoretical sense to inquire into the question of the ideas and arrangements of property that are supportive of democratic norms and aspirations. This is basically a matter of recognizing the importance of property as an institution of political economy—in any political system, let alone in a democratic one. From time to time, the argument is made that property has lost its coherence under conditions of advanced capitalism. I will be considering this argument in chapter 7. Suffice it to say for now that the coherence of property is one thing, its persistence into and through the era of advanced capitalism quite another. Coherent or not, the fact is that in one form or another property endures, and has endured, in a wide variety of politico-economic systems. And certainly at this point in history, it is hard to imagine a system in which some substantial portion of economic resources is not organized and allocated in relation to some kind of framework of property rights, claims, and interests. In fact, the spread of global capitalism is apt to make property more important as a framework within which to organize economic resources and assets.[32] By the same token, it is hard to imagine a system in which property does not provide an important institutional link between economy and polity, between processes of resource allocation and structures of authority.

It seems likely, then, that property is going to be an important part of the mix of political-economic institutions in democratic systems for the foreseeable future. To assume otherwise is to pursue a strategy of transcending property which, at best, is naively utopian and, at worst, leaves the field of property to those who either care too little for democracy or are insufficiently wary of economistic modes of thought and practice.

Recognizing the importance of property as an institution is not simply a matter of being sensitive to practical questions concerning the possibilities and problems associated with different arrangements and programs of political economy. Practicality *is* at stake here, and it is partly because of this that I have set for myself the goal of moving towards a democratic theory of property. But practicality in the context of this inquiry is not merely about things that work or are useful; it is a theoretical practicality that most interests and concerns me, a practicality in the sense of theoretical awareness of the beliefs and conditions that make democratic ideals and aspirations achievable. This is essentially a hermeneutic perspective on practicality, and my second reason for emphasizing property is its importance for the hermeneutic purpose of illuminating the "lifeworld" of democracy, that is, the background of implicit understandings that inform democratic practices and help to constitute the social and economic conditions necessary for the realization of these practices. This requires a longer explanation than the first reason.

Hermeneutics is about how we interpret things—texts, theories, language, and the world in general. In the most influential of modern philosophical formulations of hermeneutics, an interpretive engagement is characterized as something that occurs within standpoints or "horizons" of meaning and language.[33] Meaning therefore is contextual, and this is so in two ways: first, by virtue of being embedded within language and discursive practices, and second, by virtue of the fact that it develops within and through history. Hermeneutics of this type, therefore, looks simultaneously to the present and the past, or rather, the "horizonal" background of the present is seen as being conditioned by the past. Just how much the past conditions, or should condition, the present is an ongoing question for "hermeneuticists." We shall see, for example, that my own hermeneutic perspective is considerably less traditionalist than that of most civic republicans and communitarians. Right now, though, the key point is that my approach to property is one that seeks to elucidate the horizon of democracy by showing how it has developed in relation to different assumptions and beliefs about property.

At first glance, property seems to hold little promise as a subject of hermeneutic inquiry. For that matter, hermeneutics seems to have quite a bit in common with the very same post-materialist philosophical orientation that I am calling into question. In any case, property seems to fit oddly with hermeneutic notions of context, meaning, language, and interpretation. Yet the oddness of the fit can also be seen as a clue to how narrowly property has come to be viewed in the horizon of Western democracy, and how comfortable we have become with this narrow view of property. The universe of theoretical issues and conceptual possibilities expands considerably and sometimes unpredictably once property is recast along hermeneutic lines as a linguistically constituted context of meaning and interpretation. Such a contextual approach even unsettles the underlying "ontological" structure of property by revealing the "locational" dimension that marks property's placeness.

For many, talk of the narrowness of prevailing views of property is likely to evoke thoughts of the dominance of the commodity form of property under conditions of advanced global capitalism. But this is not quite what I have in mind; or rather, what I hope to do through my hermeneutic approach is uncover the background of preconceptions and implicit understandings of property and citizenship out of which, and against which, the commodification and commercialization of property emerged. Insofar as this may be seen as an attempt to get at the root of commodification in Western liberal democracy, and insofar as attempting to get at the root of something may be described as "radical," it may be said that I wish to develop a radical perspective on property.

I believe that the root of the commodity form of property, and the deeper source of narrow thinking about property, is simply the belief that property is, at its core and in its entirety, about the possession, ownership, use, and exchange of things, or (as the lawyers would remind us) the *right* to possess, own, use, or exchange things. This is a view that emphasizes the "thingness" of property. In describing an emphasis on "thingness" as narrow, I do not mean to deny that "thingness" is, and always has been, an important part of property. Nor do I wish to deny that "thingness" has taken, or can take, very different forms, depending on the theoretical and cultural beliefs and practices through which it is expressed and defined. What is of interest and concern to me is a particular form of thingness that has grown up with liberal capitalism, and that seems to be well on its way to becoming the predominant understanding of property around the world (if it is not already). I have in mind a form of thingness that is marked not only by extensive commodification but also by a pronounced tendency to occlude any deeply constitutive conceptual connection between property and political authority. Property, in this modern framework, is presumed to be about private rights to control things while political authority is public and is about the governance or control of people. For convenience (although at some risk of oversimplification) I will call this framework "modern thingness."

Although modern thingness reflects a narrow view of property, this should not be taken as evidence of rigidity or inflexibility. To the contrary, it can quite plausibly be argued that modern thingness has become a hegemonic system of property partly because it has been very adaptable and flexible. For instance, the regime of modern thingness has been quite capable of accommodating and assimilating the forms of "intangible" property (e.g., stocks, insurance, and patents) that have become important in late modern capitalism.

Viewed exclusively in terms of its close association with the modern system of commodity production and exchange, modern thingness might understandably appear to have importance for democratic theory only with respect

to the dangers of corruption and inequality that accompany self-interested acquisitiveness. This is the prevailing view of modern property in the texts of the
republican revival and post-socialism in general (that is, when property is discussed at all). This perspective is not so much wrong as it is one-sided, and the
primary reason is that it does not account for the relationship between property and political authority.

Within modern thingness, property and political authority might be seen
as related, but only contingently and indirectly. Property (as measured, say, in
levels of wealth or income) might be seen as being empirically correlated with
the authority (or power) of different families, groups, or classes. It might even
be seen as being conceptually related to authority in the sense that a system of
property functions, as a system of control over people. But property and authority are ultimately distinct entities in this view, and if property functions
as a system of authority, it does so indirectly, not as a system that is immediately and directly about control over both people and things, and certainly not
as a system of authority that is grounded in having property in people. Thus,
this modern form of thingness lacks the kind of direct or seamless conceptual
relationship between property and political authority that one finds, for instance, in traditional notions of *dominium*, which by definition involved both
ruling and ownership. In a Western context, the most visible example of such
an intermingling of ownership and rulership is probably that of feudalism.
The eminent English historian Frederic Maitland was so struck by English
feudalism's intermingling of a private sphere of property with a public sphere
of authority that it became his primary point of reference in contrasting feudal law with modern law. Thus, in their seminal history of English law, Maitland and Frederick Pollock defined feudalism in terms of "a denial" of the
modern distinction between private and public law. "Just in so far as the ideal
of feudalism is perfectly realized," they went on to say, "all that we call public
law is merged into private law: jurisdiction is property, office is property, the
kingship itself is property; the same word *dominium* has to stand now for
ownership and now for *lordship*."[34]

The example of feudalism also serves as a reminder that opposition to traditional and traditionally hierarchical and exclusionary understandings of
property and authority has been crucial to the development of norms of equal
and inclusive citizenship, and therefore crucial also to understanding the horizon of democratic citizenship. That is to say, while the shift from such traditional notions of property and authority is an important source of the narrowness of modern thingness, it is also an important source of the modern
horizon of democratic citizenship. With this shift, and because of it, democracy comes to be defined in part by a normative structure that affirms conditions of non-domination, independence, and political equality while also de-

claring it illegitimate to defend political authority as a direct and immediate entailment of wealth and property. As such, this normative structure provides some fairly specific content to a broader and looser structure of democratic skepticism and suspicion concerning paternalistic forms of rule and guardianship.

The story of how Western democracy emerged out of, and against, the feudal framework of property and authority is a long and complicated one. Fortunately, however, it is enough for the critical and theoretical purposes of the present study that we have this story in mind, or more specifically, that we have in mind the connection between democracy and the norms and beliefs through which opposition to the intermingling of ownership and lordship has been expressed. The feudal form of this intermingling is distinctive by virtue of its erasure, or at least blurring, of the differences between private and public authority. But it is not the only example of a tradition in which property and authority are closely related. Neither is it the only tradition against which the emergence of modern democratic ideals and norms of equal citizenship can be measured. Given my interest in responding to civic republicanism, the most important historical illustrations of the emergence of these ideals and norms come from the republican and liberal traditions, not from feudalism. But the larger theoretical point that I will be pressing is that a hermeneutic perspective on property and citizenship reveals to us a kind of "oppositionist moment" in the development of the democratic horizon of property and citizenship, a moment in which democratic ideals are envisioned, institutionalized, and affirmed by challenging conceptual linkages between property and authority of the type found in Western feudalism.

I hope to show that this modern moment of opposition to the premodern conflation of property and authority has been very important in establishing democratic norms of liberty and equal citizenship. However, mine is not a Whig story of steadily unfolding progress, but rather one of the decidedly mixed legacy of Western modernity's confrontation with the premodern horizon of property. Or what amounts to the same thing, mine is a story of the mixed legacy of modern thingness.

What I am suggesting is that the same modern challenges to the conflation of property and authority that were instrumental in carving out a more inclusive space of democratic citizenship also helped to give birth to the excessively narrow understanding of property that is modern thingness. By itself, this might not sound like much of a problem. After all, a narrow view of property would seem to be a small price to pay for democracy. Even when the costs of economic inequality and the corruptive power of acquisitiveness are factored in, a case could be made that the gain in democratic practices makes the price worth paying. Unfortunately, modern thingness can be, and has been, a barrier

to a fuller realization of democracy even without accounting for these costs—
in other words, even when the focus is only on the relationship between property and authority. My argument in this regard is in many respects a restatement of the standard leftist critique of the tendency within liberal capitalism to
obscure and mystify the relationship between the purportedly "private sphere"
of property and the "public sphere" of political power and authority.[35] In my
restatement, this tendency has to do with treating the conceptual separation of
property and authority within modern thingness as if it were a true, empirical
description of the world. The logic of this (such as it is) goes something like
this: "Property is one thing, authority quite another, and just because *A* has
control of a lot of property, there is no reason to think that *A* is necessarily in
a privileged position to control or dominate other people. After all, the people
that *A* wants to control are free to do something else and go somewhere else,
free also to try to make their own fortunes. And besides, *A* is not threatening
democracy so long as he does not lay claim to public authority simply on the
basis of his private property. In a democracy, it is up to the people to say
whether the *A*'s of the world should be able to rule them." Through this kind
of thinking, the oppositionist norm establishing the illegitimacy of converting
property into political authority is itself illegitimately converted into an ex-
planatory principle for describing and defending unequal relations of power
and authority. The economic bases of democratic citizenship and political authority are driven underground. As a result, equal citizenship is more likely to
be defined as a formal equality of legal rights, with little interest in, or concern
about, the ways in which economic inequality undermines democratic norms
and ideals of liberty and equal citizenship.

   All of this points to the kind of paradoxical and tragic view of the properties of democracy that I mentioned earlier. That is to say, part of what I believe
is revealed by a hermeneutic approach to property and citizenship is the paradox that many of the same background conditions and understandings that
sustain democracy also threaten it. But this is not a study in the hopelessness
of democracy, and my hermeneutic approach is as much about uncovering
new possibilities as recognizing limits. This brings us to the third reason for
emphasizing property, which is precisely the possibility at this historical juncture of developing new ways of thinking about property and its relationship
to democracy. Because property has been displaced from the central position
it had during the era when theoretical debate was dominated by the conflict
between collectivism and capitalism, issues of property can also provide a
conceptual field that unsettles new habits of thinking about democracy that
have started to form in the time since that era. In no small part, this is because
it is now possible to free our thinking about property from the theoretical and
ideological dogmatism into which discussions of property often descended

during the twentieth-century debate over collectivism. In a sense, this was a debate over the "who" of property: Who should own and control the means of production? Should the public be the proprietor of property? The state? Or private individuals and firms? And what is the proper balance between these different proprietary claims? These were important questions, and in one form or another, they are likely to remain important for the foreseeable future. But in the debate over collectivism these questions often had a curiously abstract and impersonal quality with regard to the connections between property and ideals such as freedom, justice, and democracy. I believe that this is at least partly the result of the fact that this debate proceeded on the basis of an unspoken agreement that the essential nature of property has to do with its thingness. Clearly, this agreement did not extend so far that collectivists endorsed the commodity form of property that has grown up with modern thingness. But as Alan Ryan reminds us, "It is obvious enough that socialism as practised has universally required some sort of public ownership in a form familiar from the context of private ownership. That is, officials and administrators have legally guaranteed rights to control and dispose of assets held in freehold by the state, or by some entity constituted by legislative action."[36] In other words, the basic structure of property as an object of rightful acquisition, possession, and even exchange was presupposed in modern collectivist thinking about common ownership, and to this extent anyway, it can be said that the debate over collectivism was conducted largely within the narrow framework of modern thingness.

In sum, the intense conflict over the "who" masked a common perspective on the "what" of property. So perhaps now we can reconsider the "who" and the "what" questions in light of the "where" of property—its placeness. Perhaps now we can recover a sense of the importance of the various ends and purposes of property. Perhaps also we can redescribe these ends and purposes in relation to the physical and social locations of democratic citizens.

Beyond Modern Thingness

Thus, my challenge to the terms in which property has been discussed in the debate over civic republicanism is part of a broader challenge to the terms of modern thingness. Which is also to say that it is especially in relation to the recovery and illumination of the placeness of property that I hope to chart new theoretical ground pertaining to property and democracy. Property objects exist somewhere in physical and social space, and I hope to show that the contextual "where" of property is occluded in modern thingness. Again, this is not a simple matter of rejecting thingness. Property, in my reconceptualization, is always/already about both thingness and placeness. Hence, the conceptual structure that I hope to reveal through my hermeneutics of property involves an underlying relationship between the "what" and the "where" of property, between objects of rightful possession, ownership, and exchange and the various social and institutional contexts in which they are located. This involves a large number of places of property, including households and homes, workplaces and places of business, farms, libraries, hospitals, museums, schools, the marketplace itself, and these days, many of the "virtual" places of cyberspace.

From the perspective of the law of modern thingness, this attempt to conceptualize property in terms of its locations might very well look like a serious blunder, and an obvious one at that. For some very understandable reasons, modern lawyers like to point out that, legally, property is not something that is inherent in material objects or in the physical dimensions of real property such as land. Such physicalist notions of property are common among ordinary people, they acknowledge, but they have no validity in the law. Property, from a modern lawyer's perspective, is about rights to things and the different legal processes and conditions that accompany these rights. So even real property in land has nothing to do with the physical location of the land. Rather, legal claims to land revolve around things like the number of owners, the conditions of tenure, and most of all, the "duration" of the estate (e.g., whether the tenure is hereditary, for life, or for some term of years). As the authors of one property law casebook put it: "A layperson's tendency is to define real property by its physical dimensions—its place in space. But the lawyer's 'estates' identify duration."[37]

In truth, I think that the "layperson's" perspective is deserving of more consideration than most modern legal scholars give it. For one thing, there is an important physical dimension to both thingness and placeness. For instance, the various places of property in the above list have in common a certain rootedness in physical space. The "layperson" whose illusions contemporary legal scholars love to expose is actually right to call attention to this dimension. Whereas the estate in late modern law exists as a conceptual abstraction that persists through time to varying degrees, in the layperson's experience it is usually a particular place that is inhabited by someone, even if that someone is not the owner. As Jeremy Waldron has pointed out in connection to his defense of the right of the homeless to have access to property, "Everything that is done has to be done somewhere. No one is free to perform an action unless there is somewhere he is free to perform it."[38]

The physical dimensions and locations of property are important for environmental reasons as well. The modern lawyer's perspective on property results in the abstraction of property from its ecological connections to the natural world, and in this respect, the modern lawyer is following the dubious lead of the economist who has similarly abstracted economic value from the natural world.[39]

But the point of putting forward the idea of property as a relationship between thingness and placeness is not simply to affirm the layperson's view of property. What I am really trying to get at, and illuminate, is the ontological structure of property as a rightful possession and ownership of things that necessarily occurs somewhere in both physical *and* social space. Although lawyers are apt to recognize placeness as a kind of sociological fact, they do not integrate placeness into the conceptual framework of the law of property. In other words, the deeper ontological structure of placeness tends to get lost in the legal universe of modern thingness.

On the other hand, the lawyers are right to remind us that material objects and physical places only become property by virtue of the discourses and concepts through which property claims are defined, constituted, and contested. From a hermeneutic perspective, physical objects and locations have meaning only in and through cultural horizons of understanding. Certainly, this is true of a social institution such as property. Property does not grow on trees; it grows in human communities and is defined and constituted through the discursive practices and traditions of these communities.

Thus, property locations such as homes, workplaces, and libraries are constituted less by rootedness in physical space than by rootedness within various locational contexts of economic, social, and political life. There are many such contexts, and many different possible ways of categorizing and classifying them. However, there are three groups or categories of such property-related locational contexts that are of special significance to my analysis: first, contexts of labor, work, and skill; second, contexts of dominion, jurisdiction, and authority; and third, the various arrangements, beliefs, and norms about social status, class, and political membership that establish political and civic identity. For convenience, these will often be abbreviated to labor, authority, and civic identity.

Of course, I am not the first theorist to argue for a contextual approach to property. Nor am I the only contemporary theorist to challenge the narrow framework of modern thingness. In fact, recent years have seen a small but steady stream of scholarly efforts to articulate and defend a liberal democratic system of property on normative grounds that are broader than, and sometimes at odds with, the norms associated with private, "negative" rights of proprietary control and market exchange. Some of these efforts have focused on problematizing and demystifying what Joseph Singer calls the "ownership model" of property. By this, he means the model in which the rights of private ownership are taken as the essence of property, and then normatively privileged at the expense of all the other social interests, relationships, and obligations that are associated with property.[40] As an alternative to the ownership model, Singer outlines an "entitlement model." This model seeks to account for the social and contextual aspects of property that are left out of the ownership model. Private ownership still receives protection, but with the understanding that it will "be secure in certain ways and defeasible in others."[41] Like all other property rights and rules, ownership is part of an ongoing process of social construction and reconstruction.

In a related manner, Liam Murphy and Thomas Nagel seek to debunk "the myth of ownership" in contemporary debates about taxation and justice. Focusing on the social and conventional nature of property, they develop the cogent argument that the justice or injustice of the tax system "cannot be evaluated by looking at its impact on private property, conceived as something that has independent existence and validity."[42]

Other recent challenges to modern thingness have emphasized its neglect of property's potential as a formative context of moral and civic personality. Margaret Radin has tried to carve out a non-commercial space of private property in which certain property objects are given special recognition and protection by virtue of being constitutive and expressive of personhood.[43] Frank Michelman's attempt to reappropriate the classical republican ideal of propertied independence for purposes of democratic citizenship represents an important exception not only to the rule of contemporary civic republican neglect of property, but also to the anti-liberal tendencies within civic republican thinking about property.[44] And to provide one more example, Waldron has defended a version of the Hegelian argument that individuals have a right to private property because it is one of "the conditions necessary for the full development of their autonomy, their ethical personality, and their capacity for responsible agency."[45] In Waldron's version, private property is a "general right" for all adult citizens rather than a "special right" granted to select individuals who meet specific requirements for the creation or transfer of ownership rights. As he puts it, a "general right" to private property exists "independently of the contingent events and transactions in which [the rights-bearer] is involved."[46]

These alternative theoretical perspectives on property provide a much richer conceptual and normative universe than that delineated through the dominant discourses of modern thingness. But while they sometimes hint at a locational dimension of property, they never directly or systematically question the idea that property is essentially, fundamentally about thingness. Within these perspectives, social contexts and norms surround thingness, but mainly as countervailing ideas rather than as inherent aspects of property that are partly constitutive of its meaning. When we treat these social contexts and norms as inherent and constitutive aspects of property, then property is no longer simply about relationships between people and things. It also about the purposes and practices of the property-related institutional locations that people inhabit.

Ironically, the theorist whose thinking has had the most influence on my understanding of the placeness of property is a theorist who is not very well known for her work in the area of property. That theorist is Hannah Arendt. Property, Arendt argued in *The Human Condition*, has lost its original and true meaning as a location in the world, and as result, it is mistakenly identified in the modern understanding with the accumulation of income-earning and capital-creating wealth.[47] Although Arendt captured the importance of placeness, she too failed to see that placeness and thingness are inextricably bound up together in the social constitution of property. Nevertheless, Arendt's analysis of the placeness of property provides important support for my effort to challenge and move beyond modern thingness.

Of course, recovering the placeness of property does not by itself resolve all the normative questions and disputes that surround property and its relationship to democracy and social justice. But it does provide a conceptual roadmap with which to explore a variety of normative possibilities. There are four such possibilities that I hope to illuminate through my hermeneutic redescription of property's placeness. First, the placeness of property is central to what may be thought of as an ethical form of materialism. Between the crasser forms of materialism that post-socialists criticize and their own post-materialist perspective lies a perspective on freedom, democratic citizenship, and moral personality that is sensitive to both the material circumstances of oppression and the material conditions of human development. The placeness of property helps to illuminate such a path of ethical materialism. Conditioned by its placeness, property can serve moral and civic ends while also remaining grounded in the material conditions of labor, provision, and resource allocation and distribution within which people live their lives. Of course, such ends may also be found in property regimes that emphasize thingness; "propriety" is part of the history of both thingness and placeness. But under thingness, moral and civic ends are not constitutively connected to property, and because of this, they are apt to get lost in claims and counter-claims of proprietary entitlement.

Second, the placeness of property illuminates a different understanding of civic stakes in society, one in which equal emphasis is placed on the holding of stakes and on the stakes being *in* society. Within a property regime that is based mainly on thingness, stakeholding is reduced to the proprietary claims and entitlements of citizens, usually in the form of private holdings acquired in private market transactions, though sometimes (as in left liberal ideas of "new property") in the form of governmentally established entitlements to social welfare benefits or income. Such stakeholdings are not precluded by the logic of placeness. What this logic does, though, is to redefine stakeholding in a way that accounts for the various property locations that citizens inhabit. These locations of property are, or can be, formative of stakes in the larger society, both in the sense of providing a secure basis for participation in the commonwealth and in the sense of developing a psychological attachment to or "investment" in the commonwealth.[48] In other words, one develops stakes as a democratic citizen on the basis of stakes in locations such as households, schools, libraries, and workplaces.

Third, there is a leveling potential within the placeness of property insofar as the proprietary claims and counter-claims of thingness are conditioned by and sometimes even abandoned in favor of the well-being and development of those who inhabit property locations. For example, a legal regime that emphasizes the placeness of property is more likely to recognize the property-related rights and needs of renters as householders than is the case with a regime that emphasizes thingness.[49] In such instances, the placeness of property helps to reconnect issues of social justice to democratic theory. But fourth, and finally, by redescribing property in terms of inhabitation, the logic of placeness also opens up new possibilities for environmental justice, possibilities for treating property as an instrument for the health and well-being of the physical environment. In this regard, placeness provides the kind of comprehensive theoretical framework for property that is usually missing from calls for more socially and environmentally responsible forms of stewardship and trusteeship, and without which these calls are likely to sound to many like moralistic and utopian schemes that ignore the realities of property and economics in a late modern commercial republic.

In all of these respects, placeness is integral to the democratic theory of property towards which this inquiry is heading. But the road to a democratic theory of property does not move simply or easily through the logic of placeness. Always, we are confronted with the danger of fusing property with political authority. While the relationship between property and authority is suppressed and obfuscated in the regime of modern thingness, it is apt to become more visible and pronounced in a regime that emphasizes placeness. By the same token, the closeness of the connection between property and authority is a key factor in determining the extent to which placeness comes to the fore in a regime of property. The more property comes to be seen as being inherently and directly about ruling and authority, the more difficult it becomes to make sense of property apart from the social location where property-related authority is exercised. *Dominium* requires a *domus*. The dominions of a lord or master are his dominion. And so on.

It cannot be emphasized too much that this means that there is also a mixed legacy of placeness. In recovering property's placeness, we also recover the possibility of property locations that are constituted through undemocratic and oppressive structures of labor and authority. This, we shall see, is one of the painful lessons to be learned from the tradition of Aristotelian civic humanism.

Placeness and the Messiness of Democracy

So I am not putting forward a theory of the civic placeness of property in the hope of finding a panacea for the longstanding challenge of developing forms and arrangements of property that support democracy and norms of equal and inclusive citizenship. To the contrary, my exploration of property points to an old lesson of democratic theory, that democracy is often an untidy, unsettled, rambunctious, and noisy affair that defies attempts at theoretical neatness. Much of what follows is an attempt to elaborate and support this old lesson.

At first glance, it might seem that the messiness of democracy is compatible with post-socialist political theory. Post-socialist political theory is deeply skeptical of Western modernity's grand theoretical narratives of historical progress and liberation. But their thinking represents not so much a rejection of grand theoretical narratives as a shift from the grand narrative of progressive emancipation to one of moral and civic recovery in the face of corruption. The messiness of democracy—its "dirt" as William Connelly has described it—works against both of these grand theoretical narratives.[50] Yet the kind of democratic messiness that I wish to outline and defend is not completely at odds with either the theoretical narrative of progressive emancipation or that of moral and civic recovery; rather, the messiness of my own vision of the properties of democracy derives in part from the fact that it draws on both narrative traditions while simultaneously seeing both as problematically related to democracy.

Such messiness often has been a source of frustration for both democratic theorists and activists. Yet there is a vitally important constructive dimension to the messiness of democracy, a dimension of building democratic relationships and institutions in the midst of all the tensions, ambiguities, and mixed legacies that make democracy possible. Or so I hope to show in the pages that follow.

The Plan for the Rest of the Book

In chapter 2, I elucidate the main points of my internal critique of civic republicanism and seek to show how this critique is related to my perspective on property. I start with the tasks of summarizing the contemporary civic republican vision of civic recovery and renewal, showing how this represents a post-socialist vision, and delineating the different forms of this vision within the current revival. Special emphasis is placed on the similarities and differences between "communal" and "neoclassical" forms of civic republicanism. "Communal republicans" emphasize a positive liberty of shared self-government, while "neoclassical republicans" emphasize the Roman idea of freedom as non-domination. The bulk of the chapter is devoted to elaborating my internal critique in relation to the type of hermeneutic perspective on the "situated self" that informs much contemporary civic republican thought.

In chapter 3, I develop a critical analysis of the displacement of property within post-socialist political theory. I argue that the post-socialist critique of materialism is premised on the existence of deep conceptual oppositions between property and virtue and between political economy and moral and civic culture. This dualistic perspective breaks down when property and political economy are viewed hermeneutically. In the meantime, though, the dualistic perspective of civic republicans and other post-socialists prevents them from developing adequate theoretical solutions for the problems of economic oppression and injustice. I offer the theory of ethical materialism as a corrective to the dualistic approach to virtue and political economy within post-socialist theory.

The central themes of chapter 4 have to do with recovering and theorizing the placeness of property. The placeness of property emerges dialectically through encounters with civic republicanism, first through an examination of civic republican arguments about the problem of a commercial republic, and second, though a hermeneutic redescription of the "situated self" as a relationship between the self and property-related contexts of identity formation. Focusing on Sandel's concept of the "guardianship" of communal assets, I also argue that civic republicans have not developed an adequate theoretical solution for the problem of republican paternalism.[51]

Chapter 5 is an exploration of key episodes in the history of the problem of a commercial republic. First we encounter many of the roots of classical republican thinking about the problem in Aristotle's theory of the household. This theory is a foundational expression of the placeness of property in Western (and republican) thought. The placeness of Aristotelian property goes along with a civic humanist vision of ethical materialism in which property and other external goods are reconnected to the intrinsic goods of moral and civic life. However, as a theory that was informed by a masters' vision of civic virtue, the Aristotelian theory of the household also represents a foundational expression of the problem of republican paternalism.

To an extent that is seldom appreciated by either theorists or historians of republicanism, the close relationship between a civic humanist perspective on intrinsic goods and the masters' vision of civic virtue persisted in early modern republicanism. In the second half of chapter 5, I trace this unfortunate relationship in the political thought of James Harrington as well as in Montesquieu's more commercial form of republicanism. I also show that elements of the masters' vision survived in later, and otherwise more democratic, forms of republicanism. I then turn my attention back to the unsettling implications of the problem of republican paternalism for the contemporary civic republican approach to the problem of a commercial republic. The persistence of the problem of republican paternalism into the modern era of commercial republicanism underscores the fact that it is an ongoing theoretical challenge for democratic theorists of civic virtue. In this connection, I seek to establish the importance of oppositionist forms of democratic agency.

In chapter 6, I explore the oppositionist moment of democratic agency in relation to the modern progressive self-understanding. In essence, I try to provide a counter-narrative to the history of liberal and leftist traditions that is put forward by civic republicans and other post-socialists. I offer this counter-narrative more as a hermeneutic thought experiment than as rigorous historiography. Still, the point is to show that civic republican and other post-socialist critiques of both liberalism and modern leftist political thought are deeply flawed by virtue of their failure to account for the role of these traditions in opposing concentrations of property and political authority. In my counter-narrative, Locke emerges as a foundational theorist not only in the development of possessive individualism and commercial republicanism, but also in the development of the oppositionist moment in Western political thought. I trace the "Lockean principle" of separate spheres of private property and legitimate political authority in relation to both the early liberal critique of the *ancien regime* and later leftist and left liberal arguments against capitalism. At the end of the chapter, I return to the relationship between Lockean and republican understandings of property, and seek to show how this relationship was associated with non-collectivist ideas about property and democracy in nineteenth- and twentieth-century expressions of producer republicanism and reform liberalism.

In chapter 7, I consider the question of whether property has disintegrated in the modern era. Clearly, my exploration of the relationship between property and civic virtue presupposes that it is possible—or rather, that it is still possible—to talk meaningfully about property as a coherent and more or less unified concept. However, some analysts of property claim that it has disintegrated under conditions of modern political economy. I examine two versions of this disintegration thesis. The first is Thomas Grey's argument that property has collapsed because there is no longer a unified or coherent idea of "thing ownership."[52] The other version is Arendt's argument that property has disintegrated by virtue of the almost complete disappearance of the placeness of property.[53] The thrust of my critique of Grey's version of the disintegration thesis is that a residual placeness gives some coherence and stability to property in the face of disintegrative forces at work in the late modern era. However, if Arendt is right, then the placeness of property has itself disappeared. I argue that Arendt did not appreciate the importance of thingness, and furthermore, that her physicalist view of the institutional boundaries between private property and public life prevented her from seeing that placeness is culturally constituted in relation to a variety of institutional ends and purposes. The cultural constitution of property as a relationship between thingness and placeness makes property more flexible and durable than Arendt thought, flexible enough and durable enough, I maintain, to persist under conditions of late modern capitalism.

The conclusion (chapter 8) pulls the various threads of the book together by discussing the problems and possibilities of both civic republicanism as a postsocialist theory of democracy and a democratic theory of the placeness of property. I outline an approach to property that combines rights of ownership with rights of inhabitation within various institutional locations. I seek to show that both kinds of rights are necessary to establish citizen stakes in a democratic commonwealth. I also argue that different kinds of property locations serve different ends and purposes and are related to citizenship in different ways. On this basis, I outline a sphere of property—the civic infrastructure—that is especially important for democracy, but which cuts across conventional boundaries of private and public. It encompasses not only discrete institutions such as schools, libraries, parks, museums, centers for performing arts, and the mass media, but also aspects of the governance of "private" institutions such as corporations and the marketplace itself. In all of these cases, property has valuable civic ends, and as such the civic infrastructure represents an attempt to provide concrete form to a vision of ethical materialism. But the rationale for a civic infrastructure includes more defensive and protective functions as well. The civic infrastructure is itself vulnerable to the problem of republican paternalism, and combined with its role in promoting civic ends, this vulnerability necessitates two things: institutional democracy and a background of equal rights to protect oppositionist forms of democratic agency.

Notes

1. See Alasdair MacIntyre, *After Virtue: A Study in Moral Theory,* 2nd ed. (Notre Dame, IN: University of Notre Dame Press, 1984); and Michael J. Sandel, *Liberalism and the Limits of Justice,* 2nd ed. (Cambridge: Cambridge University Press, 1998).

2. The list of theorists and scholars who have contributed to the revival of civic republicanism is quite extensive. Among the key thinkers and texts are the following: Benjamin R. Barber, *Strong Democracy: Participatory Politics for a New Age* (Berkeley, CA:

University of California Press, 1984); Barber, *A Place for Us: How to Make Society Civil and Democracy Strong* (New York: Hill and Wang, 1998); Barber, *A Passion for Democracy: American Essays* (Princeton, NJ: Princeton University Press, 1998); Ronald Beiner, *What's the Matter with Liberalism?* (Berkeley, CA: University of California Press, 1992); Beiner, *Liberalism, Nationalism, Citizenship: Essays on the Problem of Political Community* (Vancouver, BC: UBC Press, 2003); Robert N. Bellah et al., *Habits of the Heart: Individualism and Commitment in American Life,* 2nd ed. (Berkeley, CA: University of California Press, 1996); Bellah et al., *The Good Society* (New York: Alfred A. Knopf, 1991); Mary G. Dietz, "Citizenship with a Feminist Face: The Problem with Maternal Thinking," *Political Theory* 13 (1985): 19–37; Dietz, "Patriotism," in *Political Innovation and Conceptual Change,* ed. Terence Ball, James Farr, and Russell Hanson (Cambridge: Cambridge University Press, 1989); Daniel Kemmis, *Community and the Politics of Place* (Norman, OK: University of Oklahoma Press, 1990); Iseult Honohan, *Civic Republicanism* (London: Routledge, 2002); Wilson Carey McWilliams, "On Equality and the Moral Foundation of Community," in *The Moral Foundation of the American Republic,* ed. Robert H. Horwitz (Charlottesville, VA: University of Virginia Press, 1986); Frank I. Michelman, "The Supreme Court, 1985 Term—Foreword: Traces of Self-Government," *Harvard Law Review* 100 (1986): 4–77; Michelman, "Law's Republic," *The Yale Law Journal* 97 (1988): 1493–1537; David Miller, *Citizenship and National Identity* (Cambridge: Polity Press, 2000); Adrian Oldfield, *Citizenship and Community: Civic Republicanism and the Modern World* (London: Routledge, 1990); Thomas L. Pangle, *The Ennobling of Democracy: The Challenge of the Postmodern Age* (Baltimore: The Johns Hopkins University Press, 1992); Hanna Fenichel Pitkin, *Fortune Is a Woman: Gender and Politics in the Thought of Niccolo Machiavelli* (Berkeley, CA: University of California Press, 1984); Phillip Pettit, *Republicanism: A Theory of Freedom and Government* (Oxford: Oxford University Press, 1997); Robert D. Putnam, *Bowling Alone: The Collapse and Revival of American Community* (New York: Touchstone, 2000); J. G. A. Pocock, *The Machiavellian Moment: Florentine Political Thought and the Atlantic Republican Tradition* (Princeton, NJ: Princeton University Press, 1975); Michael J. Sandel, *Democracy's Discontent: America in Search of a Public Philosophy* (Cambridge, MA: The Belknap Press, 1996); Sandel, *Liberalism and the Limits of Justice;* Quentin Skinner, *Liberty Before Liberalism* (Cambridge: Cambridge University Press, 1998); Thomas A. Spragens, Jr., *Reason and Democracy* (Durham, NC: Duke University Press, 1990); Spragens, *Civic Liberalism: Reflections on Our Democratic Ideals* (Lanham, MD: Rowman and Littlefield, 1999); William M. Sullivan, *Reconstructing Public Philosophy* (Berkeley, CA: University of California Press, 1986); Cass R. Sunstein, *The Partial Constitution* (Cambridge, MA: Harvard University Press, 1993); Charles Taylor, *Philosophy and the Human Sciences,* vol. 2 of *Philosophical Papers* (Cambridge: Cambridge University Press, 1985); Taylor, "Cross-Purposes: The Liberal-Communitarian Debate," in *Liberalism and the Moral Life,* ed. Nancy L. Rosenblum (Cambridge, MA: Harvard University Press, 1989); Taylor, *The Ethics of Authenticity* (Cambridge, MA: Harvard University Press, 1991); Taylor, *Philosophical Arguments* (Cambridge, MA: Harvard University Press, 1995); Taylor, *Modern Social Imaginaries* (Durham, NC: Duke University Press, 2004); Maurizio Viroli, *Republicanism* (New York: Hill and Wang, 2002); and Gordon S. Wood, *The Creation of the American Republic, 1776–1787* (New York: W.W. Norton and Company, 1969).

3. Pocock, *The Machiavellian Moment.*

4. Hannah Arendt, *The Human Condition* (Chicago: University of Chicago Press, 1958), especially 48–49.

5. See Will Kymlicka's excellent overview of contemporary "citizenship theory" in *Contemporary Political Philosophy: An Introduction,* 2nd ed. (Oxford: Oxford University Press, 2002), 284–322.

6. Antonio Negri and Michael Hardt, *Empire* (Cambridge, MA: Harvard University Press, 2000), 69–92, 160–82, and 304–24.

7. Robert Booth Fowler, *The Dance with Community: The Contemporary Debate in American Political Thought* (Lawrence, KS: University of Kansas Press, 1991), 78.

8. See, for example, Bruce Ackerman and Anne Alstott, *The Stakeholder Society* (New Haven, CT: Yale University Press, 1999); Hernando de Soto, *The Mystery of Capital: Why Capitalism Triumphs in the West and Fails Everywhere Else* (New York: Basic Books, 2000); Joseph William Singer, *Entitlement: The Paradoxes of Property* (New Haven, CT: Yale University Press, 2000); and Liam Murphy and Thomas Nagel, *The Myth of Ownership: Taxes and Justice* (Oxford: Oxford University Press, 2002).

9. Ronald J. Terchek, *Republican Paradoxes and Liberal Anxieties: Retrieving Neglected Fragments of Political Theory* (Lanham, MD: Rowman and Littlefield, 1997), 51.

10. The exceptions that receive most of Terchek's attention involve the historical interpretations of classical republican views of property that have been put forward by J. G. A. Pocock and Quentin Skinner. See, for example, Pocock, *The Machiavellian Moment,* 333–552; Pocock, *Virtue, Commerce, and History: Essays on Political Thought and History, Chiefly in the Eighteenth Century* (Cambridge: Cambridge University Press, 1985), 51–71 and 103–23; and Skinner, "On Justice, the Common Good, and the Priority of Liberty," in *Dimensions of Radical Democracy,* ed. Chantal Mouffe (London: Verso, 1992). These are important exceptions; indeed, Pocock's interpretation figures prominently in my own analysis of civic virtue and property. However, there are also some exceptions of a more strictly theoretical nature that are deserving of attention, most notably, Michael Sandel's theoretical perspective on the "guardianship" of communal resources, Alasdair MacIntyre's communitarian (and Aristotelian) perspective on the relationship between "external goods" such as property and the "internal goods" associated with virtue, and Frank Michelman's efforts to reappropriate the classical republican model of propertied independence. Terchek notes Michelman's efforts, but they are not discussed in any detail, and there is no discussion at all of Sandel's proposed principle of guardianship or MacIntyre's framework of external and internal goods. I discuss these civic republican and communitarian views of property at many points in this inquiry. See Sandel, *Liberalism and the Limits of Justice,* 95–103; MacIntyre, *After Virtue,* 184–203; and Frank I. Michelman, "Possession vs. Distribution in the Constitutional Idea of Property," *Iowa Law Review* 72 (1987): 1319–50.

11. Sullivan, *Reconstructing Public Philosophy,* 27.

12. Sullivan, 60, 21, and 178.

13. Aristotle, *Politics,* ed. and trans. Ernest Barker (London: Oxford University Press, 1975), book VII, 1323a, 280.

14. The phrase, "formative project," is one of Sandel's terms of art. See *Democracy's Discontent,* 321–24 and 5–6.

15. Frank I. Michelman, "The Supreme Court, 1985 Term—Foreword: Traces of Self-Government," 17. Michelman's understanding of the "semantic field" of the republican tradition reflects the hermeneutic perspective that is characteristic of the revival, but which is often not fully appreciated by the critics of civic republicanism. See the discussion of civic republican hermeneutics in chapter 2.

16. The contemporary civic republican who comes closest to a theory of the placeness of property is Daniel Kemmis. His understanding of the placeness of political and economic life has been a big influence on my thinking. However, to my knowledge, Kemmis has never applied his ideas about placeness to property itself. See Kemmis, *Community and the Politics of Place*, chapters 1 and 7.

17. See Maurizio Viroli's corrective argument against his fellow civic republicans in *Republicanism*, 32.

18. See Gregory S. Alexander, *Commodity and Propriety: Competing Visions of Property in American Legal Thought 1776–1970* (Chicago: University of Chicago Press, 1997), 4–5 and 30–37; Joyce Appleby, *Capitalism and a New Social Order: The Republican Vision of the 1790s* (New York: New York University Press, 1984), 8–9; Pocock, *The Machiavellian Moment*, 361–552; Pocock, *Virtue, Commerce, and History*, 103–7; and Gordon S. Wood, *The Radicalism of the American Revolution* (New York: Vintage Books, 1991), 269–70.

19. See, for example, Alfonso J. Damico, "The Democratic Consequences of Liberalism," in *Liberals on Liberalism*, ed. Alfonso J. Damico (Totowa, NJ: Rowman and Littlefield, 1986), 178–82; Amy Gutmann, "Communitarian Critics of Liberalism," in *Philosophy and Public Affairs* 14 (1985): 308–22; William A. Galston, *Liberal Pluralism: The Implications of Value Pluralism for Political Theory and Practice* (Cambridge: Cambridge University Press, 2002), 17 and 128–30; Don Herzog, "Some Questions for Republicans," *Political Theory* 14 (1986): 473–93; and Richard C. Sinopoli, *The Foundations of American Citizenship: Liberalism, the Constitution, and Civic Virtue* (New York: Oxford University Press, 1992), 163–71. Iris Marion Young reaches the same conclusion about the dangers of an exclusionary politics of civic virtue, but as a postmodern feminist critic of both liberalism and civic republicanism. See *Justice and the Politics of Difference* (Princeton, NJ: Princeton University Press, 1990), chapter 4. Also see Bonnie Honig, *Political Theory and the Displacement of Politics* (Ithaca, NY: Cornell University Press, 1993), 1–3 and 162–99.

20. See Viroli, *Republicanism*, 3–19.

21. See Ronald Beiner's discussions of the differences between "republicanism" and "communitarianism" and why he prefers the former in *What's the Matter with Liberalism?*, and Beiner, "Introduction: The Quest for a Post-Liberal Philosophy," in *Debating Democracy's Discontent: Essays on American Politics, Law, and Public Philosophy*, ed. Anita L. Allen and Milton C. Regan, Jr. (Oxford: Oxford University Press, 1998), 1–5. Also see Honohan, *Civic Republicanism*, 2 and 9–12; and Sandel's reconsideration of communitarianism in the preface to the second edition of *Liberalism and the Limits of Justice*.

22. For neopopulism, see, for example, Christopher Lasch, *The True and Only Heaven: Progress and its Critics* (New York: W. W. Norton and Company, 1991); and Harry C. Boyte, *Commonwealth: A Return to Citizen Politics* (New York: The Free Press,

1989). The foremost expositions of "the third way" are in Anthony Giddens, *Beyond Left and Right: The Future of Radical Politics* (Stanford, CA: Stanford University Press, 1994); and Giddens, *The Third Way: The Renewal of Social Democracy* (Malden, MA: Polity Press, 1998). The foundational theorist of "maternalist" or "social" feminism in the current era is Jean Bethke Elshtain. See especially *Public Man, Private Woman: Women in Social and Political Thought* (Princeton, NJ: Princeton University Press, 1981); and "Antigone's Daughters," *Democracy* 2 (1982): 46–59. Also see Joan C. Tronto, *Moral Boundaries: Political Arguments for an Ethic of Care* (New York: Routledge, 1993). West's post-socialist project is outlined in *Race Matters* (Boston: Beacon Press, 1993). For examples of post-socialist theories of participatory democracy, see Barber, *Strong Democracy*; Jane Mansbridge, *Beyond Adversary Democracy* (Chicago: University of Chicago Press, 1983); and in many respects, Judith M. Green, *Deep Democracy: Community, Diversity, and Transformation* (Lanham, MD: Rowman and Littlefield, 1999). For examples of post-socialist forms of bioregionalism, see Kemmis, *Community and the Politics of Place*; Kirpatrick Sale, *Dwellers in the Land: The Bioregional Vision*, 2nd ed. (Athens, GA: University of Georgia Press, 2000); and Helena Norberg-Hodge, *Ancient Futures: Learning from Ladakh* (San Francisco: Sierra Club Books, 1991).

23. Robert A. Dahl, *Democracy and Its Critics* (New Haven, CT: Yale University Press), 119.

24. See Dahl, 30–33.

25. Fowler, *The Dance with Community*, 149.

26. One exception to this rule is Richard Flathman. See his compelling argument that theories of "high citizenship" are problematically bound up with ideas and practices of authority in "Citizenship and Authority: A Chastened View of Citizenship," in *Theorizing Citizenship*, ed. Ronald Beiner (Albany, NY: State University Press of New York, 1995).

27. See, for example, Bernard Bailyn's discussion of dominion in *The Ideological Origins of the American Revolution* (Cambridge, MA: Belknap Press, 1967), 55–56.

28. *Republican Paradoxes and Liberal Anxieties*, especially 80–83.

29. *Reason and Democracy*, 10. Also see William A. Galston, *Liberal Purposes: Goods, Virtues, and Diversity in the Liberal State* (Cambridge: Cambridge University Press, 1991), 213.

30. Thomas C. Grey, "The Disintegration of Property," in *Property*, vol. XXII of *Nomos*, ed. Roland Pennock and John Chapman (New York: New York University Press, 1980), 81.

31. Sullivan, *Reconstructing Public Philosophy*, 190.

32. It is significant that property has emerged as a key subject in recent scholarly thinking about economic growth in the so-called "developing world." See especially Hernando de Soto's analysis of the importance of "property systems" for the transformation of assets and labor into capital in *The Mystery of Capital*, chapters 1 and 3.

33. The foundational text of philosophical hermeneutics in the contemporary era is Hans-Georg Gadamer, *Truth and Method*, 2nd ed. (New York: Crossroad, 1989).

34. Sir Frederick Pollock and Frederic William Maitland, *The History of English Law Before the Time of Edward I*, vol.1, 2nd ed. (Cambridge: University Press, 1968), 230.

35. The *locus classicus* of this standard critique is Marx's analysis in the first part of "On the Jewish Question," in *The Marx-Engels Reader*, ed. Robert C. Tucker (New York: W. W. Norton and Company, Inc., 1972), 24–45.

36. Alan Ryan, *Property* (Minneapolis, MN: University of Minnesota Press, 1987), 124.

37. Charles M. Haar and Lance Liebman, *Property and Law* (Boston: Little, Brown, and Company, 1977), 150.

38. Jeremy Waldron, "Homelessness and the Issue of Freedom," *UCLA Law Review* 39 (1991): 295.

39. See Sale, *Dwellers in the Land*, 67–71; and E. F. Schumacher, *Small Is Beautiful* (New York: Harper and Row, 1973), 43–44.

40. Singer, *Entitlement*, 3–9 and 13–18.

41. Singer, 92. Note that Singer also criticizes the "bundle of rights" approach to property for its formalistic understanding of social relations and for perpetuating the ownership model in a new form (i.e., in the form of ownership rights to strands of property in a larger bundle). See Singer, 10–13.

42. Murphy and Nagel, *The Myth of Ownership*, 8; also see 15, 31–37, and 74.

43. Margaret Jane Radin, *Reinterpreting Property* (Chicago: University of Chicago Press, 1993), especially chapter 1.

44. See Michelman, "The Supreme Court, 1985 Term—Foreword: Traces of Self-Government"; and "Possession vs. Distribution in the Constitutional Idea of Property."

45. Waldron, *The Right to Private Property*, 23.

46. Waldron, 25; also chapter 12.

47. *The Human Condition*, especially 28–37 and 58–73.

48. See Tercheck's discussion of civic stakes in *Republican Paradoxes and Liberal Anxieties*, 48–51. Also see my discussion of "habitational stakeholding" in chapter 8.

49. See Radin's interesting discussion of the property claims of renters in relation to the issues of rent control and eviction control in *Reinterpreting Property*, 19–22 and 72–97.

50. William E. Connelly, *Politics and Ambiguity* (Madison, WI: University of Wisconsin Press, 1987), 89–96.

51. Sandel, *Liberalism and the Limits of Justice*, 95–103.

52. Grey, "The Disintegration of Property."

53. Arendt, *The Human Condition*, chapter 2.

2

Points of Departure

T HIS INQUIRY ARISES IN RELATION TO, and within, two fields of theoretical inquiry that have had very different fates in recent years. One of these fields—the civic republican field of civic virtue and the qualities of moral character requisite of democratic citizenship—has been intensively cultivated, while the other one—the field of property—has been allowed, for the most part, to go fallow, or alternatively, has been cultivated only in a very selective manner. My path to the properties of democracy is one that moves dialectically between these two fields, between issues of civic virtue and issues of property. As a traditional subject of democratic theory, property provides a means of testing and evaluating contemporary republican arguments about citizenship and civic virtue in light of some enduring issues and themes concerning the properties of democracy. At the same time, however, the civic republican project of civic recovery and renewal provides a rich theoretical vocabulary with which to chart both old and new conceptual terrain concerning property and its relationship to democracy. While property provides a helpful critical lens for examining and "re-viewing" the civic republicans' post-socialist vision of a democratic politics of civic virtue, this vision also provides a lens with which to see both property and democracy in new ways.

The aim of this chapter is to explicate this dialectic of civic virtue and property in relation to my critical perspective on civic republicanism. In particular, I want to show how the civic republicans' hermeneutic perspective on identity serves as a point of departure for a critical exploration and rethinking of the relationship between civic virtue and property in democratic politics. The precise form that this dialectic of civic virtue and property takes in this inquiry is that of a movement from an "external" to an "internal" mode of critical inquiry. Simply put, the external mode is one that criticizes civic republicanism from a standpoint outside the terms of the revival. Some degree of this form of criticism is inevitable if for no other reason than that property is generally a much lower priority for civic republicans than it is for me. Still, my method is primarily one of internal criticism in that I am developing my arguments about property and democratic citizenship by working within and through the terms of theoretical debate and discussion that civic republicans themselves have established.

Let us start by stepping back and taking a closer look at the civic republican project of recovery and renewal. Among other things, this will allow us to consider some interpretive issues concerning the different theoretical tendencies and developments within contemporary civic republicanism.

A "Formative" Politics of Civic Virtue

The civic republican project of recovery and renewal is fundamentally a project of developing a democratic political culture in which individuals acquire the habits, dispositions, and capacities for responsible civic engagement.[1] From the outset of the republican revival, this project has been presented as something that is necessary to combat the corruptive influence of liberalism. In Michael Sandel's influential terms of analysis, liberalism is said to promote a merely instrumental stance towards civic life to the extent that it posits a self whose identity and moral capacities are defined apart from, and in advance of, communal attachments and purposes.[2] For such an "unencumbered" self, practical reason based on communal conversations about moral and political ends becomes less important, giving way to technical or instrumental modes of reason and self-understanding in which emphasis is placed on the calculation and maximization of means-ends efficiency. The effect of this "complex" of atomism and instrumentalism (as Charles Taylor describes it) is to make it increasingly difficult to have a democratic politics in which identification with the shared goods of the community is constitutive of the self-understandings of "socially embodied" or "situated" citizens.[3] Unencumbered liberal citizens are left with a politics of rights retrieval and interest maximization within a framework of purportedly neutral procedures and decision rules. Or even worse, they are left with a kind of anti-politics of civic disengagement and disempowerment that leaves apathetic and often cynical citizens at the mercy of organized interest groups, manipulative bureaucracies, and the impersonal economic forces of a capitalist market system. Either way, freedom loses its communal and public dimensions as a shared practice of self-government, and unencumbered individuals are unable to acquire the habits and dispositions of good citizenship that would motivate and empower them to be actively and responsibly engaged in the political life of their community.

Thus, the civic republican project is one of revitalizing democracy by transforming disengaged, atomized, and disempowered individuals into communally "situated" citizens who are actively engaged with and for the common good. According to civic republicans, it is precisely this kind of project that was emphasized in the classical republican tradition of civic virtue. "Central to [classical] republican theory," Sandel explains, "is the idea that liberty depends on sharing in government." To share in self-government means "deliberating about the common good and helping to shape the destiny of the political community." This in turn "requires a knowledge of public affairs and also a sense of belonging, a concern for the whole, a moral bond with the community whose fate is at stake." Hence, the valuable and enduring wisdom of the republican tradition is the understanding that self-government is sustained by a "formative project" that "cultivates in citizens the qualities of character self-government requires."[4]

Post-Socialist Disenchantment and Civic Republican Political Economy

The civic republican project was born of a post-socialist disenchantment with the materialist underpinnings of modern, Enlightenment-based ideals of progress and progressive emancipation. This disenchantment was powerfully expressed by Robert Bellah and the other authors of *Habits of the Heart* in the concluding chapter of that path-breaking work:

> There is a widespread feeling that the promise of the modern era is slipping away from us. A movement of enlightenment and liberation that was to have freed us from superstition and tyranny has led in the twentieth century to a world in which ideological fanaticism and political oppression have reached extremes unknown in previous history. Science, which was to have unlocked the bounties of nature, has given us the power to destroy all life on the earth. Progress, modernity's master idea, seems less compelling when it appears that it may be progress into the abyss. And the globe today is divided between a liberal world so incoherent that it seems to be losing the significance of its own ideals, an oppressive and archaic communist statism, and a poor, and often tyrannical, Third World reaching for the very first rungs of modernity. In the liberal world, the state, which was supposed to be a neutral nightwatchman that would maintain order while individuals pursued their various interests, has become so overgrown and militarized that it threatens to become a universal policeman.[5]

This quote shows that post-socialist disenchantment covers a wide range of modern beliefs and developments. But post-socialists clearly see the beliefs and developments associated with modern materialism as especially deleterious and corruptive. Thus, when the Bellah group summarized the state of American political thought in the mid-1980s, they put it in terms of "the citizen" being "swallowed up in 'economic man.'" The prevailing forms of liberal ideology ("Neocapitalism" and "Welfare Liberalism," in their lexicon) were said to be united not only by a commitment to individualism, but also by the belief that freedom is closely connected to material prosperity. As they put it, "Both Neocapitalism and Welfare Liberalism agree about the primary aim of modern society: It is twofold: to provide physical security and material well-being for its citizens and at the same time encourage as much individual choice as possible regarding the goals of activity."[6] Hence, the only real differences between these competing ideologies involve the means to achieve individual freedom of choice and material well-being and the procedures by which to ensure fairness in their pursuit. There is no meaningful debate over the nature of freedom or its relationship to material well-being, and no disagreement over the materialistic substance of justice.

Civic republican disenchantment with modern traditions of progress and progressive emancipation is undoubtedly a reason for what, even after the emergence of virtue-centered expressions of liberal political theory, remains a very reluctant embrace of left-leaning reform liberalism. Yet at the level of proposals and programs of reform, civic republicans are also more clearly, and even more conventionally, left of center than most other post-socialists.

Some caution is always in order when discussing the ideological content of civic republicanism. Interest in a politics of civic virtue cuts across the ideological spectrum. There is also ideological diversity among those theorists and scholars who, by scholarly convention and self-identification, are most closely associated with civic republicanism. The "dominant mood" of the revival, Robert Fowler points out, is that of a "Left republicanism."[7] But as this suggests, there are other moods as well, moods of moderation and at times conservatism. A certain amount of unsettling and blurring of conventional ideological distinctions and categories is to be expected in post-socialist thought. After all, since their initial appearance during the French Revolution, these distinctions and categories have grown up with progressive modernity. There is as well a propensity towards moderation that inheres in the grammar of civic virtue, a propensity to make a virtue of setting aside narrow partisan differences for the common good. But all of this only makes the left-leaning tilt of the revival stand out all the more. Moreover, it is precisely in the area of political economy—the area that traditionally has been focal point of critical concern and theoretical and programmatic interest for leftists—that we see the left-leaning tendencies and commitments of the revival.

As post-materialist thinkers, civic republicans have considerably less to say about political economy than conventional leftists, especially in terms of the theoretical aspects of these subjects. But what they have said indicates a program in which the public morality of republican citizenship is tied to proposals of political-economic reform that have been circulating among both "old" and "new" leftists and left-leaning progressives for some time now. Specifically, civic republicans envision a "political economy of citizenship" (the phrase is Sandel's) which, while still capitalist in its basic economic organization, is also collaborative in its decision making, comparatively decentralized, and strongly committed to an agenda of community and national service, economic democracy, redistributive "civic" justice, and the empowerment of disadvantaged groups and classes through grass-roots citizen action.[8]

Thus, civic republicanism affords us the unique opportunity of studying a late modern version of the leftist, progressive program for the transformation of capitalism side-by-side with a post-socialist critique of modern understandings and ideals of progress and progressive liberation.

Variations and Commonalities

Naturally, the civic republican project of recovery and renewal has been articulated in different ways by different thinkers. Two such differences are noteworthy. First, there is a disagreement about the kinds of solidarity that are most important for the formative project of democratic citizenship. More purely communitarian republicans such as Sandel, Bellah, Taylor, William Sullivan, and Daniel Kemmis place special emphasis on the link between civic engagement and the solidaristic attachments and practices of civil society. By contrast, civic republican critics of communitarianism such as Beiner, David Miller, and Mary Dietz are less interested in building community through the social networks and associations of civil society than in fostering the democratic engagement of citizens qua citizens. In other words, the communal identity of citizenship itself is what matters most.

Yet this is a disagreement within what can be thought of as the mainstream "communal republican" position of seeking to synthesize civic solidarity with civic participation.[9] By contrast, the second difference has to do with a challenge to mainstream communal republicanism. I have in mind the development in recent years of a form of civic republicanism that is less interested in either community or participatory democracy than in the recovery of the classical republican ideal of independent citizenship. I am calling this the "neoclassical" form of contemporary civic republicanism.

Neoclassical republicans maintain that there is an early modern, classical republican understanding of freedom that departs from the Aristotelian, civic humanist conception of freedom as a positive liberty of virtuous participation in self-government. As discussed by Philip Pettit, this alternative understanding holds that freedom is fundamentally about "non-domination," by which he means "the condition under which you live in the presence of others but at the mercy of none."[10] Or as another neoclassical theorist, Maurizio Viroli, puts it, the "absence of domination" should be "understood as the condition of the individual who does not have to depend on the arbitrary will of other individuals or institutions that might oppress him or her with impunity."[11] Democracy is still valued, but it is not (as it is for most communal republicans) an essential and inherent part of freedom. Thus, Pettit argues that inclusive democratic practices of "contestation" and "deliberation" are vitally important to the goal of republican liberty, but only as a means, and only insofar as they accord with the requirements of non-domination.[12]

Neoclassical republicans would have us believe that this alternative understanding of liberty is sharply at odds with the civic humanist perspective of communal republicanism. But things are not so black and white. For one thing, there are varying degrees of civic humanism among communal republicans. In its purest and most perfectionist form, civic humanism holds that the life of active and virtuous citizenship is essential to the full development and realization of human personality. Most communal republicans don't embrace the pure form of civic humanism. Rather, most endorse only a broadly developmental vision of human personality. And viewed in this way, the disagreement with neoclassical republicanism is not as great as it first appears.

Much of the disagreement over civic humanism centers on the question of how much emphasis should be placed on the protective functions of civic engagement in preserving political liberty and self-government. Naturally, such protective functions are especially important to neoclassical republicans. Yet even neoclassical republicans agree that protective forms of civic engagement are important to human development. Pettit, for example, views non-domination as a good that is worth pursuing both as a good that promotes personal development and as a common good that is intrinsic to the well being of republican citizens. And as a common good, non-domination requires precisely the kind of developmental, formative project that we have been discussing. Thus, republican laws are said to require "habits of civic virtue or good citizenship."[13] By the same token, Quentin Skinner's neoclassical reappropriation of Cicero's republicanism has much in common with a developmental civic humanism. A Ciceronian perspective on personality is itself teleological and eudaimonist in most respects, and therefore generally quite compatible with the broadly Aristotelian perspective that predominates in the revival. Certainly, as adumbrated by Skinner, the Ciceronian "concept of *virtus*" has dimensions that other, more Aristotelian participants in the revival would find attractive:

"first that it is in fact possible for men to attain this highest kind of excellence; next that the right process of education is essential for the achievement of this goal; and finally that the contents of such an education must centre on the linked study of rhetoric and ancient philosophy."[14] I dare say that these are essentially the same ingredients that are found in Sandel's neo-Aristotelian, communal republicanism.

Cultivating a Circle of Civic Engagement

By way of summary, the civic republican project of civic recovery and renewal is simultaneously a critical project of recovering from the corruptive power and influence of liberalism *and* a constructive (or reconstructive) project of recovering a better sense of who we are as independent and engaged democratic citizens. The cultivation of civic virtue is the key to both dimensions of the project. But what exactly do civic republicans mean by "civic virtue"? Not surprisingly, references to civic virtue and to particular civic virtues abound in the texts of the revival. Indeed, it sometimes seems that civic republicans are intent on making the case for their project of recovery and renewal by stringing together as many commendatory concepts of civic virtue as possible. In addition to standard notions of public spirit and the capacity to set aside private interests for the common good, civic virtue has been associated with a benumbing variety of civic excellences, including among others: cooperation, trust, mutual respect, mutual care and concern, neighborliness, empathy, civility, patriotism, fraternity, egalitarianism, civic friendship, deliberation, dialogue, the ability to find common ground through compromise, the ability to pay attention to public problems, respect for the common laws of society, the exercise of freedom, participation in civic associations, and a willingness to be involved in the formulation and enactment of public policies.

There are lessons here regarding the plasticity of the rhetoric of "civic virtue" and the variety of ideological and political purposes for which this rhetoric may be employed. The problem for civic republicans is that their own idiom of civic virtue can be employed on behalf of ideological and political purposes that are very different than the democratic purposes that they have in mind. However, it is also true that there *is* an underlying conceptual framework that supports the civic republican understanding of civic virtue. While this framework does not solve the problem of plasticity, it does imbue the civic republicans' seemingly motley collection of civic excellences with some theoretical coherence.

This underlying framework is one in which civic virtue is viewed as a twofold civic capacity: first, as a capacity to exercise or (as with the neoclassical

perspective) protect public liberty, and second, as a capacity to exercise or protect public liberty in a spirit of responsible concern for the shared goods of the
community and its citizens. In essence, then, we are dealing with the capacity
of self-governing citizens to be engaged in public life in a public-spirited and
civil manner. Again, for most civic republicans, civic engagement revolves
around participation in practices of self-government, and it is this participatory mode of civic virtue that I want to focus on now.

It needs to be stressed that this is a two-fold capacity in the strong sense that
the two elements of shared goods and participation are seen as mutually rein-
forcing. In this regard, what is distinctive about the communal republican
politics of civic virtue is its emphasis on a dialectical relationship between the
community as a formative moral context of shared goods and the community
as a transformative (or trans-formative) context of responsible citizen participation. We can think of this as a circle of virtuous civic engagement. It is a
circle in which citizens are engaged in an ongoing project of defining themselves on the basis of shared goods that they also have a hand in determining
through collective civic deliberations. Or more simply, it is a circle in which
citizens are engaged with and for each other in the collective practice of self-
government.

As might be expected, many communal republicans see the tradition of
classical republicanism as the source of "foundational" or "paradigmatic"
statements of this circle of engagement.[15] Typical in this regard is the redescription of the republican tradition offered by Kemmis. "Republicanism,"
he writes, "was an intensive brand of politics; it was, heart and soul, a politics
of engagement. It depended first upon people being deeply engaged with one
another . . . and second upon citizens being directly and profoundly engaged
with working out solutions to public problems, by formulating and enacting
the 'common good.'"[16] In a parallel manner, Taylor underscores the connection established by classical republicans between, on the one hand, the "republican thesis" that the preservation of a free society against the threat of
despotism requires "a willing identification with the polis on the part of the
citizens" and, on the other hand, the idea that a civic capacity for "participation in self-rule is of the essence of freedom."[17]

Taylor's rendering of the circle of civic engagement reminds us that communal republicans see the recovery of civic virtue as a way of redescribing and
reconstructing positive liberty. Consider in this regard Sullivan's view of the
close relationship between civic virtue and freedom:

> For the republican tradition, civic virtue is the excellence of character proper to
> the citizen. It *is* freedom in the substantive sense, freedom understood as the ca-
> pacity to attain one's good, where *goodness* describes full enjoyment of those ca-

pacities which characterize a flourishing human life. Since humans are by nature social beings, living well requires a shared life, and a shared life is possible only when the members of the community trust and respect one another. To participate in such a shared life is to show concern for and reciprocity to one's fellows, and to do so is simultaneously fulfilling for the individual.[18]

When Sullivan made these points, the revival was just beginning to gather momentum. But this kind of analysis of the connections between civic virtue, freedom, community, and participation has played a central role throughout the course of the revival. We can get a sense of this from a description of republican citizenship that David Miller put forward several years after Sullivan wrote the above passage. "The republican conception of citizenship," Miller wrote, "conceives the citizen as someone who plays an active role in shaping the future decisions of his or her society through political debate and decision-making. It takes the liberal conception of citizenship as a set of rights, and adds to it the idea that a citizen must be someone who thinks and behaves in a certain way. A citizen *identifies with the political community to which he or she belongs, and is committed to promoting its common good through active participation in political life*."[19]

These descriptions of virtuous positive liberty show that despite their post-socialist skepticism about progressive modernity, communal republicans are committed to a goal that long has been the hallmark of both participatory democracy and left-leaning progressivism in general. It is a goal, moreover, that many critics and commentators mistakenly have assumed is not part of "communitarian" republicanism. This is the goal of social and political transformation through empowerment. True, this must be understood as empowerment that is tempered by a responsible and self-disciplined regard for the community. But it is empowerment nonetheless.

Even in its most purely communitarian expressions, the civic republican understanding of civic virtue is as much about transformative and empowering civic agency as about an attunement with the goods and ends of the community. Sandel, for example, consistently has argued that the "radically unencumbered self" of contemporary liberal thought is problematic in large part because it leaves the self "disempowered."[20] For Sandel, as for other communal republicans, democratic citizenship in its truest sense is about being empowered as a participant in the life of one's community. In the first instance, this requires what Taylor calls a "public space" of "attending-together" which "is not reducible to an aggregation of attendings separately."[21] But this becomes a democratic space when those inhabiting it are empowered as participants in the ongoing tasks of creating, defining, formulating, and enacting the ends and goods of a common public life. And with this, we come back to the circle of civic engagement. That is to say, within the communal republican vision of virtuous positive liberty, the excellence of character proper to democratic citizenship is one in which situated citizens are empowered both to develop a capacity to reflect on the goods of their community *and* to act in concert with others to determine and realize these goods within practices of self-government. And the more widely this excellence of character is cultivated, the better able we will be to recover from the excesses and distortions of liberalism. Taylor expresses this hope in terms of the potential for moving from a "vicious circle" to a "virtuous" one. The danger of a "vicious circle" has to do with the political "fragmentation" that is produced by the market mechanisms and bureaucratic structures of modern liberal capitalist societies. As he puts it, "A fading political identity makes it harder to mobilize effectively, and a sense of hopelessness breeds alienation." However, this "vicious circle" also points to its own "virtuous" solution: "Successful common action can bring a *sense of empowerment* and also strengthen identification with the political community."[22]

But what of neoclassical civic republicans? Does their rejection of the ideal of virtuous positive liberty mean that we should think of them as having a qualitatively different perspective on civic virtue? I do not think so. Certainly, there are important differences between the neoclassical perspective and the more strongly Aristotelian civic humanism of the communal republican mainstream. Neoclassical republicans are less interested in participation, more wary of tyranny of the majority, more trusting of representative forms of democracy, and more open to freedom as a form of security that is protected by the rule of law. But as neoclassical theorists describe their perspective, the key difference is a conceptual one having to do with the previously discussed question of whether democracy is an essential part of the meaning of freedom.

While the argument that democracy is only contingently related to liberty is certainly one that needs to be taken seriously with respect to philosophies of freedom, it has surprisingly little relevance to the question of whether neoclassical theorists have a qualitatively different view of civic virtue than their communal republican cousins. The reason is that the same basic theoretical structure of a circle of civic engagement can also be found in neoclassical republicanism. The pursuit of the common good of non-domination requires that citizens be engaged with and for one another in collective, public ways. It also involves the capacity of citizens to define themselves on the basis of a common good that they affirm and at least partly determine through collective civic deliberations and practices. True, it is a more defensive and protective engagement, and one in which things like direct democracy and economic democracy play less of a role. But a case can also be made that neoclassical civic engagement is very much in the spirit of positive liberty, even if this engagement is viewed as something conceptually and logically different than freedom. Some support for this comes from Skinner. According to Skinner, many early modern defenders of the "neo-roman" understanding of freedom (as he calls it) advanced the "radical thesis" that "it is only possible to be free in a free state." And how did these thinkers define a free state? Precisely by their "capacity for self-government." "A free state," Skinner says of this "neo-roman" perspective, "is a community in which the actions of the body politic are determined by the will of the members as a whole."[23] What is this if not a variation of positive liberty as political self-rule? But even if we don't accept Skinner's interpretation (or for that matter, my interpretation of Skinner) the general point is that protecting, pursuing, and promoting freedom as non-domination requires forms of engagement in which individuals, as citizens, take collective control of their lives. This is self-government. This is participation. This is civic empowerment. And in both the communal and the neoclassical branches of contemporary civic republicanism, the goal is for citizens to be politically empowered in civil and public-minded ways.

Civic Republican Teleology and the Question of Perfectionism

There is one other philosophical disagreement in the universe of contemporary civic republicanism that is relevant to this discussion of a formative circle of civic engagement. This has to do with differing civic republican perspectives on the teleological order of moral and civic ends. Adapting a distinction that Richard Sinopoli makes in his defense of what he takes to be the liberal republicanism of the American founders, it can be said that the civic republicans' circle of virtuous civic engagement is associated with two very different teleological perspectives. In some articulations, their circle evokes the "strong civic humanist thesis" of a perfectionist order of ends, while at other times, it is closer to the "weaker republican thesis" of a pluralistic and more loosely structured order of ends.[24] Whereas the first thesis treats civic virtue as a higher end within a rank order of human goods, the second one holds that while the goods of citizenship are intrinsically valuable, they are not the only important goods or even the most important ones of moral and political life. I suspect that were philosophical push to come to shove, most contemporary civic republicans would align themselves with the weaker thesis. Still, it is possible to find expressions of support for the stronger thesis, as for example when Sullivan writes approvingly of the civic humanist view that "a higher integration of the powers of the self" is "at once the goal and the effect of participation in civic life."[25]

These two perspectives are ultimately irreconcilable. Obviously, also, this is a philosophical difference with important practical implications. At some point, civic humanist perfectionism translates into real demands and burdens on citizens, and because of this, I join with Sinopoli and other liberals in worrying about the potential for coercion and oppressive conformism in the stronger civic humanist understanding of civic virtue. By the same token, I think that this is an area where the neoclassical position is the superior one in contemporary republican theory. The understanding of civic virtue that neoclassical republicans defend is one that goes out of its way to be less demanding and less onerous than ancient Greek and Roman understandings. Rather than the renunciation of private interests and self-sacrificing devotion to the common good, neoclassical virtue is grounded simply in the love of liberty and acceptance of basic civic duties to secure it.[26] But it is important that we not give too much weight to the dangers of civic humanist perfectionism when it comes to contemporary republican theory. In addition to the fact that most of today's communal republicans steer clear of a perfectionist form of civic humanism, there are a couple of other points to be made. First, it bears repeating that civic republicans share a broadly teleological perspective on morality and politics.[27] All civic republicans view civic or public virtue as an ethical disposition that helps both individuals and communities to realize valuable ends and goods. Second, there is a sense in which the issue of perfectionism, much like the question of whether democracy is an essential part of freedom, is irrelevant to the theoretical structure of civic virtue. What I mean by this is that the basic structure of a circle of engagement in which self-governing citizens are engaged with and for each other in determining the common good is not going to change depending on whether it is embedded in a perfectionist or a pluralist perspective on moral ends and purposes. The issues that are at stake with perfectionism are how the circle of civic engagement relates to other moral practices and ends and whether the ends of civic life end up crowding out other valuable ends in an oppressive and unjust manner. But the basic structure of the circle raises some issues that are logically of a different order. For instance, how are democratic norms of equal citizenship to be incorporated into the basic theoretical structure of civic republican virtue?

As this question suggests, the fact that the civic republican circle of engagement is capacious enough to accommodate very different philosophical perspectives has important implications for my critique. Specifically, it means that there is a level of critical analysis of civic republicanism at which the structure of the circle itself is what is at issue, regardless of whether the circle is elaborated along communal republican lines of virtuous positive liberty, and regardless of whether it is accompanied by a perfectionist view of the order of moral and civic ends. At this level, the flaws in this structure that are revealed by my investigation (say, with regard to threats to democratic equality) may be partly offset, but never entirely or adequately repaired by moderating the commitment to positive liberty or by retreating from the "strong civic humanist thesis" of perfectionism. It turns out that this is precisely the case with respect to the problem of republican paternalism. That is to say, I believe that the danger of an undemocratic paternalism is rooted in the very structure of the circle of engagement.

Towards an Internal Critique

My concerns about the problem of republican paternalism underscore the fact that I am a liberal critic of civic republicanism. Yet there is also much in civic republicanism with which I agree. I do not hesitate for a moment in saying that civic republicans have given us some compelling arguments and reminders about the importance of an ethos of responsible citizenship for democracy. Whatever the problems with their formative project, civic republicans have reminded us that democracy is fundamentally a shared civic affair—a *res publica*. It is more than impersonal procedures of accountability and consent, and more also than simple empowerment. Procedures and empowerment are both important. But procedures do not entail civic education or civic engagement and participation, and shorn of civic attachments and ends, empowerment can just as easily defeat democratic aspirations as enrich them.

The challenge is to engage civic republicanism in a manner that affirms its insights about democratic citizenship while also accounting for dangers that inhere in a politics of civic virtue. Too often, the debate over civic republicanism has taken the form of a neat opposition between liberalism and civic republicanism. Among other things, this has resulted in a tendency among critics to fall back on the formulaic argument that the problem with civic republicanism is a theoretically uncomplicated one of going too far in promoting civic duties and the good of the community. This argument holds that liberal ideas of individual liberty, equal rights, and tolerance emerge as crucially important checks on the civic republican tendency towards oppressive or exclusionary conformism.[28] While this way of arguing wins debating points for liberals, it also glosses over the complexity of the relationship between civic virtue and democracy.

It is in the interest of breaking free of these kinds of formulaic arguments that I am adopting the mode of internal criticism. To be sure, I cannot and will not completely bracket or suspend my liberal commitments and beliefs. But I do not want to defend these commitments and beliefs as an *a priori* perspective that is given in advance of my exploration of civic republicanism. Rather, I want to defend them through a critical, but also dialogic, encounter with civic republican arguments about civic virtue and community. The result is still a defense of liberalism—or more precisely, of a form of left-leaning democratic liberalism. But I believe that it will be a stronger defense for having been developed through an internal-critical encounter with civic republicans, in no small part because it will be a defense that is open to the civic republicans' post-socialist revisions and qualifications of liberal democracy.

A Hermeneutic Circle of Civic Engagement

From the outset of the revival, liberal critics have taken civic republicans to task for ignoring the exclusionary and conformist possibilities that accompany their efforts to re-embed the self in communal contexts of character formation.[29] I think that the critics have a point, and to some extent, my critique can be seen as an extension of their arguments about the situated self. But I also think that these criticisms have swept far too broadly, usually with little regard for the differences between civic republicanism and other contemporary theories of community, and almost always without appreciation for the hermeneutic perspective that informs the most systematic civic republican discussions of moral and civic identity.

With communal republicans such as Sullivan, Taylor, and Sandel, the general hermeneutic approach that I discussed in the Introduction is elaborated with specific reference to moral and civic identity. The basic idea is that identity formation has to do with how we understand ourselves and our beliefs and actions in relation to our history and our place in the social and political world. Hermeneutically speaking, therefore, the situated self that is described and defended by civic republicans is a self whose identity as "a self-interpreting being" is constituted through an ongoing engagement with the understandings, practices, and discursive traditions of its community.[30]

Hermeneutics is not the only way in which civic republicans have expressed their views on moral and civic personality. Nor are all civic republicans on the same philosophical wavelength when it comes to hermeneutics. Some take issue with the communal republican emphasis on particularistic contexts of self-interpretation.[31] Some show little interest in hermeneutics of any kind. And others develop arguments that are quite consistent with a hermeneutic perspective on identity, but without making the connection explicit. Still, the communal republican hermeneutics of the situated self provides an elegant and robust framework for the idea of civic virtue as a circle of engagement. The image of a circle is itself central to philosophical hermeneutics. This is the case, for example, with Hans-Georg Gadamer's extremely influential reformulation of the hermeneutic perspective.[32] While Gadamer is not the only

source of civic republican hermeneutics, looking at his reformulation and re-
structuring of the hermeneutic circle as an interpretive engagement with discursive traditions helps to bring the theoretical underpinnings of the revival
into sharper focus.

For Gadamer, as for communal republicans, human understanding has a
socially embodied and embedded quality. Specifically, communal republicans
join with Gadamer in arguing that there is no point outside of history or language from where we begin the process of understanding a text, a culture, a
social practice, a discursive tradition, or any other "object" of understanding.
Rather, the nature of human understanding is such that it occurs within, and
indeed, is made possible by, the historically and linguistically constituted
standpoint or horizon of interpretation within which we are always/already
situated. This means in turn that the task of interpretation is one of encountering "texts" which are themselves implicated in our own horizon by virtue
of having an effective or "living" historical presence in language. Consequently, "the ontological structure of human understanding" is seen by
Gadamer as being akin to a continuous circular movement between the horizon of linguistically embodied understandings or "prejudices" which we bring
to the task of interpretation and the horizon of that which we are interpreting. This continuous circular movement of understanding is what Gadamer
calls a "fusion of horizons."[33]

With civic republicans, the emphasis shifts from the general ontological
structure of understanding to an emphasis on the social ontology of moral
and civic personality. It is the communal and civic "sources of the self," and
not the sources of the human relationship to Being in general, which civic republicans are mainly interested in exploring. The same circular interpretive
structure is there, the difference being that it is a circle of moral and civic understanding and self-understanding that comes to the fore. It is in this
hermeneutic spirit, for example, that Sullivan applauds advocates of a "virtue
ethics" for recognizing that "moral understanding moves in a kind of circle in
which the practical consensus is guided by a tacit sense of importance that is
presupposed even as it is brought to light through discourse. That consensus
is ultimately not a system of beliefs, though it may be interpreted as such, but
is, rather, embedded in ways of seeing and acting. . . . Moral reflection becomes
in the first instance a task of interpretation."[34]

For Sullivan and like-minded communal republicans, therefore, civic virtue
is an ethical engagement that is both political and interpretive. To be engaged
with and for other citizens in the practice of self-government is part of, and
made possible by, an interpretive engagement with the horizon within which
citizens see and act as moral beings. Or what amounts to the same thing, civic
republicans believe that a healthy and sustainable republic is one where (at

Chapter 2

least much of the time) the political and hermeneutic modes of engagement work together. When this happens, the interpretive engagement is formative of civic virtue, and civic virtue contributes in turn to the ongoing deliberative project of recovering, revealing, refining, and redefining the moral universe of the community.

An important part of civic republican hermeneutics (and a part which shows the influence of Gadamer) revolves around the historical dimension of situated understanding and self-understanding. "We are," writes Taylor, "embodied agents, living in dialogical conditions, *inhabiting time in a specifically human way, that is, making sense of our lives as a story that connects the past from which we have come to our future projects*."[35] "Making sense" of the historical context of our lives is also the point of Sullivan's claim that a "recovery of democratic politics in America must start with reawakening a living sense of the social and historical relationships within which we stand."[36]

For civic republicans such as Taylor and Sullivan, the circle of civic engagement is one in which we encounter our republican past as a living, although half-forgotten and often occluded, presence in our own horizon of civic understanding and self-understanding. Accordingly, the civic republicans' hermeneutic encounters with the republican tradition are best seen as attempts to recover and "re-cognize" (if you will) submerged republican understandings of self-government. This would constitute a fusion of horizons. It is the hope of civic republicans that by reawakening a "living sense" of our republican heritage of civic virtue, we can begin to expose and test the individualist and proceduralist prejudices that inform so much—too much—of our current liberal democratic understanding of self-government. More than this, some civic republicans maintain that in encountering the republican tradition we are encountering a tradition that is itself hermeneutic in its approach to practical contexts of reason and understanding. "The civic tradition," Sullivan writes, "shares the [hermeneutic] understanding that practical reason moves in a circle, growing by the efforts of citizens formed by the civic *paideia* to extend and realize the ideal of a more humane and just commonwealth."[37] The excellence of character that is cultivated through a reappropriation of this circularity of practical reason involves not only the realization of our nature as social and communal beings, but also the realization of our freedom as democratic citizens.

Of all the theorists and scholars who have participated in the revival of civic republicanism, none has made more of a contribution to the civic republicans' hermeneutic perspective on personality and citizenship than Taylor. In fact, it is Taylor, and not Gadamer, who has been the main intellectual force in this area. Over a period of several years, and in numerous essays and books, Taylor has developed a theoretical framework for understanding the situated self as a "self-interpreting being" whose capacity for agency is cultivated through participation in, and interpretation of, the community's historically extended conversations about morality and politics.[38]

As is the case with other accounts of the situated self that have emerged in recent years, Taylor's is grounded in an ontological premise about the communal nature and sources of human personality. "The community," as Taylor puts it, "is not simply an aggregation of individuals; nor is there simply a causal connection between the two. The community is also constitutive of the individual, in the sense that the self-interpretations that define him are drawn from the interchange which the community carries on."[39] As this suggests, Taylor does not see the community as being constitutive of the individual merely in the sense of being the source of emotional attachments and bonds. To be sure, the community *is* constitutive of identity partly because it is such a context of belonging. But from a hermeneutic perspective this means that it is also, and more importantly, constitutive of identity because it provides conversational contexts within which self-interpreting individuals come to understand themselves as moral and political beings.

Participation in the "interchange which the community carries on" is not, by itself, a sufficient condition for the development of the various moral and civic excellences of character that Taylor and other civic republicans extol. Though relatively open-ended, the communal republican account of the situated self is not so broad or so loosely structured that it envisions or defends each and every communal interchange as a formative context of virtue. Before participation in the communal interchange can rise to this level, it must occur within languages—Taylor calls them "languages of qualitative contrast"—that promote reflective, discriminating, and socially and politically responsible forms of interpretation and self-interpretation. When this happens, we have what Taylor refers to as "strong evaluation."

Taylor contrasts "strong evaluation" with two other general approaches to moral decision-making. The first of these alternatives is what he calls "simple weighing," by which he means an unreflective and often inarticulate reliance on feelings or preferences that an individual has about the right course of action. The second alternative is evinced in much contemporary liberal theory. It is a proceduralist approach that seeks to ground practical reason either in formal criteria of right, obligation, and justice or in purportedly neutral "decision rules" such as those associated with utilitarianism. Though this proceduralist approach is far more elaborate than simple weighing, and though it is far more likely to be accompanied by the articulation of reasons and justifications for decisions and actions, it is like simple weighing in the crucial respect that it effaces the kinds of qualitative moral distinctions and contrasts that make strong evaluation a deeper and richer mode of decision-making.[40]

According to Taylor, then, unlike both the simple weigher and the procedu-ralist, the strong evaluator makes qualitative discriminations within her ethi-cal situation between higher and lower moral ends, between what is noble and base, virtuous and corrupt. Not least important in this regard is the capacity to discern the higher ends and purposes associated with popular rule and self-government—the higher ends and purposes of what Taylor calls a "citizen re-public." "The citizen republic," he writes, "is to be valued not just as a guaran-tor of general utility, or as a bulwark of rights. It may even endanger these in certain circumstances. We value it also because we generally hold that the form of life in which men govern themselves, and decide their own fate through common deliberation, is higher than one in which they live as sub-jects of even an enlightened despotism."[41]

In addition to illuminating the connection between strong evaluation and civic republican ideals, the qualitative contrast between a citizen republic and despotism serves as a reminder that the civic republican account of the situ-ated self is not just about identity in some general sense, but also more specif-ically about agency. In the civic republicans' teleological vision, the situated self is a self who develops a capacity to act responsibly in the world, not just reflect on moral ends and purposes. Or rather, reflection on moral ends and purposes is itself about the ends and purposes of moral action in the world. "By contrast with liberalism," Sullivan writes, "classical teleological reason *sit-uates achievement of an integrated self capable of self-reflection, and so of re-sponsible action,* within a continuity of life which is both social and natural."[42]

Through strong evaluation, then, individuals and citizens come to see that who they are as members of the community is very much tied to their activi-ties on behalf of the goods, ends, and excellences that define a depth of char-acter. In terms of the goods, ends, and excellences associated with a citizen re-public, the practice of strong evaluation involves both a capacity for agency as a self-governing citizen and a willingness to respect and support the processes and practices by which all are ruled. In the Aristotelian idiom of communal re-publicanism, strong evaluation promotes responsible civic engagement in the sense of a capacity to "share in the civic life of ruling and being ruled in turn."[43] Merely having a sense of identification with other citizens and with the shared goods of the civic community might make it easier to accept and appreciate public-spirited rule by others, but it would not motivate or empower citizens to "take their turn" ruling themselves. By the same token, a project that seeks to motivate and empower citizens to rule themselves is unlikely to succeed—or worse, is apt to promote a Hobbesian power struggle—unless it is accompa-nied by communal norms of mutual understanding, respect, and concern.

To summarize, the civic republican circle of civic engagement is a hermeneutic one in which "self-interpreting" citizens are simultaneously engaged with one another at the level of a common civic identity *and* engaged with one another in the shared practice of self-government. Moreover, virtuous civic engagement is linked to strong evaluation in that it involves reflective moral agents and citizens becoming engaged with and within richly textured "languages of qualitative contrast" pertaining to distinctions between what is higher and lower, noble and base, virtuous and corrupt.

The Internal Critique Spelled Out

It is easy to see how this hermeneutics of identity gets translated into an argument about the corruptive power of property in the modern liberal commercial republic. Property is corruptive not merely because the self-interested pursuit of it turns citizens away from the common good (although that is part of it). It is also corruptive—deeply corruptive—because the pursuit of it is associated with self-understandings that undermine the higher and nobler ends of strong evaluation and responsible civic engagement. But the simplicity of this opposition between property and higher moral and civic ends begins to break down when we make the internal-critical move of fully integrating property into the civic republican hermeneutics of identity. This move gives rise to two kinds of questions that are very unsettling for civic republicans. First, there are questions concerning the implications for civic republican thinking about civic virtue and the sources of civic identity. What happens to the hermeneutic circle of civic engagement when property becomes part of the project of cultivating the virtues of citizenship? And what happens when the situated self is situated within contexts of property? Second, though, there are questions about the implications for property. How does our understanding of property change when it is viewed as a potentially formative context in its own right? And what happens when property is viewed as a location within which selves are situated?

Recasting the Civic Republican Hermeneutics of Identity

My interest in introducing property into the civic republican hermeneutics of identity should not be taken as a sign that I am in complete philosophical agreement with the communal republican approach to hermeneutics. I am not so traditionalist, and I am more skeptical of particularistic communal attachments and self-understandings. In the lexicon of contemporary philosophical discussions of such things, mine is more of a "hermeneutics of suspicion" that seeks to demystify communal traditions than is the case with communal republicans, most of whom espouse more of a "hermeneutics of faith" or "recovery" that emphasizes the recovery of communal understandings.[44]

All of this raises thorny issues concerning the conflict between particularistic approaches to hermeneutics and universalistic and transcendentalist alternatives. At the risk of appearing to try to reconcile irreconcilable positions, I wish to steer a course between particularism and universalism and between embeddedness and transcendentalism. The liberal theorist William Galston has a point when he says, "the inner movement of reflective consciousness engenders a philosophically significant difference from [particularistic] local perspectives."[45] But so too does Sullivan when he argues along hermeneutic lines that "moral reflection…is inherently circular" in that it involves reflection on the same moral understandings that are embedded in our "ways of seeing and acting."[46] There is (or can be) a context-transcending moment of critical reason in socially embedded interpretation. At the same time, though, there is (or can be) a moment of linguistic and historical immanence in the creation of critical distance from "local perspectives." In saying that a deeper moral understanding necessarily involves interpretation and reflection within our own ethical situation, we need not deny that critical reason and reflection can create distance from "local perspectives." A deeper moral or political understanding can and sometimes should result in disagreement with the conventions of one's community.[47] By the same token, there is a point at which a "deeper" understanding becomes indistinguishable from a "higher" truth.[48]

I cannot hope to resolve these issues here. Fortunately, it is not crucial for the purposes of this inquiry whether the creation of critical distance from local perspectives is best seen in terms of immanence or transcendence. What matters most in this regard is the fact that a capacity for critical distance is an important attribute of democratic agency. As my critique develops, it will become increasingly clear that I do not think that civic republicans have succeeded in articulating the background conditions for such a civic capacity. Nevertheless, my critique starts with the hermeneutic belief that I share with civic republicans like Taylor, the belief that we become who we are in large part by reflecting within and on the horizon that informs our understandings. I too think that the development of identity and agency occurs within interpretive contexts of meaning and language that are in some general sense both communal and historical.[49] And like the communal republicans I think that this applies to the horizon of democratic citizenship. It is by uncovering and exploring the horizon within which democratic citizens stand and within which they see and act that I hope to be able to say something about the properties of democracy.

Thus, my internal critique starts within a broadly common framework of hermeneutics. In terms of the central themes of this inquiry, what is at issue with regard to this common framework is not that civic republicans have applied a hermeneutic perspective to matters of identity, but the selective manner in which they have done so, most especially with regard to property and property-related contexts of authority and dominion. As we have already begun to see, what emerges from this process of internal criticism is a theoretical vocabulary of democracy and hermeneutics that is very different than that of contemporary civic republicanism in several key respects. My own vocabulary is more deeply and more self-consciously informed by a left-leaning democratic liberalism, by progressive traditions of opposition to oppressive concentrations of property and political power and authority, and by the aspiration to provide ordinary citizens with propertied stakes in a democratic commonwealth. However, the point of departure for my critique is not a different vocabulary, but a rearrangement of the terms of theoretical discussion and debate that civic republicans have established through their project of civic recovery and renewal and their hermeneutics of identity. In this rearrangement, property is placed front and center, partly as a corrective to the civic republicans' generally dismissive stance on property, but also, and more importantly, for the theoretical purpose of helping to illuminate those sources, conditions, and problems of democracy that are difficult to see when property is kept in the shadows.

A couple of additional points of clarification are in order. First, in adopting a hermeneutic approach I do not mean to disparage social-scientific research on the empirical relationships between property, civic virtue, and democracy. There are well-established research agendas for investigating empirical questions pertaining to such things as cross-cultural variability in the formation of civic beliefs, the requisite degree of public spirit in a democratic civic culture, the role of voluntary civil associations in fostering attitudes and practices of civic engagement, the relationship between levels of political participation and "social capital" in the form of social networks of trust, and the relative importance of different forms of political participation.[50] These are important questions. But I am not addressing them, at least not at the level of systematic empirical research and analysis. For one thing, these are issues that should be addressed by political sociologists and others who are better equipped to deal with them. But in addition, there are lingering theoretical issues in the debate over civic republicanism that are at least as important as these empirical questions. This includes issues pertaining to the question of how civic virtue and the formative project of cultivating it should be conceptualized in relation to the background of beliefs and conditions that make democracy possible, and inform its practices. It is of course in order to illuminate this background that I am turning to hermeneutics. And it is in relation to this horizontal background, I am arguing, that property is more deeply, more complexly, and more problematically implicated than civic republicans have recognized.

Second, it needs to be kept in mind that these theoretical issues cannot be addressed or resolved simply by civic republicans putting forward more policy proposals. Civic republicans often have been accused of failing to outline a practical program of political economy, and with considerable justification in the early stages of the current revival of a politics of civic virtue. At present, though, this charge is without merit, for, as we saw earlier, there are now plenty of civic republican proposals for a concrete program of political-economic reform. It is a sign of the times that such a program can be developed with only sporadic and generally superficial attention to property itself.[51] Even so, what is at issue with respect to civic republican thinking about property is not whether they have advanced concrete policy proposals about political economy, but rather whether they have developed a theoretical framework that is practical in the sense of supporting and sustaining the expansive democratic aspirations that inform, and are reflected in, their "political economy of citizenship." I do not think that they have. More than this, I think that civic republicans have developed a theoretical framework that is as likely to defeat these aspirations as support them. And this becomes clear, I am arguing, when we look beneath concrete programs and proposals of political economy and cast a hermeneutic eye on occluded democratic understandings of property and property-related contexts of authority, labor, and civic identity. That is to say, it becomes clear when we recast the civic republicans' own hermeneutics of identity around issues of property and its relationship to democracy.

Beyond a Hermeneutics of Avoidance

We are now in a position to come up with a more precise statement of the central thesis of my critique: Property—that is, property in the broader, contextual sense that I have outlined—is associated with civic understandings and social and economic conditions which, while deeply ingrained in the horizon of modern democracy, are largely ignored and overlooked in the civic republican hermeneutics of identity. Because the "social and historical relationships within which we stand" as democratic citizens are constituted in part through property-related contexts of meaning and identity, civic republicans exclude them from their "hermeneutics of recovery" at the risk of creating substantial blind spots in their conception of the situated self. When civic republicans write of the distortions of personality and citizenship that are fostered by liberal understandings of property, they are at least implicitly acknowledging the hermeneutic importance of property. However, by selectively applying their hermeneutics of identity to "atomistic" liberal ideas of possessive individualism, and more especially, by ignoring or glossing over the ways in which property has functioned as a context of dominion and authority, civic republicans fail to reawaken "a living sense" of the practical contexts of property within which individuals in liberal democratic societies stand as self-interpreting moral agents and democratic citizens.

In order to reawaken "a living sense" of the full range of issues associated with the corruptive influence of liberal capitalism, civic republicans need to reexamine the historical background of the relationship between property and civic virtue. We shall see that starting with Aristotle's theory of the household and continuing through early modern celebrations of virtuous propertied independence, classical republicans sought to define the capacity for self-government in terms of the rule of dependent adults within locations of property. This perspective on property and self-government points to a classical republican tradition of placeness. But it also points to what I am calling, in ideal-typical fashion, a "masters' vision of civic virtue." This is a vision in which the capacity for virtuous civic engagement among free and equal male masters of households and estates was defined in relation to the virtuous deference and non-participation of those adults who, for reasons of both "natural" and socioeconomic dependency, were thought to lack the capacity for republican self-government.

True, by now most civic republicans have made a point of acknowledging and distancing themselves from the undemocratic and exclusionary possibilities of the republican tradition. The problem is that this has not been accompanied by an effort to confront these possibilities in a sustained and systematic theoretical manner. This is especially true with respect to property and the masters' vision of civic virtue. As a result, civic republicans risk transforming their hermeneutics of recovery into a hermeneutics of avoidance. For if civic republicans are right (as I think they are) in claiming that the republican tradition of civic virtue and public liberty persists as a residual idiom in Western liberal democratic cultures, then there is reason to think that republican mastery persists in submerged forms as well. In this regard, I wish to argue that the primary theoretical importance of the masters' vision has to do with the fact that it represents a foundational and paradigmatic expression of the broader problem of republican paternalism. Though rooted in the past, this problem is not to be avoided by claiming, as some civic republicans do, that it is outmoded in a modern era of democratic republicanism. This claim not only begs the question of how the horizon of modern democratic republicanism was constituted in contrast and opposition to classical republican paternalism. It also avoids difficult theoretical issues associated with the relationship between the *formative* and *distributive* dimensions of a politics of civic virtue. Theoretically, the problem of republican paternalism has to do with the fact that the project of cultivating civic virtue has distributive conditions and consequences that are problematically related to democratic norms of equal and inclusive citizenship. The problem arises not simply in bygone European or European American eras of exclusionary and hierarchical thinking about civic capacity, but also theoretically at the point where the question of the distribution of the capacity for civic virtue among different groups and classes begins to condition the question of how to cultivate such a capacity. Or what amounts to the same thing, it arises at the point where the question of how to cultivate a capacity for virtuous civic independence is answered by ascribing this capacity (for whatever reasons) to those in privileged positions of power, authority, socioeconomic status, or property.

If I am right, then the problem of republican paternalism is rooted in the theoretical structure of a politics of civic virtue. Among other things, this means that it is a problem for neoclassical theorists of non-domination as well as for the communal republican mainstream. Indeed, as a problem having to do with the capacity for independent citizenship, the problem of republican paternalism takes an especially stark form in neoclassical civic republicanism. Specifically, it becomes a problem of the capacity for virtuous non-domination being a function of the domination of those deemed to lack this capacity.

By way of summary, I hope to show that property is a doubly unsettling presence within the civic republican hermeneutics of identity: first, because it can serve as a formative location of civic virtue as well as a source of materialistic corruption; and second, because it provides a compelling example of the problematic interaction between the formative and the distributive dimensions of a politics of civic virtue. The upshot, in both respects, is that it becomes far more difficult for civic republicans to use property as an issue with which to claim the high ground of moral and civic virtue against the liberal tradition of property. But more than this, the question arises as to whether the civic republican project of recovering an ethos of civic virtue would lead to the renewal of democracy or simply to a new, virtue-centered form of the mystification of relations of power and authority. We are left with the unsettling possibility that a politics of civic virtue might become the source of property-based inequalities of civic power and authority which, while of a different kind than those which are generated by possessive individualism and a mechanistic market model of instrumental exchange relationships, are nonetheless at odds with the civic republicans' own strong commitment to equal and inclusive citizenship.

Again, what emerges from this process of internal criticism is not an argument against civic virtue. By no means do I wish to join with those libertarians and neoliberals who think that where there are appeals to civic virtue, tyranny and oppression cannot be far behind.[52] What emerges, rather, is an argument that democracy is a messy business with both enduring problems and enduring possibilities for renewal and transformation. We shall see that the placeness of property as a formative context of citizenship is a case in point. The danger of exclusionary and hierarchical forms of civic placeness is ongoing. Yet the civic placeness of property also contains enormous democratic potential. The idea of property serving as a formative location of responsible citizenship helps to illuminate a "political economy of citizenship" that empowers citizens as responsible and equal stakeholders. What is this if not a reformulation and renewal of the modern progressive tradition of social democracy?

In the end, it is a partly republicanized and more environmentally conscious, but fundamentally liberal vision of social democracy that I wish to defend. This I believe is the best we can do in meeting the difficult challenge of bringing some kind of theoretical and moral agreement between the messy pluralism of democratic liberalism and the requirements of social justice. But in the current era, it is not unremarkable to be able to say something in support of social democracy.

Rethinking the Right and the Good

There is, finally, an aspect of my critical exploration of civic republicanism that has to do with property and its relationship to the philosophical priority of the good over the right. So far I have said very little about this issue. But there is a sense in which it is central to this whole enterprise. The priority of the good is one of the areas where I am in agreement with civic republicans. By this I mean only that I agree with civic republicans (not to mention liberal theorists of virtue and most post-socialists) that theories of right and justice presuppose conceptions of the human good, and that what is right or just is so because it furthers or helps to realize this human good. But as with the civic republicans' hermeneutic perspective on identity, here too we are dealing with an area of agreement which, while substantive, is also relatively open-ended. More to the point, my focus on property represents an attempt to introduce more specificity to a philosophical debate that has tended to be very general and very abstract. In my judgment, this has left "the good" and its attendant virtues in a kind of privileged isolation from practical contexts of property, economic interest, power, discipline, and authority. By the same token, there has been a tendency to avoid the problematic interaction between the good and these practical contexts by defining and redefining the good ever more capaciously. Thus, if a particular theory of the good is criticized as being potentially too conformist, too hierarchical, or too authoritarian, the solution is simply to expand our understanding of the good to make room for values such as pluralism and diversity, and maybe even doses (although not always liberal doses) of equal rights and individual freedom. All of this is very high-minded. But at some point, this theoretical practice of reformulating the good to meet every possible objection becomes a rather unilluminating form of casuistry, with little meaningful connection to the practical existential struggles and predicaments that are part of political life. By the same token, I believe that there is a point at which we must recognize that the good is not so neatly ordered or harmonious as we might hope for as theorists and philosophers. And this too is something that property, with its dual status as a corruptive influence and an instrument of human development, helps us to see.

Thus, the theoretical priority that I am giving to property reflects a broader interest of mine in refocusing and "re-situating" discussions of the good. Now that the good has been brought back into political theory, it is time—in my view, long past time—to explicate it in relation to more prosaic contexts and concepts such as property. Just as liberal defenders of a deontological ethic of rights have to defend themselves against the charge that the imagery of property is deeply implicated in a liberal language of rights, so too is it incumbent upon theorists of the good to consider how the instrumental good of property might be implicated in their favored ethic of virtue. Over the course of the remainder of this inquiry, it will become clear that there is an important sense in which this is a matter of challenging neo-Aristotelian theorists to be simultaneously more Aristotelian in their approach to the good and more aware of the dangers of such an approach.

Notes

1. For an excellent overview of the republican revival and its historical sources, see Iseult Honohan, *Civic Republicanism* (London: Routledge, 2002).
2. See Michael J. Sandel, *Liberalism and the Limits of Justice*, 2nd ed. (Cambridge: Cambridge University Press, 1998), especially chapter 1; Sandel, "The Procedural Republic and the Unencumbered Self," *Political Theory*, 12 (1984): 81–96; and Sandel, *Democracy's Discontent: America in Search of a Public Philosophy* (Cambridge, MA: Belknap Press, 1996), chapter 1.
3. See Charles Taylor, *Sources of the Self: The Making of Modern Identity* (Cambridge, MA: Harvard University Press, 1989), especially chapter 11; and Taylor, *The Ethics of Authenticity* (Cambridge, MA: Harvard University Press, 1991), 58–59 and 93–108.
4. *Democracy's Discontent*, 5–6 and 321–24.
5. Robert N. Bellah et al., *Habits of the Heart: Individualism and Commitment in American Life*, 2nd ed. (Berkeley, CA: University of California Press, 1996), 277.
6. *Habits*, 271 and 262.
7. Robert Booth Fowler, *The Dance with Community: The Contemporary Debate in American Political Thought* (Lawrence, KS: University Press of Kansas, 1991), 69.
8. See especially Benjamin R. Barber, *Strong Democracy: Participatory Politics for a New Age* (Berkeley, CA: University of California Press, 1984); Robert N. Bellah et al., *The Good Society* (New York: Alfred A. Knopf, 1991); Daniel Kemmis, *Community and the Politics of Place* (Norman, OK: University of Oklahoma Press, 1990); Philip Pettit,

Republicanism: A Theory of Freedom and Government (Oxford: Oxford University Press, 1997); Sandel, *Democracy's Discontent*; and William M. Sullivan, *Reconstructing Public Philosophy* (Berkeley, CA: University of California Press, 1986). Pieces of the program can also be found in Ronald Beiner, *What's the Matter with Liberalism?* (Berkeley, CA: University of California Press, 1992); Mary G. Dietz, "Citizenship with a Feminist Face: The Problem with Maternal Thinking," *Political Theory* 13 (1985): 19–37; and Daniel Kemmis, *The Good City and the Good Life: Renewing the Sense of Community* (Boston: Houghton Mifflin Company, 1995).

9. My interpretation of "communal republicanism" may be contrasted with Seyla Benhabib's analysis of the difference between "integrationist" and "participationist" strands of contemporary communitarianism. Her distinction makes some sense as a first gloss on communitarianism. But in my view, it is not fine enough to capture what is distinctive about civic republicanism as a vision of community, namely, the way in which civic republicanism aims at recovering political agency within and through community. In this respect, even those I am calling "communal republicans" are "participationists." See Seyla Benhabib, *Situating the Self: Gender, Community, and Postmodernism in Contemporary Ethics* (New York: Routledge, 1992), 77.

10. Pettit, *Republicanism*, 80. Also see Quentin Skinner, *Liberty Before Liberalism* (Cambridge: Cambridge University Press, 1998).

11. Maurizio Viroli, *Republicanism* (New York: Hill and Wang, 2002), 35. I note one difference between Pettit and Viroli: Whereas Viroli sees non-domination as a variation of, and improvement on, negative liberty, Pettit insists that it should be thought of as a distinctive form of liberty that is different from both a negative liberty of non-interference and a positive liberty of self-rule. Compare Viroli, 11 and 35, with Pettit, 7–12 and 17–31. As is discussed in chapters 4 and 5, my own view is closer to Viroli's, though unlike both Viroli and Pettit I believe that the negative liberty of non-domination is closely linked to positive liberty.

12. Pettit, *Republicanism*, chapter 5, especially 183–205.

13. Pettit, 245.

14. Quentin Skinner, *The Renaissance: The Foundations of Modern Political Thought*, vol. 1 (Cambridge: Cambridge University Press, 1978), 88; also see 84–94. Iseult Honohan provides a helpful summary of the similarities and differences between the political philosophies of Aristotle and Cicero in *Civic Republicanism*, chapter 1.

15. On the idea of "paradigmatic" historical formulations of important concepts and theories, see Charles Taylor, "Philosophy and Its History," in *Philosophy in History: Essays on the Historiography of Philosophy*, ed. Richard Rorty, J. B. Schneewind, and Quentin Skinner (Cambridge: Cambridge University Press, 1984).

16. *Community and the Politics of Place*, 12.

17. Charles Taylor, "Cross-Purposes: The Liberal-Communitarian Debate," in *Liberalism and the Moral Life*, ed. Nancy L. Rosenblum (Cambridge, MA: Harvard University Press, 1989), 165 and 179.

18. Sullivan, *Reconstructing Public Philosophy*, 163.

19. David Miller, *Citizenship and National Identity* (Malden, MA: Polity Press, 2000), 53, emphasis added.

20. See *Liberalism and the Limits of Justice*, 56–59 and 177–78; "The Procedural Republic"; and *Democracy's Discontent*, 322–25.

21. "Cross-Purposes: The Liberal-Communitarian Debate," 167.

22. *The Ethics of Authenticity*, 118, emphasis added. Also see Taylor, *Philosophical Arguments* (Cambridge, MA: Harvard University Press, 1995), 281–85.

23. *Liberty Before Liberalism*, 60 and 26.

24. Richard Sinopoli, *The Foundations of American Citizenship* (New York: Oxford University Press, 1992), 10–12.

25. *Reconstructing Public Philosophy*, 167.

26. See especially Viroli, *Republicanism*, chapter 5. On the other hand, the civic republican who, in my judgment, best exemplifies the more pluralistic approach is not a neoclassical theorist, but someone with roots in communal republicanism. I have in mind Taylor. See his arguments on behalf of the importance of "diversity of goods" in *Sources of the Self*, especially chapters 18 and 25, and *Philosophy and the Human Sciences*, vol. 2 of *Philosophical Papers* (Cambridge: Cambridge University Press, 1985), 230–47.

27. I say "broadly teleological" partly because I want to accommodate those civic republicans who, while committed in some general sense to viewing politics in terms of ends and goods, eschew the kinds of metaphysical systems of thought with which teleology has been associated in the past. One thinks of the neopragmatism of Benjamin Barber in particular, but in point of fact, just about all civic republicans depart from these traditional metaphysical systems to some substantial degree.

28. This way of arguing is common not only among liberals who emphasize rights, but also among the new liberal theorists of virtue. See, for example, William A. Galston, *Liberalism and Pluralism: The Implications of Value Pluralism for Political Theory and Practice* (Cambridge: Cambridge University Press, 2002), 15–17; and Sinopoli, *The Foundations of American Citizenship*, 24–30.

29. The debate over the situated self is discussed in detail in chapter 4.

30. The foundational texts for the communal republican hermeneutics of identity are Charles Taylor, *Human Agency and Language*, vol. 1 of *Philosophical Papers* (Cambridge: Cambridge University Press, 1985); Sandel, *Liberalism and the Limits of Justice*, especially 154–64; and Sullivan, *Reconstructing Public Philosophy*, especially 172–73 and 181–84. Jurgen Habermas provides an excellent overview of the hermeneutic perspective of civic republicanism in a discussion of the differences between his theory of deliberative democracy and both liberalism and civic republicanism. See Jurgen Habermas, *Between Facts and Norms: Contributions to a Discourse Theory of Law and Politics* (Cambridge, MA: The MIT Press, 1998), 296–302.

31. Beiner, in particular, eschews a particularistic form of hermeneutics. On the other hand, Beiner joins with other civic republican "hermeneuticists" in emphasizing the importance of practical wisdom or *phronesis* as well as the hermeneutic nature of the self as a reflective and self-reflecting being. See Ronald Beiner, *Philosophy in a Time of Lost Spirit* (Toronto: University of Toronto Press, 1997), chapters 2, 6, 10, 16, and 18.

32. See especially Hans-Georg Gadamer, *Truth and Method*, 2nd ed. (New York: Crossroad, 1991).

33. See *Truth and Method*, 300–307 and 369–79.

34. *Reconstructing Public Philosophy*, 110.

35. *The Ethics of Authenticity,* 105–6, emphasis added.
36. *Reconstructing Public Philosophy,* 179.
37. *Reconstructing,* 179–80.
38. See *Human Agency and Language,* chapter 1.
39. "Introduction," in *Philosophical Papers,* 8.
40. See Taylor, *Philosophy and the Human Sciences,* chapter 9; *Human Agency and Language,* chapter 1; and *Sources of the Self,* chapters 1 and 2.
41. *Philosophy and the Human Sciences,* 245.
42. *Reconstructing Public Philosophy,* 168, emphasis added.
43. Aristotle, *Politics,* ed. and trans. Ernest Barker (London: Oxford University Press, 1975), book III, 1283a–1283b, 134.
44. See Paul Ricoeur, *Freud and Philosophy,* trans. Denis Savage (New Haven, CT: Yale University Press, 1970), 26.
45. William A. Galston, *Liberal Purposes: Goods, Virtues, and Diversity in the Liberal State* (Cambridge: Cambridge University Press, 2002), 41. Also see Beiner, *Philosophy in a Time of Lost Spirit,* chapter 16.
46. *Reconstructing Public Philosophy,* 110.
47. As Beiner himself points out, this seems to accord with Gadamer's own understanding of hermeneutics. See Beiner, *Philosophy in a Time of Lost Spirit,* 102–4.
48. Much of my own thinking in this area follows in the path of the kind of "interactive universalism" that Seyla Benhabib lays out in *Situating the Self.* Also see Jurgen Habermas's illuminating discussion of these issues in *The Philosophical Discourse of Modernity: Twelve Lectures* (Cambridge, MA: The MIT Press, 1990), Lecture XI, especially 321–26; and Habermas's discussion of "transcendence from within" in *Between Facts and Norms,* 17–27.
49. Which is not to say that hermeneutics provides an adequate or complete *psychological* theory of identity formation. Rather, a hermeneutic perspective on identity aims at a phenomenological account of the lived experience of individuals at the level of meaning and self-understanding.
50. The *locus classicus* for comparative analysis of civic beliefs relating to democracy is Gabriel Almond and Sidney Verba, *The Civic Culture* (Boston: Little, Brown, and Company, 1965). See the contrasting empirical accounts of American civic culture in William E. Hudson's civic republican text, *American Democracy in Peril,* 3rd ed. (New York: Chatham House Publishers, 2001), especially chapters 2 and 3; and Michael Schudson's defense of the evolution of American citizenship in the direction of a rights-based liberalism in *The Good Citizen: A History of American Civic Life* (Cambridge, MA: Harvard University Press, 1998). Also see Robert D. Putnam, *Bowling Alone: The Collapse and Revival of American Community* (New York: Touchstone, 2000); the essays in Theda Skocpol and Morris P. Fiorina, eds., *Civic Engagement in American Democracy* (Washington, DC: Brookings Institution Press, 1999); and William A. Galston and Peter Levine, "America's Civic Condition: A Glance at the Evidence," in *Community Works,* ed. E. J. Dionne (Washington, DC: Brookings Institution Press, 1998).
51. For example, over half of Sandel's book *Democracy's Discontent* is devoted to a contrast between liberal political economy and the republican "political economy of citizenship." Yet property barely makes an appearance in this whole discussion.

52. One of the clearest and most forceful statements of libertarian antipathy to a politics of civic virtue is found in the opening lines of *Capitalism and Freedom* (Chicago: University of Chicago Press, 1962), Milton Friedman's popular defense of libertarianism. In response to President Kennedy's famous call for civic virtue, "Ask not what your country can do for you, but what you can do for your country," Friedman wrote the following:

> Neither half of the statement expresses a relation between the citizen and his government that is worthy of the ideals of free men in free society. The paternalistic 'what your country can do for you' implies that government is the patron, the citizen the ward, a view that is at odds with the free man's belief in his own responsibility for his own destiny. The organismic, 'what you can do for your country' implies that government is the master or the deity, the citizen, the servant or votary. To the free man, the country is collection of individuals who compose it, not something over and above them. 1–2.

3
Beyond the Displacement of Property: Towards an Ethical Materialism

M Y CRITIQUE IS A RESPONSE not only to what civic republicans have said about civic virtue, but also to what they have not said about property. But civic republicans are by no means alone in neglecting property. They are participating in a broader trend involving the displacement of property, a trend that encompasses not only post-socialist theorists of virtue and community, but also much of contemporary political theory. In this chapter, I begin to develop my critical analysis of the difficulties that the displacement of property creates for civic republicans and other post-socialists. In addition, I outline a framework of ethical materialism as an alternative to the post-socialist perspective on property.

Two Senses of Displacement

In speaking of the "displacement" of property, I mean to evoke images of property being supplanted, replaced, and dislodged. The various linguistic uses and meanings of "displacement" through which these images are evoked constitute what, in Wittgensteinian terms, may be thought of as the "grammar" of the "displacement of property." However, there is a distinction within this grammar of "displacement" that is especially important to my theoretical and critical perspective on property. This has to do with the difference between property being displaced in the sense of having diminished importance in contemporary political theory and property being displaced in the sense of being viewed in isolation from institutional contexts. In the first case, the grammar of displacement has to do with property being dislodged from what was once a central, or at the very least far more important, position or role in political theory. Or what amounts to the same thing, the idea is that that property has been supplanted by other theoretical concerns. We can formalize this by thinking of the shift of priorities away from property as the *normative* displacement of property in contemporary political theory, the point being that we are dealing with normative judgments about the theoretical value or importance of property as a concept and category. By contrast, the second sense of displacement has to do with how property is conceptualized, and accordingly it may be thought of as the *conceptual* displacement of property. Here too the grammar of "displacement" evokes the idea of something being dislodged. But in this second sense, property is displaced when it is conceptually dislodged from its social and political contexts, as is the case with modern thingness.[1] In other words, what is at issue with the conceptual displacement of property is not the priority that is attached to property as a theoretical category or concept but rather how property objects are conceptualized in relation to the activities, practices, and institutional arrangements that constitute their social and political contexts.

Although we shall be considering both types of displacement in this chapter, the focus will be on the normative displacement of property. The movement away from property within civic republicanism and other episodes of post-socialist theory is the catalyst for my interest in developing a perspective of ethical materialism. The conceptual displacement of property will assume greater importance in the chapter that follows, where we return to the internal-critical task of exploring the relationship between property and the situated self.

The Normative Displacement of
Property in Contemporary Political Theory

In stark contrast to contemporary theorizing about the virtues of community life and democratic citizenship, contemporary theoretical treatments of property are often marked by large gaps and silences, and by the absence of sustained and systematic arguments. It is hard not to be struck by how this represents a reversal of the situation just a few decades ago. Despite some signs of change such as the marginal role of property in Rawls's theory of justice, it was property, not civic virtue, which was the more likely subject of theoretical interest and inquiry in the 1960s and 1970s. The displacement of property was gathering momentum, but it was by no means a pronounced tendency. On the contrary, the tendency seems to have been to assume that issues of property were central to both political theory in general and prominent theories such as

Rawls's theory of justice in particular. Apart from Thomas Grey, for instance, there is little indication from this period that commentators or critics were interested in, or even recognized, the marginal role of property in Rawls's theory.[2]

As this suggests, the shift away from property has not been accompanied by any great fanfare; there have not been any dramatic declarations or theoretical manifestos to announce the arrival of a "post-property" age of political theory. This, no doubt, is one reason that the change has been almost imperceptible. But as is often the case, with hindsight, the change appears quite dramatic.

We can get a sense of this by considering how unlikely it would be these days to find more than a handful of theorists who would say, as C. B. Macpherson did back in 1973, that "all roads lead to property" when we attempt to retrieve "a genuine theory of democracy" or "an adequate theory of liberty."[3] Today, most theorists are apt to say that in the retrieval of democracy and liberty, almost all roads—and certainly the most important ones—lead away from property. And this is true even of theorists such as the civic republicans who are fond of repeating Macpherson's argument that liberalism promotes "possessive individualism" by identifying freedom and individual rights with the acquisition and exchange of private property.[4] What was once (with Macpherson and like-minded theorists) a critique of a particular way of conceptualizing property and its relationship to freedom has become, in the hands of most of today's critics of possessive individualism, a more global critique of property and of any theory that seeks to connect freedom to property. True, this more global critique is seldom as explicit and direct as when Benjamin Barber summed up the problems with the liberal theory of possessive individualism by claiming that a "perspective on human nature that was less wary of mutuality and more inclined to integrate social dimensions of human life into the human essence would have less need for such hedonist-individualist concepts as power, property, and rights."[5] But the dismissive spirit of Barber's attack, if not the explicitness, is typical of a substantial segment of contemporary political theory.

Several years ago, the liberal political theorist Amy Gutmann captured the shift away from property issues among liberalism's critics in a discussion of the differences between the "old" communitarian critics of liberalism writing in the 1960s and the "new" communitarians of the 1980s. After pointing out that the new communitarians have rejected Marx in favor of Aristotle and Hegel, Gutmann concluded that the "political implications of the new communitarian criticisms are correspondingly more conservative. Whereas the good society of the old critics was one of collective property ownership and equal political power, the good society of the new critics is one of settled traditions and established identities."[6] This overstates the conservatism of the "new communitarians." Gutmann was referring to civic republicans such as

Charles Taylor and Michael Sandel as well as to traditionalists such as Alasdair MacIntyre, and as we saw in the previous chapter, there is a tendency to the left in most aspects and expressions of civic republicanism. Certainly also Barber's synthesis of republican virtue and participatory democracy is far from conservative. However, the residual leftist elements within post-socialist thought do not invalidate Gutmann's point about the shift away from property. If anything, they bring this shift into bolder and more dramatic relief.

Gutmann's discussion is interesting for another reason as well. Once again, we see a liberal theorist calling attention to the lack of interest in property issues among communitarians and civic republicans without considering the signs of a broader shift away from property in political theory as a whole. The case of Rawls reminds us that many contemporary liberals also have traveled down roads that lead away from property. And there are many other theoretical episodes and perspectives that could be cited as well. Some of these provide even clearer evidence of the normative displacement of property than liberalism or post-socialism. One thinks of postmodern deconstructionism, for instance.

The point of course is not that all theorists in the 1960s and 1970s assigned as much theoretical importance to property as Macpherson did. Just as there are some theorists these days who focus on property, so too were there some theorists back then who showed little interest in issues of property. The point, rather, is that a claim such as Macpherson's had considerably more resonance back then than it does now.

There are doubtless many historical, sociological, and cultural reasons for the declining fortunes of property as a category of inquiry and analysis. Thankfully, the task of providing a comprehensive account and explanation of these reasons is not one that I have set for myself. However, the task of making some sense of the normative displacement of property within post-socialist theory is pertinent to this inquiry. The starting point for this is the post-socialist reaction against modern materialism. This reaction is far broader and much deeper than anything found in contemporary liberalism. For post-socialists, the effort to combat modern materialism is inseparable from the effort to elevate moral and civic culture above matters of political economy and economics. The problem, I wish to argue, is that this post-materialist project of recovering moral and civic culture is premised on a false dichotomy of culture and political economy.

The Post-Socialist Bias against Political Economy

Simply put, most post-socialist theory is marked by a strong bias against political economy. Among most (if not all) post-socialist thinkers, the feeling seems to be that in the present age, questions of political economy are no longer imbued with theoretical significance or transformative potential. Whatever importance such questions still have is in relation to purportedly more relevant and pressing contemporary questions concerning such things as the sources of modern identity, the threats to both social and natural ecologies, the crisis of moral and spiritual belief in the face of technocratic materialism, the crisis of democratic citizenship, and the difficulties attendant to a postmodern world of non-existent foundations and indeterminate and elusive meanings. Of course, these *are* relevant and pressing issues. But too often post-socialists write as if these issues are best understood when the subject of political economy is bracketed, or worse still, as if recovering from the problems of modernity means recovering from the subject of political economy. Thus, the sociologist and moral theorist Alan Wolfe decries "the increasing hegemony of political economy" in modern social science and even argues that this is a principal cause of the collapse of the moral understandings that are fostered by civil society.[7]

Now, the mere fact that post-socialists show little interest in the technical aspects of contemporary economics and political economy is not problematic from my point of view. (As someone putting forward a rather unconventional, hermeneutic approach to political economy, I am hardly in a position to chastise post-socialists for avoiding the technicalities of economics and political economy!) The problem, rather, is that post-socialists let what is essentially a normative judgment against political economy cloud their understanding of, or for that matter, their interest in, the politico-economic conditions and consequences of their projects of recovery and renewal. This is partly a simple matter of being unrealistic. Even the most virtue-centered and most communal and ecological of social systems needs some kind of program of political economy. Beyond this, and more important in my view, is the artificial and misleading conceptual dualism of political economy and moral-civic culture to which the bias against political economy gives rise.

This dualistic conceptual structure is clearly seen in the Bellah group's complaint towards the end of *Habits of the Heart* that "much of the thinking about [American] society and where it should be going is rather narrowly focussed on our political economy." To counter this narrow focus, they "followed Tocqueville and other classical social theorists in focussing on the mores—the 'habits of the heart'—that include consciousness, culture, and the daily practices of life."[8] This would not be so troubling if the complaint was only about misplaced moral priorities. But the Bellah group's complaint sweeps more broadly than this, for it suggests a kind of ontological disjuncture between political economy and moral-civic culture. By itself, a conceptual framework that emphasizes the intrinsic goods and ends of moral and civic culture does not

rule out the possibility of treating political economy as something that is constituted within and through "consciousness, culture, and the daily practices of
life." But that is precisely what the Bellah group seems to want to do. That is
to say, their language constructs political economy as something that is somehow apart from or beneath "consciousness, culture, and the daily practices of
life." There is a ghostly and ironic materialism here, an almost inverted materialism that first seeks to confine political economy to the materiality of
political-economic structures and processes, and then seeks to situate matters
of "consciousness, culture, and the daily practices of life" on the presumably
higher (and broader) ground of moral and civic life. Nor is there any inquiry
into, or explanation of, this anti-materialist ontology. Indeed, this is an ideological analysis of political economy in the worst sense of letting prejudg-
ments about it prefigure the analysis of what it is about. It is an anti-
economism that apes its economistic counterpart in disguising ideological
thinking about economics. In the meantime, we are left with the absurdity
that political economy is not really about "the daily practices of life."

In fairness, I should point out that political economy receives considerably
more attention in *The Good Society*—the Bellah group's sequel to *Habits of the
Heart*. However, the most important issues for my argument have less to do
with how much attention post-socialists give to political economy than with
how they conceptualize it. Unfortunately, for example, *The Good Society* is
premised on the same conceptual dichotomy of culture and political economy
that is found in *Habits of the Heart*. Or to put it in the terms used by the Bellah
group itself, *The Good Society* deals with the same issues addressed in *Habits of
the Heart*, but does so in relation to institutional structures and patterns rather
than in relation to "cultural and personal resources for thinking about our common life."[9] This is certainly a commonplace distinction in social science, and
this is doubtless so for some good analytical and heuristic reasons. But it also
begs the question—the hermeneutic question—of how institutional structures
and patterns such as those associated with political economy are informed and
constituted by cultural and linguistic horizons of understanding and belief. A
hermeneutic perspective helps us to see that culture includes the culture of political economy, and furthermore, that the culture of political economy is itself
partly constitutive of politico-economic structures and processes.

This might seem like a rather peripheral issue having more to do with the
philosophy of social science than with a case study and critique of post-
socialist thought. The point, though, is that when consistently applied,
hermeneutics can help to unsettle and efface the dualism of culture and political economy, and in the process, also help to reveal weaknesses and fissures in
the post-materialist conceptual structures that support post-socialism. As I
argued in chapter 2 in relation to civic republicanism, it is these conceptual

structures, and not the presence or absence of particular proposals for politico-economic reform, that are at issue. In fact, one could compile a fairly extensive list of politico-economic reforms and economic policy proposals that have been put forward by post-socialists.[10] But these proposals and re- forms do not address the theoretical issues associated with the dualism of po- litical economy and culture. If anything, they bring into bold relief the prob- lems that this dualism creates for post-socialism. For all of their elegiac complaints and warnings about the dangers of economically oriented politi- cal thought, post-socialists nevertheless cannot do without political economy. Yet because of the dualistic structure that informs most post-socialist thought, the programs and proposals of political economy that they develop often end up being detached from the theoretical frameworks that support their projects of recovery and renewal. Put differently, these proposals often are theoretically ungrounded and unencumbered.

The Implications for Post-Socialist Views of Justice

We can get a better idea of the problems that are created by the post- socialists' dualistic perspective on culture and political economy by looking at their views of justice. There is a sense in which the post-socialist tendency to bracket political economy is not about a shift *within* the grammar of justice, but a movement *away* from justice to a cultural politics of communal virtue and corruption. However, it cannot be stressed too much that this is at most a partial movement and that it should not be confused with a lack of concern about justice. Even Sandel, who, in *Liberalism and the Limits of Justice*, comes as close as any post-socialist to making an argument pitting the ideal of moral community against justice, concedes the enduring necessity and importance of justice in light of the fact that "we cannot know each other, or our ends, well enough to govern by the common good alone."[11]

Sandel's dichotomous treatment of justice and the common good is also something of an exception to the post-socialist rule. Most are apt to redefine justice in terms of the common good rather than in opposition to it. Phillip Selznick maintains that justice is the most important of the ideals that "we as- sociate with community." According to Selznick, the "shared understandings" of justice "underpin the transactions and arrangements of everyday life."[12] For MacIntyre, one of the problems of Western modernity is precisely that it lacks the kind of communal, moral consensus that imbues justice with substantive ideas and principles of desert.[13] And to provide one more example, William Sullivan claims that the close relationship between justice and community provides additional confirmation of the civic humanist wisdom of the repub- lican tradition. "Because the *telos* of justice is fellowship," he writes of the civic republican vision of justice, "a polity must be so ordered that all citizens share the grounds for uncoerced participation."[14]

So there are good reasons to define post-socialism in terms of concerns about both corruption and injustice. Justice has not disappeared in post-socialist thought, but rather has become something that is redefined and re-valued by being viewed through the lens of post-socialist concerns about virtue and corruption. The question though is whether the post-socialist bias against political economy prevents them from developing a coherent reformulation of justice. I think it does. The problem, as I see it, is not simply that this bias results in insufficient emphasis on the distribution of economic resources and rights; nor is it simply that it results in scant attention to perennial issues of economic power. Post-socialism *is* seriously flawed in both of these respects. But the greater problem is one that is internal to the post-socialist vision. This is the problem of showing how matters of economic justice and economic power are to be addressed within the virtue-centered perspective of post-socialism. Put differently, there is an internal problem of showing how the goods of political economy are to be reconciled with the intrinsic goods of moral and civic life. The bias against political economy undercuts such a project of reconciliation because such a bias places a premium on being able to claim the high ground of virtue *against* the corruptive influence of property and political economy.

Consider the example of Ronald Beiner. Beiner writes as a strong critic of economically oriented theories of social justice, and in this respect he typifies post-socialist skepticism about what is seen as the corruptive materialism within leftist and left-liberal expressions of progressive modernity. But Beiner is also an instructive case because his skepticism about the economic framework of social justice is accompanied by some unmistakably leftist commitments and aspirations. Unlike many post-socialists, Beiner is very open to the possibility of reappropriating leftist political theory. He even seeks to identify civic republicanism with what he calls "the political argument for socialism." Basically, this argument is that socialist arrangements make for better citizens insofar as these arrangements promote solidaristic civic bonds and an ethos of public spirit and civic engagement. As Beiner puts it, "If socialism is defined in terms of shared civic responsibility rather than economic justice, then the achievement of a new socialist order will, by definition, usher in a new republicanism."[15] But as this suggests, Beiner's republicanized socialism is also put forward as an alternative to conventional arguments on behalf of socialism, arguments that, in Beiner's view, are deeply flawed by virtue of being preoccupied with an economic and materialistic understanding of social justice.

True to post-socialist form, Beiner seeks to trace the problems with this conventional socialist understanding of justice to liberalism. "The problem with basing the argument for socialism strictly on the claims of social justice,"

Beiner says, "is that this way of proceeding runs the risk of getting enmeshed in the language of rights and entitlements that defines (and in my opinion disfigures) liberalism as a political philosophy and is thus liable to distract from what Marx considered the key question about socialism, namely the quality of social relationships among human beings." Using the example of Rawls (who else?) Beiner elaborates by suggesting that the standard case for socialism suffers from the same kinds of problems—providing only "the most minimal account of shared ends" and a "thoroughly instrumentalist conception of rationality"—that afflict left liberal theories of social justice. Beiner's strategy emerges as the opposite of that pursued by Rawls and conventional socialists. The "intermediate problem" of determining a fair distribution of economic rights and entitlements is eliminated, thereby enabling Beiner to go "straight to the question of shared ends and the basis of social solidarity."[16]

Summarizing his argument in the form of a rhetorical question, Beiner asks: "Does one seek social equality for its own sake, or in relation to a further end, namely that it makes us better citizens and promotes a shared experience of political community?"[17] But having put distributive justice and social equality in their places, Beiner then goes on to outline a series of policy principles that are clearly redistributive in nature! These include a principle of full employment in which government "guarantees a job" to every "employable member of society," a principle of "decent employment" in which government "is obliged to do everything in its power to render it more likely that the kinds of jobs actually available to members of the society do not destroy the soul," and finally, a principle—Beiner calls it the "Plato principle"—that says that "social order and the health of the polity" require public action to prevent large disparities of income (he suggests a ratio of highest to lowest income no greater than five to one).[18]

Beiner maintains that under these principles, social equality and social justice are transformed into political equality and political justice. The "social question" of how society should address problems of class inequality and economic deprivation becomes a "political question." It is doubtless true that such a reformulation would have some real consequences in terms of how different life would be in a civic republican form of socialism. We can reasonably infer that there would be more emphasis on civic solidarity and citizen participation, fewer entitlements to social welfare, and a somewhat more accommodating stance on economic inequality than at least some egalitarian expressions of conventional socialism. But it is hard to escape the impression that there is a bit of a shell game going on here. True, Beiner and other postsocialists eschew collectivist systems of public ownership, and true also they see redistribution as an instrument of higher moral and civic ends rather than as a central norm around which political theory is to be developed. But traditionally the argument for public ownership has been more of an argument about political justice than economic justice. By the same token, it seems to be a quibble at best to argue that Beiner's proposals to reduce income inequality through redistributive tax policies are more about political justice than social or economic justice.

By way of summary, Beiner's own program of distributive justice (what else can it be called?) indicates that the differences between social and political justice are not as sharp as he claims. Beiner might respond by pressing the point about the difference between viewing economic redistribution as an end in itself (as conventional socialists and Rawlsian liberals purportedly do) and viewing it as a means to other, higher ends (as civic republicans and "political socialists" do). It seems to me, however, that this sets up a "straw man." It is hard to imagine any principled socialist or left liberal (including Rawls of course!) defending redistribution simply on the grounds of economic entitlement alone, as opposed to higher ends and goods like human dignity, solidarity, democracy, and justice itself.

Beiner's argument reveals the lengths to which many post-socialists will go to define their beliefs about justice in terms other than those of a tainted and corrupt progressive modernity. There is a progressive voice in post-socialist arguments about justice, but it is a submerged and often very reluctant voice of social justice in its redistributive economic sense. But why this reluctance? Why is it so difficult for post-socialists to acknowledge their progressive and sometimes even traditionally leftist commitments and aspirations in areas like distributive justice? There are doubtless many things going on here, including for example a political climate that marginalizes and often demeans leftist politics and a sense that the well of politico-economic transformation has run dry in an era of global capitalism and failed collectivism.[19] But whatever else is going on, it seems clear that the post-materialist orientation of post-socialists is associated with a grammatical shift from political economy to culture, and furthermore, that this shift is informed by a theoretical bias against political economy, and most especially against its economic elements. Of course, in saying this, I do not mean to criticize post-socialists for eschewing economistic models of social and political life. What I am claiming, rather, is that they have set up their projects partly as efforts to claim the high ground of moral and civic culture against modernity's purportedly materialist preoccupation with political economy, and that in doing so, they have failed to do justice (as it were) to the complex relationship between political economy and moral and civic culture. It is as if post-socialism were the theoretical reflex of the "culture wars" that rage on and on in contemporary American politics without any meaningful or sustained connections to issues of political economy and economic justice. This puts things too neatly of course, but I would insist that there is a grain of truth here.

The Significance of Property

What then of property? I wish to suggest that property is simultaneously a key to understanding the contradictory theoretical impulses that are created by the post-socialist bias against political economy *and* a key to seeing how political economy can be reconciled with moral and civic culture. In both respects, I wish to challenge the post-socialist tendency to view property through the dualistic lens of their critique of modern materialism.

Property stands out as a subject of political economy that post-socialists are especially reluctant to investigate. Indeed, it usually remains bracketed even when post-socialists explore issues of political economy. Civic republicans are probably the best example here. As was discussed in chapter 2, they are something of an exception to the post-socialist rule of avoiding the subject of political economy. Hence, it is significant that property plays but a marginal role in civic republican discussions of political economy. For example, property receives scant attention in *The Good Society,* and it barely makes an appearance in Sandel's lengthy exploration of "the political economy of citizenship" in *Democracy's Discontent.* At the same time, however, property has special significance within the post-socialist universe as an object of anti-materialist disdain. I mean this both in the sense of property being something about which civic republicans and other post-socialists are often disdainful *and* in the more philosophical sense of property being conceptualized in terms of an irreducible, material "objectness" or "thingness."

Property brings the issues associated with the post-socialist critique of materialism to a head because, more than with political economy in general, post-socialists are apt to see property as embodying and expressing a materiality of social and even physical processes and forces. On this view, economism appears as a kind of historical realization of the materialist essence of property. However, the intuitive sense of this view disappears when we move outside the framework of modern thingness, and when we recover the connections between property and contexts of labor, authority, and identity. When we recover these connections—when we recover the placeness of property—economism looks less like the realization of property's essential materialist logic and more like property's replacement. However, the point that needs emphasis at this time is that the bias against political economy is of a piece with a bias against property in post-socialist thought.

An Economy of Mixed Messages

What we find in post-socialism is not a simple neglect of property issues, but a theoretical structure of mixed, yet interrelated messages. Rather than property, the theoretical focus of post-socialism is on broader and purport-edly deeper ethical and meta-ethical questions pertaining to the nature and sources of identity, practical reason, and "the good" as well as on the implica-tions of these questions for political theories of community, freedom, justice, ecological interconnectedness, and democracy. At the same time, though, there is a sense in which property is at the heart of post-socialism. For while post-socialists generally treat property as if it had little or no larger theoreti-cal significance, they are often eager to evoke the linguistic and conceptual connection between liberal individualism and property. The notion that the languages and images of property are paradigmatic expressions of a liberal self who is unencumbered by constitutive communal and civic understandings, purposes, and practices is a pervasive theme not only in contemporary civic republicanism, but also in post-socialism in general. Indeed, adherence to the proposition that there is a fundamental and deep tension between virtue and liberal languages and images of property is one of the reasons for being able to speak of a distinctive and more or less unified post-socialist perspective. And more often than not, post-socialists are united in thinking not just of an opposition between *liberal* property and virtue, but also more globally of an opposition between property and virtue. Property, we are apt to be told by post-socialists, is something—and again, the emphasis is clearly on its thing-ness—that is likely to be pursued, acquired, and valued by modern "economic man," not by communal beings situated in natural or moral ecologies of virtue, and not by people who fulfill themselves as public-spirited citizens.

Sometimes post-socialist criticisms of property are quite explicit, as with Barber's claim that property is a "hedonist-individualist" concept. More typi-cally, the post-socialists' dismissive attitude towards property is an implication of criticisms of the acquisitiveness of a market culture, as when Jean Bethke Elshtain bemoans the ill effects of consumerism on civil society: "We want more and we want it now! All of life is pervaded by the market and by market imagery. Perhaps we should not be too surprised that in America's cities, young people rob, beat, and even kill one another to steal expensive sneakers and gold chains. Or that in America's suburbs, young people whose families are well off shun school and studies and community involvement to take part-time jobs to pay for extra consumer goods that their parents may be loathe to provide."[20]

It needs to be stressed that these very different messages about the signifi-cance of property have a kind of strategic significance for post-socialists. Herein lies the *economy* of their mixed messages. This has to do with both the selective and the tendentious nature of post-socialist messages about prop-erty. That is to say, it is an economy of mixed messages not simply because post-socialists are generally brief and sparing in their discussions of property, but also because they emphasize those particular property issues that are strategically most useful in furthering their critical purposes in challenging liberalism and progressive modernity. Of course, I am not suggesting that post-socialists are duplicitous. Rather, the economy of mixed messages is an *effect* of sincere theoretical beliefs and commitments.

Significantly, this economy of mixed messages is found in more moderate forms of post-socialism as well as in more radically anti-modern expressions. Take, for instance, the role of property in Taylor's inquiry into the "sources of the self" in the modern world. On the one hand, property seldom appears in what is an otherwise remarkably comprehensive and nuanced hermeneutic exploration of "the making of the modern identity." On the other hand, when property does appear, it is almost always in connection with the dangers of acquisitiveness and possessive individualism. For example, at an especially important point in *Sources of the Self,* Taylor cites Macpherson's critique of possessive individualism in arguing that one of the most influential forms of the modern disengaged self is found in Locke's proprietary model of individual freedom and rights.[21] But Taylor does not even mention the various interpretive issues that are raised by Macpherson's claims about the relationship between liberalism and possessive individualism. And rather than pausing to explore the different dimensions of the relationship between property and modern identity, Taylor proceeds immediately to the deeper problem of the "modern complex" of atomism and instrumentalism. The deeper problem, Taylor argues, is that this complex of atomist and instrumentalist ideas and self-understandings works against those modern doctrines "which have tried to recapture a more holistic view of society, and to understand it as a matrix for individuals rather than as an instrument." Not surprisingly, the first example Taylor gives of these more holistic doctrines is the civic humanist vision of a politics of civic virtue:

> The notion of citizen virtue, as we see it defined in Montesquieu and Rousseau, can't be combined with an atomist understanding of society. It assumes that the political way of life, in devotion to which Montesquieu's "virtue" consists, is in an important sense prior to the individuals. It establishes their identity, provides the matrix within which they can be the kinds of human beings they are, within which the noble ends of a life devoted to the public good are first conceivable.[22]

What is troubling about this is not what Taylor says about the larger problems of atomism and instrumentalism, but the manner in which property is discussed (or not discussed!) in relation to these problems. In effect, issues of property are displaced (both normatively and conceptually) by moving to the level of the sources of moral identity. Taylor describes this level as the "moral ontology" of the self. Yet property does not disappear entirely; rather, it remains as a disturbing, if somewhat submerged, presence—but only on the side of the moral ontology of the disengaged self.

So long as property is of secondary theoretical importance, there is no need for thorough and sustained consideration of the possibility that property might be a source of serious problems for post-socialist projects of recovery and renewal, problems that are often (if not always) of a wholly different order than those associated with possessive individualism and modern "economic man." By the same token, if the primary importance of property is its corruptive power in promoting possessive individualism and the instrumentalist mode of economic reason, then it is easier for post-socialists to claim the high ground of virtue against liberal modernity's purported tendency to become preoccupied with the pursuit of property and riches. And rather than having to explicate the theoretical rationale that supports this high ground, post-socialists need only evoke well-established (and of course often well-founded) moral and religious concerns about the debasement of personality that results from a preoccupation with material things.

As this suggests, post-socialist views of property are closely related to the dualistic framework of political economy and culture. It will be helpful to consider in this regard Barber's treatment of property in *Strong Democracy*. Both because of its influence and its content, *Strong Democracy* can be seen as a foundational text in post-socialist political theory. In contrast to other foundational texts such as MacIntyre's *After Virtue*, *Strong Democracy* is a text that combines standard post-socialist themes of socially embodied personality and communal virtue with the theme of participatory democracy. Yet it is also a text which shows that when it comes to property, post-socialist traditionalists and post-socialist democrats have a great deal in common.

Let us start with Barber's basic messages and arguments about property. Although only a small fraction of *Strong Democracy* is devoted to issues of property, there can be no doubt as to the pivotal role these issues play in Barber's arguments against the liberal vision of "thin democracy" (i.e., representative government based only on consent of the governed and the protection of individual rights). Thus, in the first chapter, Barber asserts that what is common to all of the different formulations and "dispositions" of liberal democracy is the belief that "politics is prudence in the service of *homo economicus*—the solitary seeker of material happiness and bodily security." Here we see Barber evoking the moral and religious concerns alluded to above (this despite his neopragmatist contention that the procedures of "strong democracy" are "genuinely independent of external norms, prepolitical truths, or natural rights"). The notion that liberalism debases moral personality through a preoccupation with material things becomes a more explicit theme in the next chapter, where Barber claims that "the most striking feature" of the liberal "frame of reference" is the "physicality" or "thingness" of its "language and imagery." "With a vocabulary of such materiality," Barber argues, "liberal theory cannot be expected to give an adequate account of human interdependency, mutualism, cooperation, fellowship, fraternity, community, and citizenship."[23]

Not surprisingly, Barber's first example of "characteristic liberal concepts" that are based on the "axiom of materialism" is the idea of "property as an extension of the physical self and of physical self-ownership"—in other words, Lockean possessive individualism in its basic meaning. And later, Barber draws out the implications of possessive individualism for the liberal psychology of "Man alone": "Because man is solitary, says the liberal, he is also hedonistic, aggressive, and acquisitive." Barber then goes on to discuss the relationship between property and freedom in liberal understandings of power and authority: "Power-seeking, like freedom-seeking, finds its natural extension and logical end in property-acquisition. For property is a form of cumulative power, an authoritative variety of institutionalized aggression, by which the claims of individuals to adequate means are given a permanent and legitimate home." Similarly, the "proprietary claim" defended by liberals is said to transform "power into authority, force into right, mere possession into rightful ownership."[24]

In these few passages, Barber has attempted to undergird his whole critique of liberalism by casting liberalism as a theory of possessive individualism and crass and aggressive materialism. Equally important, however, is the paucity of attention that Barber gives to property. To express this in deconstructionist language, it is the absence of property throughout most of *Strong Democracy* that (strategically speaking) marks his theory of post-socialist, civic republican democracy as a theory which, in sharp contrast to liberalism, has deeper and more important things on its mind than property. In this way, we are led to believe (with but the barest of suggestions) that in a post-socialist, civic republican regime, property would not only be given less emphasis by citizens, but would also be directed towards the intrinsically valuable ends of a more communal democracy. Thus, the only passage of *Strong Democracy* that refers to the role of property in a civic republican polity is the previously quoted one where Barber identifies property, power, and rights as the kind of "hedonist-individualist concepts" that could largely be dispensed with in a "perspective on human nature that was less wary of mutuality and more inclined to integrate social dimensions of human life into the human essence." Barber goes on to say that such a communal perspective on human nature "would use these concepts, when it did use them, to describe complex social interactions."[25] As with Taylor, the unstated implication of Barber's argument is clear: The only important problems of property in the modern world of liberal democracy are on the side of a liberal politics of unencumbered and disengaged selves, not on the side of civic republican and post-socialist virtue.

Barber's discussions of liberalism and property reveal a structure of binary oppositions that is built around the supposedly fundamental opposition between the corruptive power of property and communal, democratic virtue. In this structure, the materialism of liberal thought is homologous to property, which in turn is homologous to other "hedonist-individualist concepts" like power and rights, leading all the way down to the instrumental reason of "economic man" and the privatism of a "thinly" democratic liberal politics of disengaged individuals. Both separately and together, these manifestations of liberal corruption are presented as being in deep and fundamental opposition to the non-material, ethical situation of individuals, the non-proprietary interests of citizens, the intrinsically valuable goods of mutuality and community, and a strongly democratic politics of civic virtue.

This kind of dualistic structure is the purest and starkest form of the normative displacement of property within post-socialist thought. But notice that the entire structure depends on a non-contextual view of property as thingness. Specifically, the dualistic structure set up by Barber glosses over two very different ways in which property is about things. First, there are property-related things in the sense of objects of acquisition, possession, ownership, or exchange. This of course is the essence of modern thingness, and it is clearly such a thingness that Barber has in mind when discussing property. But second, there are property-related things in the sense of things that constitute a particular location or place in the world. We need not deny the danger that possessive individualism poses to virtue to see that there is not a single logic of corruption that is common to both thingness and placeness. A house, for example, can be a property-related thing in both senses. But obviously there is no direct (let alone logically necessary) relationship between the corruptive power of possessive individualism and being a member of a household or even *having* a home as a location of identity. Indeed, trying to fit the placeness of the house into Barber's dualistic structure would lead to the absurdity of thinking of inhabitation as a form of self-ownership.

As if to underscore his post-socialist bias against property, Barber evokes the locational dimension of things only when he turns his attention to the locations inhabited by citizens in a strong democracy. For example, he writes of the activity of democratic will formation as belonging to "the *domain* of power and action" (my emphasis). In the same vein, he writes of the need for "civic arenas" and of the importance of the project of "recreating the neighborhood as a physical public space."[26] Placeness matters greatly to Barber, just not when it comes to property. And looking beyond Barber, we need only think of the idea of a *situated* self to see that the evocation and redescription of locations and places are pervasive themes in post-socialist thought.

What we begin to see is that the dualistic structure of post-socialist thinking about property presupposes the conceptual universe of modern thingness. That is to say, post-socialists almost always bring to their analysis of property the same framework of conceptual displacement that has grown up with the commercial regime of modern thingness that they criticize. In this respect, the foundational dualism of their perspective is the assumption that property objects exist apart from, and in conceptual opposition to, the contexts of moral and civic life. This is seen, for example, when post-socialists decry the corrosive effect that property acquisition has on the bonds of civil society without ever accounting for the fact that civil society is itself a context of property— as if the civil bonds of family, neighborhood, voluntary associations, and community did not have any bases or dimensions pertaining to property!

This discussion brings us back not only to the placeness of property, but also to its formative potential in the cultivation of moral and civic personality. Barber himself calls attention to this potential when he comments rather cryptically that the "energetic entrepreneur offers a more inspiring model of self-governing citizenship than the terminally passive welfare client."[27] Coming in a section on "the problem of inequality of capitalism," and after Barber's sharp criticisms of the acquisitiveness of *homo economicus*, this is a somewhat startling assertion. But once again we find an economy of assertions in the sense of brevity of elaboration. And it is no wonder, for if Barber had explored the possibility of an entrepreneurs' vision of civic virtue, he might have been forced to abandon the dualistic structure of his critique of liberal property. He might also have had to confront the startling impracticality of his claim that post-socialist and post-liberal democrats would have little need for concepts such as property.

Yet here too we see a certain strategic advantage that results from the economy and selectivity of post-socialist messages about property. Better merely to hint at the possibility of an entrepreneurs' vision of civic virtue than to explore this possibility systematically in relation to the dangers that it and other virtue-centered approaches to property pose to the post-socialists' (submerged) progressive commitments to equality and inclusiveness. After all, as Barber is well aware, the contrast between the responsible entrepreneur and the "terminally passive welfare client" often has been employed in conjunction with invidiously discriminatory and exclusionary ideas about race, gender, and class.

In sum, by slighting the importance of property as a subject of political theory, and by participating in the modern tendency of conceptual displacement, Barber and other post-socialists are unable to bring the placeness of property to bear on their projects of recovery and renewal. Were they to do so they would have to abandon their simplistically dismissive view of property and consider the conditions under which property has functioned, and can function, as a formative context of moral and civic personality. To recognize and consider these conditions is an important step towards the recovery of a more nuanced view of property. This means moving beyond reductivist views that conflate property with modern forms of commercialism and economic reason.

Property is not just about the acquisition and exchange of commodities by *homo economicus*. But the more nuanced view of property that I have in mind is also one that accounts for the checkered history of virtue-centered approaches to property. Once this history is taken into account, the high ground of post-socialist virtue gives way to a more varied topography of possibilities and problems. And at this point, we are in a better position to see and appreciate the mixed legacy of modern property, to see and appreciate how, for all its materialistic flaws and tendencies, modern property is also associated with norms that support our understandings of equality and inclusiveness by casting doubt on the legitimacy of efforts to use idioms of virtue to translate wealth and ownership into forms of political jurisdiction, dominion, and control. Or so I am going to argue in the remainder of this book.

Summing Up: A Flawed Strategy of Transcendence

Whether they attack it directly or indirectly through an attack on commercialism, post-socialists often treat property as the disdainful object of acquisition within a crassly materialistic culture. Granted, the moral force of such attacks derives partly from the fact that the concept of property has become increasingly identified with the market in the modern and late modern eras. Still, much of what these post-socialist attacks on property gain by way of claiming the high moral and civic ground against modern commercialized thingness is lost by leaving us with an unrealistic and sanitized understanding of moral and civic life. This is seen in the propensity of post-socialists to write as if property somehow will not be needed to any great extent in their projects of recovery and renewal. This strategy of transcending property is seldom so clearly or explicitly expressed as in Barber's claim that a perspective that appreciated the social dimensions of human nature would have "less need" for property and other "hedonist-individualist concepts." More typically, the post-socialist strategy of transcendence is seen in the reluctance of post-socialists to discuss property apart from its corruptive power in a market culture. Thus, Elshtain never returned to the subject of property after castigating the acquisitiveness of contemporary American culture. And to provide another example, Beiner never gets around to discussing property in his argument that political justice is superior to economic justice.

One problem with this strategy of theoretical transcendence is that it makes post-socialists vulnerable to the charge of failing to put forward a realistic program of political economy as an alternative to the corrupt regime of liberal capitalism. On the assumption that property will remain an important feature of political economy through the late modern era, this charge will have merit unless and until post-socialists provide a detailed and theoretically coherent account of the understandings and arrangements of property that will accompany and support their projects of recovery and renewal. Here and there in the texts of post-socialist thought one finds some tantalizing hints of such an alternative regime of property—for instance, Sandel's brief discussion of a communal guardianship of assets in *Liberalism and the Limits of Justice*, a couple of paragraphs in *Dwellers in the Land* in which Kirkpatrick Sale sketches a bioregionalist system that combines communal ownership with individual and family rights of use, some passages in *The Communitarian Persuasion* where Selznick contrasts "person-centered" with "market-centered" forms of property, and Christopher Lasch's praise for the populist vision of proprietary democracy in *The True and Only Heaven*.[28] But we are left only with hints. Sandel, for instance, seems to have lost interest in developing a civic republican theory of guardianship; in any event, such a theory has not figured in Sandel's subsequent discussions of political economy. Even Lasch, after boldly (and idiosyncratically) identifying the question of "what was to replace proprietorship as the material foundation of civic virtue" as "the great question of twentieth-century politics," ended up providing little guidance for an actual theory of property.[29]

Of course, this is all part of a broader trend in contemporary political theory involving the normative displacement of property. Consequently, it would be wrong to hold post-socialism exclusively responsible for this state of affairs. Certainly, liberals and others who have engaged post-socialists in debate and discussion also have shown little interest in property. Certainly, also, there has been little of the same kind of give and take over issues of property that there has been in relation to the various new issue frameworks of post-socialist thought. It is telling in this regard that scant attention has been given to property in all the scholarly commentary that has been generated by seminal texts such as *Liberalism and the Limits of Justice* and *The True and Only Heaven*. Still, as critics of liberal capitalism, post-socialists bear a burden in providing an alternative theoretical perspective on property.

As I have stressed throughout this study, there is more at stake than the presence or absence of practical policy proposals. The problem, rather, is one of theoretical impracticality in the sense that post-socialists have failed to develop approaches to property and property-related contexts of identity, labor, and authority that cohere with, and support, their various projects of recovery and renewal. Their mixed messages on the importance of property may have given them a certain strategic advantage in their efforts to claim the high ground of virtue and community against the purported defenders of property. But the theoretical price that post-socialists have paid for this strategic advantage is very high: a dualistic perspective on property and virtue that is simplistic at best, and at worst, theoretically incoherent. In most cases, this perspective has been more of a by-product of post-socialist efforts to slay modernity's dragons of materialism and economism than a systematic attempt to theorize about property. This unsystematic approach to property is itself a major source of the difficulties that post-socialists have created for themselves in the area of property. Had they been more attentive to the theoretical implications of their claims about property, they might have realized that they have set up a logic that leaves them trapped in the same forms of materialism and economism they deplore. It is a logic of anti-materialism that mirrors vulgar forms of materialism by seeking to draw a bright line between the non-material realm of culture and the material world of property. By the same token, there is a post-socialist logic of anti-economism, which, by identifying property almost exclusively with the corruptive power of instrumental reason and commercialism, leaves the inhabitants of post-socialist communities with the unrealistic choice of pursuing a virtuous life through either the neglect of property or its transcendence.

We have seen the difficulties that confront post-socialists when they bring their dualistic perspective to bear on their efforts to reformulate the social question. Caught on the horns of unnecessarily and unjustifiably dichotomous choices between political economy and culture and between economistic views of distributive justice and the common good perspectives they wish to recover, post-socialists struggle unsuccessfully to break free of conventional leftist and left-liberal impulses and aspirations. Viewed through the reductivist lens of the post-socialists' dualistic perspective, these impulses and aspirations appear indistinguishable from the corruptive materialism of modernity. Yet the social question cannot be completely divorced from matters of political economy, and rather than transcending its more conventional leftist formulations, post-socialists are apt to smuggle them into their projects in the rather pretentious garb of moral and civic culture.

Rethinking the Post-Socialist Critique of Materialism

As an alternative to the post-socialists' dualistic framework, I offer an approach that emphasizes the interrelationship between material conditions and moral and civic purposes. At the risk of seeming tendentious, I am calling this approach "ethical materialism" in contradistinction to the "ethical anti-materialism" of most post-socialists.

Ethical materialism accepts much of the post-socialist critique of materialism. It joins with post-socialists in condemning an amoral and anti-spiritual materialism—a "crass materialism"—that precludes or forsakes higher human ends in the pursuit of material satisfactions. By the same token, a defender of ethical materialism shares the concern that the identification of progress with the efficient use of technical reason often has produced a logic of domination rather than one of emancipation. And these shared concerns go along with shared opposition to several other philosophical tendencies and commitments within modern materialism. Thus, an ethical materialism eschews any kind of economic determinism, and strongly opposes the efforts of some vulgar materialists to treat ideals such as justice as mere epiphenomenal reflections of underlying economic processes. Certainly, also, ethical materialism rejects the kind of materialist metaphysics that reduces reality to matter and its motions, and which (as post-socialists would remind us) is associated in the fields of social and political theory with a mechanistic view of social processes and forces.

What then is materialist about ethical materialism? The answer, in simplest terms, is a sustained sensitivity to the fact that moral and civic ends can be promoted but also quite often constrained by the material conditions of people's lives and labors. Such an ethical materialism is not as quick as post-socialism to rule out some role for the fulfillment of economic wants and preferences in the pursuit of both justice and democracy. But more than this, an ethical materialism appreciates the fact that for most of us, most of the time, moral and civic development occurs within the context of a struggle to make ends meet. It also realizes that for most of us, most of the time, this is a struggle which, for all the economic and technological changes of late modernity, is constant and is waged under circumstances of economic power, process, and policy that are seldom within our control as individuals.

No doubt, some will find it difficult to reconcile "materialism" with moral and civic development. I would argue that this difficulty stems from the lingering (and unfortunate) influence of the nineteenth-century terms of debate that sought to pit materialism against idealism. So long as we are forced into an either-or choice between ideas or material conditions as the constitutive elements of social life, ethical materialism is apt to appear as a contradiction in terms. But this is precisely the kind of dualistic thinking that creates so many problems for post-socialists. One could even reformulate my critique of post-socialism as an argument that post-socialists generally remain trapped in the opposition between materialism and idealism that has framed so much of the modern debate over capitalism. Theirs is an idealist critique of liberal capitalism, but one that all too often lapses into the illusion of being able to keep the ideas of moral and civic culture in splendid isolation from the material conditions and processes of political economy.

In place of the post-socialists' illusory and ultimately futile project of transcending property and political economy, ethical materialism seeks to challenge and efface the materialism-idealism opposition. An ethical materialism resists the twin temptations of viewing moral and civic life as fundamentally epiphenomenal reflections of the world of material forces and life processes *and* viewing them as fundamentally transcendental ideas that lack meaningful connections to physical existence and its material conditions. In contrast to the extremes of both modern materialism and modern idealism, ethical materialism is a pragmatic approach that envisions moral and civic life in terms of formative social practices and languages that are always/already both material and ideal. Or what amounts to the same thing, ethical materialism is concerned with the development of an ethical and civic life in the "materialist" sense of discovering the resources that sustain human life and the development of human capabilities.

But look at what has happened. We have worked our way back to the kind of formative perspective on moral personality and citizenship that is the hallmark of civic republicanism and many other post-socialist projects of recovery and renewal! The potential for an ethical materialism exists within post-socialism itself, and at times this potential is at least partially realized in the form of specific post-socialist ideas and arguments about the relationship between political economy and moral and civic culture. Certainly, for example, Sullivan evoked the spirit of ethical materialism when he cast the project of "making contact with tacit republican practices" as one of "reconstructing a public discourse that can reunite economics, power, and morality."[30] And another civic republican, Iseult Honohan, gets to the nub of things when she says, "Citizens need a material basis, not just 'social capital' or civic virtue to be able to act as active and independent citizens."[31]

This counter-tendency is one more reason for a method of internal criticism. There is something to work with in post-socialist thought as we develop the perspective of ethical materialism. Unfortunately, though, not that much. It is only a counter-tendency. And as we have seen, the problem is not simply that civic republicans and post-socialists have too little to say, but also that there are substantial lacunas in what is said. With respect to civic republicans, the lacuna with respect to property and its relationship to equal citizenship is especially problematic, for without attention to this area, it is impossible for civic republicans to develop a form of ethical materialism that is internally consistent with both their theoretical perspective on identity and their democratic aspirations.

Ethical Materialism and the "Capabilities Approach"

However, there is a theoretical approach that helps to bridge the gap between the civic republicans' formative project of post-socialist citizenship and my project of ethical materialism. I have in mind the so-called "capabilities approach" to social justice and economic development that has been elaborated in recent years by Amartya Sen and Martha Nussbaum.[32] This approach rejects both the utilitarian framework of welfare maximization and the deontological priority of the right over the good in favor of an emphasis on the actual quality of life. Quality of life is conceptualized and measured in terms of distributive schemes and policies that allow individuals to develop capabilities in relation to those forms of "functioning" that are vital to a worthwhile human existence. The list of such "functional capabilities" is fairly extensive; it covers capabilities for many spheres of human functioning, including (among others) life, bodily integrity, nourishment and good health, practical reason, affiliation with other people, caring for and being cared for by loved ones, and having and exercising agency with regard to one's own life and surroundings.[33] The purpose of politics, as Nussbaum spells it out, is to make sure that citizens "receive the institutional, material, and educational support that is required if they are to become capable of functioning in [each] sphere according to their own practical reason—and functioning not just minimally, but well, insofar as natural circumstances permit."[34]

This is precisely the kind of practical translation of the priority of the good into political economy that is central to my idea of ethical materialism, and that I have argued is sorely missing in most post-socialist thought. By focusing on the actual functionings of human beings, and by considering the societal resources that promote good functioning in different spheres of life, the "capabilities approach" meets the basic requirement of ethical materialism: sustained attention to the material conditions and circumstances of life and labor that support or constrain the moral and civic development of free and equal democratic citizens. There is even room in the capabilities approach for consideration of the different forms and arrangements of property that best promote good human functioning. In fact, property has become increasingly important in Nussbaum's formulations of the capabilities approach, as she has come to realize the importance of land reform and equal property rights for women in developing countries like India.[35]

The capabilities approach is practical not just because of its interest in political economy, but also more broadly because it opens up empirical investigation of the linkages between different goods and the effects of policies and institutions. At the same time, the capabilities approach provides a compelling normative framework for analyzing the instruments and ends of human development and well-being. Among other things, this framework makes it easier to see the connections between the social question and issues of democratic theory. It does so by showing how both moral and political agency are part of human well-being. In other words, both a just society and a democratic society require and promote the good of people in the sense of promoting their capacities to freely direct their own lives.[36]

Nussbaum's formulation of the capabilities approach is especially apropos, for it includes an Aristotelian view of the capabilities associated with engaged and socially responsible citizenship. Nussbaum does not ask the specific question of how property is to be related to the capacity for civic virtue. But property and labor *are* treated as two of the resources and activities (alongside political participation, education, and several others) which need to be provided, arranged, and distributed by the polity in order to bring free and equal citizens "across a threshold into a condition in which good human functioning, at least a minimal level, can be chosen."[37]

So there are good reasons for me to try to build on the capabilities approach. To a degree, ethical materialism can be seen as an attempt to redescribe this approach along more hermeneutic lines, and on the basis of a more systematic analysis of property. However, my redescription also stems from my belief that the capabilities approach needs to be revised in a couple of fundamental ways. For one thing, while it creates a theoretical space for issues of property, it does so largely within the conceptual confines of modern thingness.[38] What the capabilities approach provides is a way of connecting property as a "thing of utility" to different goods and ends of human flourishing. To this extent, it can be seen as an Aristotelian approach to property. The problem is that there is little attention to the complexities and complications that accompany property as a location of labor and authority. Hermeneutically, it is important to encounter such complexities and complications because they help us to understand the interpretive horizon that informs our sense of important capabilities and goods. And this points to another problem with the capabilities approach, which is that it does not have much of a hermeneutic sensibility or sensitivity. This gets us back to the kind of hermeneutic sense of practicality that I have stressed from the outset of this study. It is well and good that the capabilities approach is practical in the sense of encouraging empirical investigation of the conditions that support or constrain human development and well-being; such empirical investigation has a very important role to play in ethical materialism. But empirical investigation is not enough, for it leaves unexamined the horizonal background within which the commitments of capability theorists to things like social justice, democracy, and freedom arise. These commitments define and condition the understanding of human flourishing that capability theorists bring to their empirical investigations. By failing to encounter and explore the horizonal background of their underlying theoretical commitments, capability theorists run the risk of presupposing whatever type of horizonal background is required to support their normative framework. By contrast, a hermeneutic perspective requires us to test our prejudices in the process of encountering what we are trying to understand. Presupposing the most agreeable horizonal background obviously does not meet this requirement. The upshot is that capability theorists beg the hermeneutic question of how well their normative framework of capabilities and good functioning meshes with the actual historical horizon of freedom, social justice, and democracy. Or what amounts to the same thing, capability theorists end up treating capabilities and functionings as hermeneutically isolated and untested givens.

So as valuable as the capabilities approach is for the project of ethical materialism, it is by no means a simple corrective for the problems that we have uncovered in post-socialist thinking about property and political economy. In fact, the problems of hermeneutic *im*practicality and the neglect of the complexity of property are common to both the capabilities approach and post-socialism. This perhaps isn't surprising insofar as there is an affinity between the two perspectives. On the other hand, the civic republican hermeneutics of identity provides resources that can contribute to a form of ethical materialism that avoids the problems we have been discussing. This is especially true with respect to the placeness of property, but also with respect to the civic republican appreciation of historical context. So in that spirit, I want to spend some time introducing the problematic complexity of the Aristotelian background of ethical materialism.

The Significance of Aristotle

Whatever label is used to describe it, ethical materialism has had a long history in political and social theory. Ironically, there are large elements of it in Marx's thought. Certainly, Marx was interested in the material conditions that would promote the development of human capacities without regard to an individual's class situation. And in his own way, Marx sought to break free of the terms of debate between materialism and idealism, especially with regard to how these terms were constructed in nineteenth-century German thought. Breaking free of these terms was the whole point of his reworking of materialism in almost pragmatist terms of sensuous activity and practice. This is seen in the first of his "theses on Feuerbach":

> The chief defect of all hitherto existing materialism . . . is that the thing, reality, sensuousness, is conceived only in the form of the object or of *contemplation*, but not as *sensuous human activity*, *practice*, not subjectively. Hence, it developed that the *active* side, in contradistinction to materialism, was developed by idealism— but only abstractly, since, of course, idealism does not know real, sensuous activity as such.[39]

For Marx, both material reality and thinking are fundamentally practical in nature. So in the second thesis on Feuerbach, he went on to say that the "dispute over the reality or non-reality of thinking which is isolated from practice is a purely *scholastic* question."[40]

This much in Marx is quite compatible with my own approach to ethical materialism. However, it is Aristotle, and not Marx, who is the key figure for the vision of ethical materialism that is elaborated in these pages. There is something of a strategic reason for this: Because Aristotle is an important figure in both past and present expressions of civic-humanist republicanism, he becomes an important presence in my critique. But there are other reasons as well. For one thing, as Nussbaum would remind us, Aristotle is a foundational thinker in the effort to situate material conditions and processes within an ethical context. In this regard, it is important that Aristotle provided the kind of explicit practical philosophy of ethics and politics that often got lost in the midst of Marx's positivistic proclivities. In addition, Aristotle (more than Marx) provides specific theoretical guidance regarding the ethical possibilities and problems associated with property itself.

Whether in matters of ethics or property, Aristotle's thinking was informed by a teleological and eudaimonist approach to philosophy. Speaking broadly, this is an approach that first identifies the good with human well-being and flourishing and then seeks to uncover the conditions and practices which allow individuals to flourish by actualizing moral and civic excellences of character.[41] On my reading, this is very much about justice as well as virtue. But at this time, I want to focus on what Aristotle offers us with regard to an ethical materialist perspective on virtue. To this end, let us consider what Aristotle has to say in the *Politics* about the "constituent elements of the best life."

Aristotle discusses the "constituent elements of the best life" in terms of the relationship between three types of goods: "goods of the body" involving the health of the body and the satisfaction of basic physical needs such as hunger; "external goods" such as wealth and property, power, and reputation; and intrinsically valuable "goods of the soul" such as fortitude, temperance, justice, and wisdom.[42] Within an Aristotelian understanding of ethical materialism, the key is that both goods of the body and external goods function as "things of utility" in relation to the development and cultivation of those capabilities and excellences of moral character which constitute the intrinsically valuable goods of the soul (or internal goods for short). By contrast, a corrupt and unethical materialism arises when the acquisition of bodily goods and external goods is no longer "within moderate limits," or worse still, becomes an end in itself. The good life has been profoundly debased when the struggle to make economic ends meet is geared only to the satisfaction of physical needs, or when property, power, and reputation are acquired only because one craves riches, is power-hungry, or desires a high social status. But while bodily and external goods are marked by their corruptive potential, they nonetheless remain "constituent" rather than merely contingent elements in the good life, and this too is crucial to an Aristotelian form of ethical materialism. All three goods are necessary for human flourishing.

This last point needs emphasis. There is a simplistic form of ethical materialism—a kind of pseudo-ethical or perhaps proto-ethical materialism—which focuses almost exclusively on the relationship between bodily needs and internal goods. Put briefly, this is a perspective that attaches great importance to the fact that the satisfaction of basic bodily needs is a necessary condition for all human development, including moral and political development. This perspective must not be confused with an Aristotelian ethical materialism. While an Aristotelian ethical materialism accepts both the obvious truth and the importance of the claim that the satisfaction of bodily needs is a necessary condition of human flourishing, it does so in a theoretical context that places equal emphasis on external goods. External goods mediate the relationship between bodily needs and internal goods. More precisely, external goods represent cultural and institutional resources which, in addition to generating their own practices and standards, provide institutional contexts within which bodily needs and internal goods are brought into relation to one another. Herein lies the special significance of property within an Aristotelian ethical materialism, for of all the different external goods mentioned by Aristotle, it is property that is most directly and most consistently related to the wherewithal necessary for material provision.

Let me pause to make sure that my purpose in talking about an Aristotelian approach to ethical materialism is not misunderstood. Aristotle's account of the "constituent elements" of the good life—and especially the part of it involving the relationship between external goods and internal goods of the soul—provides a general framework within which to begin to elaborate an ethical materialism and the different issues and challenges it poses for a post-socialist theory of democracy. But this does not mean that I am endorsing all the particulars of his account, and the fact that I am drawing on it certainly does not constitute a defense of Aristotelianism in general. To the contrary, Aristotle is a decidedly Janus-faced figure in this inquiry. As will be discussed in more detail in chapter 5, both faces of Aristotle can be seen in his analysis of the constituent elements of the good life and in the historical legacy of this analysis. While his analysis provides the groundwork for an ethical materialism, it is also foundational for a tradition of thought that identifies internal goods with paternalistic and patriarchal forms of mastery. Within this latter tradition, property and power become authoritative not simply by being connected to virtue, but also by being the instruments with which institutions are ruled and their hierarchies preserved. In addition to reminding us that questions of authority are very much at stake with an ethical materialism, this tradition of paternalistic mastery provides a disturbing counterpoint to contemporary civic republican narratives and reappropriations of Aristotelian civic humanism. In chapter 5, we shall see that these narratives and reappropriations have little to say about how early modern civic-humanist republicans such as James Harrington followed Aristotle in seeking to bring property and other external goods into the orbit of the internal goods of virtuous citizenship within the institutional context of a hierarchical and *un*democratic vision of household mastery. This vision is the source of the problem of republican paternalism.

Even historians who are sympathetic to civic humanist forms of classical republicanism have been led to the conclusion that part of what defines early modern republicanism in its civic humanist form is the existence and persistence of ancient Greek and Roman beliefs concerning the unequal capacities for self-government among different groups and classes. And some of the most compelling evidence for this conclusion involves property and the project of reconciling it with the capacity for virtuous self-government. This is seen in Michael Ignatieff's explanation of why "citizenship was an exclusionary category" from its inception in the republican tradition. Taking Aristotle as the foundational thinker for the "classical republican model" of citizenship, Ignatieff summarizes the Aristotelian answer to the question of who is fit to be a citizen in the following way:

> Since Aristotle assumed that political discussion was an exercise in rational choice of the public good, he also assumed that the only persons fit for such an exercise were those capable of rational choice. And the only ones capable of rational choice were those who were free. Dependent creatures could not be citizens: slaves, those who worked for wages, women and children who were both subject to the authority of the domestic *oeconomia* were excluded from citizenship. Adult male property owners were the only persons vested with civic personality.[43]

Ignatieff has captured the main features of "the masters' vision of civic virtue." As with all ideal types, there is the danger that this vision will make a complex historical reality appear too black and white. Certainly, I would not want to say that the masters' vision of civic virtue existed in exactly the same form or to the same degree in all classical or classically inspired republican thinkers and episodes. At the same time, however, I believe that there is ample evidence to show that, in one form or another, the masters' vision of civic virtue was a persistent feature of civic humanist republicanism up to and through the efforts of classical republicans in the early modern era to address the tension between civic virtue and emerging forms of commerce.

In the end, the long historical shadow cast by the masters' vision of civic virtue will make it necessary to make room within our Aristotelian materialism for a distinctly modern moment of progressive opposition to hierarchical and exclusionary concentrations of property and authority—by no means an inconsequential or easy change to make. It is also largely because of the importance of this modern oppositionist moment for the project of advancing both social justice and democracy that there is no simple Aristotelian correction for the ethical anti-materialism of post-socialist thinkers.

Notes

1. Note that this is not a matter of ignoring empirical, causal relationships—say, between wealth and variables like political power or access to the political system. One could be very attuned to such empirical relationships while simultaneously conceptualizing property (or wealth) as a discrete "object" whose fundamental meaning is untouched by practical contexts and relationships of labor, authority, and social and civic identity.

2. Thomas C. Grey, "The Disintegration of Property," in *Property*, vol. XXII of *Nomos*, ed. Roland Pennock and John Chapman (New York: New York University Press, 1980).

3. C. B. Macpherson, *Democratic Theory: Essays in Retrieval* (London: Oxford University Press, 1973), 121.

4. C. B. Macpherson, *The Political Theory of Possessive Individualism: Hobbes to Locke* (Oxford: At the Clarendon Press, 1962).

5. Benjamin R. Barber, *Strong Democracy: Participatory Politics for a New Age* (Berkeley, CA: University of California Press, 1984), 75.

6. Amy Gutmann, "Communitarian Critics of Liberalism," *Philosophy and Public Affairs* 14 (1985): 309.

7. Alan Wolfe, *Whose Keeper? Social Science and Moral Obligation* (Berkeley, CA: University of California Press, 1989), 190.

8. Robert N. Bellah et al., *Habits of the Heart: Individualism and Commitment in American Life*, 2nd ed. (Berkeley, CA: University of California Press, 1996), 275.

9. Robert N. Bellah et al., *The Good Society* (New York: Alfred A. Knopf, 1991), 4.

10. In addition to the civic republican proposals that were discussed in chapter 2, see, for example, Anthony Giddens, *The Third Way: The Renewal of Social Democracy* (Malden, MA: Polity Press, 1998); Alasdair MacIntyre, *Dependent Rational Animals: Why Human Beings Need the Virtues* (La Salle, IL: Open Court Publishing, 1999), especially chapter 11; Kirkpatrick Sale, *Dwellers in the Land: The Bioregional Vision*, 2nd ed. (Athens, GA: The University of Georgia Press, 2000); and Phillip Selznick, *The Communitarian Persuasion* (Washington, DC: Woodrow Wilson Center Press, 2002).

11. Michael J. Sandel, *Liberalism and the Limits of Justice*, 2nd ed. (Cambridge: Cambridge University Press, 1998), 183.

12. *The Communitarian Persuasion*, 107.

13. Alasdair MacIntyre, *After Virtue: A Study in Moral Theory*, 2nd ed. (Notre Dame, IN: University of Notre Dame Press, 1984), chapter 10, especially 249–53.

14. William M. Sullivan *Reconstructing Public Philosophy* (Berkeley, CA: University of California Press, 1986), 175.

15. Ronald Beiner, *What's the Matter with Liberalism?* (Berkeley, CA: University of California Press, 1992), 148.

16. Beiner, *What's the Matter with Liberalism?*, 144.

17. Beiner, 145.

18. Beiner, 166, 167, and 160.

19. Nancy Fraser discusses this sense of skepticism in connection to what she calls "the postsocialist condition" in *Justice Interruptus: Critical Reflections on the 'Postsocialist' Condition* (New York: Routledge, 1997). I note that Fraser focuses more on postmodern expressions of identity politics than on the kinds of projects of moral and civic recovery that are at the heart of the theories that I am calling "post-socialist."

20. Jean Bethke Elshtain, *Democracy on Trial* (New York: Basic Books, 1995), 13.

21. Charles Taylor, *Sources of the Self: The Making of Modern Identity* (Cambridge, MA: Harvard University Press, 1989), 195–96.

22. Taylor, *Sources of the Self*, 196.

23. Barber, *Strong Democracy*, 20, 135, and 33–34.

24. Barber, 34 and 73–74.

25. Barber, 75.

26. Barber, 200 and 305–6.

27. Barber, 252.

28. Sandel, 96–103; Sale, 84–86; Selznick, 72–73 and 95–97; and Christopher Lasch, *The True and Only Heaven: Progress and its Critics* (New York: W. W. Norton and Company, 1991), 302, 310, 315, and 531.

29. Lasch, *The True and Only Heaven*, 531–32.

30. Sullivan, *Reconstructing Public Philosophy*, 14.

31. Iseult Honohan, *Civic Republicanism* (London: Routledge, 2002), 191.

32. See the essays in Martha C. Nussbaum and Amartya Sen, eds., *The Quality of Life*, (Oxford: Clarendon Press, 1993); Amartya Sen, *Freedom as Development* (New York: Anchor Books, 1999); Martha C. Nussbaum, "Aristotelian Social Democracy," in *Liberalism and the Good*, ed. R. Bruce Douglass, Gerald M. Mara, and Henry S. Richardson (New York: Routledge, 1990); and Nussbaum, *Women and Human Development: The Capabilities Approach* (Cambridge, MA: Cambridge University Press, 2000).

33. This list is drawn from Nussbaum, "Aristotelian Social Democracy," 217–26 and Nussbuam, *Women and Human Development*, 78–80. Also see Sen, *Freedom as Development*, 74–86.

34. Nussbaum, "Aristotelian Social Democracy," 228.

35. See Nussbaum, *Women and Human Development*, 80 and 156–57.

36. See Sen, *Freedom as Development*, especially chapters 3 and 6.

37. Nussbaum, "Aristotelian Social Democracy," 228.

38. Nussbaum edges close to placeness in her recognition of the importance of property "in developing a sense of self" as well as in her engagement with the issue of the role of property in the constitution of the structure of authority within families. But in the end Nussbaum's understanding of property remains rooted in the rightful

control of assets and land as property objects. See Nussbaum, *Women and Human Development*, 156 and 281–82.

39. Karl Marx, "Theses on Feuerbach," in *The Marx-Engels Reader*, ed. Robert C. Tucker (New York: W. W. Norton and Company, 1972), 107, emphasis in the original.

40. Marx, 108.

41. See Nussbaum, "Aristotelian Social Democracy," 208–17; Martha C. Nussbaum, "Non-Relative Values: An Aristotelian Approach," in *The Quality of Life*, ed. Nussbaum and Sen; Richard Kraut, *Aristotle on the Human Good* (Princeton, NJ: Princeton University Press, 1989); Honohan, *Civic Republicanism*, 19–21; and David L. Norton's discussion of Aristotle and eudaimonism in *Democracy and Moral Development* (Berkeley, CA: University of California Press, 1991), 1–8.

42. Aristotle, *Politics*, ed. and trans. Ernest Barker (London: Oxford University Press, 1975), book VII, 1323a, 280.

43. Michael Ignatieff, "The Myth of Citizenship," in *Theorizing Citizenship*, ed. Ronald Beiner (Albany, NY: State University of New York Press, 1995), 56.

4

Rethinking the Properties of
the Situated Self

I N CONJUNCTION WITH MY CONCERNS ABOUT PROPERTY and its displacement, I
have brought two suspicions to my critique of civic republicanism. The first
is that civic republicans are essentially correct in arguing on behalf of a formative politics of civic virtue. More precisely, I suspect that they are essentially
correct in arguing that democratic practices of liberty and self-government
require a critical mass of citizens who are educated in the habits and dispositions of responsible citizenship. The second suspicion is very different. It is
that civic republicans do not fully appreciate the extent to which issues of social justice are implicated in a formative politics of civic virtue, and that because of this, their project of civic recovery and renewal contains insufficient
safeguards against the dangers which such a politics poses to democratic understandings and norms of equal citizenship. With regard to this second suspicion, I am concerned about issues pertaining to unjust and undemocratic
forms of second-class citizenship. While this includes the standard problem of
tyranny of the majority, my suspicion is that the problem that is most distinctive of a formative politics of civic virtue is one involving too close a linkage between the capacity for self-rule and patriarchal, paternalistic, or otherwise exclusionary forms of guardianship of other adult members of the polity.

If both of these suspicions are well founded (as of course I believe them to
be), then the relationship between civic virtue and democracy is rather more
complicated and problematic than civic republicans'would have us believe. If
not a contradictory relationship, it is at least one marked by tension, paradox,
and ambiguity.

I believe that property provides a very helpful lens for seeing the tension, paradox, and ambiguity of the relationship between civic virtue and democracy. This is not to say that focusing on property is absolutely necessary in order to make the case that a formative politics of civic virtue is simultaneously essential to the maintenance of democracy and a threat to it. But precisely because the participants in the debate over civic virtue so often have treated property as a subject of dubious moral and theoretical value, it provides an unsettling and revealing counterpoint to the terms in which this debate has been conducted. Especially when we broaden the conceptual scope to include property-related contexts of labor, authority, and civic identity, we discover that an emphasis on property unsettles the all-too-comfortable (and all-too-common!) belief that the only really important issue of property is how to overcome the two-fold influence of possessive individualism and economic reason. By the same token, focusing on property and its contexts reveals substantial blind spots and gaps in both the critical and constructive programs of the participants in the debate, not just in terms of property, but also in terms of the properties of democracy in general.

The upshot of all this is that property is an important instrument and vehicle of "external" criticism of civic republicanism and related visions of politics. However, as we first began to see in chapter 2, some of the most unsettling and revealing aspects of property emerge through an "internal-critical" mode of recasting property along lines suggested by the civic republicans' own hermeneutic understanding of the "situated self."

As an internal critique, my approach is one that seeks to show the problematic implications of property for civic republicanism while simultaneously drawing on civic republicanism for ideas regarding the question of how to conceptualize property. The aim of this chapter is to spell out this dialectic of property and civic republicanism. The focus is on how the civic republican hermeneutics of the "situated self" helps us to rethink the properties of property, and how this rethinking of property also unsettles the theoretical foundations of the civic republican project of recovery and renewal.

This dialectic revolves around the idea of the placeness of property, and much of what I have to say in this chapter is about the different dimensions of this idea. I also explore the possibilities and problems of a civic republican understanding of the placeness of property in relation to Michael Sandel's concept of the "guardianship" of communal assets and resources. I start, however, by taking a closer look at the civic republican analysis of the problem of a commercial republic. The problem of a commercial republic provides a bridge between the discussion of ethical materialism in the previous chapter and my hermeneutic exploration of the properties of the situated self. Civic republicans analyze the problem of a commercial republic with many of the idioms and concepts of an ethical materialism, most especially the idioms and concepts of an Aristotelian perspective on the relationship between external and internal goods. We shall see, though, that the civic republican analysis remains trapped within the post-socialist dualism of political economy and culture. The emphasis is more on overcoming property and other external goods than on showing how these goods might serve and support formative locations of "situated" democratic citizenship. Through the recovery of its placeness, property can function as such a location. But the placeness of property also carries with it the possibility of paternalistic forms of authority and dominion, and unfortunately such structures must be counted among the properties of the civic republicans' situated self.

Civic Republicanism and the Problem of a Commercial Republic

From what has been said in previous chapters, we know that civic republican concerns about the commercial republic often bear a strong family resemblance to C. B. Macpherson's classic critique of possessive individualism.[1] Like Macpherson, civic republicans believe that liberalism committed itself to a distorted and debased understanding of moral and political life through its adoption of a proprietary model of freedom and personality. Within this model, individual liberties and rights are grounded in self-ownership and, by extension, in the acquisition, possession, and exchange of commodities in a market system. The result, in the view of both Macpherson and civic republicans, is a theory that promotes acquisitiveness, competition, and inequality at the expense of democracy. However, civic republicans offer more than a simple restatement of Macpherson's critique. Rather, their approach to the problem of a commercial republic is one that situates possessive individualism in the classical republican framework of virtue and corruption. The argument, in general form, is that the collective liberty of self-governing citizens is sustained by virtuous engagement with and for the common good, and the capacity for such a virtuous engagement is undermined by commercial values and practices that validate the self-seeking pursuit of property and other external goods.

There has been surprisingly little variation in this basic argument. The most important variation has to do with the neoclassical republicans' rejection of a positive-libertarian understanding of public liberty. Again, neoclassical republicans define public liberty more defensively and protectively in terms of a republican citizenry's freedom from subjection and domination. By contrast, the communal republican understanding of public liberty holds that "to be free is to share in governing a political community that controls its own fate."[2] At first glance, these different understandings of public liberty seem to imply substantially different approaches to the problem of a commercial republic. But this is not the case. Neoclassical republicans are not so overtly Aristotelian in their approach, and overall they seem less critical of commercial processes and practices. But they remain theorists of civic virtue who seek to protect the common good of republican liberty from the tendencies toward corruption and privatism within a modern regime of commerce. Philip Pettit, for example, affirms Sandel's argument that the project of cultivating the virtues of republican citizenship is betrayed by modern consumerism, and like Sandel, he worries that this project is undermined by the liberal attachment to a market model in which preference maximization is the norm of both economic and political decision making.[3]

This common ground between neoclassical and communal republicans extends to the ideal of independent citizenship itself. For communal republicans, freedom from domination and dependency does not rise to the level of being the central end or meaning of republican liberty; rather, it is more of a background condition of positive-libertarian civic engagement. Even so, the ideal of independent citizenship looms large in the communal republican approach to the problem of a commercial republic. For example, this ideal is central to the "political economy of citizenship" that Sandel claims has been displaced in the United States in recent decades by more proceduralist and consumerist approaches to political economy. "From the standpoint of the republican tradition," Sandel writes in *Democracy's Discontent*, "the demise of the political economy of citizenship constituted a concession, a deflation of American ideals, a loss of liberty. . . . Cultivating in citizens the virtue, independence, and shared understandings [that] civic engagement requires is a central aim of republican politics."[4]

Finally, communal and neoclassical republicans share the view that the problem of a commercial republic is partly a problem having to do with the threat to political equality that is posed by commercial values, practices, and institutions. Consider first the communal republican analysis of this threat.

Communal republicans tend to define political equality in terms of the ideals of mutuality and solidarity. Naturally, the liberal perspective that is said to inform the modern commercial republic does not measure up well against these ideals. Liberalism, on the communal republican view, offers mainly a legal framework of individual rights, equal opportunity, and market competition. Such a framework is not only conceptually at odds with an egalitarian spirit of civic mutuality, but it also undercuts this spirit by preventing the kind of "sharing of viewpoints" that occurs within practices of "collective deliberation."[5] Liberal equality, Benjamin Barber suggests, is a market-oriented equality to make private deals.[6] Equality is thereby reduced to an instrument for the more or less orderly competition among individuals for scare resources and unequal outcomes or "amounts" of freedom. Or as Wilson Carey McWilliams puts it, liberal equality is found in societies "whose institutions are based on exchange relationships." In these societies—including, of course, modern American society—"dignity is a function of one's relative power in exchange," and equality becomes a merely formal concept. By contrast, "civic, or communitarian, equality" has a classical, and most especially, an Aristotelian provenance. According to McWilliams, this civic understanding of equality is found in societies that "aim at common values and interpersonal bonds" and which derive dignity "from the quality of one's devotion to the common values."[7] Similarly, William Sullivan maintains that "equal concern and respect among citizens" is at the heart of the "shared moral order" of civic republican liberty. According to Sullivan, the "civic tradition teaches with nearly one voice" that this moral order "demands and expresses an egalitarian ideal." The problem is that this egalitarian ideal has been eclipsed and corrupted by "utilitarian individualism." "Utilitarian individualism," he writes, "has no necessary connection to equality in the civic sense. On the contrary, utilitarian social forms, in particular the market, generate moral and psychological pressures in a directly anti-egalitarian direction."[8]

Neoclassical republicans do not travel as far as communal republicans down the road towards egalitarian mutuality. But they are nonetheless intent on checking the threats to equal liberty within liberal capitalist regimes. Pettit even offers the classical republican ideal of non-domination as a weapon in the struggle against capitalist wage slavery.[9] More generally, neoclassical republicans argue that an unfettered capitalist market is apt to decrease the liberty of those who are socioeconomically disadvantaged without increasing the liberty of either advantaged groups or society in general.[10]

Of course, it is one thing to assail liberal capitalism for undermining democratic ideals of inclusion and equal liberty, and quite another to show that these ideals are supported and furthered by the civic republican project of recovery and renewal. It is primarily in relation to the latter proposition that I wish to challenge the civic republican analysis of the problem of a commercial republic. It is my contention that civic republicans have failed to show how the terms of equal and inclusive citizenship can be maintained when republican virtue is marshaled against commercial corruption. Over the course of the rest of this chapter and the two that follow, I hope to show that this is the Achilles heel of their approach to the problem of a commercial republic. But this is not a simple matter of using the problem of a commercial republic as an occasion to reiterate the well-known tension between equality and civic virtue. Rather, I believe that we can learn a great deal about the properties and sources of democratic equality when we explore both the problems and the constructive theoretical possibilities that inhere in the relationship between property and

the civic virtues of the situated self. To this end, it will be helpful to consider
in detail two theses that both communal and neoclassical republicans have advanced about property and the problem of a commercial republic.

A Critique of External Goods and the Liberal Language of Rights

The first of these two civic republican theses is essentially a reworking of
Aristotle's analysis of the "constituent elements of the best life," and especially the Aristotelian view of the corruptive power of instrumental goods.[11]
It is easy to see how we get from here to the problem of a commercial republic. The basic idea is simply that the intrinsic goods and virtues of republican citizenship are debased and corrupted by commercial beliefs and
practices that promote the immoderate pursuit of property and other
"things of utility." I am going to call this the "internal goods thesis" (or the
"IG thesis" for short).

To be sure, the relationship between civic republican views of the problem
of a commercial republic and Aristotelianism is more nuanced than this suggests. For one thing, there are civic republicans—most notably, neoclassical
republicans—who show little or no interest in reappropriating Aristotle's
thought. For another, we need to be mindful of the fact that even civic republicans who are generally Aristotelian in their approach are critical of some aspects of Aristotle's political philosophy. For example, Charles Taylor makes a
point of criticizing Aristotle's perfectionist notion of a comprehensive and
supreme good that entails "all the goods together in their proper proportions."
Citing Aristotle's defense of slavery and the subordinate role of women in the
Aristotelian polity, Taylor maintains that Aristotle's "comprehending strategy"
of affirming and harmonizing the goods of particular social arrangements
poses a threat to modern (and liberal!) understandings of justice and human
dignity. Yet Taylor is also an example of the enormous influence that an Aristotelian perspective on internal goods has had on contemporary civic republicanism. How else can we describe the higher ends and goods that are to be
apprehended and realized through Taylor's dialogic practices of "strong evaluation" if not as goods that bear a strong family resemblance to Aristotle's
"goods of the soul"? In addition to being goods that are intrinsically worthwhile, they are internal goods in the sense of being "internal to practices which
humans develop in their different societies."[12]

Even Barber, who has no interest in identifying his perspective with "republican nostalgia," evokes the Aristotelian classification of goods in his discussion of "hedonist-individualist concepts [such] as power, rights, and property." In effect, these concepts are the functional equivalent of Aristotle's
external goods within Barber's civic republican critique of liberalism, while

goods such as mutualism, cooperation, fellowship, fraternity, community, and democratic citizenship are analogous to Aristotelian internal goods.[13]

More typical of the communal republican perspective on internal goods is Sullivan's appeal to Aristotle and classical republican thinkers regarding the notion of an "intrinsic claim of quality." According to Sullivan, the "classical theorists of the [republican] tradition" held the view that "the form and the end immanent in a style of life give significance and worth to living." Sullivan argues that an "intrinsic claim of quality" holds "that an activity is important because there is some prized good which exists within and is not separable from that activity." In his view, the failure of "liberal utilitarianism" to recognize such intrinsic moral qualities places it on a slippery slope leading to a subjectivist and instrumentalist individualism.[14] Sullivan is quick to point out that the utilitarian framework of maximizing subjective preferences is the source of the "marketing orientation" within liberalism. In contrast to this orientation, "moral virtue represents a higher integration of the powers of the self." Furthermore, in the Aristotelian tradition of republicanism, this formative process of moral integration and maturation is "at once the goal and the effect of participation in civic life." Hence, participation in the civic community is itself a good that is internal to moral character. As Sullivan puts it, "collective deliberation on matters of common concern is good intrinsically, not instrumentally."[15]

Again, neoclassical republicans have little interest in reappropriating Aristotelian civic humanism. Their historical retrievals and reappropriations focus on those forms of Renaissance and early modern republicanism that were influenced by Roman thought. But the gap between neoclassical and communal republican understandings of internal goods is not nearly as great as neoclassical republicans would have us believe. For one thing, while neoclassical republicans conceptualize public liberty differently than communal republicans, they see it as an intrinsically valuable good. In the process, and almost despite themselves, they evoke a broadly Aristotelian view of the virtues of republican citizenship. We can think of it as a structural form of Aristotelianism, as opposed to a self-consciously and explicitly articulated Aristotelianism. For example, Pettit explicates a neoclassical virtue ethic that is quite compatible with the IG thesis that has been advanced by communal republicans. This virtue ethic revolves around identification with the civic community and internalization of the norms of civility, vigilance, trust, and civic virtue. Civic identification and the internalized "virtues of good citizenship" are internal goods in the sense of being intrinsically valuable habits of public liberty.[16]

For neoclassical republicans, corruption involves activities and practices (whether commercial or otherwise) in which self-seeking individuals or groups threaten public liberty. And how exactly do such self-seeking individuals or groups threaten public liberty? Through the domination and subjection of other citizens, of course, but also by possessing and using their private resources of wealth and power in a manner that, structurally if not explicitly, looks a lot like Aristotle's immoderate use of external goods. In keeping with his neo-roman orientation, Pettit calls such private resources *dominium*. Like Aristotle's external goods, *dominium* is necessary for both individual development and civic life. The problem, as with Aristotle's external goods, is the abuse of *dominium* such that it is used for illegitimate ends, or worse, becomes an end in itself.

I turn now to the second thesis. This thesis grows out of the civic republican critique of the liberal discourse of rights. Broadly speaking, this critique holds that liberal rights discourse promotes a negative liberty of non-interference in private choices at the expense of a public liberty of self-governing citizenship. Civic republicans argue that the threat to public liberty is partly the result of the close conceptual and linguistic relationship between rights and property within liberalism. I call this argument about the corruptive "intertextuality" of rights and property the "rights/property thesis" (or the "R/P thesis" for short).

We have already seen several examples of the communal republican formulation of the R/P thesis: Sullivan's critique of the "liberal emphasis upon freedom understood as security of possession"; Taylor's identification of modern rights as proprietary immunities in the Lockean tradition of possessive individualism; Barber's treatment of rights and property as fundamentally similar "hedonist-individualist concepts" and his attempt to link liberal "freedom-seeking" with "property-acquisition"; and Beiner's argument that we lose sight of the question of the quality of social relationships when we discuss justice in "the language of rights and entitlement." In these cases, and others like them, we find civic republicans viewing rights through the lens of the critique of possessive individualism. But notice also that these examples show how civic republicans move well beyond the problems of acquisitiveness and Lockean self-ownership to a more sweeping critique of the intertextuality of property and rights. The problem, from this point of view, is not just one of grounding freedom and rights in the pursuit and acquisition of property, but also a deeper one of introducing property-related ideas and imagery into the very core of liberal freedom. In the name of freedom, communal republicans complain, liberalism erects property-like fences and spaces of separation from the community. As a result, a preoccupation with external goods like property becomes part of the concept of freedom. And since it is a negative liberty of non-interference in the spaces of isolated individuals that is established, freedom loses both its public and its positive dimensions. "The ultimate battle cry of the liberal," Barber declaims, "is 'Don't cross this line!' The political slogan always reads 'Don't walk on my turf!' Liberalism is a politics of negativity, which enthrones not simply the individual but the individual defined by his perimeters, his parapets, and his entrenched solitude."[17]

For most communal republicans, rights and property are simply different types of external goods. In other words, rights and property have the same status as "things of utility." This has been expressed in different ways, and with varying degrees of opposition to both rights and liberalism. In its more extreme anti-liberal moods, communal republicanism has taken the position that rights are inherently and fundamentally corruptive. This was the position adopted by Barber when he lumped rights with property and power, and treated them all as "hedonist-individualist concepts." In a similar spirit, Beiner has affirmed the critique of liberalism that holds that its "rights discourse tends to posit forms of social life that are excessively adversarial, litigious, and geared towards modes of self-assertion of individuals or collectivities." In Beiner's view, the liberal preoccupation with rights is a key sign that contemporary liberalism is an "ethosless ethos" that is incapable of articulating any conception of the good other than the vacuous good of individual choice itself.[18] Alternatively, in its more moderate, and usually more liberal moods, communal republicanism has taken the position that the problem is not so much rights themselves, but the moral and civic context within which they are embedded. Taylor, for instance, has consistently maintained that the goal is not to eliminate modern liberal concepts such as individual freedom and rights, but "to purge" them "of their atomist distortions."[19] So too has Taylor sought to focus attention on the task of ranking certain rights and liberties. In his terms, a person who engages in "strong evaluation" rather than simply weighing personal preferences will take into account the qualitative moral distinctions between different rights—for example, the qualitative difference between the right to practice your religion and the right to be free of traffic lights when driving your car around your neighborhood.[20] And on this basis, Taylor has gone on to elaborate the possibility of a "patriotic liberal regime" in which citizens are virtuously engaged on behalf of the protection and expansion of their fundamental liberal rights and liberties.[21]

Clearly, there are some important differences here. But at the level of how rights are conceptualized in relation to civic virtue and internal goods, the gap between Taylor and thinkers such as Beiner and Barber is much less than it first appears. In both forms of the R/P thesis, there is deep skepticism about what Taylor calls theories that assert the "primacy of rights" at the expense of "our obligation to belong to or sustain a society."[22] And in both cases, this skepticism is rooted in the priority of the good over the right. Thus, while Taylor emphasizes qualitative distinctions between certain rights, he also argues that these distinctions are only intelligible against a horizon of significance regarding the intrinsic human good to be realized through the "higher" type of right.[23] The upshot is that for Taylor, a "patriotic liberal regime" is a second-best, teleologically incomplete politics of civic virtue. Specifically, Taylor says that, much like current democratic politics in the United States, such a regime will emphasize a judicial politics of rights retrieval and a politics of single-issue advocacy at the expense of a more solidaristic, egalitarian, and majoritarian "politics of democratic will-formation."[24]

What, then, of neoclassical republicans? In some respects, their perspective on rights is very different than that of their communal republican cousins. Put briefly, they are not so hostile towards rights. For neoclassical republicans, rights are part of the *dominium* through which citizens of the modern democratic republic prevent abuses of state authority while also maintaining their independence. Of course, property can serve similar functions, and to this extent, neoclassical republicans provide a more nuanced and circumspect view of the intertextuality of rights and property than one usually finds in communal republicanism. Moreover, while neoclassical republicans are critical of the liberal tradition of negative liberty, their emphasis on the protective functions of rights opens up an area of common conceptual ground with liberalism that goes beyond Taylor's idea of a second-best democratic republic of patriotic liberalism. And yet a version of the R/P thesis is never very far from the surface of neoclassical republicanism. In this version, the proprietary model of rights within the liberal tradition of negative liberty is problematic not only because of the privatism that it promotes, but also because it is ultimately ineffective.

In order to bring the neoclassical republican perspective on rights into focus it may be helpful to consider it in terms of the Lockean metaphor of "fences" of liberty.[25] Neoclassical republicans maintain—correctly in my view—that there is something valuable in conceptions of rights and liberties as property-like fences that provide protection for citizens from arbitrary forms of interference and coercion. That is to say, such fences can be a form of *dominium* that serves the good of non-domination. However, like communal republicans, neoclassical republicans worry that such fences also make it easy—far too easy—for citizens to avoid their social and civic responsibilities. As Quentin Skinner puts it in a critique of contemporary deontological liberalism, rights all too easily become "trumps" that defeat "calls of social duty."[26] Skinner argues that this is self-defeating insofar as both personal and public liberty are sustained by the same civic duties that are often de-emphasized by deontological liberalism.[27] Of course, this is consistent with the communal republican position. What is distinctive about the neoclassical version is the next step of arguing that the proprietary model of non-interference is simply not strong enough to protect personal and public liberty. The problem, on the neoclassical view, is that the enjoyment of non-interference might be contingent on the good will of the powerful. To put this in Pettit's words, "You might enjoy . . . non-interference in the actual world . . . because it happens that certain powerful individuals have a liking for you or it happens that you are able to keep out of the way of such individuals."[28] Neoclassical republicanism has little tolerance for sycophants! More to the point, there are occasions when proprietary fences can purchase non-interference only at the cost of remaining under the sway or thralldom of the powerful. The key is to move beyond the proprietary model of negative liberty to the civic model of non-domination. This means moving beyond a rights discourse of possessions, trumps, and fences to one in which rights facilitate independent citizenship by allowing citizens to be within their own power and jurisdiction.[29]

From an Analytic to a Hermeneutic Perspective

The neoclassical view of rights provides a corrective to the communal republican tendency to treat rights as necessary evils whose significance has much more to do with their corruptive potential than with their role in securing the conditions of self-governing citizenship. In general, it can be said that neoclassical republicans have moved much farther in the direction of an ethical materialism than have most communal republicans. Too often, communal republicans lapse into an ethical anti-materialism in which external goods are viewed almost exclusively as limiting or negating conditions of virtue. Neoclassical republicans recognize the corruptive potential of *dominium*, and they certainly affirm moderation in its use. But they appreciate the fact that *dominium* functions not just as an unavoidable threat to virtue, but also as a practical material condition for the realization of the intrinsic goods of civic independence and public liberty.

In the end, though, the neoclassical analysis of the problem of a commercial republic also stops short of an ethical materialism, and the reason, I wish to argue, is that like their communal republican cousins, neoclassical republicans conceptualize *dominium* and external goods in a fundamentally non-contextual and non-relational manner. Or what amounts to the same thing, both neoclassical and communal republicans have adopted a fundamentally analytic approach to the problem of a commercial republic rather than a hermeneutic one. The difference—and when we get back to the situated self, we shall see it is an important one—is that communal republicans claim that theirs *is* a hermeneutic approach. Indeed, they are apt to offer such an approach as an alternative to the analytic philosophical leanings of the liberal tradition.[30]

From an analytic point of view, the task of understanding the relationship between external goods and the internal goods of democratic citizenship is one of breaking down the relationship into its discrete parts. External and internal goods are treated as if they were logically and conceptually self-contained categories. In this way, *dominium* and external goods are conceptually and phenomenologically isolated from their practical contexts of meaning; in my terms, they are conceptually displaced from their contexts. These contexts include the various conversations and practices through which intrinsic goods such as public liberty, civic independence, and virtuous civic engagement are constituted. As a result, an analytic approach makes it difficult to see that *dominium* and external goods are situated *within* moral and civic contexts and locations, and that the ends and purposes of these contexts and locations can condition the meaning of external goods such as property and rights.

Property does seem to be the hard case here. So used are we to thinking of it as being essentially about thingness that it is difficult to think of the nature of property being conditioned by its contexts. More than is the case with rights, property appears in the modern horizon as a generalized and fungible thing of utility that exists apart from more particularistic contexts of moral and civic life. But this tells us less about the nature of property than about the degree to which the conceptual displacement of property is ingrained in the horizon of modern thingness. Which is also to say that modern thingness is closely allied with the analytic mode of reasoning. Under the influence of the analytic perspective, modern discussions and debates about property often revolve around claims and counter-claims concerning its component logical or empirical parts, its component properties, as it were. The focus is on questions such as, "What does it mean to say that property holder A has a right or entitlement to x?" and "How (if at all) is the right to x derived from other propositions, concepts, or facts?" Clearly, such questions do not preclude normative analysis of the proper scope or purposes of property. Nor, for that matter, does the analytic approach foreclose analysis of empirical and logical relationships between property and social institutions, arrangements, and processes. However, in making the first step of isolating property from its social context, the analytic method forecloses the possibility of uncovering a constitutive locational dimension to property relations. And because of this, the analytic approach tends to emphasize and reinforce the thingness of property as the dominant understanding of property in modern political and legal theory.

If the foregoing discussion is on the mark, then there is an important sense in which the civic republicans' analysis of the problem of a commercial republic is ensnared in the same discursive and theoretical framework of property that they criticize. That is to say, their analysis presupposes that property is what the analytic discourse of modern thingness claims it is. And it is precisely the analytic discourse of modern thingness that I wish to call into question by recasting the communal republican hermeneutics of the situated self as a hermeneutics of both property and identity. In part, this is simply a matter of recovering the social character of property. But hermeneutics reveals the social character of property in the specific theoretical sense of showing that the possessive relationships between property holders and their holdings are constituted by and within a social and linguistic horizon of interpretation. This means that we "experience" these possessive relationships on the basis of, but also within, the understandings and conversations that constitute them. The fact that these understandings and conversations occur somewhere in social space gives rise to the possibility of a placeness of property. But this possibility is realized as a "lived experience" when understandings and conversations about one's social location begin to constitute and define the possessive relationship itself. And it is precisely this "lived experience" of property locations that comes into view when property is fully admitted to the horizon of the situated self.

Property and the Moral and Civic Situation of the Self

Due in large part to the influence of the critiques of liberalism that were put forward in the early 1980s by Sandel and Alasdair MacIntyre, much of the early debate over both civic republicanism and communitarianism centered on questions concerning the communal sources of moral personality and the purported failure of liberalism to acknowledge and appreciate these sources.[31] There was a flurry of responses and counter-responses, with liberals of all philosophical varieties denying that the liberal self lacks or need lack constitutive communal attachments and commitments, and civic republicans and communitarians denying that their situated self is so radically encumbered by such attachments and commitments that it lacks any capacity for critical reflection and agency. Over time, this give and take resulted in a surprisingly large measure of agreement. While most liberals are still likely to press the point that the community and its traditions should be seen as contexts of self-direction, individual choice, and the capacity of individuals to use reason to revise their ends, it would be difficult to find many liberals, or at least left liberals, who would not concede the basic ontological point that communal understandings and conversations are partly constitutive of individual identities.[32] By the same token, while communitarians and civic republicans continue to insist that voluntarist and "constructivist" conceptions of moral agency provide incomplete and distorted accounts of the self, they are likely to affirm (or reaffirm) the importance of linking a more communal conception of moral personality to the capacity for critical reflection on the shared understandings and discursive traditions in which the self is embedded.[33]

It seems that what Sandel once called "the debate between unencumbered selves and situated ones" has largely run its course.[34] To be sure, it can still generate some heat, as was seen after the publication of Sandel's book, *Democracy's Discontent*, in 1996.[35] Yet the debate over the situated self has lost much of its steam. The good news in this is that the more sweeping and more reductive claims that accompanied this debate in its early stages have given way to more nuanced theoretical positions and arguments. But the debate has always had, and still has, some serious limitations and blind spots. Much like the debate between communitarians and liberals to which it has been closely related, the debate over the situated self has suffered from a two-fold tendency to be both too narrow and too broad in its focus. It has been too narrow in that it too often has avoided important philosophical issues such as those pertaining to hermeneutics. It has been too broad in that once again there has been a tendency to lump civic republicanism together with communitarianism. In addition, the interchange concerning the situated self usually has been so general and so abstract that it has begged the question of how the self is to be understood in relation to different kinds of communal contexts. Among other things, therefore, making property a focus of my critique of civic republicanism is meant to provide "the debate between unencumbered selves and situated ones" with more theoretical specificity. But my method of doing so is, of course, one of internal criticism.

A Conceptual Rearrangement

One of the metaphors that I have used to describe my internal critique is that of a "rearrangement" of the conceptual materials of civic republicanism. This metaphor is meant to capture important aspects of the process of internal criticism, the process of working within and through the terms of civic republicanism. Simply put, to rearrange is to work with materials that are already there. With respect to property, this refers to my interest in moving property from the margins to the center of the theoretical universe of civic republicanism. This is partly a matter of paying more attention to the civic republicans' own arguments about property and political economy than has been the case to this point in the discussion and debate surrounding a politics of civic virtue. But it is also a matter of rearranging the civic republican hermeneutics of identity so that it becomes a conceptual field within which to explore the properties of property and its relationship to democratic citizenship. The question then is what happens when property is viewed as one of the civic republicans' formative contexts of identity.

Almost despite the intentions of communal republicans, there are idioms and images of property lurking within the shadows of the situated self. To see what I mean by this, and in order to start the process of redescribing the situated self, it will be helpful to look at the framework of situated and unencumbered selves that informed the seminal critique of Rawls's theory of justice that Sandel developed in *Liberalism and the Limits of Justice*. At this time, my interest is not in the specific merits of Sandel's assessment of Rawls, but in what this critique says about the relationship between property and the situated self in civic republican theory.

Whether intended or not, the allegedly unencumbered Rawlsian self that is criticized by Sandel bears some striking family resemblances to the possessive individualist. In this regard, Sandel's critique of Rawls represents a variation of the R/P thesis. Specifically, the rights-bearing, "deontological self" envisioned by Rawls is said to be a "subject of possession" for whom ends and purposes can be objects of choice but never constitutive parts of who he or she is as a self-reflecting, communally situated being. For such an unencumbered self, ends and purposes can only be contingently "mine," never constitutive of a "me."[36] Extending the imagery of property that is evoked here, Sandel's argument is that the purposes of the Rawlsian self are fungible objects of choice, things which are of merely instrumental value and which may be readily possessed, discarded, or exchanged so long as the basic principles of justice are upheld.[37]

The fact that this imagery is merely evoked in Sandel's critique serves as a reminder that we are dealing with the normative displacement of property. But it is the conceptual displacement of property within Sandel's critique that is more important with respect to the internal-critical task of redescribing the situated self. What we discover in this regard is a striking affinity with the analytic approach to property that we discussed earlier. This provides additional confirmation for my claim that civic republicans have accepted and perpetuated the terms of modern thingness in their analysis of the problem of a commercial republic. But the affinity of Sandel's critique with the analytic approach reaches down to the level of Sandel's theoretical perspective on moral and civic identity. More to the point, there is an important sense in which Sandel analyzes the relationship between the subject and its possessions in terms of the same analytic logic of isolation and separation that he finds so troubling about the deontological conception of the self. Of course, one expects to find such a logic of isolation and separation in deontological liberalism (at least as deontological liberalism is portrayed by Sandel). The deontological self stands apart from, and prior to, the ends that it chooses in the same way that property-holder A stands apart from, and prior to, the property object x that A chooses to acquire, own, or exchange. What is so striking is that Sandel does not alter this analytic approach to possessive relations when discussing the relationship between property and the *situated* self.

With Rawls, possessive relations are conditioned and constrained by principles of justice (and this is true in both the original and revised versions of his theory). With Sandel, by contrast, they are conditioned by the human good of membership in a "constitutive community." Sandel defines this "constitutive community" in unambiguously hermeneutic terms. As he puts it, "what marks such a community is not merely a spirit of benevolence, or the prevalence of communitarian values, or even certain 'shared final ends' alone, but a common vocabulary of discourse and a background of implicit practices and understandings within which the opacity of the participants is reduced if never finally dissolved."[38] The problem is that Sandel never gets around to considering property as something that is constituted within such a background or horizon of discourse and implicit practices and understandings. Property is displaced from the horizon of the constitutive republican community. Consequently, in the midst of this community, one finds an anomalous series of possessive relations involving unencumbered civic republican citizens. In this regard, it is very telling that when Sandel turns (very briefly, I note) to the task of explicating an alternative understanding of property and personality, he does so not by re-describing property along more contextual and relational lines, but simply by outlining and defending the community as a "wider" and more corporate "subject of possession" than the purportedly individualistic subject of possession in Rawls's theory. This "wider" subject of possession is the basis for Sandel's theory of "guardianship." Later in this chapter, when we focus on the problems with civic republican guardianship, I will suggest that a formative placeness of property lurks within Sandel's view of property. But in terms of the issues at hand now, what needs to be stressed is that, by itself, the movement to a "wider" subject of possession leaves both property and the analytic logic of the possessive relationship untouched by the hermeneutics of identity. Property remains an object without any deeply constitutive social character, and while the subject of possession is now a corporate one, its identity is still defined apart from, and prior to, both its holdings *and* its property-related ends and purposes. Presumably, these property-related ends would include moral and civic ends that contribute to the good of the republican community.

Sandel never considers the possibility of property having a deeply constitutive social character by virtue of its socially embedded moral and civic ends. Reminiscent of the post-socialist economy of mixed messages that we discussed in the previous chapter, property is evoked but not fully or adequately integrated into Sandel's theoretical perspective on the situated self. But again the question is what happens when it *is* fully integrated. This is the question that unsettles both the conceptual universe of modern thingness and the conceptual universe of the civic republican perspective on identity. But to see why, we need to consider how, in dialectical fashion, property and the situated self end up redefining each other. For this purpose, it may be helpful to shift to another metaphor I have used to describe my critique, that of seeing things through different lenses. While property provides a critical lens for re-viewing the situated self, the communal republican hermeneutics of identity provides a helpful lens for re-viewing property.

Re-Viewing the Situated Self and Property

Let us start with the lens of property. To look at the situated self through this lens gives rise to the possibility that, given the right conditions, property might be thought of as part of the ethical and civic situation of the self; to be sure, not in the sense that the mere acquisition of property is a moral or civic end in itself, but rather in the sense—the Aristotelian sense—that it is an instrument which, when used properly, can contribute to the cultivation and practice of moral and civic virtue.

Unless and until we recognize a locational dimension to property, we might not feel comfortable thinking in terms of being ethically or politically situated "within" property itself. But there does not seem to be any reason to think that property does not meet the kind of general ontological conditions of situated identity that we have discussed in this chapter. After all, it is possible to think of property as an institution which is established by communities, which has a history, and which is constituted through language, and for that matter, partly through communal conversations pertaining to morality and politics. Besides, even without a full-blown concept of placeness, we have no problem thinking in terms of being situated within certain kinds of property *arrangements*.

Now, if this way of looking at property-related contexts of identity is at all accurate, then there are some disconcerting implications for civic republicans. For one thing, as happened in our examination of Sandel's critique of Rawls, we are confronted with the prospect of a civic republican self who, in almost all of the formulations of contemporary civic republicanism, is radically unencumbered in the sphere of property. In other words, civic republicans have posited a self whose identity is defined in advance of, and apart from, the ends and purposes that are associated with the acquisition, ownership, and use of property. For another thing, if this is true of property, could it not also be true of other goods and practices that are associated with utilitarian, instrumental reason? If property (of all things!) can be part of our "moral ecology" of shared understandings, then so too perhaps can the whole discourse of rights and entitlements of which many civic republicans are so suspicious.[39]

By itself, this is not a completely damning critique. After all, civic republicans could respond that the goods and practices of instrumental reason should not be deeply constitutive of the self. But at the very least it can be said that the lens of property reveals a more complex relationship between the world of means or instruments and the world of moral and civic ends than what civic republicans usually present. Which is also to say that the lens of property shows us that the self is situated in communal contexts that relate means to ends, not just in a fellowship of shared ends and purposes.[40]

The admission, or rather, the intrusion of property into the horizon of the situated self also brings with it some messy implications with respect to distributive justice. Civic republicans would have us believe that their project of forming and cultivating the habits and dispositions of virtuous citizenship is at a conceptual and philosophical remove from the kind of justice that is preoccupied with fair rules and principles for distributing property and other rights, entitlements, benefits, and resources among the members of the community. For civic republicans, this is part of what is entailed by the philosophical priority of the good over the right. On this view, the formative project of developing virtuous citizens is about realizing the human good in the political sense of a common good, and as such, its logic is not one of distributing and dividing resources among separate individuals. With some civic republicans—most notably Sandel and Beiner—this view is associated with an openly and strongly critical stance on distributive justice. Others see a role for rights-based and entitlement-based distributive justice as a component of a more communal and more teleological vision of civic justice. But either way, civic republicans seem to want to keep their formative project untainted (if not untouched) by what they take to be the atomist and instrumentalist tendencies within the liberal discourse of distributive justice. It is precisely this splendid conceptual and philosophical isolation that is shattered by the intrusion of property into the ethical and civic situation of the self. Not only is there the unsettling possibility of a formative role for property. There is also the unsettling possibility that the formative project is directly and inherently associated with distributive conditions and consequences. And this becomes even more apparent when we consider that in talking about property as a context of identity we are very likely talking about property-related contexts pertaining to a division of labor and a structure of power and authority as well.

But notice what has happened to property in the meantime. In looking at the situated self through the lens of property, both have taken on new appearances. For once we took the step of looking at property as potentially being part of the ethical and civic situation of the self, we also began to look at property through the lens of civic republicanism. We began to consider the possibility of property being defined in part by *its* ethical and civic situation, and therefore in part by *its* moral and civic ends and purposes. In effect, we began to look at property in the same relational and contextual way that civic republicans approach identity.

From here, it is but a short step to my argument concerning the conceptual displacement of property and the modern preoccupation with, and privileging of, a possessive and proprietary thingness. By the same token, thinking contextually and relationally about property prepares the way for the task of reconnecting it conceptually to its social locations—for instance, to households and homes, workplaces and places of business, the marketplace itself, and eventually to the commonwealth of the political community. Put briefly, we begin to see that property is about both thingness and placeness.

Daniel Kemmis's "politics of place" provides an interesting example of the dialectical interplay of property and the situated self that we have been exploring. In his environmentalist reworking of the communal republican hermeneutics of the situated self, emphasis is placed on the physical places we inhabit. According to Kemmis, "public life can only be reclaimed by understanding, then practicing, its real connection to real, identifiable places."[41] Kemmis discusses the physical placeness of market economics, but stops short of exploring the placeness of property as a social institution.[42] The fact that Kemmis does not even consider the relationship between property and "real, identifiable places" underscores both the normative and the conceptual displacement of property within civic republicanism and other forms of postsocialist thought.[43] Yet Kemmis's understanding of placeness as an important (and submerged) dimension of late modern political economy also helps to illuminate the placeness of property. In both cases, the point is to replace abstract understandings of economic activity with more concrete, particularistic understandings. Just as the impersonal market mechanism may be redescribed as a bounded and localized marketplace, so too can we replace the idea of property as an abstract objectification and internalization of economic value with the idea of property as a specific location that connects the means and ends of possession and ownership. And in both reconceptualizations, there is a new emphasis on how moral agents and citizens *inhabit* the institutions and practices of economic life. Hence, Kemmis describes his project of "reclaiming the marketplace" as "the economics of re-inhabitation." Hence, also, my theory of placeness seeks to add rights of inhabitation to the proprietary rights of possession and ownership within modern thingness.

Now, all of this might seem to suggest that the placeness of property is not only a solution to the problem of a commercial republic, but also a solution which can be fashioned out of the civic republicans' own terms of analysis. If only things were this simple! If they were, then the rest of this book could be devoted to extrapolating a theory of democratic placeness from the civic republican project of recovery and renewal. But things are not this simple, and rather than a simple agenda of extrapolating a theory of democratic placeness, the plan for much of the rest of this book revolves around showing the tensions and the complexity within the various relationships that exist between civic virtue, property, and democracy. The placeness of property is not a panacea for the corruptive power of commercialism, economic justice, or democracy any more than collectivism was, and the basic reason is the same: Whether public or private, and even when its thingness is emphasized, property is never just about the acquisition, ownership, or exchange of things. It is always also about institutional structures of power and authority which, on the one hand, establish and distribute conditions of labor and work, and, on the other hand, have an effect on the distribution of political access and influence and therefore also on the opportunity for an effective and efficacious exercise of political liberty.

So when we look more closely, and more critically, at property through the lens of civic republicanism, we see that social locations such as households, workplaces, and the marketplace are not just contexts of property but are also property-related contexts of labor and authority. If anything, a conceptual emphasis on placeness results in structures of authority and labor being drawn even more tightly into the orbit of property. What I mean is that within a regime of property that emphasizes placeness, such structures are partly constitutive of the meaning and "nature" of property; in other words, property is inherently about these and related structures. By contrast, in a regime of property that emphasizes thingness, the relationship between property and the distribution of labor and authority is constituted more along the lines of empirical correlation or causation between discrete variables.

By working through the possibilities and problems of the placeness of property from the standpoint of civic republicanism, we are led to another subtle shift in perspective. Specifically, we are led back to looking at civic republicanism from the standpoint of property. To explore the possibilities and problems of the placeness of property is, to a great extent, to explore the possibilities and problems of the civic republican project of recovery and renewal in relation to matters of property and political economy. The possibilities revolve around the development of formative contexts and practices in which external goods are not merely connected to internal goods, but are deeply conditioned by them. The problems have to do with the danger of republican paternalism that is created by these kinds of formative contexts and practices.

I will have more to say about the historical development of republican paternalism in relation to property and the problem of a commercial republic in the next chapter. But the problem of republican paternalism is fundamentally a theoretical one, and lest we think that we are dealing with matters only of historical interest, we need to explore the relationship between property and the problem of republican paternalism in relation to contemporary civic republicanism. We are going to do so by taking a closer look at Sandel's brief but very important discussion of guardianship in *Liberalism and the Limits of Justice*. But first I want to try to spell out the nature and theoretical parameters of the problem of republican paternalism with more precision.

Caregiving, Democracy, and Republican Paternalism

Clearly, there are cases when it is legitimate to deny full civic agency to members of a democratic polity on paternalistic grounds, the most obvious one being the denial of full political rights to children. Beyond this I would argue that there would be something seriously wrong with a democratic community in which citizens of all ages did not show any care or concern for one another as citizens, and did not acknowledge that the conditions of democratic citizenship include dependency and interdependency along with the capacity for independent civic agency. In the spirit of ethical materialism, we all need help from time to time, and at any given time, some of us need more help than others. Or as Martha Nussbaum puts it, "any real society is a caregiving society, and must therefore discover ways of coping with [the] facts of human neediness and dependency that are compatible with the self-respect of the recipients and do not exploit the caregivers."[44]

But set against this—or rather, uneasily juxtaposed to it—is the strong democratic presumption that all or nearly all adult members of a polity can participate in and contribute to the polity's practices of self-government. Recognition and provision of the needs of citizens are one thing; efforts to exclude adult citizens from civic life on paternalistic grounds are quite another.[45] So strong is the democratic concern about paternalistic exclusion that democratic nations almost always err on the side of conferring full political rights on adults who suffer from severe cognitive or emotional disabilities.

As was discussed in chapter 2, the problem of republican paternalism is rooted in the distributive conditions and consequences of the formative project of cultivating a capacity for civic virtue. It may be helpful to formalize this in terms of the problematic interaction between the formative and distributive dimensions of such a republican capacity. The formative dimension revolves around the question of which communal or political understandings, practices, and institutional arrangements are best suited to the task of cultivating a republican capacity for virtuous citizenship. By contrast, the distributive dimension has to do with the contexts of power, authority, discipline, labor, socioeconomic status, and property through which this republican capacity is distributed among different groups and classes. Here, the question is not *how* to cultivate a capacity for civic virtue, but *who* is seen as possessing, or having the potential for, such a capacity. Accordingly, the question of distribution is simultaneously and necessarily a question of attribution.

The problem of republican paternalism is a problem of mixing these two dimensions of republican capacity in such a way as to claim that the capacity for virtuous public liberty and self-rule is cultivated through the rule, control, or protection of adult members of the polity who are deemed incapable of independent civic engagements. Hence, from the point of view of modern democratic norms of equality, the problem of republican paternalism is a problem of second-class citizenship. Hence, also, it is a problem of democratic injustice in which the social question becomes a political question pertaining to the denial of democratic equality.

Neoclassical republicans might counter that the problem of republican paternalism is more of a problem with positive liberty than with the civic independence of non-domination. However, the problem of republican paternalism is rooted in a conceptual structure that defines the capacity for civic independence in terms of a relationship of power or control over dependent adults, and this structure is fundamentally the same regardless of whether the capacity for civic independence is conceptualized as a positive liberty of self-rule or as non-domination. Phillip Pettit's analysis of non-domination is a case in point. Pettit seems to think that non-domination is qualitatively different than both negative liberty and positive liberty, and that it therefore avoids the problems of both alternatives. I am not convinced that non-domination represents such a distinct conceptual alternative. To the contrary, I believe it makes far more sense to think of non-domination as a distinctively republican way of defining negative liberty such that the absence of domination becomes a necessary condition for the attainment of a positive liberty of civic independence and self-government.[46] But in terms of the problem of republican paternalism, the main reason for questioning the idea that non-domination is conceptually distinct has to do with the fact that it moves so easily in the direction of tying the capacity for non-domination to the domination of others.[47]

Thus, the problem of republican paternalism is fundamentally about a conceptual structure of relational hierarchy in which the capacity for virtuous republican liberty (whether as positive liberty or as non-domination) is defined relationally in terms of the civic dependency of other groups of adults (whether in the form of overt servitude or some other form).[48]

We need to be careful not to confuse this conceptual structure with the unavoidable tension between democratic equality and the different levels of civic capacity among democratic citizens and leaders. Even under ideal conditions for upholding democratic norms of equal and inclusive civic agency, there will be cases where some citizens set themselves above others in terms of civic skills and civic awareness. Whether because of inclination, ability, or experience, there will always be some citizens who are more gifted than others in practicing the democratic arts of communication, deliberation, persuasion, and leadership. By the same token, there will always be citizens who will be sought out because of the expertise or wisdom that they bring to matters of public policy and collective deliberation.

Such forms of civic excellence engender inequality, but only in a contingent way, not in a structural way. What I mean by this is that these forms of civic excellence are not defined and conceptualized in ways that directly and necessarily threaten the basic democratic structure of equal and inclusive civic agency. By contrast, the problem of republican paternalism arises precisely when civic excellence is defined and conceptualized primarily in terms of a capacity to rule over those adults deemed to be fundamentally dependent and therefore without civic agency.

Rethinking the Concept of Guardianship

Clearly, the problem of republican paternalism is not just about property. It has broader roots in the distinctly republican ideal of self-governing civic agency in which civic mindedness and public spirit are combined with an independence of civic judgment and action. The question of the relationship between property and civic virtue is part of a larger series of questions concerning the distributive conditions and consequences of the formative project of cultivating the capacity for such virtuous independence. Yet I believe that exploring the relationship between property and civic virtue illuminates the problem of republican paternalism in an especially clear and powerful way, in a way, moreover, that calls attention to issues that have received scant attention from either civic republicans or their critics.

Sandel's discussion of guardianship is a partial exception to the rule of civic republican neglect of the formative possibilities of property. To my knowledge, it represents the only effort in contemporary civic republicanism to theorize the relationship between property and personality in the framework of the situated self. There are even hints of the placeness of property in Sandel's concept of guardianship. Yet it is only a partial exception.' The issues associated with guardianship were a low priority in *Liberalism and the Limits of Justice*—they were covered in a space of about eight pages—and Sandel has not returned to the subject of guardianship in any subsequent writings. Nevertheless, his brief discussion of guardianship is instructive because it reveals the difficulties that civic republicans face in moving from being critics of liberal capitalism to constructive theorists of property and political economy.

As I suggested in the earlier discussion of Sandel, he puts forward the principle of guardianship as an alternative to what he sees as Rawls's flawed account of the relationship of the self to its assets and endowments. Sandel is well aware of the dangers of applying the critique of a pure possessive individualism of self-ownership to a Rawlsian form of modern welfare liberalism. Rawls was a critic of such a first-order possessive individualism (as it may be called). Otherwise, he could not have defended his theory of the social contract as "an agreement to regard the distribution of natural talents as a common asset and to share in the benefits of this distribution whatever it turns out to be."[49] Consequently, rather than lumping Rawls together with either classical liberal or contemporary libertarian conservative defenders of possessive individualism (as some critics of liberal individualism are wont to do) Sandel distinguishes between three different conceptions of the relationship between a subject of possession and the assets or endowments that are possessed.

First, there is a conception of possession in which the subject is the owner of his or her endowments, including, for example, special talents and a capacity to labor. This of course is precisely the type of self-ownership that is at the heart of a first-order possessive individualism. Second, there is the possibility that the self is neither the owner nor the guardian of natural or acquired assets but merely "the repository of the assets and attributes accidentally located in my person."[50] This is the flawed conception that Rawls is said to have. It represents a kind of second-order possessive individualism in that it is based not on self-ownership, but on property-like fences of right. Finally, there is Sandel's preferred alternative of guardianship. As defined by Sandel, the principle of guardianship "denies individual ownership in favor of a more ultimate [or wider] owner or subject of possession of which the individual person is the agent."[51]

Partly on the basis of this typology, Sandel goes on to argue that Rawls does not have a conception of the self that can support his implicit notion of the community as a guardian of common assets. More precisely, he argues that Rawls's commitment to a second-order possessive individualism precludes the "wider subject of possession" that his commitment to social welfare and redistribution would seem to require.

Something like Sandel's concept of guardianship would seem to be essential if civic republicans are to develop a cohesive and practical response to the problem of a commercial republic. Without such a concept, they have a "moral ecology" of shared anxieties about the corruptive power of property and commerce, but little in the way of shared understandings regarding how the instrumental goods of property and commerce are to be harmonized with the intrinsic goods and virtues of republican citizenship. And in the participatory spirit of civic humanism, Sandel's principle of guardianship has the potential of reintroducing civic agency into economic life, thereby countering the disempowerment associated with both the "invisible hand" of the market and heavy-handed collectivism. Thus, Sandel's principle of virtuous guardianship opens up the possibility of "a public discourse that can reunite economics, power, and morality."[52] But in opening up this possibility, Sandel's discussion of guardianship also discloses the structural sources of the relationship between property and the problem of republican paternalism.

The Problematic Relationship between Guardianship and Authority

The central problem with Sandel's discussion of guardianship is that it obfuscates relations of authority. Not surprisingly, I see this problem as being closely connected to the suppression of the placeness of property within Sandel's understanding of the relation of the self to its assets. Yet this is by no means a simple matter of neglect. For one thing, as I will explain shortly, there is a sense in which the problematic connection to authority is rooted in both the thingness and the placeness of guardianship. For another thing, there is a counter-tendency in the direction of placeness in Sandel's discussion of guardianship alongside the analytic logic of modern thingness. His wider subject of possession is about as close as one gets in contemporary civic republicanism to a theory of the civic placeness of property. Almost despite himself, Sandel evokes the placeness of guardianship by linking the possession of things—assets and resources—to a form of moral and civic agency that is situated *within* communal property arrangements. It is as if his civic guardians are chafing under the conceptual constraints imposed by the analytic logic of modern thingness. Certainly, Sandel's civic guardians are not radically unencumbered subjects of possession. They are *wider* subjects of possession whose identities as guardians and as citizens are bound up with the community on whose behalf they act as agents. In the end, though, it is only an evocation of placeness, only a submerged counter-tendency. The upshot, I wish to argue, is that Sandel's concept of guardianship partakes of the worst of both thingness and placeness. However, I want to set this point aside for now and discuss the relationship between guardianship and authority in more general terms.

With or without explicit recognition of its connection to placeness, guardianship always involves someone or some group who acts authoritatively, or claims to act authoritatively, on behalf of either other members of the community or the community itself. The grammar of "guardianship" is as much about representing or acting on behalf of others as it is about "expansive self-understandings that . . . shape a common life."[53] Consequently, guardianship of communal assets and resources is not only about claims or norms of virtuous regard for the shared goods of the community; it is also about claims and norms of at least a *de facto* jurisdiction over those assets and resources, or some aspect of the management, use, and disposition of them. To be sure, both dimensions of guardianship imply a wider and more corporate "subject of possession" than is found in the two orders of possessive individualism. Moreover, like Sandel, I believe that some kind of principle of guardianship or trusteeship is both necessary to, and insufficiently developed within, rights-based theories of welfare liberalism. Yet proclaiming the superiority of such a principle in the abstract is relatively easy compared to the task of showing how one avoids forms of guardianship that are undemocratically and unjustly paternalistic and hierarchical. While guardianship is constituted through expansive self-understandings, it is an open question as to the conditions under which expansive self-understandings become inclusive ones.[54]

In typical communal republican fashion, Sandel seeks to convert troublesome issues concerning property-related contexts of authority into a debate between unencumbered and situated selves, between a narrow atomistic individualism and expansive communal self-understandings. Within this theoretical framework, the principle of guardianship assumes an almost self-evident validity as a principle that simultaneously breaks down the fences of possessive individualism and transforms property into a means to higher communal ends. This seems innocuous enough when the theoretical task is limited to establishing the moral authority of communal ends in some abstract way against the atomist distortions of liberal individualism. However, when the task involves specific socioeconomic contexts of property and authority, this will not do. For at this point one must consider not only how guardianship transforms property into a means to higher communal ends, but also the means through which virtuous guardianship becomes *authoritative*. And at this point also we are left wondering how the capacity for guardianship of the common good is to be developed without tying this capacity to the paternalistic rule and guardianship of second-class citizens.

Thus, far from being a simple solution to the two orders of possessive individualism, the principle of civic guardianship is itself a potential source of the problem of republican paternalism. One need only bring the example of the Aristotelian household to mind to see how the issues associated with property-related forms of paternalism are at stake with the formative project of cultivating a capacity for virtuous guardianship. The Aristotelian household was a "wider subject of possession" for which the male master acted as an agent. The master was a guardian of the assets and resources of the household. But he was also the guardian of the other members of his household, including his wife and adult slaves. Of course, it was also largely on the basis of his capacity for virtuous guardianship of the household that the master was said to develop his capacity for virtuous self-government.[55]

Sandel's failure to consider the relationship between property and personality in terms of authority is somewhat surprising in light of the fact that he chose to identify his principle with guardianship rather than the less threatening idea of stewardship. A notion of stewardship is undoubtedly embedded in his concept of guardianship. I cannot imagine Sandel objecting to a subject of possession who has expansive enough self-understandings to act as a responsible steward of the natural environment and to make decisions about resources with an eye to the effect on future generations. And this is all to the good. But the point I wish to press now is that a civic republican theory of stewardship would not solve the problem of paternalism. To be sure, stewardship does not have the strong juridical overtones that guardianship has, and because of this, stewardship would seem to provide the kind of benign form of communal property that Sandel wants. However, stewardship is not necessarily benign. In fact, Sandel's choice of guardianship rather than stewardship is fortuitous precisely because we are more apt to be lulled into complacency about issues of authority when we think in terms of stewardship. Especially in an era of heightened concern about the natural environment, there is an understandable eagerness to interpret stewardship simply in terms of a willingness to take seriously the moral and religious responsibilities to care for and preserve land and other natural resources. But this way of thinking can also obfuscate the fact that issues of authority are as deeply implicated in the idea of stewardship as they are in guardianship. Stewardship of land and natural resources is also about stewardship of communal resources, and because of this stewardship is inevitably inscribed in property-related contexts of control and authority over the actions of other members of the community. Hence, in the context of a system of property, to be a steward of communal resources and assets necessarily overlaps with the idea of being a guardian of those resources and assets. The problem, of course, is that the grammar of both "stewardship" and "guardianship" is often associated with the paternalistic idea of protecting those who are, or are thought to be, unable to take care of themselves.[56]

The larger theoretical point here is that paternalistic guardianship (or stewardship, or trusteeship) will always be potentially problematic in a democracy. There are two reasons for this. The first has to do with the fact that even as a civic principle for adult members of the polity the grammar of "guardianship" evokes the notion of agency on behalf of the good of others. Sandel and like-minded civic republicans want us to believe that a truly civic guardianship would preserve and further equal citizenship by constituting agency on behalf of a common good, with citizens showing mutual care and concern for one another's assets and resources. The problem with this is that it overlooks the second reason, which has to do with the manner in which virtue-centered civic guardianship combines two different kinds of authority. I have in mind the standard theoretical distinction between being "in authority" and being "an authority."[57] To be "in authority" is to be authorized to make, or to participate in the making of, rules or decisions for a community. This aspect of authority is broadly concerned with the question of jurisdiction over certain classes and contexts of decision-making. As such, it is often concerned with the types of juridical and procedural issues of right that many civic republicans disdain. By contrast, to be "an authority" is to possess a special competence, ability, or capacity in a particular field of skill or training.

Within a virtue-centered form of civic guardianship, being "an authority" is closely and, arguably, unavoidably connected to being "in authority." Virtue-centered civic guardianship at the level of "an authority" has to do with claims and norms of an authoritative capacity to be virtuously and responsibly concerned with, and for, the assets and resources of the particular institution or community on whose behalf one acts as an agent. By itself, this might seem like a fairly innocuous, and even desirable, form of responsible civic stewardship. But claims and norms of an authoritative capacity for virtuous guardianship are bound up with claims and norms of decision-making jurisdiction within particular contexts and locations of guardianship. The virtuous civic guardian is *in* authority as well as being *an* authority.

And here we see the deeper structural sources of the problem of republican paternalism. The very same formative project that makes the republican tradition so appealing to contemporary civic republicans often has been a project of trying to translate the purported excellence of being "an authority" in matters of civic virtue into a special capacity and right to be "in authority" as a self-governing citizen. The ease with which this makes it possible to justify exclusionary and hierarchical attributions and distributions of the capacity for authoritative self-government is troubling enough. But when we consider how such a translation of "an authority" into "in authority" is identified with virtue in opposition to corruption, we begin to see how deeply rooted the problem of republican paternalism is in the conceptual structure of the Western tradition of republican virtue. At least since the Renaissance, republicans have used the charge of corruption to challenge and check abuses of power. True, this often was a way of defending the virtue of the people against monarchical and aristocratic corruption. But we also know that the concept of "the people" almost always has been plagued by a false inclusiveness. It seems that one reason for this is precisely the problematic connection between civic virtue and popular government, for it is in this context that the problem of determining who has authority to speak for and represent the people has appeared as the problem of determining who has the excellence of civic character to be the guardian of both the common good and the good of those (for instance, the dependents of the master of the household) thought to lack the capacity for authoritative self-rule.

Thus, there are good reasons to think that authoritative civic guardianship represents something of a paradigm case of the problem of republican paternalism. The kind of interaction between the formative and distributive dimensions of republican capacity that gives rise to the problem of republican paternalism is at the heart of the grammatical structure of authoritative civic guardianship. By way of summary, this grammar entails the distinct possibility of a republican agency on behalf of the common good being cultivated and prepared through the experience of being the authoritative agent of the good of those deemed incapable of full and equal citizenship.

Like many other communal republicans, Sandel maintains that the expansive self-understandings that promote an engagement with the common good emerge through the particularity of our ethical situations. For example, he argues that a deontological ethic of rights leaves us disempowered as citizens because it does not cultivate those constitutive understandings and attachments we have "as the particular persons we are—as members of this family or community or people, as bearers of that history, as citizens of this republic."[58] Presumably, therefore, some of the formative contexts which exist below the level of the civic republican polity itself (for instance, the family) would be formative contexts of civic guardianship as well.[59] Consequently, to link *these* formative contexts of guardianship to the moral particularity of potentially hierarchical and paternalistic relations of authority would throw a very large monkey wrench into Sandel's effort to link guardianship to a circle of formative attachments and civic-minded, democratic empowerment. In effect, Sandel is forced to leap over all the intermediate contexts and communities of authoritative guardianship into the more expansive sphere of an egalitarian, democratic form of guardianship.[60]

Guardianship and the Relationship between Thingness and Placeness

What then of the placeness of civic guardianship? At first glance, it might seem that it would be better to leave placeness lurking in the background of guardianship. After all, the more that placeness is incorporated into our understanding of property, the more property becomes identified with its structures and arrangements of authority. However, leaving placeness in the background is not a solution. For one thing, the close relationship between "an authority" and "in authority" would exist even if we could somehow limit guardianship to the thingness of communal assets and resources. Under these conditions, we would still have claims of jurisdiction over these assets and resources. But a guardianship of pure thingness is, in any event, a fantasy that does not account for the fact that placeness is built into the structure of guardianship. The aspect of the grammar of "guardianship" having to do with agency on behalf of the good of those being "guarded" necessarily entails a shift from the thingness to the placeness of property. And part of this shift is a change from a jurisdiction over things to a "situated" jurisdiction that is explicitly concerned with decision-making authority over both the things and the people within the guardianship community.

Of course, one could acknowledge that placeness inheres in guardianship without making it central to a theory of guardianship. Yet it is not at all clear that this would be the best way to proceed. Unless such a theory builds on the placeness of a guardianship community, it will be difficult to develop a strong connection between the assets of such a community and the civic purposes to be served by their guardianship. The analytic logic of modern thingness works against such a connection by severing the connection between property objects or values and the purposes of their various institutional locations. Property becomes fungible, not just because it is subsumed under economic value, but also because it is abstracted from any particular moral or civic context. To be sure, we are still left with the dangers that stem from the fact that guardians exercise agency that is often not just on behalf of other inhabitants of the location, but also over them. Yet even in this respect it may be better to move placeness to the forefront. At least then the dangers of authority will be in the open rather than being suppressed and obfuscated. In fact, some of the most disturbing examples of guardianship in the modern era involve the collectivist suppression of placeness. The collectivist state stands above the community as a kind of master manager of the community's collective assets, ignoring and eventually effacing the differences between the institutional purposes that property serves in civil society. Under such an arrangement, it is all but inevitable that the state will cease being an agent of the wider communal subject of possession and will become instead the de facto subject of possession that rules over those without any meaningful or effective authority over the resources of the community.

One of the dangers of Sandel's wider subject of possession is precisely that it can be become a new kind of collectivism—a post-socialist collectivism, as it were. Preoccupied with the challenge of discovering a communal republican alternative to the two orders of possessive individualism, Sandel makes the collectivist mistake of neglecting the relationship between property and its particular formative contexts. Nor does he evince any interest in explicating the different ways in which external and internal goods are related to each other and to relations of authority within these multiply situated forms of guardianship.

All of this suggests that Sandel's form of guardianship promotes the worst of modern thingness. Arguably, however, Sandel also promotes the worst of placeness by failing to confront the relationship between authority and the placeness of property that lurks within the theoretical framework of the situated self. We are left with a formative guardianship that mystifies and masks its own problematic connection to authority by virtue of focusing on the presumptively shared and common goods of the unequally situated inhabitants who constitute the wider subject of possession.

Whether as a post-socialist collectivism or as an authority-masking form of placeness, Sandel's concept of guardianship threatens his own commitment to democratic equality. Of course, my concerns in this area are not limited to Sandel and his concept of guardianship. Rather, we are dealing with an instance of the larger problem of the failure of contemporary civic republicans to address the ongoing danger of republican paternalism.

The Critique of Rights Revisited

The failure of communal republicans to account for the distributive conditions and consequences of their formative project casts serious doubt on their critique of rights. Without a much stronger commitment to individual rights, communal republicans leave their situated citizens vulnerable to illegitimate exercises of paternalistic guardianship. Whatever is gained in the effort to combat the corruptive intertextuality of rights and property is lost in terms of citizens being dominated by their would-be guardians. As we saw earlier, neoclassical republicans recognize this danger and emphasize the importance of rights as a resource that helps to preserve and protect the independence of citizens. Yet the neoclassical approach to rights is far from a quick fix for the problem of republican paternalism; more precisely, the neoclassical approach reveals the same kind of mixture of hopeful and worrisome theoretical possibilities that we have seen with property. On the one hand, neoclassical republicans point us in the direction of a placeness of rights that goes well beyond the space of negative liberty that is created by proprietary barriers and fences. What I have in mind is a placeness in which the capacity for independent citizenship is formatively located within a rightful jurisdiction of democratic liberty. Or to use a more familiar expression, independent citizenship is prepared by letting democratic citizens be *within* their rights. On the other hand, there is still the worrisome possibility that the virtuous independence that is gained by virtue of citizens being within their own rights may be at the expense of those adults who are excluded from republican citizenship or treated as second-class citizens. The virtuous, independent citizen envisioned by neoclassical republicans may not be alone within the jurisdiction of his rights, and as with the placeness of property, the relational dimension of the placeness of rightful jurisdiction can be bound up with exclusionary and hierarchical relations of ruling and being ruled.

Consider Quentin Skinner's analysis of the Roman provenance of early modern republican thinking about the contrast between freedom and slavery. Skinner points out that in the Roman law of persons, the "essence of servitude" was defined by "the distinction between those who are, and those who are not, *sui iuris*, within their own jurisdiction or right."[61] This distinction, Skinner goes on to argue, is the foundation for classical republican understandings of both personal and public liberty. Which is also to say that this distinction between servitude and being within one's rightful jurisdiction is partly constitutive of the civic ideal of non-domination that Skinner wishes to recover so that we might break free of the liberal idea of non-interference. Unfortunately, he does not pay enough attention to the fact that the contrast of virtuous freedom with servitude usually carried with it an acceptance of forms of servitude and "virtuous" dependency that are at odds with democratic norms of equal and inclusive citizenship. The independence of Roman and then later neo-roman masters was derived not simply from the *dominium* of their liberty as individual citizens, but also from the *dominium* they ruled. It was a paternalistic masters' vision of virtuous independence.

I turn now to an exploration of the history of the relationship between this masters' vision and the placeness of property within classical republican approaches to the problem of a commercial republic.

Notes

1. C. B. MacPherson, *The Political Theory of Possessive Individualism: Hobbes to Locke* (Oxford: Clarendon Press, 1962).

2. Michael J. Sandel, *Democracy's Discontent: America in Search of a Public Philosophy* (Cambridge, MA: The Belknap Press, 1996), 274.

3. Philip Pettit, "Reworking Sandel's Republicanism," in *Debating Democracy's Discontent: Essays on American Politics, Law, and Public Philosophy*, ed. Anita L. Allen and Milton C. Regan, Jr. (Oxford: Oxford University Press, 1998), 53.

4. Sandel, *Democracy's Discontent*, 274.

5. William M. Sullivan, *Reconstructing Public Philosophy* (Berkeley, CA: University of California Press, 1986), 182.

6. Benjamin R. Barber, "Liberal Democracy and the Costs of Consent," in *Liberalism and the Moral Life*, ed. Nancy L. Rosenblum (Cambridge, MA: Harvard University Press, 1989), 59.

7. Wilson Carey McWilliams, "On Equality as the Moral Foundation of Community," in *The Moral Foundations of the American Republic*, ed. Robert H. Horwitz (Charlottesville, VA: University Press of Virginia, 1986), 310 and *passim*.

8. Sullivan, *Reconstructing Public Philosophy*, 214.

9. Philip Pettit, *Republicanism: A Theory of Freedom and Government* (Oxford: Clarendon Press, 1997), 140–43.

10. This involves what Pettit calls "structural egalitarianism," by which he means a form of equality that maximizes social and political protection for non-domination among all groups and classes. Although such a "structural egalitarianism" sometimes requires a redistribution of economic resources, Pettit distinguishes it from the kind

of "material egalitarianism" that seeks to expand freedom for the lower classes by giving them more economic resources. See *Republicanism,* 110–19.

11. Probably the most purely Aristotelian form of post-socialist thinking about virtue and instrumental goods is found in Alasdair MacIntyre, *After Virtue: A Study in Moral Theory,* 2nd ed. (Notre Dame, IN: University of Notre Dame Press, 1984), chapter 14, and especially 189–203.

12. Charles Taylor, *Sources of the Self: The Making of Modern Identity* (Cambridge, MA: Harvard University Press, 1989), 66.

13. Benjamin R. Barber, *Strong Democracy: Participatory Politics for a New Age* (Berkeley, CA: University of California Press, 1984), 75 and 34–35.

14. Sullivan, *Reconstructing Public Philosophy,* 182.

15. Sullivan, 167 and 182. The other intrinsic goods that Sullivan mentions in this connection are friendship, the civic community, justice, and life itself.

16. Pettit, *Republicanism,* 257–60. Also see Maurizio Viroli's discussion of a neo-classical virtue ethic in *Republicanism* (New York: Hill and Wang, 2002), especially 77.

17. Barber, "Liberal Democracy and the Costs of Consent," 59.

18. Ronald Beiner, *What's the Matter with Liberalism?* (Berkeley, CA: University of California Press, 1992), 42 and 25.

19. Charles Taylor, "Introduction," in *Philosophical Papers* (Cambridge: Cambridge University Press, 1985), 8. Also see Sandel, *Democracy's Discontent,* 25–28 and 290; and Sandel, *Liberalism and the Limits of Justice,* 2nd ed. (Cambridge: Cambridge University Press, 1998), 185–86.

20. Charles Taylor, *Philosophy and the Human Sciences,* vol. 2 of *Philosophical Papers* (Cambridge: Cambridge University Press, 1985), 218.

21. Charles Taylor, "Cross Purposes: The Liberal Communitarian Debate," in *Liberalism and the Moral Life,* ed. Nancy L. Rosenblum, 175–82; and Taylor, *The Ethics of Authenticity* (Cambridge, MA: Harvard University Press, 1991), 113–14.

22. Taylor, *Philosophy and the Human Sciences,* 188.

23. Taylor, *Philosophy and the Human Sciences,* chapters 7 and 8.

24. Taylor, *The Ethics of Authenticity,* 115–21. Also see the criticisms of a judicial politics of rights retrieval in Robert N. Bellah et al., *The Good Society* (New York: Alfred A. Knopf, 1991), 126–30.

25. As Locke writes in chapter III of the *Second Treatise* in connection to the "state of war" that is created when one man forcibly enslaves another, "To be free from such force is the only security of my Preservation: and reason bids me look on him, as an Enemy to my Preservation, who take away that *Freedom,* which is the fence to it." John Locke, *Two Treatises of Government,* ed. Peter Laslett, 2nd ed. (Cambridge: Cambridge University Press, 1967), book II, 279.

26. Quentin Skinner, "On Justice, the Common Good, and the Priority of Liberty," in *Dimensions of Radical Democracy: Pluralism, Citizenship, Community,* ed. Chantal Mouffe (London: Verso, 1992), 215.

27. Skinner, 221–22. Also see Quentin Skinner, "The Idea of Negative Liberty: Philosophical and Historical Perspectives," in *Philosophy in History,* ed. Richard Rorty, J. B. Schneewind, and Quentin Skinner (Cambridge: Cambridge University Press, 1984).

28. Pettit, *Republicanism*, 24.

29. See Quentin Skinner, *Liberty before Liberalism* (Cambridge: Cambridge University Press, 1997), 38–47.

30. See, for example, Sullivan, 64–72 and 90–98. I note that I am not of that school that believes there is nothing whatsoever to be gained from the methods of analytic philosophy. My point is simply that such methods fail to capture important aspects of the various relationships and contexts associated with property.

31. The texts that sparked the debate are Sandel, *Liberalism and the Limits of Justice*, especially chapter 1; and MacIntyre, *After Virtue*, especially chapters 3 and 4. To get a sense of how the debate played itself out in the 1980s and early 1990s, see Barber, *Strong Democracy*, chapters 4, 6, 7, and 9; Robert N. Bellah et al., *Habit in the Heart: Individualism and Commitment in American Life*, 2nd ed. (Berkeley, CA: University of California Press, 1996), 75–81 and chapter 6; Seyla Benhabib, *Situating the Self: Gender, Community and Postmodernism in Contemporary Ethics* (New York: Routledge, 1992), chapter 2; Jean Bethke Elshtain, "The Communitarian Individual," in *New Communitarian Thinking: Persons, Virtues, Institutions, and Families*, ed. Amitai Etzioni (Charlottesville, VA: University Press of Virginia, 1995); William A. Galston, *Liberal Purposes: Goods, Virtues, and Diversity in the Liberal State* (Cambridge: Cambridge University Press, 1991), 154–55; Emily R. Gill, "Goods, Virtues, and the Constitution of the Self," in *Liberals on Liberalism*, ed. Alfonso J. Damico (Totowa, NJ: Rowman and Littlefield, 1986); Amy Gutmann, "Communitarian Critics of Liberalism," *Philosophy and Public Affairs* 14 (1985): 308–22; H. N. Hirsch, "The Threnody of Liberalism: Constitutional Liberty and the Renewal of Community," *Political Theory* 14 (1986): 423–49; Bonnie Honig, *Political Theory and the Displacement of Politics* (Ithaca, NY: Cornell University Press, 1993), especially chapter 6; Will Kymlicka, "Liberal Individualism and Liberal Neutrality," *Ethics* 99 (1989): 883–905; Susan Moller Okin, *Justice, Gender, and the Family* (New York: Basic Books, 1989), chapters 2 and 4; Thomas A. Spragens, Jr., "Communitarian Liberalism," in *New Communitarian Thinking*, ed. Etzioni; Taylor, *Philosophy and the Human Sciences*, chapter 7; Iris Marion Young, *Justice and the Politics of Difference* (Princeton, NJ: Princeton University Press, 1990), 228–236; Michael Walzer, "The Communitarian Critique of Liberalism," in *New Communitarian Thinking*, ed. Etzioni; and Mark Warren, "Democratic Theory and Self-Transformation," *American Political Science Review* 86 (1992): 8–23.

32. On the point about community as context of self-direction, choice, and rational revisability, see Will Kymlicka, *Liberalism, Community, and Culture* (Oxford: Oxford University Press, 1989); Stephen Macedo, *Liberal Virtues: Citizenship, Virtue, and Community in Liberal Constitutionalism*, (Oxford: Clarendon Press, 1990); Richard Dagger, *Civic Virtues: Rights, Citizenship, and Republican Liberalism* (New York: Oxford University Press, 1997), especially chapters 3 and 4; Spragens, "Communitarian Liberalism"; and Thomas A. Spragens, Jr., *Civic Liberalism: Reflections on our Democratic Ideals* (Lanham, MD: Rowman and Littlefield Publishers, Inc., 1999), chapter 5 and 260–64.

33. Taylor has always emphasized critical reflection. See the discussion of his views of "strong evaluation" in chapter 2. Also see William M. Sullivan, "Bringing the Good Back In," in *Liberalism and the Good*, ed. R. Bruce Douglass, Gerald M. Mara, and Henry S. Richardson (New York: Routledge, 1990); and Alasdair MacIntyre, *Dependent Rational Animals: Why Human Beings Need the Virtues* (La Salle, IL: Open Court

Publishing, 1999), chapter 8. Although he underestimates the degree to which thinkers like Sandel and MacIntyre have allowed for the rational revisability of communal ends, Kymlicka provides a helpful summary of the different phases of the debate over the situated self in *Contemporary Political Philosophy: An Introduction*, 2nd ed. (Oxford: Oxford University Press, 2002), chapter 6.

34. Michael J. Sandel, "Introduction," in *Liberalism and its Critics*, ed. Michael J. Sandel (New York: New York University Press, 1984), 6.

35. See Sandel, *Democracy's Discontent*, especially 11–13 and 349–51 for his most recent formulation of the "situated self." For responses, see the essays by Clifford Orwin, Richard Rorty, Bruce Frohnen, and Mary Lyndon Shanley in Anita L. Allen and Milton C. Regan, eds., *Debating Democracy's Discontent*, chapters 5 (especially 89–91), 8 (especially 118–19), 12, and 18.

36. Sandel, *Liberalism and the Limits of Justice*, 54–59.

37. Almost needless to say, John Rawls did not accept such a characterization of his conception of the self. See his discussion of the person in *Political Liberalism* (New York: Columbia University Press, 1993), 18–20 and 26–27.

38. Sandel, *Liberalism and the Limits of Justice*, 172.

39. The phrase "moral ecology" was coined by the Bellah group in *Habits of the Heart*, 40–41 and 335.

40. Ronald Terchek makes a parallel type of internal criticism when he comments that "one of the puzzling features in the communitarian debate is that for all the talk about situating, incumbering, and embedding citizens (primarily with duties and obligations), little attention is given to whether citizens have overcome necessity, are secure, and attend to the multiple needs that are important." Ronald J. Tercheck, *Republican Paradoxes and Liberal Anxieties: Retrieving Neglected Fragments of Political Theory* (Lanham, MD: Rowman and Littlefield, 1997), 48. However, Terchek does not go on to explore how all this talk about situating citizens might lead to a rethinking of property and other material needs.

41. Daniel Kemmis, *Community and the Politics of Place* (Norman, OK: University of Oklahoma Press, 1990), 6.

42. Kemmis, especially chapter 7.

43. Kemmis's neglect of property is also ironic in light of the Arendtian provenance of much of his thinking about placeness. As is discussed in detail in chapter 7, placeness is at the center of Arendt's analysis of property and its decline in the modern era. See Kemmis's adaptation of Arendt's political theory in *Community and the Politics of Place*, 5–7 and 76–82.

44. Martha C. Nussbaum, "The Future of Feminist Liberalism," in *Social and Political Philosophy: Classical Western Texts in Feminist and Multicultural Perspectives*, ed. James P. Sterba, 3rd ed. (Belmont, KY: Wadsworth, 2003), 551.

45. See Carol Gould's insightful discussion of the tensions between democracy and a care ethic in "Feminism and Democratic Community Revisited," in *Democratic Community*, vol. XXXV of *Nomos* (New York: New York University Press, 1993).

46. My view of this is similar to that of Iseult Honohan, who argues that nondomination should be seen as but one of the conditions of positive-libertarian self-direction. Honohan maintains that neoclassical republicans do not place enough emphasis on interdependence as an important condition of political freedom. She also

makes the interesting observation that autonomy is limited not only by domination, but also by "dependence on the effects, often unintended, of the actions of others." See Iseult Honohan, *Civic Republicanism* (London: Routledge, 2002), 186–87.

47. See Pettit, *Republicanism*, especially 4–7, 11–12, and chapter 1.

48. I take this to be one of the lessons of Rogers Smith's analysis of the exclusionary aspects of civic idealism in American history in *Civic Ideals: Conflicting Visions of Citizenship in U.S. History* (New Haven, CT: Yale University Press, 1997).

49. John Rawls, *A Theory of Justice* (Cambridge, MA: The Belknap Press, 1971), 179. Also see Rawls, *Justice as Fairness: A Restatement*, ed. Erin Kelly (Cambridge, MA: The Belknap Press, 2001), 74–77.

50. Sandel, *Liberalism and the Limits of Justice*, 97.

51. Sandel, 96–97; also see 103 and 141.

52. Sullivan, *Reconstructing Public Philosophy*, 14.

53. Michael J. Sandel, "The Procedural Republic and the Unencumbered Self," *Political Theory*, 12 (1984): 91.

54. Coming from a different perspective (deconstructionism), Bonnie Honig reaches a similar conclusion in *Political Theory and the Displacement of Politics*, chapter 6.

55. The Aristotelian household is analyzed more systematically in chapter 5.

56. The overlapping grammar of these two concepts is indicated by the similarities in their dictionary definitions. For example, the 1989 edition of *Webster's Encyclopedic Unabridged Dictionary of the English Language* contains the following two entries under "guardianship": "1. the position and responsibilities of a guardian, esp. toward a ward. 2. care; responsibility; charge." Compare these with the first entry under "steward": "1. one who manages another's property or financial affairs; one who administers anything as the agent of another or other." Note also the following two entries under "guardian": "1. a person who guards, protects, or preserves. 2. *Law*. one who is entrusted by law with the care of the person or property, or both."

57. See Richard B. Friedman, "On the Concept of Authority in Political Philosophy," in *Concepts in Social and Political Philosophy*, ed. Richard E. Flathman (New York: Macmillan, 1973); Richard E. Flathman, *The Practice of Political Authority: Authority and the Authoritative* (Chicago: University of Chicago Press, 1980); and Richard E. Flathman, *Towards a Liberalism . . .* (Ithaca, NY: Cornell University Press, 1989), chapters 2 and 3.

58. Sandel, "The Procedural Republic and the Unencumbered Self," 90.

59. It seems to me that this provides some confirmation of Susan Okin's argument in *Justice, Gender, and the Family* on behalf of treating the family as a "school of justice."

60. I note that this problem is not solved by talking (as Sandel does in *Democracy's Discontent*, 350–51) of "multiply situated selves." Such intersectionality certainly points to the need for a more pluralistic understanding of the sources of citizenship. But it doesn't necessarily solve the problem of republican paternalism. It all depends on the distributive conditions and consequences of the different formative situations of the self. Moreover, it is also possible that the pluralism Sandel now lauds will defeat his formative aspirations by making it difficult to develop consistent norms and practices of civic character formation!

61. Skinner, *Liberty before Liberalism*, 40–41.

5

The Problem of a Commercial
Republic in Historical Perspective

O NE SIGN THAT SOMETHING IS AMISS with the civic republicans' analysis of
the problem of a commercial republic is their sporadic and generally superficial treatment of classical republican ideas of property. Insofar as classical republican views of property were based on what are now clearly outmoded, preindustrial ideas of landed property, civic republicans certainly can
be forgiven for being reluctant to reappropriate them. Yet the failure of today's
republican theorists to confront classical republican views of property is indicative of a larger and deeper problem of failing to encounter the complex
ways in which property has been or might be implicated in the formative project of cultivating a spirit of responsible civic engagement.

I do not offer a definitive and comprehensive interpretation of the republican tradition. I am not interested in tracing all the twists and turns in this tradition from Greek and Roman antiquity through the Italian Renaissance and
into the early modern era. Nor am I interested in trying to measure the scope
and extent of the influence of the republican tradition in the development of
Western democracy. What I offer, rather, is more of a philosophical history, or
more precisely, a critical hermeneutics that seeks to illuminate theoretical aspects of the problem of a commercial republic pertaining to republican paternalism and the placeness of property that have been occluded or ignored in
contemporary civic republicanism. My philosophical history starts with an
examination of the Aristotelian household, and then proceeds to consideration of the problem of a commercial republic in the early modern political
philosophies of James Harrington and Montesquieu.

By placing so much emphasis on Aristotle, I am necessarily entering into controversies that cut across both political theory and historiography. In the process, I will be challenging the interpretive claims and theoretical conclusions of both communal and neoclassical republicans. But viewed strictly in terms of issues of historical interpretation, the emphasis on Aristotle is more directly and sharply at odds with the views of neoclassical republicans. Neoclassical republicanism has grown up with, and contributed to, the currently influential interpretation that discounts the importance of Aristotelian civic humanism in the classical republicanism of the Renaissance and the early modern eras. This interpretation holds that Aristotle's teleological account of the importance of citizenship and participation in political life was largely displaced by a form of "neo-roman" republicanism in which liberty, though still having a collective and corporate component, is more legalistic and defensive in character. As elaborated by Phillip Pettit, Quentin Skinner, and Maurizio Viroli, the central tenet of Renaissance and early modern classical republicanism was not positive liberty in the Aristotelian sense of a capacity to participate in shared practices of deliberation and self-government, but rather civic independence in the Roman sense of both individuals and states being free from domination. Aristotle is almost completely left out, and sometimes neoclassical republicans go so far as to try to expunge Aristotelianism entirely from the classical republican tradition.[1]

My primary complaint against the neoclassical interpretation has to do with the apparent assumption that Aristotelian civic humanism and classical republican non-domination were mutually exclusive frameworks that could not and did not coexist as republicanism developed into the modern era. I do not dispute the claim that non-domination became an important aspect of classical republican freedom during the Renaissance and then later in the development of early modern English republicanism. But I *am* challenging the view that Aristotelian civic humanism was thereby eclipsed in influence and rendered insignificant. Given the Roman provenance of many classical republican ideas of freedom and non-domination, and given the fact that Roman republicanism of the type represented by Cicero contained a large Aristotelian residue, we should hardly be surprised that the two would continue to develop together in subsequent eras.[2]

For the purposes of my philosophical history, it is the areas of conceptual affinity between civic humanism and the neo-roman tradition of non-domination that are most important. As was mentioned in chapter 4, one of these areas has to do with the possibility of viewing non-domination as a condition of positive-libertarian self-rule rather than as a qualitatively different form of liberty. But the area of affinity of more direct relevance to my exploration of the problem of a commercial republic has to do with the Aristotelian understanding of virtue in terms of the relationship between instrumental goods such as property and intrinsically valuable or internal "goods of the soul." If we were to confine this understanding to its original home in Aristotle's teleological metaphysics, then we would probably have to conclude that it had little influence or impact on the subsequent development of republican thinking about the problem of a commercial republic. But if we think of this understanding as a theoretical idiom within which to elaborate the relationship between republican virtue and corruption, then we begin to see a conceptual structure of Aristotelian virtue that persists and develops within different metaphysical and philosophical systems. Unfortunately, we also see the persistence of the kind of exclusionary and paternalistic masters' vision of civic virtue that informed Aristotle's original understanding of internal goods. And it is in the midst of all this that we see both the possibilities and problems of a classical republican form of the placeness of property.

By rejecting many of the central tenets of the neoclassical interpretation, and by emphasizing Aristotelian civic humanism, I am moving back in the direction of J. G. A. Pocock's path-breaking interpretation of republicanism as a tradition that runs from Aristotle and Polybius through Machiavelli and Harrington to the founding of the United States.[3] But my interpretation is by no means a simple reversion to Pocock. Pocock's civic humanism is essentially an exaltation of the political dimension of human personality. It is Aristotelian in the sense that it identifies freedom with participation in public life. But it is a Machiavellian moment of civic humanist virtue and corruption that Pocock emphasizes. Central to this moment is the capacity for manly political mastery of those historical circumstances (*fortuna*, in Machiavelli's lexicon) which, if unmastered, lead to the decay and decline of the republic. In key respects, this is simply a different aspect of neo-roman thinking than what is highlighted by Skinner and Pettit; certainly, Machiavelli saw his republicanism as being in the tradition of Roman glory. In any case, by emphasizing the Machiavellian pursuit of worldly political glory, Pocock's civic humanism leaves little room for the Aristotelian framework of instrumental and internal goods. I believe that this is a serious omission, not just because this framework proved to be remarkably durable, and not just because it allows us to see a fuller range of connections between republican liberty and ethical life, but also because this framework reveals many of the deeper sources of the problem of republican paternalism. While Pocock's interpretation takes the history of republican paternalism into account, it does not emphasize or systematically explore the sources of this paternalism within pre-political institutional locations of external goods such as the household. While such locations linked the ethical use of external goods to the formation of civic character and capacity, they did so within and through hierarchical structures and arrangements of labor and authority. The control of institutional instruments and assets was inextricably bound up with the control of people, and the historical moment of republican mastery was tied to the master's guardianship of non-citizens and second-class citizens. Nor did this masters' vision completely disappear with the advent of forms of republicanism—most famously Montesquieu's commercial republicanism—in which "liberal" and "bourgeois" ideas of economic virtue were combined with the virtues of republican citizenship. Or so I am going to argue in the course of this chapter.

The Need for a Critical Hermeneutics of the Republican Tradition

The uses and abuses of history have been central to the debate over a politics of civic virtue. The revival of civic republicanism in the 1980s was followed by a steady drumbeat of criticism of civic republican efforts to reappropriate the classical republican tradition. Critics repeatedly called attention to the hierarchical, paternalistic, patriarchal, exclusionary, racist, and oppressively conformist aspects of this tradition.[4] In the process, many critics argued, or at least implied, that the civic republican reappropriation of classical republicanism was a misguided exercise of nostalgia. Such attacks have diminished as civic republicanism has branched off into new areas such as deliberative democracy and the recovery of civil society, but they have by no means completely disappeared.[5] Not surprisingly, civic republicans sometimes have become defensive about the role of history in their project of recovery and renewal. I too am critical of the civic republicans' use of history. Yet I believe that their defensiveness is not entirely without justification. The key to this apparent paradox is the spirit of critical hermeneutics that I share with civic republicans—at least in theory.

In Gadamerian terms, a critical hermeneutics is about gaining an awareness of our horizon of beliefs by testing our conceptual and normative commitments against those aspects of our tradition that run counter to our current "prejudices." As such, a critical hermeneutics has nothing in common with what one critic of the "hermeneutic mode of debate" in contemporary political theory has described as an attempt by theorists to "find support" for their "own favored views in the ambiguous legacy of history and tradition."[6] That the "hermeneutic mode of debate" has been accompanied on many occasions by such a partisan approach to history and tradition is not something that I wish to deny, or defend. Clearly, though, this is not an argument against hermeneutics as such, but an argument against what I believe is an unfortunate tendency to lapse into a hermeneutics of avoidance. A *critical* hermeneutics requires that we put our "favored views" at risk, and expose their comforting familiarity to the unsettling strangeness of unfavored views. Support for such a spirit of critical hermeneutics comes from Gadamer himself. According to Gadamer, the "true locus of hermeneutics" is "in the play between the traditionary text's strangeness and familiarity to us."[7]

In essence, then, a critical hermeneutics of classical republicanism simply involves the willingness to encounter those aspects of the tradition that are at odds with our own democratic "prejudices," and to do so in a systematic manner. Part of what is "strange" about classical republicanism is precisely the fact that republican paternalism seldom appeared as problematic within classical republican understandings of civic capacity and public liberty. In other words, the idea that the republican capacity of political equals is best prepared within inherently unequal contexts of rule and guardianship such as the household was more likely to be seen as normatively axiomatic than as normatively problematic. But to call for a systematic encounter with this side of classical republicanism is also an internal-critical challenge to civic republicans to be true to their own hermeneutic commitments. While it is seldom recognized by critics, one of the primary goals of the civic republican recovery of classical republicanism has been, and continues to be, an enhanced and, yes, critical awareness of the historical situation of the citizens of Western liberal democracy. This goal grows out of a critique of what civic republicans see as the tendency within philosophical liberalism to view the self apart from history. Though he eschews the traditionalist hermeneutics of many of his fellow communal republicans, Barber nevertheless speaks for many of them when he says that humans "are above all creatures of time, defined by a history we make together."[8] Consequently, an important part of the civic republican project of recovery is to reconnect individuals to their own history—that is, to the history they have made together as citizens.

In such a critical spirit, Skinner looks to intellectual history to "help us appreciate how far the values embodied in our present way of life, and our present ways of thinking about those values, reflect a series of choices made at different times between different possible worlds." "Equipped with a broader sense of possibility," he goes on to say, "we can stand back from the intellectual commitments we have inherited and ask ourselves what we should think about them."[9] In a related manner, Charles Taylor maintains that "to understand ourselves today, we are pushed into the past for paradigm statements of our formative articulations."[10]

The failure of many critics to acknowledge the importance of this goal of critical historical self-awareness has been the source of frustration for civic republicans. In a tone of barely concealed exasperation, Robert Bellah responded to critics by pointing out that the attitude that he and the other authors of *Habits of the Heart* adopted towards tradition was not one of "unthinking acceptance, but active and critical reappropriation."[11] This is a fair point. Yet the critical spirit of a hermeneutic approach to history cuts both ways, for civic republicans have shown little interest in addressing the theoretical issues associated with the objectionable aspects of classical republicanism. True, most civic republicans have acknowledged these aspects and voiced their opposition to them. But it is one thing to acknowledge and criticize these aspects and quite another to show how one develops a politics of civic virtue that overcomes or avoids the theoretical difficulties that are associated with them. Without a critical appreciation of the "strangeness" of those classical republican texts that lack the background conditions of democratic equality, the civic republicans' circle of virtuous civic engagement will become a disabling prejudice that undermines their democratic aspirations.

In terms of the relationship between the problem of a commercial republic and the tradition of republican paternalism, the central theoretical issue that needs to be addressed has to do with the degree to which traditional republican ideas about property, virtuous civic independence, and public liberty were tied to the exclusion or dependency of other adult members of the polity. This issue often has been acknowledged by civic republicans but never really worked out at a theoretical level.

Consider the example of Pettit's reappropriation and redescription of classical republican ideas of public liberty. Although there is no indication that Pettit has been directly influenced by philosophical hermeneutics, his approach to history is strikingly similar to that taken by more self-consciously hermeneutical civic republicans. Pettit describes his theoretical project as one that aims "to find a new republican philosophy of government in the rich materials of the old, premodern tradition." Much like civic republican hermeneuticists, Pettit's reconstruction of public philosophy is centrally concerned with the recovery and revitalization of the language of republicanism. Politics necessarily has a "conversational, deliberative aspect," and as result, "the role of political philosophy is to interrogate the languages in which such conversation is carried forward and, if necessary, invent or reinvent terms and idioms that may aid in clarification and facilitate convergence." Pettit is quick to admit that the constituencies that participated in the premodern republican conversations about public liberty were exclusionary: "The individuals involved were always male, they were always men of substance—men of trade, men of land, men of property—and they were always, of course, members of the mainstream culture."[12] Yet Pettit insists that the classical republican language of non-domination is flexible enough to resonate with a variety of culturally, economically, and politically marginalized groups. As can be inferred from what I said in chapter 2 about the plasticity of the idiom of republican virtue, I don't entirely disagree. The problem is that other than the plasticity of classical republican language, Pettit does not offer much of an argument as to how his modern democratic republicanism will be able to avoid new forms of the premodern problem of republican paternalism. To use Pettit's own terms, how does one incorporate the "inclusivist assumption" of modern democratic republicanism while still holding on to the "old republican ideal"?[13] More to the specific point of my critique, how does one develop a republican liberty of non-domination that is not conceptually tied to the subjection and dependency of other adults? To be sure, the plasticity of the republican idiom of non-domination means that it could be used against itself in the sense that more inclusive and egalitarian expressions might challenge more mainstream ones, or exclusionary ones. But it is hard to see how a republican language with such wildly divergent views of the relationship between civic independence, equal citizenship, and social justice could serve as the basis for a defensible public philosophy.

There is no reason to single out Pettit for criticism. In fact, Pettit's appraisal of classical republicanism is more circumspect and balanced than many others—all the more reason to worry that civic republicans have not met the challenge of elaborating those properties of democratic equality and inclusion that both distinguish and protect their project of cultivating republican virtue from the exclusionary paternalism that afflicted traditional forms of this project.

This challenge cannot be met simply by mixing and matching the best of different historical idioms, or (as Pettit suggests) by finding modern institutional forms within which to re-embed "the old republican ideal."[14] Rather, this challenge is best met by moving to a level of critical hermeneutics, that is to say, by exploring and articulating the horizon of implicit understandings and self-understandings concerning civic independence and civic equality that inform democratic practices. Civic republicans have explored and articulated this horizon in a selective and tendentious manner, focusing their critical energies on the testing of liberal and liberal capitalist prejudices, but spending precious little time testing the prejudices of their own tradition of classical republicanism. Viewed through this narrow lens, virtuous republican liberty appears less as an inherently problematic ideal and more as a corrective to liberalism—for communal republicans, as a corrective to liberalism's atomist distortions; for neoclassical republicans, as a corrective to the liberal understanding of negative liberty; and for both communal and neoclassical republicans as a corrective to the excesses of a modern commercial republic. But when we look for a distinctively civic republican corrective to the problem of republican paternalism, we find various strategies of avoidance: the strategy (adopted by Pettit among others) of claiming that modern "inclusivist" assumptions have solved the problem;[15] the strategy of claiming that in its "truest" or "deepest" sense, the tradition of civic humanist and classical republicanism was fundamentally egalitarian;[16] and the strategy of separating the democratic republican wheat from classical republican chaff, or in Cass Sunstein's terms, of reappropriating only "those aspects of republican thought that have the strongest claim to contemporary support."[17] These are not the strategies of a truly critical hermeneutics; rather, they are the strategies of a partisan hermeneutics of trying to "find support" for "favored views in the ambiguous legacy of history and tradition"—a hermeneutics of avoidance that has glossed over the most unsettling theoretical implications of the history of republican paternalism.

The problem of republican paternalism will not simply go away if civic republicans shrink the historical dimension of their project of recovery and renewal. The important question never was whether civic republicans reappropriated the republican tradition, but whether, in the interest of uncovering the sources and conditions of democracy, they systematically explored both the possibilities and the problems within this tradition. In terms of the goal of critical historical self-awareness, one could even say that the worst form of a hermeneutics of avoidance is simply the avoidance of the history of a republican politics of virtuous liberty. Judging from the role of history in recent offshoots of the republican revival such as the debate over deliberative democracy and the recovery of civil society, the trend is not good. The debate over deliberative democracy has been conducted in largely ahistorical terms. And while the upsurge of interest in the relationship between civil society and civic virtue has been accompanied by a fair amount of historical sociological analysis of things like social capital, there has been little interest in encountering the "paradigm statements" of the relationship between civic virtue and social capital in the history of political theory.

Of course, the news is not all bad with respect to the republican tradition and its influence on the horizon of Western democracy. Due in large part to the efforts of today's civic republicans, democratic theorists have been sensitized (or re-sensitized) to those aspects of the Western democratic horizon that are informed by traditional republican themes such as the importance of cultivating habits of responsible citizenship, the public dimension of liberty, the connection between corruption and tyranny, the patriotism of virtuous resistance to tyranny, and yes, the threat to civic virtue and public liberty that is posed by excessive acquisitiveness and commercialism. Arguably, also, these themes all too often have been eclipsed by and within late modern liberal democratic thought and practice. And in addition to all of this, I believe that a hermeneutic encounter with the republican tradition reveals the "strangeness" of a civic conception of the placeness of property that has been all but completely occluded by the prejudices of modern thingness.

Placeness and the Aristotelian Household

With but one possible exception, Aristotle's theory of the household is of foundational significance for all that I have discussed in relation to the placeness of property, the civic republican approach to the problem of a commercial republic, and the problem of republican paternalism. The Aristotelian household is paradigmatic of the placeness of property within Western republicanism, and for that matter, within much of Western thought and culture in general. It is also the theoretical context for Aristotle's foundational statement of the internal goods (IG) thesis. And last, but unfortunately, by no means least, Aristotle's theory of the household contains a foundational expression of republican paternalism in the form of a masters' vision of civic virtue. The possible exception has to do with the rights/property (R/P) thesis. Since Aristotle did not, and could not, articulate his theory of the household with reference to the modern understanding of rights, it is not directly relevant to the issues associated with this thesis. However, it certainly has some bearing on these issues. For one thing, something like a liberal discourse of equal rights would seem to be sorely needed to counter the Aristotelian household's hierarchical and exclusionary relations of labor and authority. In addition, the Aristotelian household exposes the narrow view of property that informs contemporary civic republican thinking about the problem of a commercial republic. With regard to both the IG thesis and the R/P thesis, civic republicans assume that the universe of property is almost completely defined by the form of heavily commodified and commercialized property that I have been referring to as modern thingness. But starting with the Aristotelian household, and continuing through the propertied independence that classical republicans of the early modern era identified with the landed estate, we see that the traditional republican view of the problem of a commercial republic was not a condemnation of the pursuit of property in general, but part of a conversation about the different conditions under which different modes and arrangements of property might or might not threaten the civic virtue deemed to be necessary to sustain republican liberty.

Today's civic republicans provide us with a one-dimensional picture of the role of property in Aristotle's political philosophy. The IG thesis is clearly about property insofar as property is an important example of external goods. But true to form, this is pretty much the extent to which most civic republicans have discussed the role of property in Aristotle's political philosophy. And also true to form, the interest of civic republicans in an Aristotelian view of property is largely confined to the problem of the corruptive power of acquisitiveness. This certainly is a problem that looms large in several of Aristotle's arguments about property. But Aristotle's discussions of property cover a wide range of issues, and by focusing so much on the problem of acquisitiveness civic republicans provide a truncated account of Aristotle's thinking about property. For instance, there is little (if any) discussion of Aristotle's critique of Plato's "communism." However, the most glaring omissions have to do with what Aristotle says about property in connection to the theory of household management in Book I of the *Politics*.

Civic republicans are not the only theorists and scholars to downplay the importance of the relationship between property and household management in Aristotle's thought. It seems that neglect of this relationship has been characteristic of theoretical discussions of Aristotle's thinking about property throughout the modern era. Too often, in my judgment, modern political theorists have looked at Aristotle's arguments about property through the lens of modern debates over capitalism. Viewing things this way, the discussions of property that seem most important are those in Book II of *Politics* that touch on Plato and different systems of common property. The resulting picture of Aristotle is that of a moderate (though perhaps more of a leftist by contemporary American standards) who steers a course between the extremes of Platonic communism and unfettered private property. There are large grains of truth in this picture with respect to both the Aristotelian emphasis on moderation and his defense of a system of property that combines an emphasis on private ownership with forms of use and enjoyment that are common. But as important as the discussions of property in Book II are, they do not account for the importance of the household as the primary ethical context of property within Aristotle's thought.[18] As Alan Ryan points out in a discussion that provides a corrective to the conventional picture, Aristotle's theory of property starts with the "everyday economic activities" of the household and "the sort of property on which these depend." This, he says, provides a "different context" for discussing economic activities "from that of any modern writer." As Ryan explains, "Aristotle insists that the *point* of property is the maintenance of the family, and this gives the discussion a moral flavour which more directly economic accounts in later centuries would lack."[19]

Ryan is right to highlight the gulf that separates the art of household management from modern economics. Despite the etymological connection between *oikonomia* (the Greek word for household management) and "economics," the two are quite different, certainly with respect to the late modern science of economics. In a sense, calling into question the picture of the Aristotelian art of household management as an early (and misguided) form of modern economics is the obverse of calling into question the picture of Aristotle as a moderate defender of private property. These two pictures seem to have developed together in the modern era. Not only do they fail to do justice to the importance of the household in Aristotle's thinking about property, but both also miss the distinctive teleological framework of moral and civic ends that informs this thinking.[20] However, there is one more step that Ryan could have, and in my view, should have, taken in the process of distinguishing Aristotle's views of property from modern understandings of property and economics. The step that he did not take is one of contrasting the formative placeness of the household with the modern regime of thingness. This is the step that is suggested by my redescription of the civic republican hermeneutics of the situated self. Yet it is also a step that reveals the dangers that lie along a civic republican path to the placeness of property.

The Teleology of Property

Let us start down this path by considering the following question: Is the Aristotelian household a form of property? From the standpoint of the thingness of property, the answer is clearly no. From this standpoint, the question itself is apt to seem slightly ridiculous, and even nonsensical. After all, it makes little sense to think of the Aristotelian household as an object of rightful acquisition and ownership (let alone exchange). But viewed in relation to the placeness of property, the household becomes a constitutive dimension of Aristotelian property—to be sure, not in the sense of the household being a property object itself, but rather in the sense of the theory of the household providing a conceptual and normative framework that is constitutive of the meaning and significance of the household's property objects. Or what amounts to the same thing, the theory of the household delineates a moral context that is partly constitutive of property. Add to this the fact that the household is a formative context of identity that is constituted through relations of labor and authority, and we have all the ingredients for what we can think of as a fully developed placeness of property, or "full placeness," for short.

It needs to be stressed that what is at issue here is not whether Aristotle wrote of property in connection to objects of acquisition, ownership, or exchange. He did, and in this respect, we need to acknowledge that there is an irreducible element of thingness in his conception of property. But we should not conclude from this that thingness is the core of Aristotelian property. Rather, the conclusion that is warranted is that not all property objects reached the level of a true or ethical placeness. Let me explain.

To determine whether some property object or group of objects reaches the level of true or ethical placeness we need to consider the relationship between the object or group of objects and its moral and civic context. Critics of my idea of placeness might press the point that it is possible to think in terms of a moral and civic context for property objects or property rights within the

framework of thingness; in other words, without imbuing property with a locational structure. Fair enough, but the real questions are whether and how
the context informs the meaning of the objects. As we saw in our earlier discussions of the analytic approach to property, under the idea of thingness, the
fundamental meaning of property as an object of rightful acquisition, ownership, and exchange remains untouched and unchanged by its moral or civic
context. By contrast, under the idea of placeness, the moral and civic context
is partly constitutive of the meaning and significance of the property objects
within it. By the same token, property is defined not as an analytically isolable
relationship between the rights-bearing subject of possession and the property object, but by the relationship of the property objects to the ends and
purposes of their institutional location.

This brings us back to something we discovered in the discussion of the situated self. The full placeness of property is associated with a circular and dialectical relationship between property and its moral and civic context. The
property objects come to be defined and transformed in the image of their
context. Such a dialectical relationship is at the heart of Aristotle's theory of
the household. The key to seeing this is found in Aristotle's definition of property in Book I of *Politics*. Property, Aristotle says, is a part of the household in
the specific sense that articles of household property represent "instruments"
that are to be utilized on behalf of, and in connection with, the art of household management. As with other arts, the art of household management requires both "inanimate" and "animate" instruments, the most important (and
regrettable) example of the latter being the household's slaves. And as with
other arts, the art of household management "has a definite sphere" with a
specific "function" or purpose. The relevant "sphere" of a practical art "must
be furnished with the appropriate instruments if its function is to be dis-
charged." The "function" of the household is the life of its members, and property is a key instrument of and for this function. Hence, Aristotle concludes,
"property in general is the sum of such instruments" for sustaining life.[21]

Strictly speaking, therefore, property for Aristotle is not about things or
rights to things, but about instruments. This is consistent with Aristotle's understanding of external goods as "things of utility." But we must be careful not
to think of the utility or instrumentality of Aristotelian property as if it were
akin to instrumentalist utilitarianism in the modern sense. This, indeed, is
how civic republicans and many other post-socialist thinkers are apt to view
the external good of property. This leads to the kind of dualistic perspective
on property and virtue that we uncovered in relation to the ethical anti-
materialism of civic republicanism and other forms of post-socialist thought.
Aristotle, by contrast, does not simply posit property as an always/already corruptive thing of utility. Rather, he considers the utility of property in terms of

the good of sustaining the life of the members of the household. To be sure, Aristotle worries about acquisitiveness and other situations in which the pursuit of "things of utility" takes precedence over, and undermines, cultivation of "goods of the soul." It is quite legitimate for civic republicans and like-minded theorists to derive the IG thesis from Aristotle. However, this does not obviate the point that for Aristotle, external goods such as property can, and should, serve as instruments for the cultivation of internal goods. This is partly a matter of external goods being pursued "within moderate limits."[22] But here too we must be careful not to construe Aristotle's meaning in terms of a global confrontation between virtue and instrumental reason. Moderation, for Aristotle, is not about some grand project of checking and countering an instrumentalist worldview. Rather, moderation is fundamentally about the kind of disposition that accompanies a well-constituted practical art. Accordingly, one of the conditions of moderation is having instrumental goods such as property constitutively connected to the ends and functions of their practical arts. Although she misses the importance of placeness, Martha Nussbaum gets to the nub of the Aristotelian understanding of the instrumental value of property in the following summary: "Land, money, and possessions are just things, and have no intrinsic worth. Thus there is no absolute right to property in the Aristotelian conception. The claim citizens have is to sustenance in their various essential functionings: to be brought across the threshold into capability for good human functioning. And the question about property must simply be, what form or forms of ownership best promote this situation?"[23]

The goal, then, is not to overcome property, but to have forms or modes of property that are useful for the maintenance and development of human life. In the parlance of economics, this is property's "use value." It follows for Aristotle that "true wealth" comprises those articles and objects that are "necessary for life and useful to the association of the *polis* or the household."[24] As something that is "necessary for life," property is, in the first instance, an instrument for "goods of the body." But over and above this, "true wealth" serves the end of cultivating the "moral goodness" of the members of the household in relation to the good life of the polity. At this point, we are back to property serving as an instrument for the internal goods of the soul. Or as Aristotle summed things up in Book I, the business of household management "is more concerned with the good condition of human beings than with the condition of property."[25]

I can almost hear civic republicans and like-minded post-socialist thinkers exclaiming that this sums up their own view of property as well. There is indeed a family resemblance, as I have already acknowledged. But the resemblance is superficial with regard to the meaning and nature of property.

The post-socialist effort to claim the high ground of virtue and moral recovery against the corruptive influence of the desire for property presupposes a property regime of universal thingness. Property is always/already corruptive because, at its core, the nature of property is always/already the same thing. There is a kind of unchanging, universal property object *x*, and the only important questions are whether people are moderate in the pursuit of *x* and whether any given *x* is used for promoting the good condition of human beings. At first glance, this seems to be a perspective that is fully in accord with Aristotle's. Again, there is some degree of thingness in Aristotle's view of property, and arguably, even when property objects are redescribed as instruments, there is a sense in which they have some common, universal attributes. But there is another, and I contend, deeper understanding of property in which Aristotle has in mind qualitatively different forms and types of property. At this deeper level of the meaning of property, we are not dealing with better and worse uses of a universal object or instrument *x*, but rather with better and worse forms of property.

It might seem that something has to give here, that we cannot think of Aristotle's theory of property at these two very different levels of meaning. Short of a semantic sleight of hand, how is it possible to think in terms of some universal form of thingness that remains constant in the midst of different uses while simultaneously thinking of qualitatively different forms and types of property? But there is no need for a semantic sleight of hand, for this apparent contradiction disappears when we think in terms of Aristotelian property as a movement from thingness to placeness. Viewed in this way, the description of property as an instrument is far more than simply a way of connecting property to the higher ends of human well-being. It is that, but it also a way of capturing the change from property as objects of a general and amorphously similar type to property in its more fully developed form as articles of use within and for specific locations, and especially within and for household locations.

Without the placeness of the household, Aristotle's account of "true wealth" makes little sense except as a metaphorical way of describing the good use of property. In effect, I am suggesting that Aristotle also meant to say that true wealth really is a different kind of property, a kind of property whose very nature is constituted by the practical arts of household management and statecraft.

This way of looking at Aristotle's theory of property gains support when we consider the teleological metaphysics of natural ends and functions that informs all of Aristotle's thought. There are two ways in which Aristotle's teleological perspective is associated with, and gives rise to, the placeness of "true wealth." First, it is the source of the normative framework of Aristotelian property. Aristotle's teleological perspective entails a deeply normative view of human activities and associations. The ends and functions that are naturally associated with an activity or an association are their *proper* ends and functions. And this "normative ontology" of natural human arts and associations prefigures and informs the nature of property as well. So even though property itself is only an instrument for higher, intrinsically valuable ends and functions, it nonetheless is inextricably connected to a normative structure of proper versus improper modes and forms of property. Simply put, property can never be viewed as a neutral instrument that has no normative significance in and of itself. The very meaning of Aristotelian property is normative in the sense that property instruments must be understood in relation to the question of whether the ends and functions they promote are natural and proper. True wealth is wealth that is proper by virtue of being truly natural.

Of course, this normative ontology of property also applies to forms or modes that are unnatural and therefore of dubious propriety. The chief example of this is the "chrematistic" practice of moneymaking, which, by making the accumulation of money an end in itself, is a debasement of all that is natural and proper in well-functioning households and polities. I will have more to say about this shortly.

The second way in which Aristotle's teleological perspective is associated with the full placeness of "true wealth" has to do with its role in establishing the context dependency of property instruments. Aristotelian property is defined not simply in relation to moral and civic ends in general, but also in relation to the particular ends of particular contexts. Without this context dependency, the relationship between property and moral or civic ends would not necessarily develop into a clearly defined placeness. To see this, one need only imagine a relationship between property and a transcendental order of ends—say, Kant's kingdom of ends among purely rational beings. Rightful property objects are in some sense those that serve, or more likely, are consistent with such an order of ends. But precisely because the ends are transcendental, their connection to property does not imbue it with any locational specificity. Hence, placeness is downplayed and submerged (if not completely obliterated). By contrast, Aristotelian ends are embedded in particular practices and associations such as those of the household, and this gives Aristotelian property—or at least property in the form of "true wealth"—a clearly defined locational dimension. Put differently, there is an institutional topography of placeness, with the household, the *oikos*, at the center.

The context dependency of Aristotelian property is an organic outgrowth of the normative ontology in which it is grounded. To some extent, it can even be said that we are dealing with two different ways of saying the same thing. To say that the nature of property is constituted in relation to the ends of the human associations and practices it serves is also to say that property cannot be understood apart from these associational and practical contexts. However, this analytic equivalence does not get us to the level of the dialectical relationship between property and its moral and civic context. This dialectical relationship is the most important aspect of the context dependency of Aristotelian property. Again, I am talking about a relationship in which property is transformed in the image of its moral and civic context. In terms of the Aristotelian teleology, this has to do with the fulfillment and realization of the nature—the true nature—of property within its proper moral and civic context, its proper location. This implies a movement from the potential to the actual. Hence, the context dependency of Aristotelian property is about the movement from the potential wealth of mere property objects to the true and actual wealth of property as a set of instruments within and for a well-functioning location such as the household.

One way to see this movement towards "true wealth" is to consider the reverse process of the debasement and corruption of property. It is at this point, of course, that the problem of acquisitiveness comes to the fore. But we need to be careful here. Acquisitiveness is always bad in Aristotle's view, but *acquisition* is not necessarily bad. It depends on the form it takes, which is to say, it depends on its relationship to the contexts of the household and the *polis*. The most purely natural form of the art of acquisition has to do with simple, one could even say primitive, activities relating to the provision of life-sustaining resources and articles for the household or the *polis*. This is a form of acquisition in which the exchange of goods has no role; rather, there is only a direct appropriation of resources by the manager of the household or the statesman, for instance, through hunting, gathering, or harvesting.[26] The more problematic cases of acquisition involve exchange relationships, and the most problematic of these is "retail trade" that is geared to moneymaking. Now, even acquisition based on exchange is not necessarily bad, and not necessarily unnatural, so long as it is limited to serving the proper ends and functions of the household and the *polis*. The problem is that what starts as simple bartering "to satisfy the natural requirements of sufficiency" becomes a form of "long-distance trade" based on the use of currency, and this in turn gives rise to the artificial and corruptive practice of moneymaking.[27] The danger, of course, is that a commercial regime of moneymaking will lead to a situation where the accumulation of wealth (and especially money) becomes an end in itself rather than an instrument to be moderately employed on behalf of higher ends. But this can also be seen as a debasement of property, a debasement of "true wealth." By making the accumulation of wealth its own end, moneymaking reduces property to the accumulation of objects with an artificial exchange value. Property, in other words, is reduced to a debased and artificial thingness. By the same token, the property objects of moneymaking are context-less and placeless. To use one of my terms, moneymaking represents a pure case of the conceptual displacement of property. Certainly, it is no accident that Aristotle emphasizes the connection between moneymaking and long-distance trade, for trade of this type and scale produces an actual physical placelessness of property, a transgression and breakdown of the physical boundaries within which Aristotelian property finds its true home. Yet the placeness of "true wealth" is defined much more by the moral and civic ends it serves than by its physical location. Thus, the placelessness of the property objects of moneymaking is primarily and fundamentally about the absence of a constitutive connection between the instrumental good of property and the moral and civic ends of the household and the *polis*.

In sum, Aristotle did not seek the transcendence of property, but its transformation and elevation into "true wealth." When this happens, as it does in a well-functioning household, property as thingness does indeed seem to disappear, or more precisely, it seems to persist only in a residual form. "True wealth" is wealth that is enveloped and conditioned by the moral and civic properties of the household and the *polis*. Hermeneutically and phenomenologically speaking, property becomes a "living presence" by virtue of being conditioned as an instrument for life and the good life. Or what amounts to the same thing, property as thingness all but disappears when property has been put in its proper place.

Aristotelian Placeness and Republican Paternalism

So far so good in terms of the democratic potential of Aristotelian placeness. But the Aristotelian theory of the household is paradigmatic of the dangers that placeness poses for democracy as well as its fruitful possibilities. Never mind that Aristotelian placeness seems to be of dubious relevance to a late modern commercial economy in which long-distance trade rules. Even before we get to that issue, we are confronted with the relationship between the placeness of Aristotelian property and the problem of republican paternalism. The master of the Aristotelian household—let us call him ancient "oikonomic man" to distinguish him from modern "economic man"—was thought to have developed his capacity for self-governing citizenship by virtue of his capacity to manage and rule over the members of the household, including his wife and his adult slaves. The household was formative of civic identity in this way as well.

The problem is that the placeness of the Aristotelian household is constituted not simply in terms of the ends and functions that are embedded and realized within it, but also in terms of the relations of labor and authority through which household functions are organized. Moreover, the organization of labor is itself inscribed in relations and practices of authority. In this respect, authority is the more important of these two dimensions of Aristotelian placeness. One could even say that what we moderns are apt to think of as a division of labor was, for Aristotle, about relations of ruling and being ruled.

Within Aristotle's "normative ontology," proper ends and functions are also authoritative ones, and they become authoritative partly by virtue of being in locations that have the proper and appropriate relations of ruling and being ruled. Hence, the household is a property-related context of authority in the specific sense that it is largely through and within household relations of ruling and being ruled that the ends of sustaining life and promoting the good life are served. By the same token, a well-constituted household is, for Aristotle, one ruled by those men (and only men) who are fit to be masters. The master of the household is both "an authority" in the art of household management and "in authority" in the sense of ruling over the other members of the household.

We can get a better sense of how authority and property are related to Aristotle's teleology of natural ends and functions by considering the household in terms of his analysis of natural associations. In addition to being a location of property, the household is an association. More specifically, it is an association that is the product of several "elementary associations": between husband and wife, between parents and children, and between master and slaves.[28] All of these elementary associations revolve around the distinction between "natural" rulers and "natural" subordinates. As we saw in the earlier discussion of the masters' vision of civic virtue, Aristotle argues that the capacity for ruling over other human beings is directly related to the faculty for rational deliberation. This faculty is the "ruling" element of the soul.[29] On this basis, Aristotle seeks to show that there are different degrees and types of "moral goodness" among the different members of the household. The rulership of the male head of the household is said to be natural and proper by virtue of the fact that he, and only he, possesses "moral goodness in its full form." And why is this? According to Aristotle, it is because the master's "function, regarded absolutely and in its full nature, demands a master-artificer, and reason is such a master-artificer."[30] In other words, only male masters have enough of the ruling element of reason to rule over other members of the household. It falls upon the male master, therefore, to manage the animate and inanimate instruments of the household. But for Aristotle, the management of household property instruments is of a piece with the virtuous rule of the household. Ultimate responsibility for these two tasks cannot be separated or delegated to different members of the household. Also, while the linkage between these two tasks is most obvious and direct in the master-slave relationship, it is found in all other relationships and associations within the household as well. The master of the household is simultaneously the manager-guardian of household properties and the ruler-guardian of the other members of the household. It is, indeed, a masters' vision of guardianship. And since it is only the masters of households who are deemed fit for citizenship in the full sense of "taking turns ruling and being ruled," it is also a masters' vision of civic virtue. Oikonomic man is the model citizen in Aristotelian civic humanism.

This brings us back to civic identity. The household is a property-related context of identity in two interrelated senses: first, in the sense of a formative context for cultivating the habits and dispositions of good citizenship, and second, in the sense of a context that allocates and distributes the capacity for citizenship on the basis of purportedly natural relations of ruling and being ruled. Viewed by itself, the first of these senses appears as a fairly innocuous case of the dialectical relationship between property and the situated self. Because the members of the Aristotelian household are situated within a location of property that is a deeply and constitutively moral and civic context, the household represents a property-related context of character formation. Thus, the master's civic identity has little to do with being the proprietor of the household and its property articles and instruments, but a great deal to do with his guardianship of, and within, the household. However, the connection to guardianship reminds us that the Aristotelian household is a formative context with problematic distributive implications concerning who is admitted to the public realm of self-governing citizenship and who is excluded. At one level, this sense of the household as a property-related, distributive context of identity has to do with a familiar story of how a privileged position in property arrangements gets translated into a privileged social and political status in the community. But as we have seen, the deeper sources of the problem of republican paternalism lie at the level of the *interrelationship* of the formative and distributive dimensions, for at this level, the formation of the habits of citizenship is tightly bound up with hierarchical relations of labor and authority in the household. Simply put, the problem is that the master develops the capacity for public-spirited citizenship by ruling over and managing second-class citizens and non-citizens.[31]

To formalize things, the masters' vision of civic virtue that emerges from Aristotle's theory of household management has two interrelated dimensions. First, it is characterized by a hierarchical view of civic capacity in which the capacities of free and equal masters are developed and defined in terms of their rule over those members of the household (and by extension, the polity) who are deemed to lack the capacity for self-government. Second, it is a vision of guardianship in which masters develop a capacity for civic-minded guardianship of the common good in part through the experience of being the virtuous guardians of dependent members of the household.

Now, there are some neo-Aristotelian theorists who think that we can clean up much of the problematic messiness that emerges from Aristotle by expunging the flawed metaphysical assumptions about nature and human nature from his practical philosophy of ethics and politics. On this view, we can extract the essence of Aristotelian practical philosophy from Aristotelian metaphysics merely by thinking of practical wisdom (*phronesis*) as an ongoing encounter with, and within, particular ethical situations.[32] I do not believe that Aristotle's metaphysics are easily or cleanly separated from his practical philosophy. At a minimum, his practical philosophy seems to be dependent on the metaphysical assumption of a teleological design to nature and human nature. After all, Aristotle's practical philosophy is concerned with practical wisdom about the *good* life, and as we have seen, the Aristotelian view of the good life is bound up with ontological claims about ends and functions that are simultaneously proper and natural. In essence, the neo-Aristotelian project of expunging metaphysics represents an effort to jettison what is proper from its Aristotelian moorings in nature and then reinscribe it in cultural practices and traditions. Rather than a simple separation, this is a violent divorce that damages the very core of Aristotelian practical philosophy. But for purposes of my critique of civic republicanism, there is an important sense in which this is a moot issue. It would certainly make things a lot easier if we could confine the problem of republican paternalism to flaws in Aristotelian metaphysics, or for that matter, if we could confine it to Aristotle. Unfortunately, the problem of republican paternalism has been a recurrent one in the long tradition of classical republicanism, certainly through the early modern era, and arguably beyond. To be sure, Aristotle is a foundational thinker for thinkers in this tradition, and as will be discussed shortly, his normative ontology left a rather large residue on some classical republicans of the early modern period. Yet something besides Aristotelian metaphysics is going on here. What we see is a kind of political sociology of civic capacity that makes its way from one episode of republican theory to another, and does so in the midst of many metaphysical twists and turns. And to a remarkable degree, we also see similar forms of analysis concerning the sources of civic capacity and the presumed incapacities associated with things like gender, occupation, property, race, and nationality. It is a republican sociology of the internal goods of "oikonomic man."

Tracing this republican sociology of paternalism gets rather complicated when we move from Aristotle's thought to classical republican expressions of civic humanism during the Renaissance and early modern eras. Clearly, Aristotle and these later episodes are separated by enormous differences of content and context. In addition, classical republican idioms and ideas were almost endlessly reformulated and revised throughout the early modern era.

This resulted in an enormous amount of diversity and fluidity in these idioms and ideas. And there is the additional complicating factor of republican ideas and idioms being combined (if not always harmonized) with non-classical and non-civic humanist ideas and idioms such as early modern reworkings of natural law and views of individual freedom and limited government that begin to look a lot like what we now think of as liberalism. Among other things, these new ideas and idioms led to the introduction of the language of rights into conversations about the corruptive power of acquisitiveness and a commercial regime of moneymaking and long-distance trade. Yet in the midst of all this change there is also a remarkable degree of continuity with respect to the basic Aristotelian structure of internal goods, so much so that elements of this structure outlast the household economy of "oikonomic man" and find their way into the defense of the modern commercial republic.

The Fate of Aristotelian Placeness in Early Modern Republicanism

As interpreted by Pocock, the problem of a commercial republic developed in the early modern era as a confrontation between classical republicanism of the civic humanist type represented by James Harrington and the ideologies and practices of an emergent regime of commerce.[33] Like their Italian Renaissance predecessors (most notably, Machiavelli) the lesson that early modern republicans drew from their study of Greek and Roman antiquity was that political order had to be achieved in a world characterized by constant change and the ever-present danger of a cycle of corruption, dependency, and despotism. This made the task of maintaining a republican form of government especially daunting, for rather than relying, as corrupt Court politicians did, on force, fear, and the dependency of their subjects, republican government required the exercise of virtuous independence by citizens, both collectively and individually. Most important in this regard was the willingness and capacity of citizens to serve the common good, in short, their civic virtue. Within this reformulated civic humanist framework, commercial understandings and modes of property were problematic insofar as they undermined the virtues and constitutional arrangements necessary to sustain the public liberty of a self-governing people. The "passions" and "fantasies" unleashed by commercial exchange and speculation were a threat to the self-restraint and rational self-determination that made civic virtue possible. Of particular concern was the danger posed by "luxuries," a concern, for instance, which prompted many American republicans during the revolutionary era to support sumptuary laws.[34] But even if these passions and fantasies were harnessed and transformed into a civilized pursuit of self-interest (a hope entertained by Montesquieu among others), there was still the disconcerting prospect of too many citizens being too specialized in their activities and too preoccupied with private concerns to allow for participation in, and for, the common good.[35] Finally, insofar as commercialism arose and developed in conjunction with systems of public finance (as happened in England in the latter part of the seventeenth century) there was the additional concern that the attendant use of executive patronage would lead to new forms of political dependency and corruption.

No doubt, this picture is overdrawn in key respects. Early modern republicanism was not nearly so anti-commercial as it suggests. One can also quibble with Pocock for giving too little emphasis to the neo-roman ideal of non-domination and for not seeing how readily classical republican idioms were combined with jurisprudential and even Lockean idioms of rights. But I think that at least some of the distortions in Pocock's interpretive picture can be corrected if we stop thinking so much in terms of a heroic Machiavellian mastery of circumstances and more in terms of a structural Aristotelianism having to do with the placeness of property, the relationship between instrumental and internal goods, and the republican sociology of paternalism. Let us start by taking a look at Harrington's seventeenth-century English republicanism.

James Harrington's Reappropriation of "Ancient Prudence"

Within Harrington's republicanism, the Aristotelian vision of household mastery was recast as an attempt to ground republican virtue and liberty in freehold estates.[36] As explained by Pocock and others, the idea of virtuous independence that is supported by non-dependent tenures of real property exercised considerable influence on English and American republicans who worried about the corruptive power of a political economy organized around movable property, trade, and credit.[37] Thus, for early modern republicans of the type represented by Harrington, the value of independent ownership of land had considerably less to do with the opportunities it created for commercial gain than with how "it anchored the individual in the structure of power and virtue, and liberated him to practice these activities."[38]

The importance and influence of the early modern ideal of virtuous propertied independence has been amply documented by historians, and not just those like Pocock who are associated with so-called "republican synthesis" in contemporary intellectual history. In fact, this is an area where there is widespread agreement among historians. Some of the strongest critics of the republican synthesis agree that the ideal of virtuous propertied independence played a central and often decisive role in the development of the early modern republican perspective on the problem of a commercial republic.[39]

Given this preponderance of historical evidence and opinion, and given the reliance of many contemporary civic republicans on republican historiography, one might reasonably have expected that the early modern ideal of virtuous propertied independence would play a prominent role in civic republican discussions of the problem of a commercial republic. Yet this ideal seldom has been discussed by either civic republicans or their critics, and when is has been discussed, it usually has been treated in a cursory and highly selective manner, with little or no attention to its problematic connection to republican paternalism.[40]

The avoidance of Harrington's formulation of the ideal of virtuous propertied independence is especially unfortunate, not simply because he was one of its most influential expositors in early modern republicanism, but also because he is an interesting transitional theorist who connects Aristotelian civic humanism to the advent of the modern commercial republic. Notwithstanding the efforts of neoclassical republicans to enlist Harrington as an example of the neo-roman form of classical republicanism, there can be no doubt as to Harrington's own belief that he was writing in a tradition that was rooted in Aristotelian civic humanism.[41] As Harrington made very clear in the opening pages of his chief work of political theory, *The Commonwealth of Oceana*, his republican solution to the post-revolutionary crisis of authority in seventeenth-century England was based on the recovery and reformulation of what he called "ancient prudence." Aristotle was not Harrington's only exemplar of "ancient prudence"; it was also exemplified by the likes of Cicero, Livy, and Machiavelli. But it was Aristotle who provided the main foundation for his theoretical reconstruction of the English polity along republican lines.

Harrington defined "ancient prudence" by counterpoising it to "modern prudence." "Modern prudence" was exemplified not only by what we would call feudalism, but also by Hobbes. This seems like a very odd combination to modern liberal democratic ears accustomed to hearing a Whig story of Western progress on the road to liberty. But Harrington saw feudalism and Hobbes as two examples of political philosophies that exalt rule in the "private interest" of a man or a group of men. This is the essence of corruption on the classical republican view, and for Harrington, as for many other classical republicans, it was the root cause of the cycle of decay and degeneration leading to despotism and tyranny. By contrast, "ancient prudence" made "popular government" possible by virtue of viewing government as "an art whereby a civil society of men is instituted and preserved upon the foundation of common right or interest."[42]

According to Harrington, a government based on the ancient art of ruling in the common interest is also a government based on the "empire of laws and not of men."[43] And he made a point of citing both Aristotle and Livy as the primary sources of the close connection between "ancient prudence" and the rule of law. This is significant in light of the efforts of contemporary neoclassical republicans to remove Aristotelian civic humanism from the picture of the classical republican vision of "justice and liberty under the rule of law."[44] But in the context of my rethinking of the problem of a commercial republic, I am more interested in the relationship between Harrington's understanding of virtuous propertied independence and five other aspects of Aristotle's thought: first, the conceptual structure of internal goods; second, the art of household management; third, the placeness of property; fourth, the positive liberty of participation in the deliberations of the polity; and fifth, the absence of a discourse of rights.

More than his support for a politics based on the common good and the rule of law, it is Harrington's reappropriation of the conceptual structure of internal goods that marks his theory as a form of Aristotelian civic humanism. It is in this framework that Harrington developed his influential account of republican property arrangements. Specifically, he discussed property in terms of the unmistakably Aristotelian relationship between "external goods of fortune" and "internal goods of the mind."[45] As with Aristotle, this is a relationship between utilitarian instruments and the virtues of a good life. Hence, Harrington identified "internal goods of the mind" with "natural or acquired virtues" such as wisdom, prudence, and courage.[46] However, Harrington redescribed and thematized the relationship between external and internal goods in terms of a correlative relationship between power and authority. External goods are about power, and internal goods are about authority. Or as he put it: "To the goods of the mind answers authority; to the goods of fortune, power or empire."[47] This changes the relationship between property and power. For Aristotle, property and power were equal as things of utility in the cultivation of virtue. But Harrington broke the general category of external goods down into a causal and historical relationship between property and power. Technically, it was a causal and historical relationship between "dominion" and power. For Harrington, though, "dominion" was nothing other than "property real or personal."

Thus, the Aristotelian relationship between property and formative locations of ruling and being ruled (for example, the household) becomes in Harrington's scheme a movement and transformation from property-based power to moral and civic authority. Or what amounts to the same thing, property provides the power that becomes the basis for the virtuous, disciplined, and civic-minded independence of self-governing citizens in a commonwealth. Since a republic is a form of "popular government," the capacity for virtuous independence must exist among "the many" and not just "the one" or "the few." Following Machiavelli, Harrington said that there must be a large enough number of citizens with the resources and the motivation to bear arms in defense of public liberty. But for Harrington, the key to both citizen militias and republican government was the availability of property. Property, and especially property in land, must be distributed widely enough to provide for popular government.

It is at this point that the Machiavellian moment of mastery of historical circumstances was evinced in Harrington's thought. Republican property arrangements were seen as the product of historical processes through which fortune distributes and redistributes property, and especially property in land. Furthermore, it was axiomatic for Harrington and other classical republicans of the early modern era that property is the source of both power and authority. Consequently, in distributing or redistributing property, fortune was also thought to be distributing and redistributing power and the capacity for those with property and power to realize themselves as authoritative, self-governing political beings. It was Harrington's hope—and conviction—that the historical distribution of property in seventeenth-century England was such that the balance of proprietary dominion over land had shifted in the direction of the many rather than the one or the few, and that this created propitious circumstances for the creation of a commonwealth, a republic: "And if the whole people be landlords, or hold the lands so divided among them, that no one man, or number of men, within the compass of the few or aristocracy, overbalance them, the empire (without the interposition of force) is a commonwealth."[48] The implication was clear: The time had come to seize the moment made possible by historical circumstances and establish a republic in England.

This is evidence of the kind of commitment to a rough equality of conditions that attracts some of today's civic republicans to the tradition of civic humanist prudence.[49] This commitment led Harrington to propose an "agrarian law" limiting the size of landed estates.[50] But what contemporary civic republicans have failed to confront is the fact that this commitment was bound up with a masters' vision of civic virtue, which for classical republicans like Harrington meant that the macro-level, constitutional mastery of historical circumstances provided by a propitious "balance" of property needed to be supported by paternalistic rule and guardianship at the micro-level of the household estate. The following characterization of Harrington's understanding of property by Pocock underscores this point in dramatic, if overstated, fashion: "Property and power are the prerequisites of authority and virtue. They discharge no other function than that of the *oikos* in Aristotle and need not (although they do) possess any other social or 'economic characteristics than those which distinguish masters from servants."[51]

Pocock goes too far in suggesting that the only really important function of the Harringtonian freehold estate had to do with distinguishing masters from servants. For one thing, this seems to identify Harringtonian republicanism with the Aristotelian defense of slavery, when in fact part of the significance of Harrington's thought for us is precisely that it shows that the early modern republican defense of oikonomic man need not be accompanied (although it sometimes was of course) by a defense of slavery itself. In addition, Pocock's description does not do justice to the conceptual structure of internal goods in Harrington's thought. Pocock would have us believe that Harrington's theory contained an early version of Hannah Arendt's sharp separation of the private and public spheres, and that like Arendt, Harrington conceptualized republican virtue in terms of citizens emerging from the private realm of power relations pertaining to the provision of bodily needs into the public realm of action among civic peers.[52] This is clearly seen in another of Pocock's descriptions of Harrington's vision of propertied independence: "Property brings power: the power of masters over servants, the power of masters over themselves; but whenever fortune has brought about the existence of a sufficient number of masters, these may leave the domain of power and enter that of authority."[53] The problem is that this leaves out the formative dimension of the relationship between property and internal goods. Harrington's citizens did not magically acquire authoritative civic virtue simply by leaving the household and entering the public sphere of positive-libertarian engagements. Rather, the movement from dominion to power to authority involved the formation of virtue *within* the sphere of dominion. More to the point of the masters' vision of civic virtue, Harrington's "landlords" emerged as citizens with a capacity for virtuous civic independence after having had the formative experience of being the virtuous guardian of the household estate and its inhabitants.

Harrington did not have the same teleology of property as Aristotle, but there is nonetheless a teleological trajectory in Harrington's vision of propertied independence that connects property as dominion to the cultivation of virtue. The favorable distribution of property through history made it possible for "the many" to be *in* authority (at least to some extent). But without the widespread development of the capacity to be *an* authority with the virtues and excellences of republican character, historical circumstances could not be mastered and the cycle of corruption and decay would set in.

So for reasons both theoretical and practical, the recovery of "ancient prudence" involved the recovery of both the art of governing in the common interest and the art of household management. In contrast to most post-socialist philosophers and theorists who have appealed to Aristotle (including, of course, many contemporary civic republicans) Harrington evinced an awareness of the importance of household management within the Aristotelian understanding of practical reason.[54] For both Aristotle and Harrington, this meant that a preoccupation with acquisitiveness, moneymaking, or luxury was contrary to the virtuous governance of a household or estate. But for both, it also meant that the civic capacity of free masters was defined in relation to the presumed incapacity of those who were not master-guardians of households or estates or, more broadly, those who, for "natural" or social reasons, were presumed to be in a situation of civic dependency.

"If a man has some estate," Harrington once wrote in a collection of aphorisms, "he may have some servants or a family, and consequently some government; if he has no estate, he has no government."[55] For early modern classical republicans such as Harrington, the notion of having "some government" (and someone to govern) was of singular importance. A man with "some estate" to govern would be better prepared for self-government, particularly if the estate being governed was a freehold. It was hoped that by owning and governing such estates, freemen would have the experience, the leisure, and, of course, the independence deemed necessary for the deliberations and the defense of a "popular commonwealth." Take away this governance of estates, and the capacity for virtuous independence is endangered. It is homeless and groundless; or to use the language of contemporary postsocialist thought, it is in danger of becoming "socially disembodied" and "radically unencumbered." But with a sufficiently large number of independent masters and household guardians, corruption and despotism would be less likely and public liberty more secure, although still a difficult art.

Clearly, then, the question of the distribution of "goods of fortune" was necessarily also a question of the distribution of civic capacities. And these questions were related in turn to the question of which modes of property were most compatible with the "natural and acquired virtues" necessary for the difficult art of public liberty. Thus, Harrington was "of Aristotle's opinion, that a commonwealth of husbandmen . . . must be the best of all others."[56] By the same token, he shared Aristotle's skepticism regarding the capacities of menial laborers and ordinary mechanics for virtuous participation in the debates and deliberations of the commonwealth. As Harrington put it in connection with a defense of a "natural" aristocracy: "Your mechanics, till they have feathered their nests—like the fowls of the air, whose whole employment is to seek their food—are so busied in their private concerns that they have neither leisure to study the public, nor are safely entrusted with it . . . because a man is not faithfully embarked in this ship if he have no share in the freight."[57]

In addition to household relations and occupational status, there were other dimensions of mastery that were common to Aristotle and Harrington, most notably, those pertaining to race and gender. With Harrington, as with Aristotle, race and gender often were closely linked to property-related, distributive contexts of civic capacity. For example, when Harrington wrote that "paternal power is in the right of nature" and is "the natural root of a commonwealth," he was not only expressing deeply rooted patriarchal assumptions.[58] He was also evoking the context of estate governance spelled out in the above aphorism.

Reading Harrington's aphorism in light of its Aristotelian provenance, we get a good sense of the relative ease with which the conceptual structure of internal goods could be used to defend and rationalize the emerging system of modern slavery.[59] After all, we are dealing with a masters' vision of civic virtue. In my view, the connection between classical republicanism and modern slavery has received far too little attention in the texts of the contemporary revival of republican virtue. To encounter this connection is to bring the classical republican horizon of civic independence and socio-economic dependency into bold and dramatic relief. Within this horizon of relational hierarchy slavery appeared to both Aristotelian and neo-roman classical republicans as the very antithesis of liberty, the pure case of oppressive subjection and dependency, of being subject to the arbitrary will of rulers.[60] But precisely because classical republican identity was built on a foundation of relational hierarchy, the contrast between freedom and slavery could also be deployed in defense of slavery, say, among southern slaveholders in the Americas.[61] David Hume may not have been sufficiently evenhanded or circumspect but he was not entirely off the mark when he made the following observation about civic humanist republicanism and slavery: "some passionate admirers of the ancients, and partizans of civil liberty . . . cannot forbear regretting the loss of this institution; and whilst they brand all submission to the government of a single person with the harsh denomination of slavery, they would gladly reduce the greater part of mankind to real slavery and subjection."[62]

Yet Harrington's aphorism is also important because it reminds us that the problem of republican paternalism is not only a problem of slavery. It may well be that Harrington and some of the thinkers who were influenced by him regretted aspects of the loss of ancient Greek and Roman systems of slavery. Harrington certainly seems to have thought that household servants—or indeed all those who lacked the economic resources necessary for civic independence—were akin to the slaves of the Aristotelian household with respect to their dependency.[63] But Harrington is also one of many early modern classical republicans who affirmed a new, more modern form of oikonomic mastery without at the same time affirming a slave economy. The masters' vision of civic virtue was articulated within a broad discursive framework of republican paternalism. It was a framework that, alas, was capacious and flexible enough for a defense of slavery. But as with Harrington, it was also capacious and flexible enough to defend virtuous propertied independence without explicitly defending slavery. And with Montesquieu, we find a thinker who combined a variation of republican mastery not only with strong and quite explicit moral opposition to slavery, but also with a defense of the modern commercial republic. Again, the language of civic virtue cuts in many different directions.

Of course, the removal of slavery from the masters' vision of civic virtue did not put an end to exclusion and marginalization on the basis of things like race, gender, occupation, and economic class. Even without slavery, relational hierarchy remained at the core of the classical republican response to the corruptive power of acquisitiveness and commerce. And Harrington's aphorism underscores this as well. The estate that Harrington idealized as a formative context of governance was constituted on the basis of a hierarchical structure of labor and authority that at the very least had a strong family resemblance to the structure affirmed in Aristotle's theory of the household. It was men who he hoped would have "some estate to govern," and this meant that these male masters would be governing their wives and their servants as well as their children.

These property-related contexts of labor, authority, and civic identity are also constitutive of the placeness of Harringtonian property. Perhaps because he was writing so much closer to the era of modern thingness, the placeness of Harrington's freehold estate seems even stranger (hermeneutically speaking) than the placeness of Aristotle's household. It is as if Harrington would have us believe that one governs the things and objects of property. And we want to say, no, people are governed; property is about things that are acquired, possessed, exchanged, or otherwise controlled, but not governed.

Writing in the context of mid-seventeenth century English political and legal culture, it was impossible for Harrington to discuss property without a large measure of proprietary thingness. But unless we recognize the placeness of property within his theory, it is almost impossible to make sense of his claim about the close relationship between having an estate and having some government. From the vantage point of modern thingness, this relationship appears as being at most a contingent empirical one having to do with causality or probabilistic correlation—for instance, that a man who owns an estate is more likely to have family or servants to govern. Clearly, however, Harrington did not have in mind a merely contingent, empirical relationship between having an estate and having some government. Rather, he had in mind a structural, conceptual relationship. Having some estate *means* having some family or servants to govern; having some estate *means* having some government. One does not simply own an estate; one governs it as a landlord and master, and this act of governance helps to constitute the estate as a location of labor and authority, and ultimately, as a location within which the capacity for republican engagements is constituted.

One way to make sense of Harrington's understanding of property is to think of it as an inscription of Aristotelian placeness into the framework of real and personal property. While Harrington identified the "dominion" of property with both real and personal property, the former was clearly privileged in his theory of virtuous propertied independence. More precisely, Harrington privileged real property in the form of a freehold estate in land. This represents a substantial revision of Aristotelian placeness. Recall that for Aristotle the key question for making distinctions relating to property had to do with how different property instruments served the ends and purposes of the location. Hence, the full placeness of the household was not defined by the household's status as an appurtenance of the land on which it rested, but rather by how adequately the "animate" and "inanimate" instruments served the household's moral and civic ends. Still, Harrington's emphasis on real property helps to þring his Aristotelian theory into the modern conceptual range. Governance of a landed estate evokes notions of the inhabitation of land that are part of the residuum of modern real property. The distinction between real and personal property also makes the idea of the corruptive power of commerce more accessible. After all, a commercial republic represents the triumph of personal property, and one cannot govern personal property in the same way that real property can be governed. Personal property is by definition movable property, and as such it always threatens to transgress and efface the boundaries of inhabitation that make it possible for estates to be governed.

For classical republicans like Harrington, the freehold estate seemed to provide a stable location for the cultivation of moral and civic virtue. It might be said that real property was the ground of virtuous liberty. But this ground was not only an object of claims and rights. It was also a place to be ruled and governed by master-guardians. Without the placeness of guardianship, it would be especially difficult to bring about the harmonization of "external goods of fortune" with "internal goods of the mind." By the same token, threats to the placeness of the estates of master-landlords—whether in the form of government policies that promoted financial speculation or simply the inordinate pursuit of movable property—generated anxieties in which fear about corruption was bound up with fear about the enslavement and dependency of masters.

The placeness of the Harringtonian estate also helps to illuminate the broadly Aristotelian understanding of positive liberty within Harrington's classical republicanism. Today's neoclassical republicans want to claim Harrington as one of their own in matters of liberty. This is not entirely unjustified. There are numerous signs of the neo-roman ideal of non-domination in Harrington's thought: the emphasis on property as a source of dominion and independence, concern about arbitrary rule, the contrast between independence and slavery, and Harrington's famous argument (contra Hobbes) that the freedom enjoyed in a popular government is necessarily greater than that enjoyed in a monarchy because in the latter even a man with considerable wealth and status lives "at the will of his lord."[64] But non-domination was not the sum total of Harringtonian freedom. Although undoubtedly important in and of itself, non-domination was conceptually bound up with liberty in the positive sense of being empowered to act as an authoritative, self-governing citizen. This was not some exaggerated idea of positive liberty as self-sacrificing devotion to the commonweal. Still, it was about citizens—or rather male citizen-masters—being virtuously empowered to bear arms and participate in elections and other public engagements in a manner consistent with common right and interest.

Even in its positive form, Harringtonian liberty was by no means purely Aristotelian. In some respects, the close connection between liberty and power sounds more like the modern understanding of positive liberty as empowerment than the Aristotelian understanding of collective deliberation. It is helpful here to call to mind the early modern republican axiom (as John Adams expressed it) that "power always follows property."[65] (Here, as in many other areas, Adams was following Harrington.) Now, this axiom certainly has elements of non-domination, and perhaps even some classical liberal negative liberty. For instance, one of its implications was that property should be kept out of the control and "lordship" of government officials and ministers. Propertied independence, it must be kept in mind, was defined in relation to dependency on government officials as well as in relation to dependents. Propertied *dependency* in any form was to be avoided, and as a condition among those men with the capacity for self-government, was a sign of corruption and a portent of slavery as well. And yet to say that power always follows property was also to say that male masters and landlords would be empowered to exercise their liberty as self-governing citizens by virtue of the dominion of their property.

As with the relationship between having some estate and having some government, the key to the relationship between property and positive-libertarian empowerment has to do with the fact that, under the idea of placeness, this relationship becomes a structural, conceptual one rather than one of empirical causation or probability. True, one could take the axiom that power always follows property as a form of hyperbole that, for the sake of scoring rhetorical points, overstates the empirical link between property and power. There probably was some of this going on with this axiom. But this certainly was not the end of the matter for early modern republicans of Harrington's type. And once again the reason has to do with the fact that the property that led to power was about both thingness and placeness. If Harrington had had only the thingness of property in mind when he wrote, "domestic empire is founded on dominion," his claim would have amounted to nothing more than that material holdings and assets are likely to cause or be associated with power. Power or its exercise, in this version, would not be conceptually entailed by the dominion of property. This way of looking at things would move Harrington's ideal of propertied independence closer to negative liberty and non-domination and farther way from positive liberty. In order for propertied independence to become a form of positive-libertarian empowerment, the exercise of power must be part of the propertied independence, whereas with both negative liberty and liberty as non-domination, liberty is defined not by the agent's exercise of power but by how others exercise power in relation to the agent. Having property or power might make it easier not to be interfered with or dominated by other actors, but it would not be integral to or constitutive of freedom itself. But clearly Harrington also had something in mind besides a contingent, empirical relationship between power and property, something that drew first power, and then authority, into the conceptual orbit of the domain of the estate and its inhabitants. Having and exercising power and authority thus become constitutive features of the independence and liberty of the master.

This brings us to the last area of comparison between Aristotle's and Harrington's thought I wish to explore, namely, the lack of a significant role for rights. The language of rights certainly can be found in Harrington's texts, as indeed we would expect in light of the ever-increasing presence and influence of rights in early modern European thinking about property and politics. But this makes it all the more striking that rights play a relatively minor role in Harrington's arguments about propertied independence. His is a decidedly virtue-centered rather than a rights-based approach to property. To draw once again on terms of analysis used by Pocock, it is a "civic humanist" rather than a "jurisprudential" perspective on property.[66] Especially noteworthy in this regard is the absence of natural law understandings of property of the type found in Grotius, Pufendorf, and Locke, among others.[67] Harrington employed the idea of natural rights in only two circumstances. First, there was a "common right" or "law of nature" that referred simply to that "interest of the whole, which is more excellent, and so acknowledged to be by the agents themselves, than the right or interest of the parts only."[68] In other words, Harrington saw it as a law of nature that the common good is more than a summation of the interests of individual citizens. Second, there was the aforementioned "right of nature" regarding "paternal power." As for property itself, its source was not a natural right established in a state of nature, but rather the distribution of property-related civic capacities by historical circumstances, as modified by the agrarian law that would guarantee a "sufficient" number of masters.

Natural Rights, Property, and the Persistence of Republican Paternalism

It would make things much easier for a defender of rights such as myself if

the growth of rights discourse in the early modern era provided a simple solution for the traditional problem of republican paternalism. But this is not
the case. In this regard, it is important to keep in mind that the small role
given to natural rights in Harrington's thought was something of an exception
to the rule within early modern classical republicanism. Natural rights took
on an increasingly important role as civic humanism moved in both neo-
roman and "liberal," Lockean directions, as for instance happened with the development of English Whig opposition thought in the latter part of the seventeenth century and throughout the eighteenth century.[69] There is an
important and troubling lesson here regarding the adaptability of republican
paternalism as it moved outside the theoretical and practical contexts of ancient oikonomic man and a household economy. This lesson will become especially clear when we turn to Montesquieu's more "liberal" and "bourgeois"
brand of commercial republicanism. But it is also a lesson about the relative
ease with which republican paternalism withstood the blending of civic humanist idioms of virtue and a jurisprudential discourse of natural rights.

Harrington's defense of the "natural right" of paternal power is itself an example of how a jurisprudential discourse of rights could support a masters'
vision of civic virtue. But a better example is provided by the eighteenth-
century English Whig opposition journalists, John Trenchard and Thomas
Gordon—or to use their more famous pseudonym, "Cato."

The authors of *Cato's Letters* had no difficulty characterizing property in
both Lockean terms of natural rights to the security of possession and person
and in classical republican terms of virtuous independence and the cultivation of civic capacity. Echoing Locke, Cato maintained that the people have as
"their highest Aim" the "Security of their Persons and Property." But echoing
Harrington, Cato argued that "the first Principle of all Power is Property."
Moreover, because "it is foolish to think that Men of Fortunes will be governed by those who have none," this first principle was very much one involving dominion over both people and things. "Men," Cato wrote, "will ever govern or influence those whom they employ, feed, and clothe, and who cannot
get the same necessary Means of Subsistence upon advantageous terms elsewhere. This is natural power, and will govern and constitute the political, and
certainly draw the latter after it, if Force be absent."[70]

A different, rather less liberal, but also very telling example is found in John
Adams's Calvinist form of classical republicanism. Building on Harrington,
Adams reformulated Aristotle's conceptual structure of internal goods in
terms of the relationship between "principles of power" and "principles of authority."[71] Under the former, Adams included wealth and the relations of
power, influence, and dependency growing out of the distribution of wealth.
By contrast, "principles of authority" referred to "virtues of the mind and

heart," including the "republican virtues" of frugality, prudence, temperance, and industry. With Adams, the civic humanist dialectic of external and internal goods moved in a more traditionally conservative direction than one finds in either Harrington or Cato. In Adams's view, inequalities of wealth were necessary and desirable for the establishment of a "natural aristocracy." At bottom, this was because "all the rich men will have many of the poor, in the various trades, manufactures, and other occupations in life, dependent upon them for their daily bread."[72] Here we see the relational hierarchy of the masters' vision of civic virtue being extended well beyond the household estate to the context of a more elaborate and more modern division of labor. But the key point right now is that Adams freely and frequently combined his "puritanical republicanism" (to use Forrest McDonald's term) with the language of natural rights.[73] Property itself was based on a natural right according to Adams, as were its alienation and transfer.[74]

By way of summary, classical republicans of the early modern era were often quite concerned with a *rightful* dominion over things, in the hope, furthermore, that this dominion would be secure from government authority and especially from the encroachment of a centralized executive. Again, Harrington himself seldom employed jurisprudential language of the type associated with negative rights. But so-called "neo-Harringtonians" such as Cato and Henry Neville frequently used the language of natural and "unalienable" property rights and even, on occasion, wrote of property in terms of a state of nature. It is also certainly the case that American republicans combined jurisprudence (both natural and otherwise) with classical idioms and understandings of virtuous independence. Moreover, as with the English opposition thinkers and republicans who influenced them, American republicans were anxious to have a security of person and property against government encroachment.[75]

Classical republican usage of the language of jurisprudence added a new wrinkle to the tension between the external good of movable, personal property and the internal goods of virtue. It became possible to conceptualize this tension as one involving property rights in conflict with virtue insofar as the former referred to commercial and mercantile modes of property. Cato called for both the security of commercial property rights *and* for public-spirited and manly resistance to luxury. Cato argued along neo-roman lines that the civil liberty of republican government would make for a flourishing regime of trade, and that this was impossible under arbitrary government. But commerce was also in tension with manly virtue because it "is a coy and humorous Dame, who must be won by Flattery and Allurements."[76] In a manner more akin to Montesquieu's defense of "economic commerce" (see below) than Harrington's balance of freehold estates, Cato believed that the key was to leave the task of flattering and alluring the dame of commercial *fortuna* in the hands of the free masters and master-proprietors of a republic.

Adams was also concerned about the effect of commercial property on republican virtue, although in his case it was the threat to "natural" aristocratic virtue that was most important. Clinging to a static view of political economy while simultaneously upholding the fundamental right to transfer and alienate property, Adams worried that the transfer of property would entail the transfer of the internal goods of republican virtue. Like many other early modern republicans, Adams was especially concerned about a political-economic system of credit and speculation. He feared that such a system would create too many economic opportunities for those who did not have "republican virtues" such as industriousness and frugality, thereby undoing the dialectic of principles of power and principles of authority.[77]

Yet in extolling "republican virtues" like industriousness, temperance, and frugality, Adams was also extolling virtues that we have come to associate with the rise of commercial economic man in Western history. This evocation of the Protestant work ethic fits nicely with Adams's Calvinism. However, it also points to another variation in classical republican thinking about property and commerce. I am referring to the efforts of early modern republicans to redeploy the virtues of oikonomic mastery on behalf of republican commerce. This puts it too baldly. As the case of Cato suggests, the process of moving towards a commercial republicanism was halting and ambivalent. A flourishing regime of trade and commerce was to be desired, but given the effeminate characteristics of commerce, it also had to be mastered. (This is not commercial republicanism with Adam Smith's invisible hand, or for that matter, the visible hand of Smith's scientific legislator.) Moreover, a simple project involving the redeployment of oikonomic virtues was impossible given the inherent mobility of commercial property and personality. For Adams and many others, the virtues of republican oikonomic man were in deep conflict with the mobility of economic property and personality.

But these tensions notwithstanding, it is possible to find the virtues of an emerging commercial economic man alongside the virtues of oikonomic man. And this too is an aspect of the republican tradition that rarely appears in contemporary civic republican narratives of their tradition. Indeed, the possibility that classical republicanism made its own contributions to the rise of a "liberal" regime of commerce is anathema to most present-day civic republicans.[78]

As contradictory as it first seems, Harrington's republicanism should itself be seen as making contributions to this more modern commercial republicanism.[79] One reason for this is that within Harrington's thought, the classical oikonomic virtues of household management appeared in conjunction with, and not in complete opposition to, economic virtues such as industriousness, self-reliance, and frugality. Both types of virtue were seen as supporting the order, the discipline, and the internal goods of republican liberty. This interaction between oikonomic and economic virtues points to the persistence of the masters' vision of civic virtue even as classical republicanism was reformulated in the form of a more commercial republicanism. That is to say, this reformulation did not mark the disappearance of the masters' vision so much as a shift in its location from the household to the market.

Republican Mastery in the Market: Montesquieu's Commercial Republicanism

This brings us to Montesquieu. He provides the best example of a commercial republicanism, for in his thought, oikonomic man begins to assume the guise of a republican merchant and the virtues of oikonomic mastery exist alongside an appreciation for the distinctive virtues of merchants as well as the virtues of commercial institutions and instruments such as banks and bills of exchange.

As Albert Hirschman has shown, Montesquieu was a major figure in the eighteenth-century project of defending commerce as a peaceful and civilizing force, which, at least in its "economic" forms, would promote a marriage of rational self-interest with good republican government.[80] It is possible to see this in terms of a tension in Montesquieu's thought between its civic humanist and liberal dimensions. This interpretation is suggested by some civic republican narratives of the history of the problem of a commercial republic.[81] Alternatively, it could be argued that Montesquieu was simply recognizing what more aristocratic classical thinkers were unable to recognize, namely, that so long as self-interested acquisitiveness is constrained and supported by economic virtues and the constitutional procedures of limited representative government, it will promote both republican liberty and prosperity.[82]

The problem I have with both of the above readings of Montesquieu's commercial republicanism is not that they are completely wrong, but that they are incomplete to the point of obscuring the problem of republican paternalism. More precisely, they leave out the commercial republican reformulation of the masters' vision of civic virtue that is contained in *The Spirit of the Laws*. To be sure, this vision is accompanied by a rather attenuated form of the Aristotelian structure of internal goods. There is less emphasis on positive liberty, and also of course far greater emphasis on instrumental economic virtues of the type associated with a capitalist market economy. Moreover, Montesquieu's commercial republicanism does not have a teleology of the market to replace Aristotle's teleology of household-based property. The Aristotelian household is not about things like profit, so "true wealth" in the household is defined in terms of service to the non-economic ends and goods of the household and its members. Even so, the structure of internal goods persists in Montesquieu's commercial republicanism, and in one respect at least, Montesquieu is more purely Aristotelian in his approach to external and internal goods than Harrington. Unlike Harrington, Montesquieu does not seek to ground this relationship in the framework of real versus personal property. Naturally, it is movable, personal property that comes to the fore in Montesquieu's political economy. While this translates into a decidedly un-Aristotelian emphasis on the commercial mobility of property in the form of "long distance trade," it also means that property and its values are once again being defined as instrumentalities within and for the infrastructural, institutional locations that connect economic life to public life. The difference—and it is an enormous one—is that the most important of these infrastructural locations is now the market rather than the household. Yet Montesquieu shows us that civic virtue and paternalistic republican guardianship can be integrated into the modern commercial republic—a rather different possibility than what contemporary civic republicans have in mind when they enlist the support of traditional republican views of the problem of a commercial republic.

Let us look first at what Montesquieu says about the corruptive power of "the spirit of extreme equality" in so-called "democratic republics": "As far as the sky is from the earth, so far is the true spirit of equality from the spirit of extreme equality. The former consists neither in making everyone command nor in making no one command, but in obeying and commanding only one's equals. It seeks not to have no master but to have only one's equals as masters."[83]

This passage shows us that the classical paradigm of mastery has by no means completely dropped out of sight in Montesquieu's thought. However, things get rather more complicated when we consider what Montesquieu had to say on subjects closer to his heart—for example, the separation of powers and the civilizing effects of commerce. Specifically, we discover a reduced commitment to the civic humanist understanding of the intrinsic moral excellence of participatory public liberty. In this respect, we find a tendency in Montesquieu's thought in the direction of the same kind of "transvaluation of public and private" which Isaac Kramnick has uncovered in the commercial republicanism of the American founding.[84] In the case of Montesquieu, this tendency is evinced in the identification of political liberty with an almost Lockean affirmation of the private security of person and property, or the "opinion" and expectation thereof.[85]

As this suggests, there is also something of a transvaluation of classical republican understandings of property and property-related locations of virtuous guardianship. Property is not only linked more closely to a juridical idiom of rights and the rightful ownership of things. It is also more closely, and more affirmatively, associated with its commodity form. For the most part, Montesquieu was a theorist of modern thingness rather than ancient placeness. However, these transvaluations are far from total in Montesquieu's vision of a commercial republic. There is an important counter-tendency in the direction of civic understandings of liberty, virtue, and even property. This counter-tendency is not unique to Montesquieu's brand of commercial republicanism. But what Montesquieu provides us with is a clear picture of how it was associated with a reformulation of the two key dimensions of classical mastery: a vision of civic capacity as a hierarchical relationship between independent masters and their dependents, and a formative project of paternalistic guardianship.

Perhaps the most obvious example of this reformulation is found in Montesquieu's discussion of the legislative power in what he took to be the English system of separated powers. The discussion starts with a reaffirmation of the civic humanist ideal of positive public liberty: "As, in a free state, every man, considered to have a free soul, should be governed by himself, the people as a body should have legislative power."[86] Having said this, Montesquieu immediately begins to elaborate a hierarchical view of civic capacity in which the capacity of the voting public for self-government is restricted to choosing their deputies in the representative body of the legislature. Along the way, he defends a separate legislative assembly for "persons distinguished by their birth, riches, or honors." The guardianship functions of this body of "nobles" would be largely negative, limited to "tempering" and vetoing the powers of the executive and the popular assembly. Still, Montesquieu leaves no doubt as to his continuing concerns about "the spirit of extreme equality." If those distinguished by "birth, riches, or honors" are "mixed among the people and if they had only one voice like the others, the common liberty would be their enslavement."[87]

This sounds like a reworking of classical republican ideas of "mixed" government—and it is. But unlike Aristotle, Polybius, Machiavelli, and Harrington, Montesquieu was explicitly defending a commercial republic. It can be said that he was searching for ways to combine the personal rule and guardianship of a "moderate" republican mastery with the security, prosperity, and peaceful mores that he associated with an impersonal system of market exchange. In part, this was simply a matter of appropriating mercantilist ideas of state regulation for the purpose of a republican superintendence of commercial growth and development.[88] But Montesquieu also expressed support for two less state-centered and more distinctively republican possibilities. First, there was the possibility of recasting the masters' vision of civic virtue on behalf of the civic leadership of merchants. To support the spirit of republican economy, Montesquieu argued, commerce should be carried on by the "principal citizens" of the republic, and most especially by those merchants whose "great enterprises . . . are always necessarily mixed with public business."[89] In effect, the masters' vision was in the process of going underground and reappearing as a purportedly "softer" merchant's vision, with the location of virtuous guardianship shifting from classical (and aristocratic) households to what we would think of as one's market position.

Second, there was the possibility of a more systemic form of mastery whereby the discipline that is necessary to sustain a "free state" is promoted through practices of market competition. Here, Montesquieu was less forthcoming. Still, the basic message is clear: In conjunction with the civic-minded guardianship of leading merchants and other distinguished citizens, what is needed is a general public which has received a civic and economic education in the discipline and instrumental virtues of "frugality, economy, moderation, work, wisdom, tranquility, order, and rule."[90] Or in contemporary conservative parlance, what is needed is a public that is constrained and motivated by "market incentives." And according to Montesquieu (and many contemporary conservatives), so long as the virtuous discipline of market competition remains intact, there is no need to be concerned about the corruptive power of large accumulations of wealth.[91]

To be sure, there are deep and probably irreconcilable tensions within this emerging paradigm of economic mastery. For one thing, there is a tension between even the attenuated civic virtues of economic discipline and the type of self-interested acquisitiveness which, for example, Montesquieu associated with the spirit of English commercialism.[92] In addition, there is a tension between the effort to retain some political control of the market through a visible hand of guardianship and the encouragement of an impersonal market system characterized by the heightened mobility of both property and personality.[93] Writing at what might be called the "rosy dawn" of commercial republicanism, Montesquieu seems not to have been completely aware of the depth of such tensions. Nevertheless, Montesquieu's vision of commercial republicanism has some unsettling implications for the current revival of civic virtue. Especially in a conservative era when the moral and civic virtues of market discipline and business success are so often celebrated, it should not surprise us to discover that our republican heritage has made its own contributions to the ideological defense of Western capitalism and its structures and mechanisms of power and authority.[94] But more than this, Montesquieu's commercial republicanism shows us that, contrary to the views of many contemporary republican theorists and historians, the republican tradition of civic virtue survived into the modern era of the commercial republic in the form of a vision of paternalistic civic guardianship, and not simply as a lingering civic humanist critique of privatism and acquisitiveness. In fact, there is an important sense in which the forms of economic mastery within modern commercial republicanism are even more hierarchical and exclusionary than the oikonomic mastery of Harrington's type. The percentage of household masters in a Harringtonian republic would necessarily be much greater than the percentage of merchants in Montesquieu's commercial republic. Hence, the shift in the location of republican mastery from the household estate to economic institutions such as the business firm or the corporation represents a shift in the "balance" of property-based dominion from "the many" to "the few." Recall in this regard Adams's astute observation about how "all the rich men will have many of the poor, in the various trades, manufactures, and other occupations in life, dependent upon them for their daily bread."

Of course, modern republican mastery has taken economic forms that neither Montesquieu nor Adams could possibly have imagined. But it is not all that difficult to see the persistence of republican mastery when we are attentive to it. For instance, it is easy enough to imagine a late-modern corporate managers' vision of civic virtue in which the model of good government is a well-run business corporation and in which a company's market position is seen as an important indicator of a business leader's capacity for authoritative management of the government. This vision, or something very much like it, seems to have considerable currency among conservatives and "centrists" in contemporary American politics. Alternatively, there is a vision of politics that has grown up with the mass media of consumer capitalism. I have in mind a celebrities' vision of civic virtue in which the model leader is a master communicator who manipulates images and symbols so as to sway and rule citizen-consumers. Civic capacity might be linked to market position in this vision as well, but more immediately it is determined by market penetration in the sense of an ability to "capture" a substantial segment of the voting market.

Republican Paternalism and the Oppositionist Self

The point of all this is not, of course, that today's left-leaning civic republicans are themselves advocates of a hierarchical, paternalistic, and patriarchal vision of property and citizenship. The point, rather, is that today's civic republicans have failed to answer the question—indeed, they seldom have asked the question—of how one addresses the dangers of possessive individualism without creating new forms of republican paternalism.

The classical republican paradigms of oikonomic and economic mastery provide compelling evidence that the relationship between external and internal goods is far more complex than today's civic republicans believe. For classical republicans, the cultivation of internal goods was inextricably connected to the arrangement and organization of external goods. The formative project was simultaneously a distributive project by virtue of the fact that the cultivation of internal goods occurred within property-related structures of labor, dominion, and authority. In sharp contrast to today's theorists of republican virtue, classical republicans quite self-consciously and quite systematically explicated their formative project as one with inherent distributive conditions and consequences. And this points to a significant contrast between classical and contemporary accounts of the relationship between the formative and distributive dimensions of a politics of civic virtue. Whereas today's civic republican theorists focus exclusively on the formative dimension of republican capacity, or at most, see this dimension as only contingently related to the distributive dimension, classical republicans saw these dimensions as being structurally and constitutively related to one another. This, it might be said, is what gave the classical republican vision of a politics of civic virtue its socioeconomic "teeth" as a perspective in search of practical ways to ensure the conditions of virtuous republican agency and liberty in the face of corruptive tendencies toward tyranny and despotism.

"The classical republican tradition," the American historian Linda Kerber has written, "assumed that deliberation was possible only in small and exclusive communities; the absence of dependent classes—defined by race, gender, and property—was *essential* to the republican view of the world, not an easily correctable accident."[95] Of course, things were a bit more complicated than this suggests. Still, there is a very large grain of truth in Kerber's analysis. Translated into my terms, her point is that the question of how to cultivate a republican capacity (e.g., through "small and exclusive communities") was essentially (i.e., structurally rather than merely contingently) conditioned by a hierarchical distribution of republican capacities among different groups and classes.

The larger theoretical lesson here is that the greater the extent to which the formative and distributive dimensions of republican capacity are seen as structurally conditioning one another, the greater the likelihood that republicanism will move in the direction of a hierarchical and paternalistic conception of citizenship. If this is the case, then it follows that the shift from a republican equality among masters and guardians to a more inclusive modern democratic understanding of equal citizenship is a change of major proportions with respect to the horizon of implicit understandings pertaining to civic identity and agency.

Some might object at this point that I have focused too much on the "darker side" of the republican tradition. Perhaps, for example, the problem of republican paternalism could be addressed simply by broadening the encounter with the republican tradition to include more democratic and egalitarian expressions of civic virtue, for example, Jeffersonian republicanism or, better yet (in light of Jefferson's racism), the various nineteenth-century movements of producerism and populism. After all, the insights and idioms of *these* episodes have also been recovered in the texts of the revival.[96] While I agree that there have been important expressions of republican virtue that are more democratic and egalitarian, there is an important sense in which such a broadening of the tradition merely raises an additional question regarding the new understandings of property and identity which accompanied, and made possible, this movement away from the masters' vision of civic virtue. In this regard, there is reason to think that this "gestalt shift" in the practical meaning of republican virtue and independence is associated with a reordering of property as a context of republican identity. What I have in mind is a shift from property as a two-fold dominion over things and persons to property as a dominion of ownership, which, in principle at least, is separate from jurisdiction over other citizens.[97]

It will be helpful at this point to look at the efforts of the civic republican legal theorist Frank Michelman to develop a distinctively republican conception of property rights. Michelman is one of only a handful of contemporary civic republicans who have encountered Harrington's thought in a sustained manner.[98] To my knowledge, he is also the only civic republican who has approached the problem of a commercial republic from the point of view of a reappropriated understanding of virtuous propertied independence.[99] According to Michelman, "in a republican perspective," property rights "become a matter of constitutive political concern as underpinning the independence and authenticity of the citizen's contribution to the collective determinations of public life."[100] Aware of the darker possibilities within the republican tradition, Michelman seeks to separate his approach from what he terms the "exclusionary" republican "strategy." This strategy "lets property distribution be determined extrapolitically, by the family and market, and then restricts the franchise to persons whose resultant holdings meet a minimum standard."[101] Instead, he reappropriates the "inclusionary" republican "strategy" which "strives through public law for the broadest feasible distribution of whatever property in whatever form is considered minimally prerequisite to political competence."

This strikes me as a valuable corrective to the abstract moral authority of Sandel's public-spirited guardianship community. By emphasizing propertied independence along with more expansive civic understandings, Michelman provides the self who is situated in a paternalistic and hierarchical context of guardianship with conceptual and practical resources of opposition that are not necessarily available to the situated self envisioned by Sandel and many other communal republicans. However, Michelman begs the question of how an "inclusionary" vision of propertied independence is to emerge from the "exclusionary" foundations of a masters' vision of civic virtue. This indeed is another example of the hermeneutic strategy of avoiding an encounter with the tradition of republican paternalism by reappropriating only the democratic potential of classical republicanism. In Michelman's own terms, it is a strategy of attempting to "extract" only "the best" that the republican tradition "has to offer us."[102]

In part, the problem is that Michelman has interpreted the "exclusionary strategy" of the republican tradition as one based on the "extrapolitical" factors of the family and the market, when in fact there was nothing at all "extrapolitical" about the family and the market in the paradigms of oikonomic and economic mastery we have considered in this chapter. Michelman seems to be saying that the contexts of the household and the market are illegitimate insofar as they are hierarchical or "exclusionary" contexts of civic capacity and guardianship. This brings us to the crux of the problem, which as I see it, is that the movement from a masters' vision of virtuous propertied independence to Michelman's "inclusionary" vision involves a profound reordering of the practical meaning of "independence" in relation to property-related contexts of authority, jurisdiction, and guardianship. We have seen that within the masters' vision, independence is both defined and constituted in relational terms of the dependency of those people deemed to lack the capacity for republican engagements and civic guardianship. In other words, starting with the classical household and continuing through the commercial marketplace, independence is defined and constituted in relational terms of ruling and being ruled. Necessarily, therefore, Michelman's inclusionary strategy involves a form of independence in which the self is defined apart from such property-related contexts of ruling and being ruled. And at this point, we begin to catch a glimpse of a self whose agency is something other than that of the model citizen whose "ancient prudence" today's civic republicans have sought to reappropriate for democratic ends. I have in mind a moment of democratic agency—an oppositionist moment—in which the self stands apart from, and in opposition to, the ends and purposes of her would-be guardians.

Such an oppositionist self bears a family resemblance to the unencumbered, rights-bearing self who is the object of so much communal republican criticism. But the resemblance is a superficial one that does not reach the ontological depths of an atomistic individualism. No, the oppositionist self is very much a social and political being, and she is quite capable of solidaristic attachments with other citizens who share her fate of being excluded or marginalized as a second-class citizen. But these attachments are born of the desire to claim (or reclaim) one's rightful jurisdiction and independence as a democratic citizen, and one's dignity as a human being.

I have no doubt that the classical tradition of civic humanist republicanism has made its own contributions to the development of this oppositionist moment in Western history. What is the classical republican ideal of virtuous resistance to tyranny if not an expression—indeed, a revolutionary expression—

of oppositionist political agency? The oppositionist self also bears a strong affinity to the neo-roman understanding of civic independence as non-domination. In both cases, the self is empowered as an independent guardian of her assets. As we have seen, however, the problem of republican paternalism is one that is faced by neoclassical republicans no less than communal republicans. The independence of the oppositionist democratic self is not—must not be—constituted on the basis of the dependency of other, second-class citizens. And such a democratic form of independence is a rather more involved and complicated change in the democratic horizon than a simple preference for the inclusionary aspects of the republican tradition.

None of this means that an undemocratic paternalism always lurks in each and every one of the particular formative contexts mentioned by civic republicans—for example, the formative contexts of civic education in schools, community or national service, economic democracy, participation in civic associations, or, to use one of Daniel Kemmis's examples, barn raising in Montana.[103] What I am arguing, rather, is that the manner in which civic republicans have articulated the IG and R/P theses begs the question of the background of understandings and practices which would prevent the problem of republican paternalism. In other words, it is a question of the coherence of the civic republicans' vision of democratic citizenship, not necessarily a question of the normative commitments and particular policy proposals of civic republicans.

Conclusion

A critical hermeneutics requires that civic republicans confront not only the prejudices of the republican tradition, but also the prejudices of their own more or less submerged commitments to progressive modernity. Among the latter prejudices is that on behalf of modern thingness. Much of what contemporary civic republicans say about the problem of a commercial republic presupposes a regime of modern thingness. This is hardly surprising since modern thingness is hegemonic in late modern capitalism, and since late modern capitalism is the context within which civic republicans have developed their arguments about the corruptive power of commerce. But the presupposition of modern thingness also gives civic republican arguments about the problem of a commercial republic an appearance of elegance, order, and symmetry that masks the historical and theoretical complexity of the problem. Even my brief philosophical history of the problem shows that its development defies the kinds of sharp and neat moral distinctions between property and virtue, rights and virtue, and commerce and virtue that civic republicans are wont to make.

Viewed through the lens of modern thingness, the problem of a commercial republic looks like a fairly straightforward (if not easily overcome) problem of cultivating civic virtue to counter liberty-threatening values and practices pertaining to acquisitiveness, economic inequality, a proprietary model of rights and negative liberty, and a market model of social and political life. Property appears as the quintessential external good, a mere thing of utility that is always/already corruptive. And rights appear (at least to many communal republicans) as a necessary but also morally and civically dangerous analogue to property—possessions in their own right, and therefore with a corruptive potential that is essentially the same as that of property. But this picture becomes rather muddled when we approach the problem of a commercial republic from the point of view of the placeness of property as well as that of modern thingness. When we look at things this way the civic republican approach appears as a doubly misguided effort: first, because it reads modern thingness into the Aristotelian structure of external and internal goods; and second, because it reads the placeness of Aristotelian property *out* of this structure.

These misreadings of modern thingness and Aristotelian, civic humanist placeness allow civic republicans to claim the high ground of virtue against possessive individualism and commercialism. But the placeness of property, and for that matter the market, reveals how shaky the foundations are that support this claim. These foundations are constructed largely on the basis of a dualistic rather than dialectical approach to external and internal goods. To encounter the civic humanist tradition of placeness is to see that locations like the household and in a more limited way, the market itself, have been, and still can be, practical contexts of meaning within which external and internal goods are related to each other. The failure to account for such property-related institutional locations makes it even more difficult for civic republicans to develop a convincing alternative theoretical perspective on property and democratic citizenship. Such a theoretical perspective must deal with both the formative possibilities of property and its problematic possibilities with regard to the distribution and attribution of civic capacities among different groups and classes. We have seen that when civic republicans have sought to develop an alternative perspective on property—as with Sandel's concept of guardianship and Michelman's reappropriation of the ideal of propertied independence—they have overlooked the problematic connection between property and authority in the history of paternalistic guardianship. This is one more sign of the civic republicans' prejudice on behalf of modern thingness. Modern thingness not only privileges the commodity form of property, but also obscures the relationship between property and authority.

So the prejudice on behalf of modern thingness simultaneously privileges property as an object of exchange and an authority-less context. But the relationship between property and authority is also a big reason why the placeness of property is such a complicating and unsettling dimension of the problem of a commercial republic. We know that the placeness of property is not simply about formative contexts within which people learn how to use things of utility in a virtuous manner, but also about identity-forming structures of labor and authority. And as we have seen in the course of this chapter, the placeness of property in the tradition of civic humanist republicanism is grounded in a relational hierarchy of virtuous independence and virtuous dependence. Placeness, therefore, is partly about the potentially undemocratic distributive conditions and consequences of the formative project of developing an authoritative capacity for the use, management, and guardianship of things of utility. And this is an important reason for affirming oppositionist modes of democratic agency.

Notes

1. Maurizio Viroli goes so far as to claim that it is "a historiographical error" to interpret republicanism "as a form of political Aristotelianism." Viroli, *Republicanism* (New York: Hill and Wang, 2002), 65.

2. See my discussion in chapter 2 of the affinity between Quentin Skinner's defense of Cicero and civic humanism. Also see the discussion of Aristotle and Cicero in Iseult Honohan, *Civic Republicanism* (London: Routledge, 2002), 39–41.

3. J. G. A. Pocock, *The Machiavellian Moment: Florentine Political Thought and the Atlantic Republican Tradition* (Princeton, NJ: Princeton University Press, 1975).

4. See, for example, Amy Gutmann, "Communitarian Critics of Liberalism," in *Philosophy and Public Affairs* 14 (1985): 308–22; Don Herzog, "Some Questions for Republicans," *Political Theory* 14 (1986): 473–93; H. N. Hirsch, "The Threnody of Liberalism: Constitutional Liberty and the Renewal of Community," *Political Theory* 1986 (14): 423–49; Ruth H. Bloch, "The Gendered Meanings of Virtue," *Signs* 13 (1987): 37–58; Joan R. Gundersen, "Independence, Citizenship, and the American Revolution," *Signs* 13 (1987): 59–77; Jeffrey C. Issac, "Republicanism vs. Liberalism? A Reconsideration," *History of Political Thought* 9 (1988): 349–77; Linda Kerber, "Making Republicanism Useful," *The Yale Law Journal* 97 (1988): 1663–72; and Richard C. Sinopoli, *The Foundations of American Citizenship: Liberalism, the Constitution, and Civic Virtue* (New York: Oxford University Press, 1992).

5. Just how close to the surface such concerns are became clear in the wake of Michael J. Sandel's efforts to redescribe and reappropriate an American tradition of civic republicanism in *Democracy's Discontent: America in Search of a Public Philosophy* (Cambridge, MA: Belknap Press, 1996). See the various critiques of this project in Anita L. Allen and Milton C. Regan, Jr., eds., *Debating Democracy's Discontent: Essays on*

American Politics, Law, and Public Philosophy (Oxford: Oxford University Press, 1998).

6. Thomas Spragens, Jr., *Reason and Democracy* (Durham, NC: Duke University Press, 1990), 6. I note that Spragens intended this as a criticism of both post-socialist thinkers and liberal theorists like Rawls who have looked to history to help ground political principles.

7. Hans-Georg Gadamer, *Truth and Method*, 2nd ed. (New York: Crossroad, 1989), 295.

8. Barber, *Strong Democracy: Participatory Politics for a New Age* (Berkeley, CA: University of California Press), 90.

9. Skinner, *Liberty before Liberalism* (Cambridge: Cambridge University Press, 1997), 117. For a similar view of the functions and benefits of intellectual history, see Honohan, *Civic Republicanism*, 3–4.

10. Charles Taylor, "Philosophy and its History," in *Philosophy in History*, ed. Richard Rorty, J. B. Schneewind, and Quentin Skinner (Cambridge: Cambridge University Press, 1984), 26.

11. Robert N. Bellah, "Citizenship, Diversity, and the Search for the Common Good," in *"The Constitution of the People": Reflections on Citizens and Civil Society*, ed. Robert E. Calvert (Lawrence, KS: University Press of Kansas, 1991), 59. Also see Cass R. Sunstein's defense of his effort to redirect liberal constitutionalism along some traditional republican paths in "Beyond the Republican Revival," *The Yale Law Journal* 97 (1988): 1539–41.

12. Philip Pettit, *Republicanism* (Oxford: Clarendon Press, 1997), 129, 130–31, and 133.

13. Pettit, 110 and 129.

14. Pettit, 129.

15. For other examples of this strategy, see Sandel, *Democracy's Discontent*, 318; Honohan, *Civic Republicanism*, 190–91; and Charles Taylor, *Modern Social Imaginaries* (Durham, NC: Duke University Press, 2004), 146–49. Sandel's approach is especially revealing. He identifies the influence of the Western Enlightenment as the primary reason that republicanism moved away from the undemocratic view that the capacity for civic virtue is rooted in "fixed categories of birth or condition." One problem with this claim is that it overlooks distributive contexts of civic capacity such as property that were not constituted by classical republicans solely or entirely on the basis of fixed and "incorrigible" categories. In addition, there is the perplexing fact that Sandel links the democratization of the republican tradition to the very same Enlightenment that he and so many other post-socialist thinkers have seen as the principal source of the problems with liberal and progressive modernity. See Sandel's critique of the Enlightenment vision as one of "a universe empty of *telos*" in Michael J. Sandel, *Liberalism and the Limits of Justice*, 2nd ed. (Cambridge University Press, 1998), 175–78.

16. See, for example, William M. Sullivan, *Reconstructing Public Philosophy* (Berkeley, CA: University of California Press, 1986), 175–78 and 181; and Robert N. Bellah et al., *Habits of the Heart: Individualism and Commitment in American Life*, 2nd ed. (Berkeley, CA: University of California Press, 1996), 143–44 and 285.

17. Sunstein, "Beyond the Republican Revival," 1541. For other examples, see Frank I. Michelman, "Law's Republic," *The Yale Law Journal* 97 (1988): 1518; and Mary G.

Dietz's argument that the subjection of women plays "no necessary part" in Aristotle's "argument concerning politics and citizenship," in "Citizenship with a Feminist Face: The Problem with Maternal Thinking," *Political Theory* 13 (1985): 28.

18. See, for example, Richard Schlatter, *Private Property: The History of an Idea* (New Brunswick, NJ: Rutgers University Press, 1951), chapter 1, who does not even discuss Aristotle's theory of the household in his classic history of private property. On the difference between modern collectivism and the Aristotelian conception of common ownership, see Martha C. Nussbaum, "Aristotelian Social Democracy," in *Liberalism and the Good*, ed. R. Bruce Douglass, Gerald M. Mara, and Henry S. Richardson (New York: Routledge, 1990), 231–32.

19. Alan Ryan, *Property* (Minneapolis, MN: University of Minnesota Press, 1987), 16.

20. See William J. Booth, "The New Household Economy," *American Political Science Review* 85 (1991): 113–29.

21. Aristotle, *Politics*, ed. and trans. Ernest Barker (London: Oxford University Press, 1975), book I, 1253b, 9.

22. Aristotle, VII, 1323a, 280.

23. Nussbaum, "Aristotelian Social Democracy," 231.

24. Aristotle, *Politics*, I, 1256b, 21.

25. Aristotle, I, 1259b, 33–34.

26. Aristotle, I, 1256b, 21.

27. Aristotle, I, 1257a, 23–24

28. Aristotle, I, 1253b, 8–9.

29. Aristotle, I, 1254a–1254b, 11–14.

30. Aristotle, I, 1260a, 35.

31. Jurgen Habermas captured the ancient Greek formulation of the masters' vision of civic virtue in the opening pages of *The Structural Transformation of the Public Sphere: An Inquiry into a Category of Bourgeois Society*, trans. Thomas Burger (Cambridge, MA: The MIT Press, 1989), especially 3.

32. See, for example, Alasdair MacIntyre, *After Virtue: A Study in Moral Theory*, 2nd ed. (Notre Dame, IN: University of Notre Dame Press, 1984), chapter 12; Ronald Beiner, *Philosophy in a Time of Lost Spirit* (Toronto: University of Toronto Press, 1997), chapter 10; and Hans-Georg Gadamer, *Truth and Method*, 2nd ed. (New York: Crossroad, 1989), 312–24.

33. The discussion that follows is an extremely condensed and simplified account of the subtle and complex interpretation that has been developed by Pocock over the course of several years. In addition to *The Machiavellian Moment*, see J. G. A. Pocock, *Virtue, Commerce, and History: Essays on Political Thought and History, Chiefly in the Eighteenth Century* (Cambridge: Cambridge University Press, 1985); and his "Historical Introduction" in *The Political Works of James Harrington*, ed. J. G. A. Pocock (Cambridge: Cambridge University Press, 1977).

34. See Forrest McDonald, *Novus Ordo Seclorum: The Intellectual Origins of the Constitution* (Lawrence, KS: University of Kansas Press, 1985), 15–16 and 88–90.

35. See the discussion of Montesquieu in Pocock, "The Mobility of Property and the Rise of Eighteenth-Century Sociology," in *Virtue, Commerce, and History*, 111–14.

36. See James Harrington, *The Commonwealth of Oceana*, in *The Political Works of*

James Harrington, ed. J. G. A. Pocock (Cambridge: Cambridge University Press, 1977), 163–73; and Harrington, *A System of Politics Delineated in Short and Easy Aphorisms. Published from the Author's Own Manuscript,* in *The Political Works of James Harrington,* ed. Pocock, 835.

37. Pocock, *The Machiavellian Moment,* especially chapters 13 and 14. Also see Gordon S. Wood, *The Creation of the American Republic, 1776–1787* (New York: W. W. Norton and Company, 1969), especially 53–70 and 409–25; Lance Banning, *The Jeffersonian Persuasion: Evolution of a Party Ideology* (Ithaca, NY: Cornell University Press, 1978); Drew R. McCoy, *The Elusive Republic: Political Economy in Jeffersonian America* (Chapel Hill, NC: University of North Carolina Press, 1980); and McDonald, *Novus Ordo Seclorum,* especially chapters 3 and 4.

38. Pocock, *The Machiavellian Moment,* 391.

39. Compare, for instance, Pocock, *The Machiavellian Moment,* chapters 13 and 14 to Joyce Appleby, *Capitalism and the New Social Order: The Republican Vision of the 1790s* (New York: New York University Press, 1984), 9; Appleby, *Liberalism and Republicanism in the Historical Imagination* (Cambridge, MA: Harvard University Press, 1992), 124–39; and John P. Diggens, *The Lost Soul of American Politics: Virtue, Self-Interest, and the Foundations of Liberalism* (Chicago: University of Chicago Press, 1984), 143. Also see Ronald J. Terchek's discussion of the contrast between contemporary and classical republican views of property in *Republican Paradoxes and Liberal Anxieties* (Lanham, MD: Rowman and Littlefield, 1997), 6–8.

40. Two partial exceptions are Terchek and Frank Michelman. But they are only partial exceptions, Terchek because (as was discussed in chapter 1) he ends up concluding that the idea of propertied stakes in society is irrelevant to the conditions of late modern political economy, and Michelman because (as is discussed later in this chapter) he avoids encountering the connection to republican paternalism.

41. For the neoclassical view of Harrington, see Pettit, *Republicanism,* 28–29 and 32–33; and Skinner, *Liberty before Liberalism,* especially chapter 2. I do not deny the influence of neo-roman ideas in Harrington's thought, but I must insist that his thought is fundamentally Aristotelian. My emphasis on Harrington's Aristotelianism is also sharply at odds with the interpretation offered by Paul A. Rahe in *New Modes and Orders in Early Modern Political Thought,* vol. 2 of *Republics Ancient and Modern* (Chapel Hill, NC: The University of North Carolina Press, 1994), 179–96. Rahe concedes that the "classical elements" of Aristotelianism "within Harrington's discussion are many and obtrusive," but concludes that these elements "are, in fact, peripheral to his overall scheme." Rahe, 178. Rahe seems to think that it is dispositive that Harrington never made reference to the specific passage in the *Politics* where Aristotle claims that man is a "political animal." Rahe, 178. Yet as Blair Worden pointed out in response to Rahe, the "aim of Harrington's commonwealth is Aristotle's aim: the good life." Worden parts ways with Pocock as well, claiming that while Harrington's Aristotelian "aspiration merges with a Machiavellian concept of military commitment and public liberty," his "philosophy is more Aristotelian or Ciceronian than Machiavellian." Worden, "Harrington and 'The Commonwealth of Ocean,'" in *Republicanism, Liberty, and Commercial Society, 1649–1776,* ed. David Wootton (Stanford, CA: Stanford University Press, 1994), 106–7. It almost goes without saying that my interpretation of Harrington follows Worden's

with respect to the question of the Aristotelian provenance of his thought.

42. Harrington, *The Commonwealth of Oceana*, 161.

43. Harrington, *Oceana*, 161.

44. Viroli, *Republicanism*, 65.

45. Harrington, *Oceana*, 163.

46. Harrington, *Oceana*, 163.

47. Harrington, *Oceana*, 163.

48. Harrington, *Oceana*, 164.

49. See, for example, Bellah et al., *Habits*, 280.

50. Note though that this was not because of a leveling impulse, which, for Harrington, was akin to an impulse towards robbery. Rather, it was because such an agrarian law would contribute to the constitutional stability and balance of the republic. *Oceana*, 292. Also see the discussion of Harrington in Alan Ryan, *Property*, 28–31.

51. Pocock, *Virtue, Commerce, and History*, 106.

52. See the discussion of Arendt in chapter 7.

53. Pocock, *Virtue, Commerce, and History*, 106.

54. See Harrington, *Oceana*, 161–63.

55. James Harrington, *A System of Politics Delineated in Short and Easy Aphorisms*, 835.

56. Harrington, *The Commonwealth of Oceana*, 304.

57. Harrington, *Oceana*, 259.

58. Harrington, *Oceana*, 216.

59. The most purely Aristotelian example of an early modern defense of slavery is probably found in the writings of the Scottish political theorist Andrew Fletcher. See John Robertson, "The Scottish Enlightenment at the Limits of the Civic Tradition," in *Wealth and Virtue: The Shaping of Political Economy in the Scottish Enlightenment*, ed. Istvan Hont and Michael Ignatieff (Cambridge: Cambridge University Press, 1983). For a discussion of the role of classical republicanism in the defense of slavery in eighteenth-century American political thought, see McDonald, *Novus Ordo Seclorum*, 51–55.

60. The contrast between republican freedom and slavery is central to the interpretations of early modern republicanism that are developed in Skinner, *Liberty before Liberalism*; and Alan Craig Houston, *Algernon Sydney and the Republican Heritage in England and America* (Princeton, NJ: Princeton University Press, 1991).

61. McDonald points out that at the Constitutional Convention, Colonel Charles Pinckney appealed to the experience of the ancient republics of Greece and Rome in support of his argument that republican liberty and slavery are quite compatible. See *Novus Ordo Seclorum*, 51. But note also that Pinckney cited reasons of commercial policy as well. See James Madison, *Notes of the Debates in the Federal Convention*, (New York: W. W. Norton and Company, 1966), entry for August 22, 505.

62. As quoted in Istvan Hont and Michael Ignatieff, "Needs and Justice in the *Wealth of Nations*: An Introductory Essay," in *Wealth and Virtue: The Shaping of Political Economy in the Scottish Enlightenment*, ed. Hont and Ignatieff, 13, n. 40.

63. See the discussions of Harrington's views of slavery in Pettit, *Republicanism*, 32–33; and Worden, "James Harrington and 'The Commonwealth of Oceana,'" 100–101.

64. Harrington, *Oceana*, 170. Also see Pettit, *Republicanism*, 32–33; and Skinner, *Liberty before Liberalism*, chapter 2.

65. As quoted in McCoy, *The Elusive Republic,* 67.

66. Pocock, *Virtue, Commerce, and History,* 103–5.

67. Although I think he underestimates the degree to which Harringtonian republicanism influenced subsequent Whig opposition thought in England and America, Michael P. Zuckert provides a cogent and comprehensive interpretation of the relationship between republicanism and early modern rights-based reformulations of natural law in *Natural Rights and the New Republicanism* (Princeton, NJ: Princeton University Press, 1994).

68. Harrington, *Oceana,* 171.

69. See Shelley Burtt, *Virtue Transformed: Political Argument in England, 1688–1740* (Cambridge: Cambridge University Press, 1992); Houston, *Algernon Sydney and the Republican Heritage in England and America*; Skinner, *Liberty before Liberalism,* 18–21; and Zuckert, *Natural Rights and the New Republicanism.*

70. John Trenchard and Thomas Gordon, *Cato's Letters,* in *The English Libertarian Heritage,* ed. David L. Jacobsen (Indianapolis, IN: The Bobbs-Merrill Company, Inc., 1965), 62 and 211. My interpretation of Cato is different than that of Zuckert, who sees Cato as almost exclusively Lockean. See Zuckert, *Natural Rights and the New Republicanism,* 297–319. My position is closer to Shelley Burtt, who argues that Cato makes "the case for the self-interested roots of virtuous public action." See Burtt, *Virtue Transformed,* 83 and chapter 4 *passim.*

71. John Adams, *Defence of the Constitutions,* in *The Works of John Adams, Second President of the United States,* vol. IV, ed. Charles Francis Adams (Boston: Little, Brown, and Co. 1853), 427.

72. Adams, 392.

73. McDonald, *Novus Ordo Seclorum,* 70–74.

74. See Leslie Wharton, *Polity and the Public Good: Conflicting Theories of Republican government in the New Nation* (Ann Arbor, MI: UMI Research Press, 1980), 47. I have benefited greatly from Wharton's analysis and interpretation of Adams' views of property and political economy.

75. See especially Bernard Bailyn, *The Ideological Origins of the American Revolution* (Cambridge, MA: The Belknap Press, 1967), chapter 3; and James T. Kloppenberg, "The Virtues of Liberalism: Christianity, Republicanism, and Ethics in Early American Discourse," *The Journal of American History* 74 (1987): 9–33.

76. Trenchard and Gordon, *Cato's Letters,* 145.

77. See Wharton, *Polity and the Public Good,* chapter 3.

78. Neoclassical republicans are an exception in this regard. See Viroli, *Republicanism,* 32 and 73–74. Yet it is also the case that neoclassical republicans are apt to overlook the problem of paternalism within commercial forms of classical republicanism.

79. See Harrington, *Oceana,* 310–11. This side of Harrington is not always sufficiently appreciated by historians who see his subsequent followers—the so-called "neo-Harringtonians"—as reactionary, nostalgic defenders of country gentlemen. Also see the discussions of commercial republicanism in Harrington's thought and in general in Issac, "Republicanism vs. Liberalism? A Reconsideration," 349–77; and Istvan Hont, "Free Trade and the Economic Limits to National Politics: Neo-Machiavellian Political Economy Reconsidered," in *The Economic Limits to Politics,* ed. John

Dunn (Cambridge: Cambridge University Press, 1990).

80. Albert O. Hirschman, *The Passions and the Interests: Political Arguments for Capitalism before Its Triumph* (Princeton, NJ: Princeton University Press, 1977), especially 70–81.

81. See Sullivan, *Reconstructing Public Philosophy*, 69, 71, and especially 202–3. I note that neoclassical republicans have shown little interest in Montesquieu's commercial republicanism, preferring instead to focus on Montesquieu's arguments about public spirit, liberty, and constitutional design. See, for example, Pettit, *Republicanism*, 18–21, 153–57, and 177–80.

82. See Michael Novak, "How to Make a Republic Work: The Originality of the Commercial Republicans," in *"The Constitution of the People": Reflections on Citizens and Civil Society*, ed. Robert E. Calvert.

83. Montesquieu, *The Spirit of the Laws*, ed. and trans. Anne M. Cohler, Basia Carolyn Miller, and Harold Samuel Stone (Cambridge: Cambridge University Press, 1989), book 8, chapter 3, 114; also see book 8, chapter 2, 112–14.

84. Isaac Kramnick, *Republicanism and Bourgeois Radicalism: Political Ideology in Late Eighteenth-Century England and America* (Ithaca, NY: Cornell University Press, 1990), chapter 8, and especially 273–79.

85. Montesquieu, *Spirit*, book 12, chapters 1–2, 187–88, and book 20, chapter 4, 340–41.

86. Montesquieu, book 11, chapter 6, 159. Montesquieu maintained that it was the existence of this popular legislative power that made England a republic, or more precisely, a republic that "hides under the form of monarchy." Montesquieu, book 5, chapter 19, 70.

87. Montesquieu, book 11, chapter 6, 160.

88. Montesquieu, book 20, chapter 12, 345.

89. Montesquieu, book 5, chapter 6, 48, and book 20, chapter 4, 340–41.

90. Montesquieu, book 5, chapter 6, 48.

91. Montesquieu, book 5, chapter 6, 48.

92. Montesquieu, book 19, chapter 27, 325–26.

93. See Anne M. Cohler, *Montesquieu's Comparative Politics and the Spirit of American Constitutionalism* (Lawrence, KS: University Press of Kansas, 1988), 120.

94. See Appleby, *Liberalism and Republicanism in the Historical Imagination*, especially chapters 1 and 3.

95. Linda Kerber, "Making Republicanism Useful," 1665.

96. See Bellah et al., *Habits of the Heart*, 30–31 and 258–62; Daniel Kemmis, *Community and the Politics of Place* (Norman, OK: University of Oklahoma Press, 1990), chapters 2 and 3; Frank I. Michelman, "Possession vs. Distribution in the Constitutional Idea of Property," *Iowa Law Review* 72 (1987): 1319–50; Sullivan, *Reconstructing Public Philosophy*, 220–21; and Michael Sandel, *Democracy's Discontent*, chapters 5 and 6. Also see Charles Taylor's discussion of the hierarchical aspects of early modern republicanism in *Modern Social Imaginaries*, 148–52.

97. See Gordon S. Wood, *The Radicalism of the American Revolution* (New York: Vintage Books, 1991), especially chapters 9–10, 13–15, and 18.

98. See especially Frank I. Michelman, "The Supreme Court, 1985 Term—Foreword:

Traces of Self-Government," *Harvard Law Review* 100 (1986): 4–77.

99. See Frank I. Michelman, "Property as a Constitutional Right," in *Washington and Lee Law Review* 39 (1981): 1097–114; and "Possession vs. Distribution in the Constitutional Idea of Property."

100. Michelman, "Law's Republic," 1535.

101. Michelman "Possession vs. Distribution in the Constitutional Idea of Property," 1330.

102. Michelman, "Law's Republic," 1518.

103. Kemmis, *Community and the Politics of Place*, 70–73.

6

Property, Authority, and the Oppositionist Moment of Progressive Modernity

W E KEEP BUMPING UP AGAINST THE FACT that civic republicans assume too much about the compatibility of their project of civic recovery and renewal with democratic norms and practices of civic equality and inclusion. This problem is especially pronounced with communal republicans, who are apt to assume that a spirit of egalitarian mutuality is the natural outcome of their formative project of cultivating a capacity for virtuous liberty. To provide but one of many possible examples, in *The Ethics of Authenticity*, Taylor stipulates (almost in passing) that a "highly democratic" society is an "egalitarian" one. But he makes no attempt to show that such an egalitarian democracy is the necessary outcome of his "virtuous circle" of stronger civic identification and civic empowerment.[1] Unfortunately, we cannot assume such an outcome. Certainly, the historical record of classical republicanism casts doubt here. But the larger theoretical problem for today's civic republicans has to do with the threat to equal and inclusive citizenship that is posed by the distributive conditions and consequences of their project of recovery and renewal. With communal republicans, this is a matter of putting the cart of egalitarian mutuality before the horse of minimal forms and conditions of democratic equality. This is seen in some of the stronger criticisms of liberal equality and liberal rights discourse that have been made by thinkers such as Sullivan, Barber, and Beiner. But the threat to democratic equality also exists in expressions of civic republicanism that are not so stridently anti-liberal. Most civic republicans, regardless of whether they are communal or neoclassical republicans, accept the need for a minimal level of democratic equality, and do so without questioning whether such a minimal level is tainted by its association with liberalism. But this does not address the question of how to make sure that this minimal level of democratic equality is upheld in the face of the paternalistic tendency within a formative politics of civic virtue.

Amy Gutmann provides a helpful point of departure for understanding the basic forms and conditions of democratic equality in her discussion of the nature of "ethical agency" within a "just democracy." She points out that "civic equality" is an important principle of ethical agency within democratic cultures. As she defines it, "civic equality" involves "the obligation of democracies to treat all individuals as equal agents in democratic politics and support the conditions that are necessary for their equal treatment as citizens."[2] This definition allows for more expansive understandings of equality in terms of positive liberty and mutuality, but it grounds these more egalitarian possibilities in the basic requirement of according all citizens of a democratic political association the status of equal agents. Clearly, then, Gutmann's definition entails a fundamental democratic norm of political inclusion. In order for individuals to be treated as "equal agents in democratic politics," they must be admitted to, and included in, the civic spaces and practices within which democratic agency is or can be exercised. Inclusion in these civic spaces and practices is presumptively the *rightful jurisdiction* of individual members of the political community, certainly with respect to the adult members of the community. By the same token, adult individuals must first be within their rightful jurisdiction as democratic citizens if they are to have the opportunity to participate in the decisions that are binding on them.[3]

These basic forms and conditions of democratic equality all too easily become distant and even uninspiring abtractions. To prevent this, it is helpful to situate them in relation to the lived experience of citizens who have struggled against oppressive and exclusionary arrangements of property, power, dominion, and authority. The various understandings and self-understandings that inform these struggles constitute what I am calling the "oppositionist moment" in the democratic horizon.

In the spirit of critical hermeneutics, I want to rexamine and redescribe expressions of this oppositionist moment that have a direct bearing on the civic republican critique of progressive modernity. In the civic republicans' post-socialist narrative, the various tensions and conflicts between liberalism and socialism that dominated much of the modern era of Western politics are misleading insofar as they mask a deeper level of overlapping commitments to materialism. Both liberalism and socialism are said to have debased and corrupted the emancipatory project by tying it and the idea of progress itself to materialist views of economic growth, technological development, and the technical mastery of both the social and the natural worlds. This narrative certainly has its grains of truth. But it grossly underestimates both the importance of the oppositionist moment and the role of modern progressive traditions such as liberalism and socialism in promoting oppositionist democratic agency.

Hence, I am interested in exploring the oppositionist moment as a moment within the modern progressive self-understanding. The modern progressive form of the oppositionist moment was shaped by the political struggles against traditional social and political structures such as European feudalism. In this early phase, the oppositionist moment helped to establish minimal standards for equal liberty. The initial formulations of these standards were not themselves egalitarian or inclusive in any modern liberal or leftist understandings of these terms. These early formulations were nonetheless important to the development of modern leftist and left liberal expressions of the progressive self-understanding. Adapting terminology used by Michael Walzer to describe the "abolitionist politics" that has accompanied progressive modernity, it can be said that oppositionist ideals of equal liberty have served a "powerful negative purpose: they are meant to bring an end to all the forms of human subjection and servitude." But as Walzer went on to say, this "negative purpose" has not only been directed against "the inequalities of traditional societies" such as feudalism, but also against "the inequalities of capitalism itself."[4] It is precisely this translation and adaptation of oppositionist ideals of equal liberty into opposition to capitalism that marks the modern left. Accordingly, I will have something to say about both of these phases of the oppositionist dimension of the progressive self-understanding.

While oppositionist democratic agency takes many forms and has many sources, much of its historical significance has to do with opposition to concentrations and combinations of property and political power and authority.[5] Certainly, this aspect often has been central to how members of progressive political movements have understood themselves. In this regard, it is my contention that civic republicans and other post-socialists have glossed over and at times completely missed the contributions to democracy that have been made by both liberal and socialist forms of opposition to the translation of private property and wealth into political authority. Thus, my counter-narrative (as it were) focuses on the things that liberals and progressive leftists share in the area of property and authority. In the Western world, the oppositionist moment was born in thinkers like John Locke, and there is a level at which Locke and Marx can and should be seen as fighting on different fronts of a common battle to prevent private property and wealth from being illegitimately converted into political authority. In the process, both thinkers—or more accurately, many of the thinkers who subsequently constructed the modern ideological systems of liberal capitalism and socialism on the basis of Lockean and Marxian theories—also paved the way for the hegemony of thingness and an economistic materialism. And at this point, but only at this point, we reenter the post-socialist narrative. In the meantime, however, we will have discovered once again that post-socialists are not so far removed from progressive modernity as they would have us believe or as they want to believe. They too must rely on the oppositionist moment of democratic agency—if, that is, they are to address the problem of paternalism in their own traditions.

Beyond Whiggism and Counter-Whiggism

Now, in making this argument, I do not wish to be cast as an apologist for progressive modernity or its European roots in the Enlightenment. My philosophical history is not a "whiggish" story of steadily unfolding progress in the modern Western world. There are countless instances of how Western modernity's promise of progressive emancipation has been, or has become, a sham. There are as well countless instances of how it has been used to marginalize and oppress various groups and cultures. In truth, though, a kind of counter-whiggism has become the dominant story of Western modernity in much of the academy, and it does not take a great deal of effort these days to convince most political theorists and analysts of the problems with Western modernity; these problems have received more than ample documentation in the texts of contemporary philosophy, political theory, and social science. What seems more difficult for many to see—or rather, to appreciate and accept—is how the promise of progressive liberation has been kept. In this connection, defenders of progressive modernity commonly cite things like economic prosperity, scientific and technological advances, and greater material welfare. To the extent that such developments and benefits have reduced human suffering and promoted human development, I think that they deserve to be included among the examples of how modernity has kept its promise of progressive emancipation. More than this, I think that many post-materialist thinkers are deservedly chided for their moralistic insensitivity to the importance of prosperity, economic security, labor-saving and health-promoting technology, and material welfare in the lives of ordinary middle- and lower-class citizens of all different cultures. However, such benefits are not the focus of my argument, for I am mainly interested in showing how the promise of progressive emancipation has been kept in terms of fundamental ideals of political freedom and equality. It is in relation to these ideals that I am developing my points about the oppositionist moment.

To be sure, a certain amount of both post-socialist and postmodern skepticism is in order here. It is difficult at this historical juncture to think in terms of the complete liberation of this or that country, people, class, or group.

There is much that rings true in Milan Kundera's lament that modernity's "Grand March" towards emancipation has in many ways become "playacting" in the face of "mute power," akin to "the struggle of a theater company that has attacked an army."[6] It is, in any case, all too clear by now that even the most dramatic triumphs of progressive modernity have been difficult to sustain. Or if they have been sustained, they seem to live on in moral shades of gray much more than in the bright colors of liberation. Certainly, we are no longer dealing with the attainment of some kind of eschatological end state. No, the promise of progressive liberation has been kept in the more prosaic sense of many small and partial liberations, often ambiguous and frequently compromised, but nevertheless important in promoting freedom, equal liberty, equal citizenship, and human development. Whether our difficulty in appreciating these more prosaic "micro-liberations" is a matter of familiarity breeding contempt I do not know. But it does seem clear that we are dealing with patterns of thought and life that are very familiar in the two-fold sense of being deeply ingrained *and* carrying with them presumptive (if not always practiced or followed) norms of conduct and institutional design. Because of this familiarity, and because we are also accustomed to the fact that the norms of progressive liberation are compromised and incompletely realized, it is easy to lose sight of the importance of these norms in constituting practices of democracy and equal citizenship. Certainly, their importance does not shout out with the sense of urgency that is heard (quite understandably) in discussions of things like the triumph of instrumental reason and technocracy, the spread of shallow forms of emotivism and value relativism, the exclusion and marginalization of particularistic cultural identities in the name of a false universalism, the growth of political cynicism, the destruction of the environment, and the increasingly global hegemony of consumerism and the market model of social and political life. But the urgency of these and other problems of Western modernity does not diminish the importance of modernity's partially successful project of progressive liberation, and to try to analyze and address the problems of Western modernity without accounting for the instances of "micro-liberation" is tendentious at best, and in any case, does more to obfuscate and mystify both the modern democratic horizon and the modern predicament than to illuminate them.

Part of the importance of property for this inquiry, then, is that it provides interesting and theoretically significant examples of the mixed legacy of progressive modernity and of the more prosaic patterns of life and thought in which one finds the partly realized promise of progressive liberation. By the same token, property provides interesting and important examples of both the submergence of progressive thinking within post-socialism and the problems that this submergence creates for post-socialist projects of recovery and renewal such as civic republicanism. In their statements of concern about the dangers of Western materialism, civic republicans and other post-socialists point us in the direction of the negative side of the legacy of modern regimes of commercial property. But these statements are not only unsystematic and superficial as critiques of modern capitalism. They are also informed by extremely selective views of property that leave out of account those property-related understandings and norms that have helped Western modernity to deliver on its promise of liberation, however incomplete and contradictory the results have been.

The Significance of Locke

Let us start with Locke. Within the post-socialist narrative of materialistic progressive modernity, the primary role of Locke has to do with the contribution he made to possessive individualism through his proprietary model of personality and freedom. Here too I think there is a grain of truth. Locke certainly grounded private property rights in the ownership of one's labor and body, and he certainly saw property and its "fences" of security as crucial supports for freedom. But this is far from the whole story. Over the last several decades, Locke scholarship has revealed a far more complicated picture of Locke as a theorist influenced by the modern tradition of natural law, by both Christian and humanist ideas of virtue, by English opposition thought, and even by neo-roman ideas of civic independence. So we must be careful not to collapse Lockean property completely into the subsequent history of possessive individualism. Possessive individualism is part but only part of the complex protean legacy of Locke's thinking about property. In addition, and more to the point of this chapter, Locke's arguments about private property were not just about how individuals establish original rights to own things by "mixing" their labor with common resources.[7] They were also political arguments about the relationship between ownership and arbitrary political power, and more specifically, about the threat to liberty that is posed by efforts to convert claims of private ownership into claims of public authority. These arguments have a very different legacy than possessive individualism. Their legacy is that of the tradition of oppositionist democratic agency in the face of oppressive and undemocratic concentrations of wealth and power.

Post-socialist political theory is almost completely devoid of historical and theoretical appreciation for what Locke contributed to the progressive project of securing equal liberty against concentrations and consolidations of property and political authority. Significantly, this is true of both post-socialists who persist in interpreting Locke as a theorist of possessive individualism (including most civic republicans) and those (Christopher Lasch, for one) who treat him as a Calvinist proponent of the work ethic who had religious concerns about capitalist acquisitiveness.[8]

It is my contention, then, that Locke should be seen as a foundational thinker in the tradition of oppositionist democratic agency. But just as we have to be careful not to collapse Locke's account of property and freedom into the tradition of possessive individualism, so too must we be careful not to conflate what Locke said about private property and political authority with the *democratic* ideas and ideals of the oppositionist moment. Locke did not see himself as a democrat, and he certainly was not committed to democratic norms of civic equality and inclusion. It is the democratic *legacy* of Lockean ideas about property and political authority that is most important for my philosophical history. Locke developed these ideas well before the progressive self-understanding in this area crystallized. On the other hand, the fact that Locke wrote when progressive modernity was inchoate is also part of the significance of Locke for this inquiry. That is to say, he provides a bridge between the early modern conversations and debates about property, civic virtue, and public liberty that we examined in the preceding chapter and our exploration of the modern oppositionist moment in this chapter. By looking at his role in these earlier conversations and debates, we will be in a better position to consider the oppositionist moment in light of civic republican themes.

Locke, Classical Republicanism, and the Project of Progressive Emancipation

Let us consider, then, how Lockean ideas of propertied independence compare to Harrington's. There are some striking differences. Locke's proprietary understanding of identity and freedom leaves far less room for civic humanist ideals of participatory freedom and the cultivation of internal civic goods. Naturally, Locke's emphasis on proprietary rights of possession and ownership also translates into a more prominent role for thingness at the expense of the placeness of the household estate. This shift away from civic humanist placeness goes along with a shift away from the idea of property as a formative context of civic capacity within which power is transformed into authority. In this regard, Locke's understanding of propertied independence is sharply at odds with Harrington's idea of civic independence being grounded in the governance of estates. And this gets us to the nub of Locke's importance as theorist of oppositionist civic agency. In contrast to Harrington's vision of property as a dominion to be both owned and governed, Locke appears as a theorist who wishes to separate private ownership from political forms of governance and jurisdiction. Indeed, an important aspect of Locke's attack on

Sir Robert Filmer's defense of patriarchal political authority is found in the idea that "Property and Fatherhood [are] as far different as Lord of a Manor and Father of Children."[9] But more important than this (which still leaves both lordship and patriarchy, though in different institutional contexts) Locke argues that "no Man could ever have a just power over the Life of another, by right of property in Land or Possessions." In this way, Locke wove an argument on behalf of Christian charity into the political fabric of opposition to property-based forms of sovereign authority. Such a form of sovereignty, Locke insisted, would be illegitimate even if the would-be ruler had proprietary dominion over "the whole Earth." As he put it, "The most specious thing to be said, is, that he that is Proprietor of the whole World, may deny all the rest of Mankind Food, and so at his pleasure starve them, if they will not acknowledge his Soveraignty, and Obey his Will."[10] When Locke moved in this direction, he was striking at the core of the relational hierarchy within classical republicanism. He was opening up a horizon of challenges to lordship, slavery, paternalistic guardianship, and arguably to "liberal" forms of patriarchy as well, regardless of countervailing tendencies in his thought. Property as a context of belonging was, at a normative level, being sundered from property as a context of explicitly political governance and jurisdiction.

In sum, Locke provided a normative framework that separated property from fatherhood while simultaneously declaring that the attempt to gain sovereign control over the life of another on the basis of either property or fatherhood was an unjust exercise of power. We may even refer to the oppositionist idea that exclusive rights of private property and public authority should not be converted into one another as the "Lockean principle of separate spheres."[11]

This principle has important implications for civic personality. In effect, Locke was attempting to constitute a relationship between property and personality in which identity is defined not simply in terms of self-ownership, but also in terms of being unencumbered by unjust attributions and distributions of political authority *through* private property. Or what amounts to the same thing, Locke conjoined ownership and jurisdiction at the level of the self-sovereign individual while sundering private ownership from a public sphere of jurisdiction at the level of constitutional arrangements.

With Locke, then, we see an embryonic form of the oppositionist democratic self whose independence is not defined in terms of the dependency of other adults, and who, on the basis of norms of equal independence and equal liberty, challenges undemocratic and oppressive forms of superintendence and domination.

As always, though, we need to be mindful of the complexity of the interaction between Lockean and classical republican idioms and ideas. There are areas of overlap and cross-fertilization as well as striking differences, and this is especially true when we broaden our comparison beyond Harrington to include other thinkers and episodes in the tradition of early modern classical republicanism.

We saw in the previous chapter that classical republicanism in the early modern era often employed the same jurisprudential language of natural rights and negative liberty that was so important to Locke. We should also keep in mind that Locke sometimes moved in the direction of a virtue ethic, even if not its Aristotelian, civic humanist form. Locke's justifications for the accumulation of money and property notwithstanding, in the process of re-formulating natural-law understandings of property rights, he also developed a theory of the moral and civic duties attendant to both property and to one's God-given calling as a laborer.[12] The upshot is that "republican virtues" such as industriousness and frugality are also found in Locke. This, no doubt, is one reason that the radical Whig thought of American Revolutionaries could so readily encompass (at the level of ideology if not logic) both classical republican and Lockean conceptions of propertied independence and connect both to religious understandings of virtue. Here, as elsewhere, the virtues of early American political thought and culture were both liberal and civic humanist, secular and religious.[13]

By the same token, it would be a mistake to identify Locke's theory of property as one exclusively concerned with jurisprudential thingness. Although it is a theory in which thingness is at the forefront, elements of placeness are clearly in evidence. True, it is difficult to find in Locke a positive-libertarian placeness that is centrally concerned with the cultivation of civic virtue and other internal goods. But when present-day civic republicans emphasize the physicality and privatism of Lockean "fences" of property, they leave out that these fences looked both inwardly and outwardly in the sense of establishing a communal and civic identity. In some respects, at least, these fences are similar to those surrounding the Harringtonian freehold estate. Once again, it is American Revolutionaries who best make this point; or rather it is best made by Gordon Wood in his discussion of the conception of property held by American republicans of the Revolutionary era:

> Eighteenth-century Whiggism had made no rigid distinction between people and property. Property had been defined not simply as material possessions but, following Locke, as the attributes of a man's personality that gave him a political character. . . . It had been thought of generally in political terms, as an individual dominion—a dominion possessed by all politically significant men, the 'people' of society.[14]

To this it may be added that with Locke, we enter upon a complex history involving an incipient placeness of the labor that one "owns." No doubt, a labor theory of property leads, in many instances, to possessive individualism, a mystifying contractualism, and a merely formal equality to compete in the race of capitalist life. But the evocation of a placeness of labor pointed in other directions as well. For example, the notion of a personal and civic estate in one's trade or craft played an important role in the development of artisan republicanism in America.[15] And to look even farther down the road, there are echoes of this placeness of labor as well as echoes of classical republican opposition to aristocracy within nineteenth-century working-class and Populist celebrations of the "citizen-producer."[16]

I will return to these overlapping trajectories of Lockean and republican ideas about property towards the end of this chapter. There is an important lesson here about the difficulty of neatly separating liberal and republican ideas as the modern era develops. But the historical evidence also seems to support the contemporary civic republican claim (or lament, more precisely) that more purely classical (i.e., Aristotelian and Roman) themes and idioms became increasingly marginal and submerged in modern European and American political life. For the most part, this is a matter of the displacement of these themes and idioms by others. But one also sees evidence that there was a tendency among some modern students of politics to lump classical republicanism together with aristocratic and elitist threats to the advance of democratic equality and the emancipatory project of equal liberty. (This way of framing things was not entirely without justification!) Consider the description of American political culture that was penned in the 1920s by Vernon Parrington, one of the leading "Progressive historians" in America during the first half of the twentieth century. Parrington argued that from the beginning of their history Americans have been divided into "two main parties," one that has always been the party of the reigning "aristocracy" and one that has been "the party of the commonality." "The one," he explained, "has persistently sought to check and limit the popular power, to keep the control of the government in the hands of the few in order to serve the special interests, whereas the other sought to augment the popular power, to make government more responsive to the will of the majority, *to further the democratic rather than the republican* ideal—let one discover this and new light is shed on our cultural tendencies."[17] True, the language of the many versus the few betrays a republican provenance that Parrington appears not to have acknowledged. But the importance of this passage for us is what it says about the increasingly diminished stature of the "republican ideal" in the progressive self-understanding during the modern era. By the 1920s there were fewer and fewer political observers, let alone ordinary citizens, who would even make a point of referring to classical republican ideals in relation to democracy.

Of course, the development of the progressive self-understanding into the twentieth century was also marked by the diminished status of Locke in some respects, certainly within leftist and left-leaning forms of progressivism. But even in these forms, and even when Locke himself was dismissed or demonized, the Lockean norm of the illegitimacy of translating wealth into exclusive political authority continued to exercise considerable influence. I wish to suggest that the continuing influence of this norm was related to the emergence of a distinctly modern (i.e., nineteenth- and twentieth-century) version of the Whig narrative of historical progress. Within the new version, the oppositionist Lockean norm was redeployed on behalf of a struggle that embraced but was also far more global than the struggle of seventeenth-century Lockean Whigs against the threat posed to both ancient and natural liberty by arbitrary and "unreasonable" forms of hereditary rule. The new Whig narrative was about the march of progress towards such recognizably modern ideals as equal liberty, democracy, and human freedom from suffering, oppression, and exploitation—namely, the ideals of the modern project of progressive emancipation. But this modern narrative of progressive emancipation was not simply forward-looking. To the contrary, it derived much of its power by measuring progress against the standard of the benighted past. Of particular importance was the power of feudalism as a negative construct against which various kinds of progressive movements defined themselves. Even when feudalism was viewed as a "necessary" stage of history, it provided the modern progressive imagination with an array of negative ideas and images, not just the ideas and images of stagnation, disease, and ignorance that took on exaggerated and distorted significance within a hubristic modern consciousness, but also the political-economic ideas and images of aristocracy and lordship and bondage.

As we saw in the previous chapter, Harrington also held up feudalism as a negative category. However, Harrington's type of republicanism did not fit well with the new story of progressive emancipation. For one thing, Harrington's idea of "progress" was actually more in line with the older, cyclical view of a return to origins. So for Harrington "modern prudence" *was* the problem, and the movement towards republican liberty was one that went backwards through "ancient prudence" even as it required the mastery of ever-changing historical circumstances. In addition, it would be hard for modern progressives to make much sense of Harrington's civic humanist understanding of propertied independence. While Harrington was acutely aware of the difference between his Aristotelian view of the governance of freehold estates and the manorial system of feudal property, modern progressives would be apt to see this as a distinction without much of a difference. Both were about mastery and lordship, and as such both were at odds with progressive norms of independence and equal liberty. Nor would the Aristotelian placeness of Harringtonian property have much of an impact on the progressive critique. The progressive self-understanding was and still is largely a product and reflection

of the era of modern thingness, and this has always made it difficult for progressives to incorporate the placeness of property into either their opposition
to efforts to translate wealth into political control or their efforts to develop
alternative arrangements of property and political authority.

By contrast, Lockean ideas about property and political authority were a
pretty comfortable fit with the progressive self-understanding. The elements
of placeness in Locke's theory were never that pronounced, and could easily
be ignored. In any case, for the purposes of progressive emancipation, the key
in matters of property was to challenge the kind of combination of ownership
and lordship that was the hallmark of feudal property, and which would provide progressives of all kinds with a negative metaphor and analogue for their
various struggles against more modern systems of property-based control and
authority. And for these purposes, the Lockean separation of ownership and
political jurisdiction worked very well. Which is also to say, it resonated well
beyond the immediate intellectual and political context of Locke's life.

Adam Smith is another early modern thinker whose role in the theoretical
construction and defense of liberal capitalism has often obscured his contributions to the oppositionist moment of democratic agency. In this regard, it is
important that we remind ourselves that his "invisible hand" was directed not
only at a state-supported system of mercantilism, but also against feudalism
and related systems that fused property and jurisdiction. This is clearly seen in
the discussion in *The Wealth of Nations* of the rise of towns as centers of commerce and manufacturing, where Smith argues that "commerce and manufactures gradually introduced order and good government, and with them, the
liberty and security of individuals, among the inhabitants of the country, who
had before lived almost in a state of continual war with their neighbors, and of
servile dependency upon their superiors."[18] The Lockean principle of separate
spheres was very much a part of Smith's political economy.[19]

Again, classical liberals like Locke and Smith only take us partway towards
the modern democratic ideals of equal liberty, inclusion, and civic equality.
Moreover, the Lockean principle of separate spheres points to the familiar
problem within classical liberalism of positing a formal equality of jurisdiction and agency while simultaneously denying that property arrangements
entail substantive inequalities of both economic opportunity and effective
civic capacity and agency. Therefore, classical liberals like Locke and Smith do
not by themselves provide the theoretical resources with which to secure even
the minimal terms of equal liberty and political equality within the progressive self-understanding. But this does not obviate the fact that classical liberal
thinking about property and political authority played an important role in
the construction of the oppositionist moment as a project of emancipation
from feudalism and similar conditions of "servile dependency." To see how

early liberal thinking about property and political authority contributed to more democratic and inclusive visions of progressive emancipation, we need only think of the liberal aspects of the heroic nineteenth-century struggles against slavery and patriarchy. When, in 1852, Frederick Douglass challenged white America to think of what the Fourth of July means to the slave, he established liberal ideas of natural rights, equal liberty, religious liberty, "rightful" ownership of one's body, and wage labor as the standards by which to measure American hypocrisy. "Go where you may," he went on to say, "search where you will, roam through all the monarchies and despotisms of the old world, travel through South America, search out every abuse, and when you have found the last, lay your facts by the side of the everyday practices of this nation, and you will say with me, that, for revolting barbarity and shameless hypocrisy, America reigns without rival."[20]

A liberal form of the oppositionist moment was also in evidence when, the same year as Douglass's address, Elizabeth Cady Stanton defended equal political and civil rights for women in a speech to the members of the state legislature of New York. Calling attention to the fact that even without full legal and political equality, women have outstripped the achievements of men in many areas, Stanton posed the following question: "Can it be that here, where we acknowledge no royal blood, no apostolic descent, that you, who have declared that all men were created equal—that governments derive their just powers from the consent of the governed, would willingly build up . . . an aristocracy of the sons above the mothers that bore them?" And later in this speech, Stanton made it clear that she thought that property was the key to overturning the aristocracy of undeserved male power and authority: "The right to property implies the right to buy and sell, to will and bequeath, and herein is the dawning of a civil existence for woman, for now the 'femme covert' must have the right to make contracts. . . . The right to property will, of necessity, compel us in due time to the exercise of our right to the elective franchise, and then naturally follows the right to hold office."[21] There is an echo here of Harrington's argument that property is the basis for power and political authority. But Stanton's understanding of the nature and importance of propertied independence was far closer to Locke and Smith than to Harrington. Stanton's propertied independence was not grounded in the relational hierarchy of governing estates; rather, it was about the security of person and possession that allows a woman to be her own person, to be judged on her own merits, to enter into her own contracts in the market, to give her own consent to government, and to have an equal opportunity to assume political authority. In fact, one suspects that there was a level at which Stanton was challenging the "headship" of men within both classical republican and lingering feudal, aristocratic visions of the household.[22]

By way of summary, these challenges and the frameworks of belief and justification that informed and accompanied them constitute the historical basis for the emergence of the oppositionist moment of the progressive self-understanding. This is a moment which, in the name of the progressive realization of "masterless" liberty and equality, challenges the legitimacy of institutional arrangements in which property and political authority are translated and converted into one another: Control of things is one thing, political control of people quite another, and it is wrong to allow one to define or condition the other. Or to look at it from a slightly different angle, this moment views combinations and fusions of ownership and political jurisdiction as illegitimate insofar as they undermine the progressive principle of equal liberty.

Leftist and Left Liberal Opposition to Capitalism

The oppositionist moment is capable of accommodating different views of liberty and equality. It can be said that this moment contains the general promises of equal liberty and democratic equality but without specifying the precise manner in which these promises are to be kept. Thus, to assert freedom from and against an oppressive fusion of ownership and jurisdiction can be construed as striking a blow either for a "negative liberty" of non-interference in individual choices and actions or for a "positive liberty" of being empowered to develop one's nature as a rational, social being and to govern oneself without fear of domination. Either way, it would seem to be striking a blow for equality as well, for clearly the challenge to these arrangements and understandings entails a certain amount of leveling of social, economic, and political inequality.[23] And here too, the oppositionist moment is capacious enough to encompass theoretical and ideological differences. On the one hand, challenging the conjoint authority and proprietary claims of lords and masters might prepare the way for a more conservative liberal view of an equality of legal rights and a formal equality of opportunity to compete for highly unequal outcomes. On the other hand, it might also prepare the way for more egalitarian projects such as equalizing opportunities through the redistribution of unequal outcomes (as with egalitarian left liberals) or achieving a communal, classless society through the equalization of the actual conditions of power, income, wealth, education, and social welfare (as with socialists). In fact, merely sundering the connection between ownership and political jurisdiction is a way of equalizing conditions of wealth and power.

With all of these different possible paths, it is hardly surprising that the oppositionist moment has proved to be remarkably durable and fecund. Long after the distinctive arrangements and understandings of the *ancien regime* had receded from everyday experience, the arguments that had been directed against it were redeployed against what were seen as analogous cases of feudalism, aristocratic lordship, and "economic royalism" (to use Franklin Roosevelt's phrase). However, there have also been limits to the ideological plasticity of these arguments, and as they came to be redeployed against corporate capitalism (as with Roosevelt) they also came to define the distinctions between right and left and between classical conservative liberals and modern left liberals that have been at the heart of ideological and political debate and conflict for many years. It is true that under the influence of Marx, the left often has eschewed the strategy of reformulating and redeploying the old arguments against the *ancien regime* in favor of developing new arguments about the distinctively modern forces and contradictions at work in the capitalist stage of history. But well into the twentieth century, many leftists and left-leaning liberals were also fond of drawing explicit parallels between corporate capitalism and the *ancien regime*, as for example when the liberal legal theorist, Morris Cohen, described the "character of property as sovereign power compelling service and obedience." In Cohen's view, as in the view of many other progressive critics of the new order of corporate capitalism in the 1920s and 1930s, this quasi-feudal aspect of property "may be obscured for us in a commercial economy by the fiction of the so-called labour contract as a free bargain and by the frequency with which service is rendered indirectly through a money payment." "But," Cohen went to say in what now reads like an almost prototypical statement of the oppositionist moment in the era of corporate capitalism,

> not only is there actually little freedom to bargain on the part of the steelworker or miner who needs a job, but in some cases the medieval subject had as much power to bargain when he accepted the sovereignty of his lord. Today I do not directly serve my landlord if I wish to live in the city with a roof over my head, but I must work for others to pay him rent with which he obtains the personal services of others. The money needed for purchasing things must for the vast majority be acquired by hard labour and disagreeable service to those to whom the law has accorded dominion over things necessary for subsistence.[24]

I believe that despite all of the changes in the techno-economic structure and culture of capitalism since Cohen first put forward this analysis in a lecture in 1926, it retains much of its cogency and critical force. These days, we might be inclined to take as our examples computer keyboard operators or hotel and restaurant workers rather than miners and steelworkers. And it may be true that the conditions of labor and service in advanced capitalist countries such as the United States are not so hard or disagreeable for so vast a majority now, and that there are compensating consumer satisfactions for at least the better off members of the working class. Yet the basic capitalist structure of property and authority described by Cohen remains intact, and clearly there are vast numbers of workers who continue to engage in hard labor and disagreeable service, and who do so more out of compulsion than out of a free bargain. In fact, it can be argued that Cohen's conception of property "as sovereign power compelling service and obedience" has acquired even more meaning with the shift to a service-based economy in which the fiction of consumer sovereignty works in conjunction with the fiction of free (and equal) bargaining power to obscure the power and authority of "those to whom the law has accorded dominion over things necessary for subsistence." The masters to whom we provide service in corporate capitalism are sometimes abstract and impersonal, but they are masters nonetheless.

Marxist true believers are apt to dismiss the analogy between corporate capitalism and feudalism as an unscientific account of the processes and stages of historical development. And if the aim is precise and "scientific" historical accuracy, then clearly the analogy between feudalism and corporate capitalism is well off the mark. As both Marxists and pro-capitalist liberals and conservatives are likely to point out, the analogy downplays the significance of the spread and entrenchment of the beliefs and practices of contractual and competitive market exchange. Fair enough. Nevertheless, the point of the analogy is not, and never was, positivistic precision or scientific accuracy. Rather, the point has always been to provide a measure of historical and critical insight into the problems of corporate capitalism through an appreciation of the bitterly ironic similarities between it and the very same feudal structures of property and authority from which capitalism is supposed to have liberated us. Moreover, the underlying strategy of seeking to unmask capitalism by holding it up to its own emancipatory ideals and aspirations has been employed by a variety of leftists, including many Marxists. That is to say, the analogy with feudalism is but one example of a strategy by which leftists have sought to show that the ideological defense of capitalism is contradicted by the actual socioeconomic conditions that it has engendered. And this means that it is a strategy that has derived much of its critical power from the same progressive ideal of masterlessness that is proclaimed by the ideologists of capitalism. Thus, the point of the analogy with feudalism—the ironic point—has been that, yes, being without a master in the sphere of property and authority is a mark of freedom and dignity, but rather than realizing this ideal as it claims, corporate capitalism has established forms of mastery and subordination that are reminiscent of feudalism. However, leftists have made the point with similar effect when they have abandoned the analogy with feudalism and concentrated on the contradictions that emerge in the capitalist "stage" of history, as when they have argued that the equal liberty and emancipatory freedom that are proclaimed and exalted by the theorists of liberal capitalism are abstractions that are contradicted by material conditions of property, class exploitation, and egoistic competitiveness.[25]

Civic Republicanism and the Oppositionist Moment

As post-socialists, civic republicans share many of the old leftist concerns about liberal capitalism. These concerns are now expressed in the idioms of moral and civic recovery and renewal, and partly because of this they lack the radical oppositionist edge of their old leftist formulations. But this softening of the critique of liberal capitalism is not as worrisome as the fact that in their eagerness to expose and destroy the materialist core of progressive modernity, civic republicans have done considerable damage to the liberal foundations of both modern democratic equality and oppositionist democratic agency.

Some of the worst of this damage has been done through the communal republican critique of liberal rights. It is difficult to imagine what other discourse civic republicans could use to ensure equal and inclusive terms of citizenship in the face of the paternalistic understanding of civic capacity that is deeply rooted in their own tradition. Harrington's "foundation of common right or interest" is inadequate for this purpose, for in establishing the shared normative understanding of a common good that is grounded in the rule of law, this foundation does not by itself create the conditions that would support and protect the agency of all adult citizens. In addition, civic republicans overlook the oppositionist resources that individual rights provide to those struggling against oppressive and exclusionary combinations of property and authority. Most important in this regard is their failure to appreciate the subtle interaction between property and an ethic of equal rights. What appears to communal republicans as a corrupt elaboration and extension of the "logic" of the thingness of property can also be seen as a basis for challenging hierarchical and paternalistic forms of the placeness of property, including of course those forms associated with a masters' vision of civic virtue. And here too there are historical lessons to consider. Most important in this regard are those occasions when an ethic of equal rights has been employed against property-based claims of dominion and authority. At least since the Putney Debates of the English Revolution, the language of equal rights has been used by the propertyless to lay claim to a stake in society and to counter the claims of proprietors and landlords that the propertyless do not have such a stake.[26] In these cases, the language of equal rights has functioned more as a fence of inclusion than as a fence of exclusion and "entrenched solitude." And far from being a simple elaboration of the logic of property, the ethic of equal rights has functioned as what Kenneth Minogue describes as a "property substitute."[27] Not least important in this regard is the notion of rightful independence as a "substitute" for subjection and subservience to authoritarian guardianship, both inside and outside the household. More generally, as Minogue puts it, an ethic of equal rights has been employed as part of the effort of the many "to engineer the conditions for the defense of liberty while abolishing the very classes hitherto so closely associated with its defense."[28]

Blinded by their preoccupation with the evils of possessive individualism, communal republicans have grossly underestimated those aspects of the intertextuality of property and rights that can contribute to the creation of an inclusive democratic community. But one of the lessons of our exploration of early modern republicanism in the previous chapter is that the presence of a discourse of rights is not enough to remove the danger of republican paternalism. Even if we assume that the civic republican polity is supported by something like rights-based liberal understandings of equal jurisdiction—as, for example, one finds with neoclassical republican ideas of the rightful jurisdiction of independent democratic citizens—there is still the possibility that the cultivation of authoritative civic excellence will end up undermining these background understandings of equal jurisdiction, or will reduce them to a merely formal legal condition. That is to say, there is still the possibility that even within a legal liberal regime of equal rights the cultivation of authoritative civic excellence will be based on the "formative" or "educative" experience of ruling over other citizens.

Once again, it is helpful to think in terms of the relationship between "in authority" and "an authority." There is an important sense in which the civic republican circle of virtuous civic engagement with and for the common good is designed to be formative of the capacity to be *an* authority in matters of public liberty and self-government. Specifically, it is an authoritative *excellence* of civic character that civic republicans are interested in cultivating. This in itself contains a threat to equal citizenship that is glossed over, and seldom even acknowledged by civic republicans. As Richard Flathman has observed about the grammar of "an authority," there is an important sense in which the competence of one person is rendered authoritative by the deference of others who recognize and accede to this competence.[29] This is confirmed by William Sullivan who, in a rare moment of allowing issues of authority to enter into his defense of civic republicanism, argues that the non-contextual liberal view of rational agency leaves out of account the "the defining, authoritative role of . . . substantive paradigms of the good society, the good person, and good life practices."[30] What Sullivan leaves out of account is how civic republicans are to avoid a hierarchical, paternalistic, or exclusionary politics of deference to authoritatively "good" persons.[31] At the very least, we need to know how the model citizens and civic leaders of Sullivan's polity are to be held accountable to other citizens.

However, the more serious difficulties with civic republican authority have to do with the ways in which authoritative excellence is implicated in the patterns and relations of jurisdiction that are associated with being "in authority." The classical republican dream of a "natural aristocracy" of virtuous and talented civic leaders notwithstanding, in politics, authoritative excellence is not like the excellence of an accomplished pianist or a master bridge player. On the contrary, it is constituted within and through relations of ruling and being ruled in which individuals or groups have, or are subject to, various kinds of decision-making jurisdiction. Thus, the citizen of the Aristotelian republic developed his authoritative civic excellence by virtue of being both an authority and in authority in the "formative" context of the household.

This brings us back to the problem of republican paternalism as a problem of tying the cultivation of civic virtue too closely to distributive contexts of property, power, dominion, and authority. Such a close structural relationship between the formative and distributive dimensions of republican capacity threatens the underlying jurisdictional equality of democratic citizens. The problem for civic republicans is that other than implying some vague notion of the sovereignty of equal citizens they do not show how the cultivation of authoritative civic excellence is to be achieved without compromising this jurisdictional equality.

Herein lies the importance of the oppositionist self for the project of civic recovery and renewal. The understandings and self-understandings of such a self must be admitted to the democratic horizon as part of the ongoing challenge of creating and ensuring a contingent relationship between the formative and distributive dimensions of civic capacity. Again, it is difficult to imagine the oppositionist self except as a rights-bearing self. And this probably carries with it a measure of second-order possessive individualism. But the rights of the oppositionist self are not reducible to property-like fences of negative liberty. Rather, the oppositionist self bears rights in the senses of having and being within her rightful jurisdiction as a democratic citizen. This presupposes a commitment to the good of democracy. But more than this, there are specific goods associated with oppositionist agency. I have in mind such well-known civil libertarian goods as dissent, protest, and resistance to oppression and injustice. As participatory practices of civil liberty, these goods establish a direct connection between non-domination and positive liberty. But they are also necessarily instrumental goods. To transform practices of protest, dissent, and resistance into ends in themselves or into mere instruments of self-aggrandizement would subvert them into anti-social activities— no less a form of corruption than that of capitalist acquisitiveness. The oppositionist goods must remain instruments of democratic liberty and democratic justice.

There are virtues associated with these oppositionist goods—courage for one, and the patriotism of resistance to undemocratic and unjust forms of second-class citizenship for another. These and other oppositionist virtues have a formative dimension in that they are necessarily learned within (if not always affirmed or prescribed by) one's community. Yet the goods and virtues of the oppositionist self are not a good fit with the civic republican project of recovery and renewal. There is indeed a profound rupture in the hermeneutic circle that connects identification with the good of the community to engagement on behalf of that good. Existentially, the oppositionist self is born of alienation and estrangement from one's community, and from its prevailing norms and understandings of both virtue and the common good. So civic republicans are in a bind. On the one hand, by establishing, or rather, by implying and presupposing, a merely contingent relationship between the formative and distributive dimensions of civic virtue, they change the background conditions of classical republican citizenship in a fundamental and far-reaching way. Such a change is an essential condition for an oppositionist moment of democratic agency. On the other hand, the circle of virtuous civic engagement is constitutive of the republican revival, and civic republicans can keep this circle intact only by glossing over or neglecting the problematic interaction between the formative and distributive dimensions of civic capacity. And this creates the conditions for new forms of republican paternalism that would suppress the moment of oppositionist agency.

Ethical Materialism Revisited

If the analysis of republican paternalism and guardianship that I have developed in this chapter and the preceding ones is essentially correct, then there are good reasons to think that contemporary civic republicanism is based on a deeply flawed account of the nature and sources of civic independence in a democracy. In their different ways, both communal and neoclassical republicans seek to cultivate and support civic independence through the development of a stronger sense of *public* liberty and *shared* practices of self-government. They envision civic recovery and renewal in terms of a movement from a disengaged, competitive, and dominating "I" to a relational (if not always deeply communal) "we." I have gone out of my way to say that there is much of value in the civic republican perspective on democracy. More than this, my understanding of the placeness of property can be seen as an attempt to redescribe property along civic republican lines. But it is also when we incorporate property and other distributive contexts of civic identity into the formative project of civic republicanism that we see how difficult it is to develop a democratic "we" that is non-hierarchical and inclusive as well as relational.

Always, we come back to the messiness of democracy. The historically constituted horizons that are encountered through hermeneutics never come in neat little boxes of syllogistic reasoning, and this is especially true of the democratic horizon. The horizonal background of democracy is one of real—that is, practical—complexity. It contains many different practical understandings of moral and civic life and identity, many of which sit well together, but many of which are the stuff of both political and theoretical tension, struggle, and conflict. No doubt, democracy would be far less messy were it not for all the struggles to transform traditionally exclusionary (and often racist and patriarchal) ideals of popular government into democratic ideals of equal liberty and equal and inclusive citizenship. But without these struggles there would not be much distinctive substance to the concept of democracy.

Ethical materialism is also necessarily messy. After all, it must account for and incorporate the messy conditions and capabilities of democracy if it is to be based on a comprehensive view of human development. A democratic vision of ethical materialism grows out of a commitment to affirming, protecting, and supporting the agency of self-governing citizens. This commitment sustains democratic norms and ideals of civic independence and civic equality. Yet it often coexists uneasily with ideals of social justice that involve caregiving and communal provision to support citizens in need. Largely because our practices of "strong evaluation" in these areas of social justice are informed by norms and ideals of both civic independence and civic equality, the challenge (to quote Martha Nussbaum again) is to cope with the facts of "human neediness and dependency" in ways "that are compatible with the self-respect of the recipients and do not exploit the caregivers." This is often difficult enough. But there is an even deeper background of messiness out of which the challenges of caregiving and civic friendship arise. The same norms and ideals of independence and equality that condition (or should condition) our practices of caregiving and civic friendship coexist uneasily with each other.[32]

Fortunately, there are some foundations for ethical materialism that are not so messy or difficult. In truth, some of what we have accomplished so far in developing these foundations has been pretty straightforward. It is not all that difficult or complex to defend the basic claim that the ethical situation of the self is in some fundamental sense always/already a material situation pertaining to modes of labor, provision, and resource allocation and distribution. And once the relationship between external and internal goods is given more than the superficial theoretical treatment that it usually is given by post-socialists, it is not all that difficult to make the case that the instrumental value of property and other external goods is not something to be transcended as a form of crass materialism, but rather is simply one part of a larger picture involving the means and ends of moral and civic life. If these basic claims on behalf of ethical materialism result in consternation or strong opposition, it would seem to have less to do with the substantive merits of the claims than with the substance, structure, and influence of post-materialist thought in the current era. That is to say, if they seem like problematically complex claims, that probably is a reflection of the fact that much of the political theory of late modern capitalism seems stuck in a polar universe of economistic commercialism and anti-economic post-materialism. But when we step outside this universe, the material situation of ethical life and the importance of treating property in terms of a relationship between instrumental goods and things like virtue and fundamental rights is pretty easy to see, and pretty easy to square with most beliefs about democracy, justice, and human development.

Things get more difficult when we turn to the hermeneutic and phenomenological tasks of showing the conceptual interaction and interrelationship between external and internal goods and recovering the placeness of property and other external goods. Through these tasks, we come back to the problematic complexity of modern democratic identity within European-influenced cultures such as the United States. What we begin to see is not simply the depth and scope of modern Western commitments to things like independence and equal liberty, but also, and more importantly, how these commitments are associated with resistance to oppressive and unjust masters. In ways and for reasons not fully appreciated by civic republicans and other post-socialist thinkers, progressive modernity has fostered an ethos of and for those whom Hobbes described as "masterless men."[33] What I have in mind is an ethos concerned with the conditions of civic and political agency, not the condition of men in a state of natural warfare that Hobbes had in mind. But the emphasis also has to be placed on how ingrained this ethos of "masterlessness" is, for we are talking about deeply and often unconsciously held beliefs and understandings that are woven into the lived experience of individuals. What is ingrained at this deeper, hermeneutic level is more than the commonplace suspicions and fears of centralized and concentrated power. As important as these suspicions and fears are in modern political life, they are but the tip of the horizonal iceberg. Below the surface, we find a conceptual world in which resistance to masters is about resistance to the kind of inscription of authority in social relations that we see in Aristotle. By the same token, it is a deeply ingrained resistance to having one's identity defined in terms of property-related locations of mastery and authority.

To be sure, the close association between this ethos of opposition to masters and Western culture needs to be kept in mind. It may be that there are non-European alternatives that can help us to get to both democracy and ethical materialism without all the tensions and messiness that exist in European traditions. One could perhaps find a non-European cultural tradition—one thinks of the Iroquois confederation—in which civic independence is more seamlessly integrated into communal practices. Perhaps also, as Russell Fox has tried to demonstrate with his creative redescription of Confucianism as a theory of democracy, it is possible to reduce the tension in democracy between independent ethical agency and authority by developing ritualistic practices that are more participatory, communal, and creative than most European forms of authority.[34] An exploration of such alternatives is well beyond the scope of the present inquiry. I will confine myself to two points. First, it seems to me that civic republicans and other post-socialists would do well to encounter non-European traditions and perspectives in a more sustained and systematic manner. After all, ideas of virtue, community, socially embedded personality, and moral recovery and renewal have deep roots in many non-European traditions and perspectives. But second, based on my own encounters with such traditions and perspectives—and I confess to still being at the beginning of the learning curve in comparative political theory—it seems unlikely that we will come across any silver bullets of democratic theory that will make it unnecessary to support democracy with spaces and modes of oppositionist agency and civil liberty. To the contrary, it seems likely that we will discover the importance of such spaces and modes in non-European practices of self-government as well. For example, it hardly seems coincidental that for the Iroquois, "the autonomous individual, loyal to the group but independent and aloof, was the ideal."[35] There is in fact a strong family resemblance between the Iroquois spirit of liberty and the classical republican ideal of liberty as non-domination. Thus, while Iroquois boys were taught to be "loyal, selfless members of the clan," it was also made clear to them that they "were not respected if they were dependent, submissive, or cowed by authority."[36] This also suggests an awareness of authority as an ongoing threat to independence. Be that as it may, it seems likely that encounters with non-European traditions and perspectives will reveal problems of hierarchy and exclusion similar to the problem of republican paternalism. Even Fox tempers his enormous optimism about the potential for Confucian democracy with caveats about the inequality of Confucian social relations and the continuing danger of authoritarian forms of Confucianism.[37] Consider also what Nussbaum discovered about the politics of property in India:

> Property rights in India have traditionally belonged to families as organic wholes, and women have little or no control over the family unity or 'coparcenary,' which is run by its male members. Demands by women for land rights have frequently been greeted with the claim that this would 'break up the family.' And certainly the demand, if accepted, would transform the internal governance of that structure.[38]

What does all of this mean with respect to my rethinking of property? There is a close, but not entirely comfortable, relationship between the oppositionist ethos of democracy and the regime of modern thingness. In both cases, identity is defined in terms of a subject of possession who stands apart from property objects and their contexts. However, the relationship is also an uneasy one, partly because we must remain open to the possibility that the placeness of property can provide resources for resistance to masters—in the form, say, of civic stakeholders asserting their rights as inhabitants of property arrangements—but also because modern thingness can foster its own forms of unjust and undemocratic mastery.

There is no neat and simple trade-off between modern thingness and the recovery of placeness. Messiness lurks here too. Both modern thingness and placeness have benefits and gains, and both also have risks and losses. Viewed against the hierarchical and paternalistic tendencies within civic guardianship, modern thingness appears as a source of equal justice and democratic equality. But the explicit connection between property and authority within placeness also seems more honest and open than the formal equality that often accompanies modern thingness. And always there is the problem of acquisitiveness and crass materialism within modern thingness. Viewing it in relation to placeness, we see how easily modern thingness results in the suppression of the ethical aspects of material practices and conditions. Placeness, on the other hand, allows for embedded forms of strong evaluation and ethical agency in which the means and ends of moral and civic life can be connected. What Fox says about the ordering of the Confucian community through social roles and rituals could just as easily be said about the placeness of property: "Certainly belonging to a group circumscribes possibilities, but the act of normative 'closure' transforms an open plain into a particular space, and the goods of ordered communities only exist in such spaces."[39] And yet in matters of democracy and ethical materialism, we also need to be aware of the possibilities that may be foreclosed and suppressed. Whether in the placeness of Confucian rituals or the placeness of property, agency is conditioned and sometimes constrained within contexts of authority and labor that can undermine the democratic rights and the dignity of their inhabitants.

Different Paths

But where does this leave us with respect to progressive modernity and the relationship between property and authority in the progressive self-understanding? While messy complexity is the primary lesson that emerges from my philosophical history, this is not a lesson that teaches resignation in the face of the dominance of free-market capitalism in this largely post-collectivist era. There are, and always have been, programmatic and theoretical alternatives to both classical liberal capitalism and bureaucratic collectivism. We can get a sense of this by sketching some alternative liberal paths in which property became a framework within which to relate (if not completely harmonize) propertied independence and the ideal of a democratic commonwealth. This brings us full circle back to the relationship between Locke and classical republicanism, for the paths that I am sketching often were formed by the intersecting legacies of Locke and a residual republicanism.

In its specifically Lockean formulation, the normative separation of ownership and political jurisdiction undoubtedly creates conditions for a first-order possessive individualism that both promotes and obfuscates inequalities of effective freedom and political power. Add to this Locke's defense of private economic virtues, and we begin to see how a Lockean perspective was able to contribute not only to a libertarian privatism but also to modern conservative expressions of commercial republicanism. In this regard, the Lockean separation of private ownership and political jurisdiction opened up possibilities for reformulating and "softening" republican mastery in an era marked by the growing influence of the values of popular sovereignty and equal rights and opportunities. This is seen, for example, in the commercial republicanism of James Madison. In Madison's hands, the Lockean principle of separation is redescribed in the form of a tension between the rights of private property and the rights of persons.[40] Although the connection between property and civic virtue is much weaker in Madison's vision of an extended commercial republic than in classical republicanism, the special emphasis and protection given to property rights creates the conditions for submerged forms of republican mastery. Yet by defining both property rights and personal rights in terms of the rightful freedom of all citizens apart from property-based forms of political jurisdiction, Madison was able to ground republican authority in the self-sovereignty of the people.[41]

Set against all this, however, is the fact that with Locke we enter upon a complex history of democratic republicanism in which workers and farmers challenge the ways in which owners and managers of property exercise an unjust dominion over second-class citizens. By asserting the dignity of the labor that is "owned" by productive citizens, these traditions of producerism and labor republicanism also show that Lockean understandings of property and personality contributed to the search for a democratic conception of productive property in the era of industrial capitalism.[42] Adapting some of Jeremy Waldron's terminology, this democratic conception of property reflects a shift within the Lockean framework from Locke's own view of property as a "special right" that confers protection and privilege on particular individual laborers to a "general right" that exists, or should exist, for all citizen-producers as stakeholders in a democratic commonwealth.[43]

Clearly, these broadly, and sometimes loosely, Lockean voices of democratic opposition are not easily disentangled from the voices of commercial republicanism. This, it seems to me, is the irony, at times perhaps the tragic irony, at the heart of the problem of a commercial republic. In other words, while there is ample reason to agree with civic republicans that a commercial republic promotes the submergence of democratic initiative, there is also ample reason to believe that the commercial republic and its democratic critics have some common ideological and normative sources. Consider in this regard what the American historian, Leon Fink, has to say about the nineteenth-century American tradition of working-class republicanism:

> The language of labor republicanism itself reflected the internal crisis and attempted restructuring of liberal political ideology. The labor theory of value, for example, underwent a subtle transformation. A mere strand of individualist Jeffersonian thought (and one that disappeared in neoclassical economics), it became a moral pillar of the collective claims of the laboring classes.[44]

Traditions of labor republicanism were characterized by a reworking of traditional republican themes as well as liberal individualist ones. Historians such as Fink who have studied nineteenth-century producer republicanism in America have discovered a language and ideology of dissent within which modern industrial capitalism appears as a corruption of the first principles of republican government, in part because it threatens the virtuous propertied independence of "honest laborers."[45] As William E. Forbath has shown with respect to the working-class republicanism of the Knights of Labor in the 1880s, traditional republican themes pertaining to "economic independence" in the form of "ownership of productive property" provided conceptual and normative materials with which to oppose the emerging Lockean justification of corporate capitalism.[46]

Equally significant is the qualitative shift away from a vision of civic mastery and deferential dependency. This shift was by no means total. At times, working-class republicans contrasted their own propertied independence with the corrupt dependency and untrustworthiness of the "propertyless 'servant' or 'hireling.'"[47] These traces of mastery and dependency—relational hierarchy, to use my term of art—suggest a tension between the producers' ethic of equal rights and their ethic of situated virtue.[48] Nonetheless, within working-class republicanism of the Gilded Age, propertied independence was exercised by industrial workers who claimed equal rights and equal stakes in a democratic republic. And rather than celebrating the leisure and political capacities that come from the governance of servants and dependents, working-class republicans challenged "wage slavery" by asserting their control of the productive process, by pushing for reforms such as the eight-hour work day, and in some cases, by establishing worker cooperatives as model forms of the placeness of property in a "cooperative commonwealth." Again, Lockean fences look both inwardly to the sphere of personal security and outwardly to the community.

For us, the particular configuration of liberal and republican themes is not so important as the fact that these movements of producer republicanism were sustained in part by the type of normative framework of rights and propertied independence that civic republicans and other post-socialists are inclined to see as an important source of the corruptive power of progressive modernity. Without denying the corruptive power of this framework, I have tried to show that it nonetheless has provided crucial support for the oppositionist moment of democratic agency. In the case of producer republicanism, this support manifested itself in workers and farmers who asserted their independence from oppressive forms of guardianship as well as from the expansive, but undemocratic, self-understandings of deferential obedience that accompanied them.[49] Yet movements such as those associated with producer republicanism also reveal the civic possibilities within the old ideal of stakes in society. As is discussed in detail in chapter 8, the notion of stakes in society implies a form of agency that is more independent than that exercised in a communal republican engagement on behalf of collective liberty. At the same time, though, because they are stakes *in* society, independent agency is exercised within a context of civic interdependence.

The project of conjoining propertied independence with the civic life of a democratic commonwealth was also characteristic of some expressions of modern reform liberalism in the first half of the twentieth century. To trace the various twists and turns in the history of reform liberal arguments about property would be well beyond the scope of this book. But it is worth calling attention to the fact that for earlier reform liberals such as Cohen, Adolf Berle, Gardiner Means, L. T. Hobhouse, A. D. Lindsay, and (for a time anyway) Walter Lippman, the importance of property lay in the challenge of responding to both the classical liberal defense of *laissez-faire* and the rise of statist collectivism. Speaking broadly, this meant, on the one hand, criticizing classical liberalism for its denial of the "social character" of property as well as for its failure to take into account the unequal relations of power within a capitalist economic system; and, on the other hand, trying to find ways of incorporating the social character of property into more equitable legal and economic structures without at the same time making the collectivist mistake of denying the value of private property in areas of personal use and consumption.

Consider in this regard the path-breaking analysis of the modern "corporate system" that was put forward by Berle and Means in 1932. Berle and

Means claimed to have discovered a new system of "quasi-public" property tenure and economic organization comparable in its scope and historical importance to the system of feudalism. As they famously argued, the combination of large-scale factory production and the multiplication of owners had created a new structure in which ownership and control of the corporation were largely separate.[50] In the meantime, the modern corporation had become an institution that rivals the medieval church and the modern nation state with respect to both its concentration of power and the diversity of group interests under its control. The difference, Berle and Means contended, is that the corporation had not yet been "subjected to the same tests of public benefit" that reformers of these other institutions were eventually able to establish. Berle and Means called for a renewal of this spirit of reform to meet the challenges posed by corporate power. In their view, communist collectivism was simply "the most extreme aspect" of the desire of many in the 1930s to make the economic power of corporations accountable to the "common interest."[51] But their own approach was a fundamentally reformist, liberal one in which the structure of corporate property was redefined on the basis of "community obligations" relating to things like fair wages, job security for employees, and "reasonable" public service requirements for corporations.[52]

Here then is a very different path from property to the welfare state than that which liberalism eventually took. Rather than positing civic responsibilities and social rights that trump property rights on the basis of economic justice and the common interest, Berle and Means posited economic justice and the common interest as civic responsibilities entailed by property. This is the path not taken by contemporary liberals (not to mention most civic republicans and post-socialists).[53]

True, there is some continuity with recent liberal theory as well as discontinuity. When John Rawls criticizes a conservative "meritocratic society" for creating conditions under which "the culture of the poorer strata is impoverished while that of the governing and technocratic elite is securely based on the service of national ends of power and wealth," and when Thomas Spragens chides libertarian conservatives for making property rights "too sacrosanct" and points out that a "rational society need not timidly worry whether it has any business intruding obligations of civic respect and equality into what is seen as almost exclusively private terrain," they are giving expression to concerns that have animated the programs and policies of reform liberalism for over a century.[54] However, in contemporary liberalism, these concerns lack an organic connection to a comprehensive theory of property. Property, in other words, is not the central, organizing concept that it often was in the formative period of modern reform liberalism. Consider in this regard the evocation of both the thingness and the placeness of property in Hobhouse's description (written in 1913) of the challenge for liberals under the "new" conditions of industrial capitalism: "The problem of modern economic reorganization would seem to be to find a method, compatible with the industrial conditions of the new age, of securing to each man, as a part of his civic birthright, a place in the industrial system and a lien upon the common product that he may call his own, without dependence on private charity or the arbitrary decision of an official." And shortly thereafter, he goes on to say that in order to "restore the contact between the individual and the instruments of labor," "we need to restore to society a direct ownership of some things, but an eminent ownership of all things material to the production of wealth."[55]

This is precisely the type of "wider conception" of property that Rawls and most other contemporary liberals rule out.[56] Yet it is neither libertarian conservatism nor bureaucratic socialism. It is a liberal vision that evokes both a broadly proprietary model of labor and traditional republican themes pertaining to the constitution of civic stakes in a commonwealth, where "commonwealth" retains its connection to the property holdings of both independent and interdependent citizens.[57] This vision accords due respect to the private sphere of personal property. However, it places equal emphasis on the search for ways in which to give institutional expression and embodiment to the social character of property.

Of course, the contrast applies to today's civic republicans as well. For all their talk of economic democracy and a civic spirit of equality, civic republicans provide their citizens with little in the way of economic stakes in their political community. We have seen that with notable exceptions such as Michelman, the dominant tendency is to treat rights and property not as civic stakes, but as corruptive external goods which, while necessary, stand in fundamental normative opposition to the internal goods of democratic citizenship.

Yet it also true that producerist ideals of a democratic commonwealth and democratic stakeholding do not resonate very clearly or strongly in the economistic universe of late modern thingness. This perhaps is one reason that civic republicans and other post-socialists have been so tempted by a strategy of overcoming and transcending property. In addition, we may have reached the point where the scope and size of most modern nation-states are simply too great to support more communal and egalitarian forms of liberal democracy. I cannot even attempt to settle the question of the empirical conditions and circumstances under which liberal norms of equal rights, civil liberty, and oppositionist agency might be harmonized with the quest for more egalitarian and communal forms of democracy. But it can be said with confidence that things have not changed so much in the late modern world that it is no longer possible to combine the independence and equal rights of potentially oppositionist citizens with the norms and responsibilities of a democratic commonwealth. Not least important in this regard is the continuing importance of the welfare state (however it is theorized in relation to property). Programs for the communal provision of social welfare have had, and will continue to have, their abuses and their economic disincentives. But these programs have also filled very real gaps in what the market can and does provide, and the abuses and disincentives need to be assessed in relation to the fact that the modern welfare state has promoted security and developmental capabilities for literally tens of millions of citizens around the world.

There also continue to be programmatic alternatives that are more directly and explicitly about the creation and encouragement of democratic stakes in the economic system. Workplace democracy is one such alternative. Cooperative forms of economic organization are another. And in the United States in recent years, we have seen the emergence and growth of one of the most promising innovations in the area of property in a very long time: the community land trust. The basic idea of a community land trust is to set up an institutional structure such as a non-profit organization through which to combine communal ownership of land with long-term renewable leases for the use of buildings and other "improvements" of the land. In this way, the propertied independence of those who lease and inhabit the land is organically connected to civic ends such as the provision of low-income housing, local control of economic life, and environmental stewardship.[58]

With its emphasis on a civic context of inhabitation, the community land trust also points to the possibility of building on (!) the placeness of property for contemporary democratic purposes. It is my contention that despite its illiberal and undemocratic historical roots, the placeness of property is crucial to the development of a democratic theory of property in the late modern world, and furthermore, that the placeness of property potentially is more in keeping with liberal aspirations and ideals than is the case with the economistic universe of modern commercial thingness. Much of what I have to say in the next chapter and in the conclusion will be for the purposes of elaborating and defending these claims about the democratic potential of placeness. However, in charting this course we come upon a potentially substantial obstacle to any effort to develop a democratic theory of property. I have in mind the possibility raised by some theorists and analysts that we already live in a post-property age in the sense that property has lost it conceptual coherence in the late modern era. So an obvious next step in this inquiry is to elucidate my views of thingness and placeness by way of responding to this "disintegration thesis."

Notes

1. Charles Taylor, *The Ethics of Authenticity* (Cambridge, MA: Harvard University Press, 1991), 3 and 118–20. On the other hand, Taylor is also something of an exception to the rule in that he has discussed the complexities of democratic equality to a much greater extent than other civic republicans. Especially in the more liberal republicanism of his later writings (roughly speaking, those starting with the publication of *The Sources of the Self* in 1989) Taylor has devoted a substantial amount of attention to the good of equal respect for all individuals and its complex, and often conflicting, implications for modern identity. Even so, this has not produced (at least as of this writing) a systematic and comprehensive analysis of the relationship between civic virtue and equality. See especially *The Sources of the Self: The Making of Modern Identity* (Cambridge, MA: Harvard University Press, 1989), 11–15 and 65–71; Taylor, "The Politics of Recognition," in *Multiculturalism and "The Politics of Recognition"*, ed. Amy Gutmann (Princeton, NJ: Princeton University Press, 1992; and Taylor, *Modern Social Imaginaries* (Durham, NC: Duke University Press, 2004), especially chapters 9 and 10.

2. Amy Gutmann, *Identity in Democracy* (Princeton, NJ: Princeton University Press, 2003), 26.

3. See Robert A. Dahl, *Democracy and Its Critics* (New Haven, CT: Yale University Press, 1989, 107–8 and chapters 8 and 9. I note that I see these ideas of political inclusion and rightful jurisdiction as foundations for the possibility of establishing what Carol C. Gould calls "equal positive liberty," by which she means simply "equal rights to the conditions of self-development." See Gould, *Rethinking Democracy: Freedom and Social Cooperation in Politics, Economy, and Society* (Cambridge: Cambridge University Press, 1990), 60–71.

4. Michael Walzer, "Socialism Then and Now," *New Republic*, November 6, 1989, 77.

5. I note that my emphasis on property and authority distinguishes my own perspective from some recent theoretical explorations of the oppositionist sources and aspects of democracy. See especially Chantal Mouffe, *The Democratic Paradox* (London: Verso, 2000), 21–22, 69–74, and 98–105; and Ian Shapiro, *Democratic Justice* (New Haven, CT: Yale University Press, 1999), 29–31 and 39–45.

6. *The Unbearable Lightness of Being*, (New York: Harper and Row, 1984), 268.

7. John Locke, *Two Treatises of Government*, ed. Peter Laslett, 2nd ed. (Cambridge: Cambridge University Press, 1967), book II, chapter V, 285–302.

8. See Christopher Lasch, *The True and Only Heaven: Progress and Its Critics* (New York: W. W. Norton and Company, 1991), 197–202.

9. Locke, *Two Treatises of Government*, book I, chapter VII, 195.

10. Locke, book I, chapter IV, 170 and 169.

11. I have been greatly influenced in this analysis of oppositionist thinking about property and political authority by Michael Walzer's discussion of the relationship between property and power in *Spheres of Justice: A Defense of Pluralism and Equality* (New York: Basic Books, 1983), 291–303. I am not sure, however, whether Walzer would accept my analysis of the foundational significance of Locke in this area!

12. See for example John Dunn, *The Political Thought of John Locke: An Historical Account of the Argument of the 'Two Treatises of Government'* (Cambridge: Cambridge University Press, 1969); Dunn, *Locke* (Oxford: Oxford University Press, 1984); and James Tully, *A Discourse on Property: John Locke and His Adversaries* (Cambridge: Cambridge University Press, 1980).

13. See James T. Kloppenberg, "The Virtues of Liberalism: Christianity, Republicanism, and Ethics in Early American Discourse," *The Journal of American History* 74 (1987): 9–33.

14. Gordon Wood, *The Creation of the American Republic, 1776–1787* (New York: W. W. Norton and Company, 1969), 219.

15. See Eric Foner, *Tom Paine and Revolutionary America* (New York: Oxford University Press, 1976), especially chapter 2; Howard B. Rock, *Artisans of the Republic: The Tradesmen of New York City in the Age of Jefferson* (New York: New York University Press, 1984), especially chapter 2; and Sean Wilentz, *Chants Democratic: New York City and the Rise of the American Working Class, 1788–1850* (New York: Oxford University Press, 1984), especially chapter 1. For a discussion of the importance of artisanal imagery in Locke's labor theory, see Tully, *A Discourse on Property*, especially 144–45.

16. For a general discussion of producer republicanism in nineteenth-century America (although one which does not discuss the possibility of a radical Lockean provenance) see William E. Forbath, "The Ambiguities of Free Labor: Labor and Law in the Gilded Age," *Wisconsin Law Review* (1985): 777–815. Also see Leon Fink's classic study of the producer republicanism of the Knights of Labor in *Workingmen's Democracy: The Knights of Labor and American Politics* (Urbana, IL.: University of Illinois Press, 1983). On the rise and fall of producer republicanism, see David Montgomery, *Citizen Worker* (Cambridge: Cambridge University Press, 1993); and Victoria C. Hattam, *Labor Visions and State Power: The Origins of Business Unionism in the United States* (Princeton, NJ: Princeton University Press, 1993). Gareth Stedman Jones discusses republican themes in the Chartist movement in nineteenth-century England in *Languages of Class: Studies in English Working Class History 1832–1982* (Cambridge: Cambridge University Press, 1983), chapter 3. The classic study of republican themes in American Populism is Lawrence Goodwyn, *The Populist Moment: A Short History of the Agrarian Revolt in America* (Oxford: Oxford University Press, 1978).

17. As quoted in Richard Hofstadter, *The Progressive Historians: Turner, Beard, Parrington* (New York: Vintage Books, 1970), 438, emphasis added.

18. Adam Smith, *An Inquiry into the Nature and Causes of the Wealth of Nations*, vol. 1, ed. Edwin Cannan (Chicago: University of Chicago Press, 1976), 433.

19. Smith's concern about "servile dependency" also evokes the neo-roman ideal of non-domination!

20. Frederick Douglass, "What to the Slave Is the Fourth of July?: An Address Delivered in Rochester, New York, on 5 July 1852," in *The Frederick Douglass Papers*, vol. 2 of *Series One: Speeches, Debates, Interviews*, ed. John W. Blassingame (New Haven, CT: Yale Unversity Press, 1982), 371. There is a sense in which the whole speech is a litany of liberal values that are contradicted and betrayed by slavery. But see in particular 369–71, 376–77, and 382–84.

21. Elizabeth Cady Stanton, "Address to the Legislature of New York on Women's Rights," in *Elizabeth Cady Stanton/Susan B. Anthony: Correspondence, Writings, Speeches*, ed. Ellen Carol DuBois (New York: Schocken Books, 1981), 45 and 48. I note that this speech also evinced some exclusionary views of class, race, and alienage. Unfortunately, there were numerous "inter-sectional" barriers on the road to equality in the development of the oppositionist moment.

22. The term "headship" is Stanton's. See Elizabeth Cady Stanton, "Home Life," *Elizabeth Cady Stanton/Susan B. Anthony*, 133. Consider also Susan B. Anthony's defense of propertied independence in the form of home ownership for women in "Homes of Single Women," Stanton, 146–51. Note that neither Stanton nor Anthony believed that rights-based oppositionist agency precluded virtue or visions of moral and civic community. In most respects, Stanton's liberal feminism was more radically oppositionist than the classical liberalism of either Locke or Smith. But this did not prevent Stanton from combining a defense of women's rights with a vision of the morality of more egalitarian and inclusive forms of family and community life. See especially "Home Life," 132–33.

23. For a similar argument, though without consideration of the relationship between property and political authority, see Charles Taylor's discussion of the linkage between personal independence and equality in the modern era, in *Modern Social Imaginaries*, 150–52.

24. Morris R. Cohen, "Property and Sovereignty," in *Readings in Jurisprudence and Legal Philosophy*, ed. Morris R. Cohen and Felix S. Cohen (New York: Prentice-Hall, 1951), 27. And later on in the same essay, Cohen extended the analysis to the modern commercial system of advertising. The "modern captain of industry and finance" does not have the ancient lord's power of "direct sumptuary legislation," Cohen conceded. "But those who have the power to standardize and advertise certain products do determine what we may buy and sell." Cohen, 28.

25. See in particular Karl Marx, "On the Jewish Question," in *The Marx-Engels Reader*, ed. Robert C. Tucker (New York: W. W. Norton and Company, Inc., 1972).

26. See Richard Ashcraft, *Revolutionary Politics and Locke's Two Treatises of Government* (Princeton, NJ: Princeton University Press, 1986), chapter 4.

27. Kenneth R. Minogue, "The Concept of Property and Its Contemporary Significance," in *Property*, vol XXII of *Nomos* (New York: New York University Press, 1980), 22.

28. Minogue, 22.

29. Richard Flathman, *Towards a Liberalism* . . . (Ithaca, NY: Cornell University Press, 1989), chapter 2, especially 51–52.

30. William M. Sullivan, *Reconstructing Public Philosophy* (Berkeley, CA: University of California Press, 1986), 112.

31. See Benjamin R. Barber's all-too-brief discussion of these kinds of dangers in *Strong Democracy: Participatory Politics for a New Age* (Berkeley, CA: University of California Press, 1984), 227.

32. See Chantal Mouffe's discussion of the tensions between liberty and equality in liberal democracy, in *The Paradox of Democracy*, especially 2–6.

33. Thomas Hobbes, *Leviathan* (London: Penguin Books, 1968), 266.

34. Russell Arben Fox, "Confucianism and Communitarianism in a Liberal Democratic World," in *Border Crossings: Toward a Comparative Political Theory*, ed. Fred Dallmayr (Lanham, MD: Lexington Books, 1999), 193–96 and 200.

35. Gary B. Nash, *Red, White, and Black: The Peoples of Early America*, 3rd ed. (Englewood Cliffs, NJ: Prentice Hall, 1992), 22.

36. Nash, 22.

37. Fox, "Confucianism and Communitarianism," 194–95 and 203–4.

38. Martha C. Nussbaum, *Women and Human Development: The Capabilities Approach* (Cambridge, MA: Cambridge University Press, 2000), 281–82.

39. Fox, "Confucianism and Communitarianism," 200.

40. See Jennifer Nedelsky's discussion of the role of property in Madison's thought in *Private Property and the Limits of American Constitutionalism* (Chicago: University of Chicago Press, 1990), especially chapter 2. For an interpretation of Madison's defense of private property in the 1780s as an instance of the "increasing conflict of his liberal with his majoritarian commitments," see Lance Banning, *The Sacred Fire of Liberty: James Madison and the Founding of the Federal Republic* (Ithaca, NY: Cornell University Press, 1995), 135–37 and 181–84.

41. See Banning, *The Sacred Fire of Liberty*, 183.

42. For a discussion of the malleability of Locke and his legacy in nineteenth-century American political thought, see Laura J. Scalia, "The Many Faces of Locke in America's Early Nineteenth-Century Democratic Philosophy," *Political Research Quarterly* 49 (1996): 807–35. Also see Kenneth Minogue's discussion of Locke in "The Concept of Property and Its Contemporary Significance," 17.

43. Jeremy Waldron, *The Right to Private Property* (Oxford: Clarendon Press, 1988), 106–15.

44. Leon Fink, "The New Labor History and the Powers of Historical Pessimism," *The Journal of American History* 75 (1988): 122–23.

45. See the sources cited in notes 9 and 10 above.

46. Forbath, "The Ambiguities of Free Labor," 767–815

47. Forbath, 774–75 and 813–14.

48. Such tensions are examined in Michael Kazin, *The Populist Persuasion: An American History* (New York: Basic Books, 1995).

49. Examples such as this underscore the fact that the problem of republican paternalism cannot be addressed simply by redescribing civic virtue in more "liberal" terms as a collective engagement on behalf of shared rights and liberties. Quentin Skinner tries to make the case for such a redescription in "The Idea of Negative Liberty: Philosophical and Historical Perspectives," in *Philosophy in History*, ed. Richard Rorty, J. B. Schneewind, and Quentin Skinner (Cambridge: Cambridge University Press, 1984).

50. Adolf A. Berle, Jr. and Gardiner C. Means, *The Modern Corporation and Private Property* (New York: Commerce Clearing House, Inc., 1932), 1–9, 127–52, and 333–57.

51. Berle and Means, 353.

52. Berle and Means, 356.

53. Among post-socialists, Phillip Selznick is an important but also only partial exception. Selznick draws on Berle and Means in the process of outlining a communitarian vision of socially responsible economic enterprise. But what he draws from

them is not their effort to redefine property and the responsibilities that attend to it, but their institutionalist approach to the corporation. The problem is that these two things went together in Berle and Means's analysis. See Phillip Selznick, *The Communitarian Persuasion* (Washington, DC: Woodrow Wilson Center Press, 2002), 98–99.

54. John Rawls, *A Theory of Justice* (Cambridge, MA: Belknap Press, 1971), 106; and Thomas Spragens, Jr., *Reason and Democracy* (Durham, NC: Duke University Press, 1990), 217. Also see Rawls, *Justice as Fairness: A Restatement*, ed. Erin Kelley (Cambridge, MA: Belknap Press, 2001), 137–40.

55. L. T. Hobhouse, "The Historical Evolution of Property, in Fact and Idea," in *Property: Its Duties and Rights* (London: Macmillan and Co., 1913), 31.

56. Thus, while Rawls defends a basic liberty of personal property, he makes a point of distinguishing such personal property rights from two "wider conceptions" of property: the conservative conception that extends protection to fundamental private rights of acquisition, bequest, and ownership of the means of production and natural resources; and the more egalitarian view of an "equal right to participate in the control of the means of production and natural resources, which are to be socially owned." John Rawls, *Political Liberalism* (New York: Columbia University Press, 1993), 298; also see *Justice as Fairness*, 115. Significantly, one finds the same bifurcation of property into fundamental rights to personal property and more limited and circumscribed rights to property outside the personal sphere in virtue-centered forms of contemporary liberalism. See, for example, Spragens, *Reason and Democracy*, 217–20.

57. See Frank I. Michelman, "Possession vs. Distribution in the Constitutional Idea of Property," *Iowa Law Review* 72 (1987): 1319–50.

58. For a helpful introduction to community land trusts, see Tom Peterson, "Community Land Trusts: An Introduction," *Planning Commissioners Journal* (1996): 10–12. Also see the information provided by the Institute for Community Economics at www.iceclt.org/clt.

7

Hannah Arendt and the
Disintegration of Property

I T IS A SIGN OF THE DIMINISHED STATUS OF PROPERTY that the possibility of its disintegration has barely caused a ripple in the texts and debates of contemporary political theory. I confess that it has crossed my mind that this reflects the strategic value of property for post-materialist thinkers. If property has disintegrated, then they will have lost something that has served as the focal point of moral outrage about acquisitiveness and economic self-seeking for centuries. Of course, this is far too cynical an explanation. In truth, if property is as great a danger as many post-materialist thinkers suggest, then there would not be much reason to mourn its passing. It is reasonable to suppose, therefore, that post-materialist theorists have neglected the disintegration thesis for the same reasons they have neglected the general subject of property.

Just as I have argued that property is deserving of more attention than it has received in contemporary theoretical debates such as that over civic republicanism, so too do I wish to argue that the disintegration thesis is deserving of more attention. It is often the case that the nature of something becomes more clear when we encounter the prospect of its disappearance. This I believe is the case with property, for when we consider the prospect of its disappearance we are able to see more clearly the relationship between thingness and placeness. I hope to show that this relationship makes it very unlikely that property will disintegrate in the near future. Beyond this, I hope to show that there are good reasons to question whether the disintegration of property would be a desirable development with regard to democracy and attendant ideals of freedom and equality.

There are two versions of this thesis that concern us. One is Thomas Grey's argument that property has collapsed because there is no longer a unified or coherent idea of "thing ownership." The other version is Hannah Arendt's civic republican argument that property has disintegrated by virtue of the almost complete disappearance of the idea of property as a location in the world. Both versions deserve our serious and sustained attention. But it is primarily around Arendt's version that this chapter is organized. There are several reasons for this. For one thing, Arendt is a thinker who has had, and continues to have, considerable influence on the various discussions and debates that have accompanied the revival of civic republicanism. In addition, the fact that Arendt developed a concept of the placeness of property has obvious relevance to this inquiry. Although there are some important differences in our respective approaches to property, my understanding of placeness owes a great deal to Arendt. And this debt extends beyond her specific ideas about placeness to her broader theoretical analysis of property and its fate in the modern world. By exploring this broader analysis, we are able to look at a variety of perennial property issues in new ways.

I turn first, though, to Grey's influential elaboration of the disintegration thesis. Sorting through his arguments about the incoherence of thing ownership will help to frame the issues at stake not only with Arendt's analysis of the decline of property in the modern world, but also with my hermeneutic perspective on the relationship between thingness and placeness.

Grey on the Disintegration of Thingness

In contrast to Arendt's analysis of the disintegration of property, Grey's has received considerable attention from the group of theorists and scholars who remain interested in issues of property.[1] This is not all that surprising in light of the fact that Grey frames his version of the disintegration thesis within (as well as against) the legal discourse of modern thingness. As an analyst in the liberal tradition of legal realism, Grey seeks to debunk the formalist illusion of "unified thing ownership" that has accompanied and supported modern thinking about property. According to Grey, property in the era of advanced market capitalism has become so complex, so technical, and most of all, so fragmented that it no longer has either the coherence or the political and moral resonance that it once had. In Grey's terms, the modern legal conception of property reflects a two-fold disintegration of the original "classical liberal" conception of property "as *things* that are *owned* by persons."[2] First, it dissolves and fragments the traditional understanding of unified "rights of ownership." Specifically, the notion of a clearly identifiable property owner who possesses clearly identifiable rights to the exclusive control of something gives way to the "more shadowy" idea of a divisible and transferable "bundle" of rights, uses, and interests.[3] Second, the traditional connection between "property rights and things" ("thing ownership," as Grey calls it) gives way to a modern legal and economic regime in which most property is "intangible"—for instance, in the form of stocks and bonds, insurance policies, bank accounts, franchises, patents, and copyrights.

As we saw earlier, Grey uses the diminished role of property in Rawls's theory of justice to support his argument. However, the thrust of Grey's analysis is to trace the disintegration of thing ownership in relation to broader economic forces and tendencies within modern capitalism. Citing capitalism's "progressive exploitation" of the division of labor and its reliance on economies of scale, Grey maintains that "the collapse of the idea of property" is "intrinsic to the development of a free-market economy into an industrial phase."[4]

Grey does not mourn the "death of property" in late modern capitalism. This is partly because he sees it as a more or less inevitable outcome given the increasingly complex and technical nature of modern economic tasks and organizations. But more than this, Grey thinks that there are important benefits to be gained from the disintegration of property. He maintains that the fragmentation of property makes it easier to face up to and accept the legal and institutional realities of late modern political economy. This is in keeping with his legal realist interest in showing just how far removed the formalist ideal of unified thing ownership is from empirical reality. In addition, Grey believes that the "death of property" opens up a path of pragmatic liberal reform that avoids the pitfalls of both classical liberalism and Marxian collectivism. Grey maintains—correctly in my view—that the classical liberal defense of capitalism and the Marxian vision of a collectivist alternative are rooted in, and suffer from, the same "thing-ownership conception of property." Grey's hope is that the disintegration of this conception will help to clear away ideological and political resistance to pragmatic liberal efforts to combine elements of the capitalist market with elements of collective decision-making. He acknowledges that there would still be important differences between these two "methods of organizing and operating enterprises." But these differences would no longer be exaggerated and distorted by the myth of unified thingness; or as Grey puts it, "the idea that natural necessity somehow imposes a stark choice between organizing an economy according to one or the other mode becomes less plausible, once the single-owner presupposition is dropped."[5]

There are echoes here of Berle and Means's analysis of the modern corporation. Berle and Means were also responding to the more complex institutional and organizational structure of modern capitalism. They too claimed that this new reality had rendered obsolete the traditional (i.e., classical liberal) understanding of property, and they too sought to steer a pragmatic path between, and away from, the ideological poles of classical liberalism and collectivism. But where Berle and Means focused on developing a new approach to property that recognized and incorporated the new institutional and organizational realities of corporate capitalism, Grey is content to let property die.

It almost goes without saying that I think that Grey is far too optimistic about both the sources and the prospects of a property-less form of liberal theory. One problem in this regard is that he glosses over the ideological dimension of the decline of property. Grey would have us believe that the decline of property is the result of economic imperatives within the development of late modern capitalism, and that the only problems of ideology have to do with the blinders that the thing-ownership conception of property has created for classical liberals and collectivists. But the decline of property is not simply an epiphenomenal reflection of underlying economic forces and developments; it is also a reflection of theoretical and ideological commitments. The subsumption of property under the terms and categories of mainstream capitalist economics is itself partly ideological in that it is based on the belief that politics should be guided by these economic terms and categories. Hence, it is an *economistic* subsumption, an *economistic* redescription of property as an institutional form of economic value within the framework of a market economy. This means in turn that the fragmentation of property is not the boon to reform liberalism that Grey hopes. The experience of left-leaning reform liberalism in America in recent years shows all too well that an economistic approach to public policy is more likely to defeat left liberal aspirations for economic justice and democracy than to bolster them. And in the meantime, citizens are forced to rely on formalist illusions of thing ownership as they try to make sense of the property arrangements within which they find themselves.

I will have more to say about the dangers of a post-property era at the end of this chapter. At this time, though, we need to focus on the prior question of whether property has disintegrated or is likely to disintegrate in the foreseeable future.

My primary reason for rejecting Grey's analysis is his neglect of placeness. The displacement of property is not just about its declining influence. It is also about how thingness is privileged at the expense of property-related contexts of identity, authority, and labor. In other words, it is about the conceptual displacement of property as well as its normative displacement. Grey's analysis perpetuates the conceptual displacement of property that is at the heart of modern understandings of thingness. But more to the point of my critique of the disintegration thesis, even modern (i.e., commercial) thingness cannot subsist without the placeness of property. I wish to argue that this residual placeness is one of the factors that prevent the collapse of thing ownership.

In order to see how placeness prevents the disintegration of thingness, we need to avoid three possible errors pertaining to the conceptual relationship between thingness and placeness. First, we need to avoid thinking of the distinction between thingness and placeness as if it refers to two different types of property. The distinction between thingness and placeness is not analogous to legal distinctions such as that between "real" and "personal" or "movable" property. Rather, it refers to different ways of understanding the relationship between a person who is in a position of claiming proprietary rights or entitlements and the objects of such rights or entitlements. Hence, both the thingness and the placeness of property revolve around a possessive relation between property holders and what is held.

At first glance, this seems to efface the very distinction I am trying to make; that is to say, it seems to collapse placeness into thingness. However, the distinction quickly reappears when we ask the question: Where, in social or socially constituted physical space, does the possessive relation take place? In essence, the distinction between thingness and placeness revolves around two different ways of responding to this question, or more precisely, two different views of the importance of this question for understanding what property is about. Under the idea of thingness, the immediate location or social context of the possessive relation might be of interest, and perhaps even of intense interest, but not in the deeper, constitutive sense of informing and defining the very nature and purposes of the relation. Again, the questions that count most are the "how" and especially the "what" of possession, ownership, and transfer. Because of this, there is a level at which both the subjects (i.e., the holders) and the objects (or holdings) retain their fundamental meaning apart from their context.

By contrast, under the idea of placeness, the immediate social location or context is partly constitutive of both the self-understandings of subjects and the nature of the objects. In keeping with my rethinking of the situated self, the possessive relation is socially embodied. This, it needs to be stressed, does not mark the disappearance of questions associated with the thingness of property. There is what might be thought of as an incipient thingness within the placeness of property. Consequently, the "what" and the "how" of possession, ownership, and exchange remain very much at issue. However, the way in which these questions are posed and addressed is shaped by the purposes and practices of the social location in which property holdings are held.

A second possible error to be mindful of has to do with hermeneutic versus analytic approaches to property. It is tempting to think in terms of neat and simple correlations between placeness and hermeneutics and between thing-ness and an analytic approach. However, things are not so neat and simple. One of the aims of this chapter is precisely to expose the problems with such a binary perspective, first by showing the problems with Grey's analytic ap-proach to modern thing ownership, and second by challenging Arendt's own hermeneutics of property for its one-sided focus on placeness. To be sure, modern thingness is bound up with an analytic approach to property, and I trust it is abundantly clear by now that I am very critical of this approach. However, it is not just placeness that is revealed by hermeneutics, but a *rela-tionship* between thingness and placeness. For reasons that I have spelled out in previous discussions of thingness and placeness, this relationship is far more likely to be uncovered through hermeneutics than through an analytic approach to property.

One final error to be avoided is thinking of the relationship between thing-ness and placeness as if it were static. Property is an institution with countless cultural and historical variations. Beyond this, there is considerable fluidity built into the structure of thingness and placeness. In addition to not being separate types of property, thingness and placeness are not quite mutually ex-clusive conceptual dimensions of property. Thus, along with an incipient thingness, it is also possible to think of an incipient placeness within the thingness of property. For instance, the same boundary-creating features of the proprietary model that critics of classical liberal property excoriate simul-taneously evoke images of location *and* images pertaining to the right of the property holder to exclude others from the use of the thing. And a similar point can be made about the possessive relation that is characterized by an emotional attachment to property holdings. On the one hand, such an emo-tional attachment can take the form of a kind of debased thingness—for in-stance, a Silas Marner type of attachment to gold—thereby sparking moral concern and criticism concerning the dangers of crass materialism and pos-sessive individualism. On the other hand, it is also possible to have emotional attachments to things—for instance, a home—which help to foster the type of constitutive locations of property that are characteristic of placeness.[6]

For us, the key point in all this is that the "lived experience" associated with property involves a dynamic relationship between thingness and placeness. By focusing only on thing ownership, Grey is neglecting not only placeness, but also, and more importantly, the fluid relationship between them.

Placeness and the Reintegration of Thing Ownership

Viewed through the lens of a hermeneutics of thingness and placeness, Grey's argument appears as a story about the disintegration of thingness that is told from the very same analytic perspective on property that is so closely associated with modern thingness. Taking classical liberal property as his baseline of analysis and comparison, Grey seeks to show that both sides of the possessive relation between property holders and their holdings have disintegrated. In other words, the idea of a self-contained property holder with a unified and complete set of rights to discrete material things has collapsed. However, if we look at late modern property in terms of a complex interaction between dominant understandings of thingness and submerged and incipient understandings of placeness, a very different set of possibilities emerges. On the one hand, we begin to see that the integrative effects of a residual placeness might be countering the tendency towards disintegration, and may, indeed, be helping to sustain the dominant understandings of thingness. On the other hand, there is the possibility that what is threatened by the disintegrative forces of an advanced market capitalism is not so much the thingness of property but those understandings and conversations which explicitly link property to the moral and civic purposes of its social locations and embodiments.

I would like to try to establish the plausibility of both these possibilities by examining two questionable assumptions within Grey's legal realist version of the disintegration thesis. First, there is the assumption that technical legal discourse about property holds the key to understanding the conceptual status and condition of property in society at large. Now, I certainly do not want to deny that specialized discourse concerning intangible property or fragmented bundles of property rights has rendered the law of property somewhat confused, if not completely incoherent. Neither do I wish to deny that legal discourse helps to shape institutional arrangements of property or (within limits) social understandings of property. However, this privileging of technical property discourse runs afoul in two ways. First, lawyers and legal specialists continue to talk about property (for instance, in the area of takings) in ways that not only presuppose a workable degree of coherence, but also presuppose the possibility of incorporating elements of ordinary thing ownership into more specialized vocabularies.[7] Second, unless we are content with a simple "false consciousness" explanation of ordinary understandings of property, we must at least seek to account for them as part of the analysis. As Joseph Singer points out in a discussion of the defects of the legal realist model of property, "It fails to recognize the cultural endurance of the concept of property for both citizens and judges. The ownership idea—for good or for ill—is extremely powerful and affects the way legal and social problems are analyzed. Demonstrating that ownership can be deconstructed does not deprive it of force as an organizing category."[8] We must, in other words, account for the persistence of meaningful property discourse both inside and outside the discursive field of the law. The property rights movement is one kind of example

of this, but so too is the environmentalist who claims that the value of ecology requires that the (more or less unified) rights of *particular* property owners must at times be regulated and restricted for the public good of environmental sustainability. What these two groups end up saying in court is a rather
different matter. But my point is simply this: Once specialized legal discourse
is no longer privileged over other types of property discourse, we are led to ask
why property has not disintegrated, or rather, why it is has not disintegrated
to the extent suggested by technical property discourse?

One possible response to this question is that property (meaning unified
thing ownership) exercises a mythic and mystifying hold on the imaginations
of both ordinary people and many lawyers. In other words, people stubbornly
cling to the illusion of possessive relations organized around unified thing
ownership.[9] This of course raises the false consciousness issue again. However,
without denying the mythic power of thing ownership in societies such as the
United States, I believe that the integrative effects of a residual placeness of
property provide a simpler (if not total) explanation.[10] Consider the case of a
homeless family that desires a home. No doubt, this family wants a house or
apartment in the sense of a property holding to which it can claim some entitlement. Yet it is equally plausible, if not more so, to think of this family as
wanting a piece of property in the sense of having a place to call their own.

As important as such cases of an emotional attachment to actual or potential surroundings are, they are not the only examples of the integrative effects
of the placeness of property. There are more impersonal cases as well, including the incipient placeness of the modern business corporation itself. Just as a
household gathers together and integrates its various property holdings for
the ends and purposes of household members, so too is it possible to think of
the corporation as gathering together and integrating its various bundles of
property rights for its corporate purposes. Of course, this may not involve
what we would think of as higher purposes. And again, what the corporation
says about property in its legal expressions and conflicts is not likely to emphasize placeness. But even corporate managers and corporate lawyers have
understandings of their social location that are not confined to those contained within technical legal discourse.

When we displace property from its social context and seek to resolve it analytically into discrete, non-contextual possessive relations, the integrative effects of placeness will not be seen. This points to the somewhat ironic possibility that the dominance of thingness in our culture is sustained in part by the
integrative effects of a submerged and often unacknowledged placeness, a self-
effacing placeness as it were. If this is the case, then, yes, there is a mythic and
illusory quality to the "official" liberal capitalist discourse of unified thing ownership. However, the illusion does not lie in the persistence of property so

much as in the belief that property is only about thingness, a thingness so pure that it need not exist in any particular social location to remain intelligible. The irony of course is that this illusion is parasitic on the placeness of property.

This brings us to the second questionable assumption within Grey's version of the disintegration thesis. This is the assumption that it is impossible to re-describe the ideal type of full classical liberal thingness in such a way as to account for developments like the rise of intangible property or the "bundle of rights" approach. In this regard, it is important to keep in mind that Grey's argument implies that property has lost its coherence in the specific sense that there is a gap between the classical liberal theory of property and the actual legal practice of ownership.[11] Even if there was a period in history in which there was no such gap (and I am not convinced that there was) this criterion of coherence is extremely problematic. This becomes clear if we suspend our hermeneutic perspective for a moment and think of the ideal type of full and unified thing ownership in more formal and analytic terms as a simple logical relationship between any property holder A and any property holding x. This of course is the basic possessive relation within any theory of thingness. But notice how easy it is to develop a theoretical redescription of this possessive relation so that it coheres with the very same changes in property that Grey says are a sign of its collapse. For one thing, and by way of elaboration of a point I made earlier, the formal possessive relation between property holder A and property object x can easily accommodate both tangible and intangible property. Formally speaking, the "objectness" of the property holding in this relationship consists only in something to which the owner can claim rights of ownership, and this need not be a tangible physical thing.

In addition, and even more unsettling, it is possible to develop a theoretical redescription of the modern "bundle of rights" approach to ownership so that it too coheres with the logic of classical liberal thingness. For Grey, the fact that ownership and its accompanying rights of control, use, and disposition can be divided and transferred among several different legal persons is a sign that advanced capitalism has largely dispensed with, and can do without, a unified and unitary subject of ownership. Instead of the fee simple estates and family-owned businesses of classical liberal theory and practice, we have the condominium and the corporation. But consider what the libertarian conservative legal theorist Richard Epstein has to say in response to Grey's argument: "The condominium and the corporation are created by the repeated use of the rights of disposition that are inherent in private property—rights that are transferred and not lost by their exercise. The protean ways in which vested entitlements can be recombined show the flexibility, not the unintelligibility, of the institution of private property."[12] In essence, Epstein is saying that there *is* a unitary subject of ownership for each and every particular "vested" right, that is, for each and every strand or stick in a larger bundle of rights.

The key for Epstein, as it is for other libertarian conservatives such as Robert Nozick, is the existence of one foundational right, which, in the midst of all the bundles of modern property, is indivisible. This is the right (with very few limits) to transfer tangible and intangible property objects through contractual market agreements. It is a market model of property in the specific sense that any particular object that has market value among consenting and of course self-owning adults is thought of as a vested entitlement. As legal realists and many contemporary liberals would be quick to point out, this is hard to square with classical liberalism of the type represented by Locke, or even Smith for that matter.[13] Even so, it does have a formal coherence.[14] And judging from recent political developments in the United States, it continues to resonate in some fairly large political circles.

Both the ease and the popularity of the libertarian conservative redescription of classical liberal property serve as a reminder that possessive individualism rushes in where liberals, post-socialists, and other contemporary post-materialists fear to tread. Moreover, the popularity of this redescription provides a dramatic refutation of the idea that the disintegration of thing ownership is an irreversible process that is built into the economic processes and arrangements of advanced market capitalism.

It might seem that Grey's version of the disintegration thesis has itself disintegrated. And it has as a thesis about the thingness of property. Yet it still has some application to the disintegrative effects that a market model of property has with regard to the moral and civic purposes that are associated with more fully developed forms of the placeness of property. In my view, the most valuable kernel of truth in Grey's argument—and it is a kernel that is not often recognized in the standard critiques of possessive individualism, economism, and modern materialism—is the idea that there is a close but also very uneasy relationship within capitalism between the market and property. For Grey, this means that the commodification of property objects leads to the unraveling of thingness; in other words, he thinks there is a sense in which thingness deconstructs itself. However, my analysis indicates that the tendency towards disintegration is more a matter of both commodified objects and their holders becoming increasingly detached from the ends and purposes of particular social locations of property. In this regard, it is hardly surprising that the locational "where" of the possessive relation almost completely disappears in the libertarian conservative redescription of classical liberal property. Indeed, places such as condominiums and corporations function only as bundles of objects that are created through the transfers of radically unencumbered property holders. In this market model of property, the concept of commonwealth is resolved into the sum of transferred and transferable wealth. The commonwealth is it-self a divisible object of wealth, not a location of citizenship.

But perhaps libertarian conservatism and other forms of neoliberal capital-ism are simply the fullest and purest ideological expressions of a process of disintegration that has more to do with the decline of placeness than with thingness. Perhaps therefore Grey was right to see the disintegrative effects of the capitalist market, but wrong to see this as being mainly or deeply about the collapse of the modern myth of unified thing ownership. And perhaps I am wrong to see a residual placeness that holds property together in the era of ad-vanced capitalism. These are possibilities that are suggested by Arendt's analy-sis of the disintegration of property in the modern era.

Recovering Arendt's Critique of Modern Property

Part of Arendt's significance for this inquiry is simply that her analysis of property has received comparatively little attention in the enormous body of interpretation and commentary that has grown up around her work in the last few decades.[15] This reminds us of how topsy-turvy the world of political the-ory has become under the influence of post-materialist thinking about prop-erty. Consider this: Rawls, the premier theorist of distributive justice in the late modern era, had little to say about property though he is often identified by his critics with the liberal tradition of possessive individualism. Arendt, perhaps the leading theorist of civic virtue in the last sixty years, had a great deal to say about property, though both her defenders and her critics are apt to identify her with post-materialist criticisms of property!

Of course, it is the substance of Arendt's analysis that most interests me, most especially with respect to her conceptualization of the placeness of prop-erty and her argument about its disintegration.

Arendt is famous for her argument in *The Human Condition* that the "pub-lic realm" of citizen action has been debased and impoverished by the rise of a "social realm" of behavioral conformity, statistical regularity, mindless labor, and mass consumerism.[16] What is seldom recognized, or at least seldom dis-cussed, is that Arendt organized this argument around a critique of modern property.

It may be helpful to think of this critique as occurring on two levels. The first level has to do with Arendt's broader critique of "the social" while the sec-ond level has to do with the decline of the placeness of property. On the first level, the problem with modern property involves the colonization of public life by activities that, in Greek and Roman antiquity, were confined to the pri-vate realm of the household. The rise of the social, in Arendt's view, is about the rise of a kind of insidious form of mass "housekeeping" in which matters of family life and biological necessity become public concerns. The connection to property is simply that these are matters that were once carried on in the context of managing the private property of the household. Hence, the rise of the social "coincided historically with the transformation of the private care for private property into a public concern."[17] What makes this transformation so insidious is that the life of self-governing citizenship is a life of action, which for Arendt means that it is a life not of necessity, but of the free and unpredictable initiation of "new beginnings" in public spaces where one can be "seen and heard" by other citizens.[18] Better for public life, therefore, when matters of housekeeping and biological necessity remain in the private realm of property. This not only preserves and protects public liberty from the normalizing influence of the social realm. It also preserves and protects the role of the household in providing for those biological needs that must be mastered if an individual is to be able to enter the public realm of freedom. As she puts it: "To own property meant here to be master of one's own necessities of life and therefore potentially to be a free person, free to transcend his own life and enter the world all have in common."[19]

It is at this first level that we see the connection between property and Arendt's well-known and controversial contempt for the "social question." From her point of view, the progressive modern impulse to address the social question perverts and undermines freedom by redefining it as physical emancipation from poverty and scarcity. These are precisely the kinds of housekeeping matters relating to the biological life process that used to be, and were more appropriately, associated with management of private property in the household. So naturally Arendt maintains that the result of the modern preoccupation with the social question "was that necessity invaded the public realm, the only realm where men can be truly free."[20]

Even though students of Arendt's thought usually have downplayed the connection to property, many of the general themes at this first level of her critique have been worked over extensively. But to focus only on this level is to miss the importance of the fact that Arendt challenged the modern understanding of property itself. Without accounting for this challenge, Arendt's views on property are apt to appear as a nostalgic defense of private property in the form of premodern households. No doubt, there is some degree of nostalgia in Arendt's critique of modern property. But she was not interested in returning to the slave economies of classical Western antiquity. Such a project was morally repugnant to her, and in any event, she did not think that it would be possible because of what had happened to property in the modern world.

This brings us to the second level of her critique. At this level, Arendt argues that modern property is a debased form of property, so debased, in her view, that it has essentially disintegrated. The fundamental problem, Arendt maintains, is that property as "a tangible, worldly place of one's own" has all but disappeared in the modern world.[21] In other words, the crisis of modern property is a crisis of its placelessness.

For Arendt, the history of property is largely one of the triumph of wealth at the expense of the placeness of property. It is within the framework of this history that she expresses her concerns about the disintegration of property. "The development of the modern age and the rise of society," she worries, " . . . may make it doubtful whether the existence of property as a privately held place within the world can withstand the relentless process of growing wealth."[22] "Wealth," in Arendt's lexicon, has to do with the generation, acquisition, and accumulation of assets. Its most important form in capitalism is capital itself. But its more general modern form (that is, in both capitalist and collectivist societies) is any form of accumulation that is a source of livelihood.[23] According to Margaret Canovan, Arendt's distinction between property and wealth revolves around the difference between "stability and process." Canovan elaborates as follows:

> By "property" [Arendt] means, as she claims pre-modern men also meant, a privately owned place in the common world, something stable, marked off from the property of others: a place to dwell in, not just to possess. "Wealth," by contrast, is something insubstantial, not tied to any particular location, and its most characteristic form is capital, the function of which is to generate more wealth in an endless process.[24]

This captures the basic distinction very nicely, but it also overstates the clarity of what Arendt has to say about the matter. The manner in which Arendt uses the terms "property" and "wealth" suggests a relationship between them that is more subtle, but also more elusive and elliptical. Sometimes Arendt treats property and wealth as completely different things ("It is easy to forget . . . that wealth and property, far from being the same, are of an entirely different nature.") while at other times she suggests that placeness and wealth represent "two types of property."[25] What *is* clear is that Arendt believed that wealth is, at best, an inferior form of property, and that the nature of true (or truer) property revolves around location and place. We also can say with certainty that she believed that placeness was the original form of property, and that this original placeness played an important role in constituting public life in the polities of the ancient Western world. "Originally," she writes in reference to the ancient Greek household (*oikos*), "property meant no more or less than to have one's location in a particular part of the world and therefore to belong to the body politic, that is, to be the head of one of the families which together constituted the public realm."[26] In the modern world, by contrast, the private placeness of the household has been absorbed within, and over-whelmed by, an ersatz public realm of mass housekeeping, and property in its original form has given way to a seemingly endless process of appropriating and accumulating wealth.

Arendt traces the tension between property and wealth to the privacy of the placeness of property. While true property is formative of the civic capacity of the masters of households, and while it plays an important role in delineating the boundaries of public life, it is, in Arendt's account, fundamentally private. As a location of property, the household has both an interior and an exterior. The exterior of the household establishes a physical boundary that helps to demarcate the public realm, but the interior "remains hidden and of no pub-lic significance." Here, as elsewhere in Arendt's thought, private and public life support each other through the starkness of their opposition: "Privacy was like the other, the dark and hidden side of the public realm, and while to be political meant to attain the highest possibility of human existence, to have no private place of one's own (like a slave) meant to be no longer human." The problem with respect to wealth is that its nature is to transgress and efface the boundaries of private life. Nor does it matter whether we are dealing with in-dividualist or collectivist modes of appropriation. "Individual appropriation of wealth," Arendt argues, "will in the long run respect private property no more than socialization of the accumulation process." And why is this so? Arendt's answer, not surprisingly, has to do with the rise of the social. Here is how she explains things: "It is not an invention of Karl Marx but actually in the very nature of [modern] society itself that privacy in every sense can only hinder the development of social 'productivity' and that considerations of pri-vate ownership should therefore be overruled in favor of the ever-increasing process of social wealth."[27] In other words, the process of accumulating social wealth is of a piece with modern housekeeping; both undermine the relation-ship between private and public life through the social management of the needs of the laboring masses, and this is true of both collectivist and liberal capitalist regimes. Mass housekeeping is about providing for the needs of the populace in predictable ways, and the promotion and management of social wealth is essential to this task.

It may be helpful to shift to more of an economic analysis of the relation-ship between wealth and true property. Both wealth and true property involve the utility or use value of what is owned, and in both cases, Arendt associates use value with forms of consumption that are facilitated by ownership. But it is the nature of true property that the use values associated with it are defined, constituted, and confined by property's location in the world. Use value, in other words, is situated or embedded in property locations such as the house-hold. This gives use value a "worldly character," but in the specific sense of providing it with a stable and more or less permanent framework for the impermanence of biological needs. The household quite literally houses the forms of consumption that make it possible "to be master of one's own necessities of life and therefore potentially to be a free person." So once use value is removed from the constraints and boundaries of its location—once it breaks free of its housing, as it were—we are on the way to the modern identification—or rather, misidentification—of property with wealth. By the same token, wealth differs from true property precisely because the forms of consumption associated with wealth no longer have worldly boundaries and purposes. Hence, the progressive "transformation of immobile into mobile property" provides an important marker for the effacement of the distinction between property and wealth in the modern era.[28] Hence, also, it is significant that the leading modern theorists of property (specifically, Locke and Marx) abandoned the idea of property as a "fixed and firmly located part of the world acquired by its owner in one way or another" and sought, instead, to ground property "in man himself, in his possession of a body and his indisputable ownership of the strength of this body."[29] This not only threatens true property as placeness, it also threatens wealth itself. The threat to wealth has always been there, but it becomes more urgent in the modern era. The problem is that wealth is measured by possessions that are themselves impermanent things that must be used and consumed if they are to have any value. So the danger that confronts wealth is that, lacking a worldly location, it becomes unable to sustain itself. Ironically, the disintegration of property as placeness threatens the disintegration of wealth.

This last claim might seem like a rather strange one to make in light of the obvious possibility of accumulating more possessions than one consumes. Arendt was well aware of this possibility. Her point about the impermanence of wealth was a conceptual one having to do with the essential placelessness of wealth and its use values. It is the nature of wealth that it must be consumed, and this, combined with the fact that wealth does not require the stability of a worldly location, is precisely what creates the imperative to accumulate more and more wealth. So accumulation is not merely causally related to wealth; it is an integral part of it. But more than this, in a world without worldly boundaries for property, the process of accumulation must of necessity be one with no end in sight, for the moment the process of accumulation stops is the moment that wealth begins to disintegrate.[30]

Again, true property—that is, property in its original sense of placeness—is also about the use values associated with consumption. But these use values are—or were—constituted and conditioned by precisely the kind of "stable structure" that wealth, by its nature, is apt to transgress, and which over the course of history has been almost completely overwhelmed by social

processes of accumulation.[31] In the modern capitalist market system, the social process of accumulation is organized around the ongoing exchange of
commodities, and in this respect at least, Arendt accepts the modern economic analysis of the increasing importance of exchange value at the expense
of use value. So too does she acknowledge that in an economy organized
around market exchange, money itself provides a certain amount of stability
and predictability. However, the stability provided by money is fleeting at best,
and as Canovan indicated in the quote above, it is capital and not money that
emerges in Arendt's analysis as the main bulwark of the modern accumulation
process. Capital provides wealth with a measure of permanence in the face of
the ever-present danger of disintegration. In the meantime, though, property
itself has disintegrated. As summarized by Arendt, the history of modern
property is one where property "lost its private use value which was determined by location and acquired an exclusively social value determined
through its ever-changing exchangeability whose fluctuation could itself be
fixed only temporarily by relating it to the common denominator of money."[32]

Rethinking Arendt's Analysis of Property

Despite my obvious and large debt to Arendt, there are also rather large areas
of disagreement between us with regard to the nature and fate of property. The
fundamental difference has to do with the fact that my hermeneutics of property is more contextual than hers. Whereas Arendt sees placeness in terms of
physical locations of property that sharply delineate private and public life, I
see placeness in terms of multiple locations that are constituted in ever-
changing ways in relation to a variety of social contexts of identity, authority,
and labor. As a result, the institutional topography of placeness within my approach is more varied and fluid than hers. In fact, one would be hard pressed
to come up with an example of Arendtian placeness other than the household.

Once we see that placeness can be found in a variety of property locations
other than the household, and once we absorb the importance of the fact that
we are dealing with socially and culturally constituted places, it becomes clear
that placeness is more resistant to modern economic forces and beliefs than
Arendt thought. It also becomes clear that the placeness of property retains
some of its integrative qualities in the era of advanced capitalism. If I am right,
and placeness is still part of the conceptual universe of property, then property is still important for political life. By the same token, if property as placeness has not disintegrated, then there are good reasons to take seriously the
possibility that property is about rights of inhabitation as well as rights of proprietary control. Rights of inhabitation have less to do with dominion over
things than with how we live among them.

There is a lot to unpack here. What I want to do now is break my critique of Arendt down into five areas of disagreement.

First, I think that Arendt erred in drawing such a sharp distinction between wealth as a debased form of property and placeness as its true or authentic form. Whether modes and understandings of property that emphasize placeness should be considered morally superior to those that do not is a legitimate and valid question. But Arendt did not really address this question; instead she transcribed it into an ontological key concerning the true nature of property. Clearly, I join with Arendt in thinking that placeness is part of the nature of property, and clearly also I join with her in thinking that there is a lacuna regarding placeness in most modern understandings of property. But there is a kind of ontological sleight of hand in Arendt's analysis. Rather than trying to explore and elaborate her claims and suggestions about placeness as the true form of property, she simply created a semantic distinction between property and wealth. Merely calling the forms of possession associated with income, money, and profit something besides "property" does not establish the validity of the ontological claim. Arendt was eager to get beneath the surface of modern thinking about property and wealth, and she succeeded in doing so. Yet she also did so at the price of giving insufficient attention and emphasis to the conventional view of wealth as an attribute of property. In seeking to integrate this conventional view of the relationship between property and wealth, we need not go on to conclude that the sole or even most important function of property is to generate wealth or possessions. Accumulation of wealth in Arendt's sense is certainly a primary function of property in the modern era. But even in a capitalist market system, there can be other functions of property. By the same token, there are forms of property in the modern world of capitalist market systems that are not just about accumulation. Some people purchase homes as an investment, some do not!

The grammar of "wealth" is actually far more nuanced than is suggested by Arendt's analysis. Of particular interest to us are those uses of "wealth" that are associated with "true" wealth or "true" riches as the properties of a life that is more meaningful or more deeply ethical and moral than a life spent on the acquisition of possessions and money. To put this in the terminology of Taylor's framework of "strong evaluation," the grammar of "wealth" is associated with "qualitative contrasts" between higher and lower forms of wealth. As we saw in chapter 5, such a contrast between true and base forms of wealth was at the heart of Aristotle's view of property. The larger point, though, is that this grammar of "wealth" and "true wealth" has been an important medium through which property has been evaluated and assessed. The question that arises in this connection is how property is related to the attainment of true wealth. Certainly, this question has always been linked to concerns about acquisitiveness.

But that is not the only dimension of this question. There is also a dimension pertaining to the different modes or arrangements of property that promote or facilitate true wealth. The reductivist views of property that have grown up with modern thingness and the post-materialist reaction against it sometimes prevent us from seeing this second dimension of the question. Recovering the placeness of property helps to bring this occluded dimension to the fore, which is to say that under the idea of the placeness of property, we can consider how true wealth is related to different locations of property.

Ironically, therefore, Arendt's concept of placeness helps us to look beyond the problem of acquisitiveness to the question of how true wealth is related to different modes and arrangements of property. But because of her preoccupation with the threat that is posed by a placeless modern process of accumulating wealth, she wound up with a strangely truncated view of property in which it is essentially "object-less" or "thing-less." She imbued wealth with aspects of thingness, but the thingness of Arendtian property is less certain than its placeness. As a result, Arendtian property is close to being a location without any objects of possession, acquisition, and ownership. To the extent that this is the case, one has to wonder what distinguishes it from any other location of activity. But we can prevent this deconstruction of Arendtian property simply by recognizing that property is structured around both placeness and thingness. Wealth, then, can be seen as an attribute of property in the specific sense of being an attribute that takes different forms depending on the nature of the relationship between thingness and placeness. The question then becomes: What is the relationship between the thingness of property and its placeness in terms of realizing true wealth?

This brings us to the second area of disagreement, which has to do with my emphasis on the relationship between thingness and placeness. Here, too, there are tensions, but they are tensions within the structure of property, not between property and wealth. The relevant questions concerning the structure of property are of the following kind: In what ways, and to what extent, are the rights to things defined and conditioned by the locations of these things? And to what extent are these locations and the social relationships within them undermined by rights to things, or particular forms of these rights?

What is at issue with these questions is not just our understanding of property, but also whether we recognize and account for the deeper phenomenological connection between things and places. Insofar as things exist in a world, they have a location. There is a lesson to be learned here from Arendt's mentor, Martin Heidegger. In his essay "Building Dwelling Thinking," Heidegger uses the example of a bridge spanning a stream to make the point that "only something *that is itself a location* can make space for a site. The location is not already there before the bridge is." To see what he means, it is helpful to distinguish between the idea of the bridge as something occupying one of many possible spots along the stream and the bridge as something that creates and constitutes a location within the world. "Thus," Heidegger writes, "the bridge does not first come to a location to stand in it; rather, a location comes into existence only by virtue of the bridge." Heidegger's point here is not simply that placeness emerges from bridges and other things in the world. Rather, he is seeking to illuminate the constitution of placeness as an aspect of things. Placeness, Heidegger is saying, is part of the essence of things. Western thought, he claims, usually has overlooked the essential placeness of things because it has treated things as isolated and contentless abstractions. As he puts it, "The consequence, in the course of Western thought, has been that the thing is represented as an unknown X to which perceptibles are attached."[33]

I have no interest in the mysticism in which Heidegger enshrouded his analysis of the inherent placeness of things.[34] But his account of the deep phenomenological interdependence of thingness and placeness provides important support for my own efforts to develop a hermeneutic alternative to modern analytic thinking about property. It also provides a corrective to Arendt's tendency to expunge thingness from "fixed and firmly located parts of the world." To recognize that placeness inheres in things is to recognize the content of thingness.

Of course, Heidegger was not talking about property. But while property requires that we be especially attentive to the cultural constitution and construction of things and places, it does not require that we abandon our interest in understanding the "lived experience" of the possessive relation between holders and holdings of property. And so long as property involves such a possessive relation, it is necessarily about both thingness and placeness. The possessive relation is like Heidegger's bridge, though the location it constitutes is one that exists within and through social practices, beliefs, and discourses.

Arendt's tendency to posit an "objectless" property not only begs the question of what exactly distinguishes locations of property from other locations. It also makes it impossible to sort through the proprietary and possessive aspects of property locations. Take her paradigmatic case of the household. The household itself is not, and cannot be, an object of acquisition, possession, or ownership (not to mention exchange). The household is about the "where" of property; the "what" of property in this context has to do with the things that the household acquires, possesses, or owns, including, but not limited to, the physical abode inhabited by the members of the household.

With Arendt, it is the physical boundaries of property locations that matter, not their status as objects of acquisition, possession, or ownership (which status, of course, would constitute them as wealth in her analysis, not property). With this, we arrive at a third area of disagreement. Simply put, I believe that Arendt's phenomenology of the placeness of property is too physicalist. To be sure, the physicality of boundaries is an important part of the placeness of property; indeed, it is partly constitutive of it. Even the "virtual" places of property in the age of the internet exist somewhere in physical space. But the "where" of property is not reducible to a lived experience of pure or unmediated physicality. Property, after all, is a social and political institution, and what really matters with respect to property's placeness is that it has to do with culturally and socially constituted locations of (more or less institutionalized) human activity and interaction. Accordingly, the placeness of property is defined more by the social purposes and ends of the location than its physical boundaries. So too is it defined by the relations of labor and authority within the social location.[35] And in both of these respects, the placeness of property is about the formation of the civic identities of those who inhabit the locations.

But, fourth, if we are to take seriously the idea that placeness is about the constitution of locations of purposeful human activity and interaction, then we must also question Arendt's efforts to limit property and its placeness to a purely private realm of household labor. At this point, we enter into a longstanding controversy surrounding Arendt's thought. One of the criticisms that has always been made of her theoretical perspective is that it draws too bright a line between private and public life, and that because of this bright line, her accounts of action and public life do not allow for the public airing of grievances and issues pertaining to family life, economics, and social justice in general.[36] I think that this criticism has considerable merit. But we need to be careful not to overstate or oversimplify the case. We know from what was said earlier that Arendt saw private and public life as closely related to one another in many respects. Indeed, she took pains to show that the private life of the household had "nonprivative" characteristics. The household is not only the place where biological needs are satisfied. It also provides citizens with an understanding of the contrast between biological necessity and the freedom that is experienced in public life. So too does the household provide citizens with the kind of "reliable hiding place," without which citizens could not understand freedom as the emergence into public spaces, and without which, also, public life would become both superficial and oppressive. These are the "prepolitical" virtues of the private property of placeness. Clearly, though, they are not simply private virtues; rather, they are civic virtues in the sense of being formative of a capacity for the public life of citizenship. Nevertheless, critics have good reason to be concerned about the limitations that Arendt placed on the space of allowable public deliberation. The problem, as I see it, is that she insisted on imbuing public life with a kind of purity, a purity that is ontological as well as normative. Hence, along with her insistence that private and public life are interrelated, Arendt also took great pains to argue that matters concerning biological necessity, labor, and the accumulation of wealth should not, and ontologically, could not be matters of public concern and debate. The rise of the social is so deeply debasing in Arendt's view precisely because it reaches the level of an ontological transgression of the line between what is private and what is public.

How, then, does my reformulation of the placeness of property challenge Arendt's bright line between the private and the public? The answer to this question follows from what I have said about property and wealth, thingness and placeness, and the physicalism of Arendt's conception of placeness. If I am right about these things, then there really isn't any reason to assume that the only real or true form of property is that which is located in a private realm of labor relating to biological necessity. Or to spell it all out, when we break free of the notion of a simple or neat opposition between wealth and property, when we recognize that thingness and placeness are inextricably bound up with each other in the conceptual structure of property, and when we see that the placeness of property is not established by physical boundaries alone, then it becomes clear that the functions and locations of property are not limited to those associated with the demarcation of private and public realms of activity. The boundary between private and public begins to blur, certainly with respect to property, but arguably also in a larger sense as well. To say this is not to deny either the influence or the ancient roots of the private/public split in Western culture. Nor for that matter do I wish to deny either the distinctiveness or the importance of public life. The point, rather, is that we are dealing with cultural understandings of what is public and what is private, and because of this, we should not think of the idea of a private/public split as something that has ontological substance by virtue of being grounded in the physical boundaries of private and public life.

While it is certainly possible that the cultural norms, purposes, and practices that constitute placeness might privilege private locations, there is nothing in the nature of the placeness of property that requires that property be located in a private sphere. This would be true even if we accepted Arendt's bright line between private and public life. After all, wherever we may stand in the various debates over private and public ownership of assets and resources, the simple truth is that we can speak of public property without being faced with an ontological or epistemological rupture. And once we get past the circular argument that any form of possession or ownership outside the private realm is wealth and not property, we can then face up to the possibility of the placeness of public property.

Let us step away from this dense thicket of connections between ontology, physicality, and culture and take a look at an example of property. Consider libraries as a form of property. Libraries do not fit very well into Arendt's schema of property and wealth. A library is not a hidden location of family life and biological processes, and therefore does not qualify as property of the household type.

One possible alternative is to think of libraries (or at least those outside of the household) as part of what Arendt called the "common world." She believed that the common world is one of two phenomena that define and sustain a public life of action, the other one being the publicity of being seen and heard by other citizens. The common world, in Arendt's view, comprises the public places that are fabricated for civic activities as well as the activities themselves. Ironically, it was in this context rather than the context of property that Arendt showed an appreciation for the inextricable relationship between things and their locations. This is seen in the famous passage in *The Human Condition* where the common world is likened to the table around which citizens meet. "To live together in the world," Arendt wrote, "means essentially that a world of things is between those who have it in common, as a table is located between those who sit around it; the world, like every in-between, relates and separates men at the same time."[37]

Obviously, modern libraries serve private, personal purposes as well as public ones. Still, the modern institution of the library clearly has elements of Arendt's common world. Citizens gather at libraries and both literally and figuratively they sit at tables in ways that relate and separate them from each other. My own view is that libraries are extremely important institutions within the common world of democratic citizenship. I even go so far as to say that while the household is the paradigmatic form of the private placeness of property, the library is a paradigmatic form of the civic placeness of property. This represents a radical departure from what I take to be the Arendtian view, and this is so for three reasons. First, a library violates the Arendtian idea of a revelatory politics of being seen and heard by other citizens. Libraries are quiet places of study, reading, and contemplation, and while this also distinguishes libraries from most households, it means that libraries are like households in that they too involve locations that are hidden from the life of civic action. Second, then, libraries cannot be fully part of an Arendtian common world because this common world is about the life of action (the *vita activa*, as she expressed it), not the life of contemplation (the *vita contemplativa*). And finally, my view of libraries depends on the possibility of public and civic forms of property, whereas Arendt viewed the common world of public life as property-less, indeed, as a world standing in sharp ontological contrast to the private world of property. Not surprisingly, the first definition of the "common world" provided by Arendt in *The Human Condition* was "the world itself, in so far as it is common to all of us and *distinguished from our privately owned place in it.*"[38]

In one respect, Arendt and I probably would be in complete agreement. I have in mind the relationship between libraries and the accumulation of wealth. Libraries are not associated with the kind of acquisitive and profit-seeking behavior that is evoked by Arendt's condemnations of the modern process of accumulating wealth. Quite to the contrary—and here we come back to my different view of the grammar of "wealth"—libraries are usually associated with the promotion of "true wealth" in the sense of a life made more meaningful and richer through study, reflection, learning, and the pursuit of knowledge. By the same token, if libraries were to be organized around the pursuit of wealth in its more material form, we would (or should) see this as a deep corruption of the purposes and practices of a library. But the corruption would not lie simply (as contemporary civic republicans and post-socialists are wont to believe) in an inordinate emphasis on property. A library is always/already immersed in and constituted by contexts and relations of property. It is easy enough to see the thingness of library property. The physical structure that houses it, the equipment, the supplies, the collections of materials (its holdings!), and data bases are all defined in terms of various property rights of acquisition, ownership, leasing, or access. And what is it that gives coherence and cohesiveness to this assortment of rights and holdings if not the placeness of the library? Yes, this is partly about the physical location (or locations) of the library. But a library is not a warehouse, and in the end, it is the purposes and practices around which a library is organized that are constitutive of its placeness.

To be sure, there is no ontological imperative requiring public ownership and control of libraries. This in itself unsettles the fixity of the Arendtian boundaries of private and public life. Yet there is a long tradition (fortunately, in my view) of public libraries, a tradition that undoubtedly draws some of its strength from the belief that the purposes and practices of libraries have a substantial public dimension pertaining to the preservation and accessibility of culture, knowledge, and information. Such purposes and practices create a presumption that a well-functioning democracy will have libraries that are open and accessible to citizens and that the materials and holdings of these libraries will either be in the public domain or subject to reasonable restrictions on their use until they become part of the public domain.[39] Furthermore, the public purposes and practices of a library must not be undercut and corrupted by the private pursuit of material wealth and profit. So even in the absence of ontological imperatives, it matters greatly whether libraries are private or public forms of property. It matters because what is at issue with libraries and other locations of property in the civic infrastructure is nothing less than the possibility of constituting a political community as a common-*wealth* of and for citizen-stakeholders.

This vision of commonwealth is the culmination of my challenge to the Arendtian framework of private property and public action. It is here that the differences between our perspectives are most starkly revealed. Arendt held the idea of commonwealth in what can only be described as contempt. At first glance, it seems strange that someone so closely identified with the republican tradition should have felt this way. But it makes perfect sense when placed in the broader framework of her critique of modern property. After all, a commonwealth is still about wealth, and in the modern era, this means that it is part of the perversion of public life through the rise of the social. "Common wealth," Arendt argued, "can never become common in the sense we speak of a common world." In her view, "commonwealth" is simply a euphemistic way of describing the modern theory of government as a form of protection for the property rights of its wealth-seeking subjects. Here is how she put it: "When this common wealth, the result of activities formerly banished to the privacy of households, was permitted to take over the public realm, private possessions . . . began to undermine the durability of the common world."[40]

Arendt's critique of "commonwealth" not only ignores the plurality of property locations, it also neglects the civic dimension of property within the infrastructure of institutional contexts and practices—including, but not limited to libraries—that support and sustain the common world of citizenship. The "table" of public life is by no means a mere object of proprietary control, but it is nonetheless a property-related location of citizenship.

In contrast to Arendt, my own theoretical perspective on property places considerable emphasis on the possibility of a democratic commonwealth of self-governing citizens who are stakeholders in a common project of seeking true wealth for their community as well as for themselves. I suppose this makes me something of a republican democrat. But as a liberal democrat, I am also suspicious of republican views of property and commonwealth because of their longstanding association with the problem of republican paternalism. And with this, we come to the fifth and last area of fundamental disagreement. This has to do with my belief that Arendt's critique of modern property glosses over the danger of true property (i.e., property as placeness) functioning as a context of paternalistic rule and guardianship.

In this context, libraries are not the best example of placeness. The issues of inequality and paternalism are not so deeply and problematically implicated in the purposes and practices of libraries as they are with many other property locations. True, it is easy enough to imagine libraries being administered in authoritarian and censorial ways as well as in ways that involve the exploitation of laborers and workers. But to see how Arendt glosses over the problem of republican paternalism, it will be better to focus on her own example of the household.

Arendt was well aware of the inequality of authority and labor within the households of classical Western antiquity. The ancient "household," she observed, "was the center of strictest inequality."[41] Arendt called attention to the fact that the division of labor was based not only on slavery but also on a profoundly patriarchal division of the tasks for men and women. And she went out of her way to describe the authority of male masters as a form of absolute, and even despotic rule.[42] One even gets the impression that she exaggerated the harshness of the master's rule in the interest of shaking up the smugness of modern democratic thinking about the importance of social and economic equality. Political equality, for Arendt, is about political peers who gain confidence in each other as a result of their shared commitment to the practice of public freedom.[43] Arendtian equality is not grounded in nature or natural rights. It is artificial in the sense of being a condition that is created and affirmed by citizens in their shared civic spaces of participation. And Arendt took this locational dimension of equality quite seriously. Equality, in her view, is limited to action and interaction in civic spaces.[44] The modern progressive project of promoting democratic equality through the equalization of social and economic conditions is not merely irrelevant to Arendt's purely political form of equality. It is also a threat to political equality because it brings with it the type of mass housekeeping and the conformist views of the general welfare that are definitive of the modern social realm's debasement of public life.[45] Hence, her disdain for the social question.

However, there is something terribly wrong with this picture of political equality, not just on broad normative grounds, but also with respect to the relationship between property and authority. For one thing, it begs the question of the conditions under which the placeness of the household promotes (or hinders) access to the public realm. Arendt herself endorsed what she characterized as "the modern and revolutionary tenet that all inhabitants of a given territory are entitled to be admitted to the political realm."[46] So even on her own terms, there is reason to be concerned about property functioning as a boundary of exclusion as well as a gateway of admittance to the public realm. The conditions of labor and authority in "prepolitical" locations of property are very relevant to the goal of political equality, and this is true not because democracy involves some radically egalitarian idea of substantive equality of power and ability, but simply because social and economic inequality in places such as households threaten what we now see as a very moderate tenet of equal access to the public realm.

Arendt would have us believe that citizens simply become equal after emerging from the hidden locations of private household property, and that this happens through the revelatory process of being seen and heard in public life. As even the most sympathetic of Arendt's critics have pointed out, this glosses over the fact that some members of the political community are not allowed to enter the public realm.[47] But there is a deeper problem here. This has to do with the danger of property locations such as the household promoting exclusionary beliefs and practices in the process of cultivating the capacity for public freedom. The barriers to public life in the ancient Greek *oikos* or in any other patriarchal and paternalistic location of property are not simply physical obstacles. Nor are we just dealing with rules of admission that can be easily revised to allow more people to enter public life. Rather, as we saw in our previous explorations of the problem of republican paternalism, the barriers have a deeper, structural basis in the distributive conditions and consequences of a formative politics of civic virtue. That is to say, property locations like the household are problematically related to democratic norms of equal citizenship because they carry with them the potential of cultivating an exclusionary and hierarchical understanding of what it takes to be a qualified participant in practices of republican liberty.

By failing to confront this mixed legacy of the placeness of the household, Arendt undercut her critique of modern property. One is left wondering whether modern property is that bad after all! At the very least, it is legitimate to ask whether modern property, for all its flaws, also is associated with the kinds of conceptual and normative resources—the resources of oppositionist democratic agency—that empower citizens to oppose and challenge paternalistic, patriarchal, and generally exclusionary forms of republican mastery. There is as well the question of the role of property in an Arendtian republic. Would property have any formative significance in such a republic? And how would locations of property serve and promote basic democratic norms of equal access and inclusion?

One senses that Arendt didn't see the need to get into these issues because true property was lost to the modern world, and probably lost forever. We are left only with the tantalizing hint in *On Revolution* that in an age when property has devolved into mere wealth, the best hope for creating the boundary lines of private and public life involves civil liberties such as those in the American Bill of Rights.[48] I think that Arendt was right to emphasize the importance of the Bill of Rights in this connection, but wrong to dismiss the continuing importance of property, and wrong also in her view that the placeness of property has disintegrated in the modern world. Rather than showing that property has disintegrated, she simply redefined it out of existence, first, by casting wealth out of the universe of property, second, by suppressing thing ownership as an important dimension of property, and last, by reducing placeness to premodern spaces of private life. Having consigned property— that is, true property—to the trash heap of history, there was no need for Arendt to show what property arrangements would be like in an Arendtian republic, and no need also to show how public life would be constituted so as to avoid the problem of republican paternalism.[49] As we have seen, today's civic republicans make the same mistakes. They make them for different reasons— for instance, out of a desire to transcend or at least limit the corruptive power of property rather than on the basis of property's purported disintegration. But they too are apt to leave us wondering exactly what property arrangements would be like in their republic, and they too end up positing and presupposing the existence of democratic equality rather than showing how it emerges from the background of hierarchical and exclusionary arrangements of property and authority.

Beyond the Disintegration of Property

Where does all this leave the disintegration thesis? The Arendtian possibility that property has disintegrated because its locations have been displaced and overwhelmed by the modern pursuit of wealth has evaporated for many of the same reasons that the possibility of the disintegration of thingness evaporated. Both versions of the disintegration thesis suffer from insufficient appreciation of the flexibility and adaptability of property, whether (as with Arendt) in the face of the rise of capitalist processes of wealth accumulation or (as with Grey) in the face of the fragmentation of unified thing ownership in the late modern era. And in both cases, the failure to appreciate the flexibility and adaptability of property is related to a failure to appreciate the conceptual interdependence of property's thingness and its placeness. Arendt failed to see that the wealth of thing ownership creates and requires its own forms of placeness, while Grey missed the importance of placeness in providing coherence and cohesion to modern bundles of property rights and interests.

In the midst of all the cultural and historical variations of property, there is an ineluctable structural relationship between thingness and placeness. This, it might be said, is the ontological limit within the structure of property that the disintegration thesis bumps up against. To be sure, this limit could be breached. It *is* possible that property as both thingness and placeness could disappear. But one of the lessons of hermeneutics is that property is constituted through the discursive practices in which both its use and exchange values are given practical life and meaning. Consequently, property will persist so long as these practical property discourses persist. And they do persist, not just as ordinary lay discourse about thing ownership, but also in technical areas of law, public policy, and even economics.

The fact that property persists into the era of late modern capitalism does not mean that it is in good condition. The relentless commodification, the long and now global reach of commercialism, the fragmentation of property rights and interests, the economistic redescription of property as the internalization of economic benefits, and post-materialist neglect of property issues—all have made it increasingly difficult to develop or sustain the idea of property as a location with ethical and civic use values.

Another Look at the Libertarian Conservative Redescription of Thingness

The libertarian conservative defense of thing ownership against the forces of fragmentation provides important (if inadvertent) support for the claims I have been making about the structure of property and its bad condition in the late modern world. That it has been relatively easy to redescribe the classical liberal vision of thingness in terms of a market model of multiple subjects of ownership with vested rights to different sticks or strands of property shows both the flexibility and persistence of property discourse. Yet the libertarian conservative redescription is only formally coherent. It is substantively incoherent because it does not account for the background of placeness that makes property an intelligible concept. This means that despite their best efforts, libertarian conservatives and other neoliberal defenders of private property are parasitic on placeness. For one thing, the market itself is a social location—a market*place* as Daniel Kemmis has reminded us.[50] In addition, there is a certain luxury of placeness (and sometimes a placeness of luxury) for those who are able to translate a dominant market position into the type of privileged social locations and statuses that are not available to those whose primary stake in society is that of a formal (and often merely formal) right to engage in competitive market exchange.

Viewed against the background of the conceptual structure of thingness and placeness, there is something almost pathetic about the neoliberal champions of private property storming the academic and ideological barricades in defense of private property as an internalization of market benefits or as a vested right to a stick within a mixed bag of property sticks. Be that as it may, this background exposes the contemporary market model of thingness as a fundamentally ideological attempt to abstract the market from other social and political locations of property. This is not simply about glossing over the locational dimension of property; it is also about abstracting the market from the different moral and civic purposes of property locations such as households, workplaces, and libraries. From this perspective, the world that is envisioned by the market model of property is a world of and for absentee landlords, but not citizens.

This does not mean that the market model of thingness is completely amoral. There is a kind of ethos of proprietary responsibility on which it draws. The proprietor has a responsibility to maintain dominion over one's things. There is as well a responsibility to follow basic market rules such as prohibitions against force and fraud. But because the acquisition and exchange of property sticks are severed from non-market locations and responsibilities, they are also severed from broader social and civic responsibilities pertaining to either the maintenance of non-market property locations or provision for those who lack privileged market positions.

To be sure, the discourse of modern commerical thingness has made at least some room for these kinds of responsibilities. That is the point of legal rules about nuisances and easements.[51] Such lingering restrictions on proprietary authority reveal aspects of a right of inhabitation lurking within modern thingness itself. But under the influence of libertarianism, such rules are apt to be viewed as outdated nuisances by most contemporary free-market conservatives. They either impose irrationally high "transaction costs" on market participants or they threaten proprietary autonomy. Either way, broader social and civic responsibilities are viewed as hindrances on private property rather than responsibilities that are entailed by it. In a word, they are redefined as externalities.

Here too, though, the libertarian conservative redescription is formally coherent, but substantively incoherent. Once placeness is readmitted to our horizon of property, we see that even libertarian conservatives need to establish background conditions for the inhabitation of the marketplace. What is more, the logic of these conditions starts to look strangely similar to the logic of the broader social and civic responsibilities that they treat as oppressive and irrational encumbrances on property. For instance, the libertarian conservative redescription of thingness is premised on at least a formal equality of access to the market. Yet what is this if not a kind of easement that prevents proprietors from excluding others from using the common wealth of the market?

At this point, we begin to see something strange about the relationship between the conservative redescription of classical liberal thingness and contemporary left liberal views of property. There is a sense in which we are dealing with mirror images of the displacement of property. That is to say, there is an ironic sense in which contemporary liberalism remains within a normative framework of classical liberal thingness, the difference being that contemporary liberals view the possessive relations of property as the more or less arbitrary creations of society and its legal system. Herein lies the deeper connection between Grey's liberal version of the disintegration thesis and the displacement of property within contemporary liberalism as a whole. In both cases, society functions as the ultimate property holder in the sense of being the ultimate arbiter of the meaning and value of property. And what society has created, society can destroy.[52] I suspect that this way of looking at things (and thingness) has its basis in an understandable interest in attacking the Lockean notion of nature-like origins for what is, after all, a social institution. In the meantime, however, both the idea and the ideal of a commonwealth lose their moral and civic substance as a property-related location of democratic citizenship.[53] The irony, of course, is that this is the same outcome as with the conservative redescription and defense of classical liberal thingness.

The same could be said of both Arendt and contemporary civic republicans. Yet by redescribing the Arendtian phenomenology of property in terms of the kind of contextual hermeneutics that is characteristic of much contemporary civic republicanism, we have been able to uncover the persistence of property's placeness in the late modern era. Recognizing the persistence of placeness allows us to break free of the constraints and distortions of modern thingness. Which is also to say that it allows us to see that the possibility of property as a right of inhabitation remains alive though not all that well in the late modern world.

Notes

1. See, for example, Jennifer Nedelsky, *Private Property and the Limits of American Constitutionalism* (Chicago: University of Chicago Press, 1990), 231–40; Margaret Jane Radin, *Reinterpreting Property* (Chicago: University of Chicago Press, 1993), fn. 85 and 216; and Joseph William Singer, *Entitlement: The Paradoxes of Property* (New Haven, CT: Yale University Press, 2000), 81–84.

2. Thomas C. Grey, "The Disintegration of Property," in *Property*, vol. XXII of *Nomos* (New York: New York University Press, 1980), 69–70.

3. Grey cites three different types of fragmentation in this regard: First, a particular thing might be divided up among several different owners. Second, an owner might sell off a particular aspect of his or her control, for example, particular uses or the right to profit from something. And third, ownership rights might be divided up temporally, or as Grey puts it, "you might sell your control over your property for tomorrow to one person, for the next day to another, and so on." Grey, 69.

4. Grey, 81 and 74.

5. Grey, 80–81.

6. For a very interesting discussion of the issues associated with emotional attachments to property, see Radin, *Reinterpreting Property*, especially chapter 2.

7. See Nedelsky, *Private Property and the Limits of American Constitutionalism*, chapter 6; Bruce A. Ackerman, *Private Property and the Constitution* (New Haven, CT: Yale University Press, 1977), especially chapters 2 and 5; and Radin, *Reinterpreting Property*, chapter 4.

8. Singer, *Entitlement*, 83.

9. See Nedelsky, *Private Property*, chapter 6.

10. Radin argues that "thing-ownership" is deeply rooted in our understanding of the relationship between the self and objects of the external world. Thus, in response

to Grey's argument, she notes that "thing-ownership seems embedded in the ideas of self-constitution through object relations." *Reinterpreting Property*, 216, n. 85. I suspect that this is right. However, I would argue that self-constitution in relation to property objects is also bound up with placeness, not only in an ontological sense, but also in a psychological sense. This is seen, for instance, in those emotional attachments to property objects that Radin sees as the source of a special category of non-fungible "personal property." The attachment itself transforms the object from an impersonal, external object into an object that is internal to, and partly constitutive of, the social situation of the self. Such attachments are a way of inhabiting the world, not just possessing it. Not surprisingly, therefore, the development of attachments to things often goes along with the ideational construction and reconstruction of physical locations that are associated with the object.

11. One problem that I am not emphasizing in this discussion is that the "full," classical liberal understanding of property (or what is taken to be the classical liberal understanding) is privileged by Grey as the baseline of analysis and comparison. Keep in mind that there is an ellipsis whereby the disintegration of *classical liberal* property becomes the disintegration of property. The problem is that if we rely solely on classical liberal property as our baseline, then we would have to conclude that, say, feudal or certain non-Western understandings of property are incoherent, fragmented, and so on.

12. Richard Epstein, *Takings: Private Property and the Power of Eminent Domain* (Cambridge, MA: Harvard University Press, 1985), 23.

13. See, for example, Grey, "The Disintegration of Property," 73–76. Also see Jane Radin's incisive analysis of the "strategy" of "conceptual severance" in conservative forms of the contemporary American jurisprudence of takings. "To apply conceptual severance," she writes, "one delineates a property interest consisting of just what the government action has removed from the owner, and then asserts that that particular thing has been permanently taken." Radin, 127–28. This of course makes it easier to defend private property interests against government regulation. But it also underscores how easy it is to redescribe thing ownership in terms of particular sticks in larger bundles of property rights.

14. Correctly, in my view, Joseph Singer criticizes the legal realists' understanding of property as a "bundle of rights" for failing to break free of the classical liberal model of ownership. See Singer, *Entitlement*, 10–13 and 81–84.

15. The displacement of property from Arendt's critique of modernity is seen across the spectrum of interpretive perspectives. See, for example, George Kateb, *Hannah Arendt: Politics, Conscience, Evil* (Totowa, NJ: Rowman and Littlefield Publishers, 1984); Dana R. Villa, *Arendt and Heidegger: The Fate of the Political* (Princeton, NJ: Princeton University Press, 1996); Seyla Benhabib, *The Reluctant Modernism of Hannah Arendt* (Thousand Oaks, CA: Sage Publications, 1996); and Margaret Canovan, *Hannah Arendt: A Reinterpretation of Her Thought* (Cambridge: Cambridge University Press, 1992). Of these authors, Canovan comes closest to appreciating the importance of property in Arendt's critique of modernity. But while she makes very insightful connections between what Arendt says about property in *The Origins of Totalitarianism*, 3rd ed. (New York: Harcourt Brace Jovanovich, 1973) and what Arendt says in *The Human Condition* (Chicago: University of Chicago Press, 1958), Canovan does not

linger on Arendt's analysis of property long enough to explore most of the issues it raises. See Canovan, 19 and 83. Still, I benefited greatly from her interpretation.

16. Hannah Arendt, *The Human Condition*, chapter 2.

17. Arendt, *The Human Condition*, 68.

18. See *The Human Condition*, 184 for Arendt's view of action as a "new beginning," 50 and 57 on being "seen and heard," and 30–31 and 175–88 for an overview of Arendt's ideas concerning action and freedom in relation to the disclosure of the agent.

19. *The Human Condition*, 65.

20. Hannah Arendt, *On Revolution* (New York: Viking Press, 1963), 111 and chapter 6.

21. *The Human Condition*, 70.

22. *The Human Condition*, 112.

23. *The Human Condition*, 61, 64, and 66.

24. Canovan, *Hannah Arendt*, 82.

25. *The Human Condition*, 61 and 66; also see 69–70, 110, and 112.

26. *The Human Condition*, 61.

27. *The Human Condition*, 63, 64, and 67.

28. *The Human Condition*, 69. Also see Arendt, *The Origins of Totalitarianism*, 145.

29. *The Human Condition*, 70.

30. See *The Human Condition*, 68–69.

31. *The Human Condition*, 69.

32. *The Human Condition*, 69.

33. Martin Heidegger, "Building Dwelling Thinking," in *Martin Heidegger: Basic Writings*, ed. David Farrell Krell (New York: Harper and Row, 1977), 332 and 331.

34. For Heidegger, the "gathering essence" of a thing has to do with how it assembles "the fourfold" of "earth and sky, divinities and mortals." Heidegger, 332 and 331.

35. Although it is not crucial to the current discussion, Arendt and I also have different views of labor. For Arendt, labor is essentially about biological necessity, and as such is of a lower order than work. Whereas the laborer produces in an endless process of consumption, the worker fabricates durable things for a common world. I think the distinction has a point insofar as it evokes different levels of skill and creativity in work. But I also think that the relationship between labor and work is more complex and more ambiguous, with considerable overlap as well as tension. Put briefly, I do not wish to press the distinction between skill in a craft and drudgery for the sake of biological survival so far as to obscure the multiple forms and levels of the relationship between work and labor. See Arendt's discussion in *The Human Condition*, especially 93–101 and 118–59.

36. The classic discussion of these issues is Hanna F. Pitkin, "Justice: On Relating Private and Public," *Political Theory* 9 (1981): 327–52. I note that property is not even discussed by Pitkin. See Jurgen Habermas's alternative account of "the social" with respect to the creation of the rules of private interaction as a subject of public discussion in *The Structural Transformation of the Public Sphere: An Inquiry into a Category of Bourgeois Society*, trans. Thomas Burger (Cambridge, MA: The MIT Press, 1989), especially chapter IV. Also see Seyla Benhabib's discussion of the private and the public spheres in Arendt's political theory in *Situating the Self: Gender,*

Community, and Postmodernism in Contemporary Ethics (New York: Routledge, 1992), chapter 3.

37. *The Human Condition*, 52.

38. *The Human Condition*, 52, emphasis added.

39. I note that the trend in the area of intellectual property in the United States has not been a favorable one with respect to recognition of the public nature and purposes of culture, knowledge, and information. As Lawrence Lessig observes, "The unavoidable conclusion about changes in the scope of copyright's protections is that the extent of 'free content'—meaning content that is not controlled by exclusive right—has never been as limited as it is today." Lawrence Lessig, *The Future of Ideas: The Fate of the Commons in a Connected World* (New York: Random House, 2001), 110 and *passim*.

40. *The Human Condition*, 68.

41. *The Human Condition*, 32.

42. Arendt, *The Human Condition*, especially 27–88, 30, and 32. Also see Habermas's Arendtian analysis of the structure of the *oikos* in *The Structural Transformation of the Public Sphere*, 3–4.

43. Arendt, *On Revolution*, 282.

44. *On Revolution*, 33 and 279–83.

45. *On Revolution*, 23 and 273, and chapter 2.

46. *On Revolution*, 275.

47. See, for example, Pitkin, "Justice," and Benhabib, *Situating the Self*, 90–95.

48. Arendt, *On Revolution*, 256.

49. It is worth noting in this connection that Arendt thought that authority had disintegrated in the modern era along with property, and for essentially the same reasons. In its original and true forms, Western authority had sources outside the sphere of power; it legitimated power and its exercise by providing external foundations such as religion and tradition. Much like true property, the foundations of true authority "gave the world the permanence and durability which human beings need precisely because they are mortal . . ." Hannah Arendt, *Between Past and Future* (New York: Penguin Books, 1954), 95. The rise of "the social" undermines the permanence and durability of both property and authority. Nor is this a coincidental connection, as is clear from Arendt's observation that "the most significant symptom" of the crisis of authority in the modern world is its decline in "such prepolitical areas as child-rearing and education"—in other words, in areas that were originally within the confines of household property. Arendt, *Between Past and Future*, 92. I believe that Arendt's view of authority suffers from the same kind of non-contextual essentialism that mars much of her thinking about property. A more contextual approach suggests the need to think of authority more pluralistically (if also more loosely) as being about legitimating norms of ruling and being ruled. It is hard to imagine that authority in this sense has completely disappeared; indeed, the persistence of placeness suggests that authority even in a broadly Arendtian sense of permanence persists into the modern era.

50. Daniel Kemmis, *Community and the Politics of Place* (Norman, OK: University of Oklahoma Press, 1990), chapter 7.

51. See Singer, *Entitlement*, 39–44 and 87–91. Also see my discussions of the rights and responsibilities of stakeholding and the civic infrastructure in chapter 8.

52. One is tempted to say that it is Hobbes and not Locke who lurks within the contemporary liberal displacement of property.

53. See Harry C. Boyte, *Commonwealth: A Return to Citizen Politics* (New York: Free Press, 1989), chapter 2.

8

Conclusion:
Towards a Democratic Theory of Property

I N *WOMEN AND HUMAN DEVELOPMENT*, Martha Nussbaum writes about how she came to believe that issues of property are far more deeply implicated in theories of human development than she once thought. She explains that in earlier formulations of her "capabilities approach," property received very little attention. It "was merely an instrument of human functioning," and was subsumed with other instruments "under a general capability to lead one's own life." Nussbaum remarks perspicaciously that the marginal role that she previously assigned to property was partly the result of her experience as a law professor: "when one teaches in a modern American law school one hears constant reference to the central importance of property rights in connection with a libertarian attack on the redistribution of wealth and income." Under the influence of this picture of property, Nussbaum recounts, she failed to see "the interest of poor people in having some property in their own names." As a result of a very different set of experiences—traveling in India and observing and working with various women's development projects while there—Nussbaum's thinking about property changed dramatically. Her conversations with Indian women showed her that "women attach intense importance" to the propertied independence afforded by ownership of land and equal rights of property and inheritance. As she tells it, "I came to the conclusion that my own thinking had simply been muddled in this area; the evidence of desire led me to see something that I had refused to see before. Property rights play an important role in self-definition, in bargaining, and in developing a sense of self."[1]

My own path to awareness of the importance of property was very different than Nussbaum's—far more academic I confess, though also influenced by my own personal experiences with Indian culture. But there is much in Nussbaum's account of her changing views of property that overlaps with the analysis of property that I have developed in this book. I too have sought to break free of the one-sidedly negative picture of property as a necessary evil that always/already threatens freedom, democracy, social justice, and human development. We have seen that this distorted picture has had considerable influence on contemporary social and political theory, certainly inside American law schools, but also in many other academic quarters as well. It is indeed a picture that has developed alongside a broad tendency of post-materialist thought.

Much like Nussbaum, I believe, and have argued in the course of this inquiry, that property should be seen as an important context within which the material conditions of life and labor are linked to the moral and political goods of human development. It is largely because of this linkage that property has "use value" as well as "exchange value." While there are certainly forms and arrangements of property that undermine the goods of human development, it is equally certain that there are forms and arrangements that promote and enhance them. Whether in land or its movable forms, property can provide resources—*dominium* in the neoclassical republican sense of the word—in support of personal and civic independence and therefore dignity as well. By supporting independence, property can also play a role in securing the terms of civic equality. Propertied independence can support civic equality by making it easier for disadvantaged individuals and groups to develop and exercise civic capacities in a variety of areas: political dialogue and deliberation, expressing political views with less fear of reprisal, and bargaining with the powerful in contexts ranging from the family to the workplace to government. Not least important in this cross-fertilization of independence and civic equality is the role that democratic forms and understandings of propertied independence can play in promoting oppositionist political agency in the face of hierarchical and exclusionary combinations of property and authority. The contemporary struggle of Indian women to gain and assert their propertied independence against the patriarchal structure of property and authority in the traditional Indian family is part of a long history of oppositionist democratic agency.

In all of these ways, propertied independence can function as an external good that supports the internal goods of both social justice and democracy. But Nussbaum's account of her changing views of property also points to something else that I have tried to illuminate and explicate about property. There is a level—a phenomenological level—at which the relationship between property and internal goods is not merely instrumental in nature, but also dialectical. Property is a condition of the realization of moral and civic ends, but the same moral and civic ends also condition property. Of course, it is not quite so abstract as this. Real human beings are at the center of this dialectic of property and its ends. Property is held by and for people. Nussbaum captures part of the significance of this when she notes that property plays an "important role in self-definition . . . and in developing a sense of self." Property, in other words, is a formative context of identity. This reveals aspects of property that are usually suppressed in the economistic and commercialized understandings and idioms that have come to dominate property discourse in the late modern era. But as we have seen in the course of this inquiry, the idea of property as a formative context of moral and civic identity also reveals a locational dimension of property that unsettles and challenges the deeply rooted prejudice on behalf of thingness within the horizon of late modern property. The more that property comes to be defined by cultural beliefs about its moral and civic ends, and the more that property functions as a formative context of identity, the more its inherent placeness comes to the fore. Property objects and holdings come to be seen in terms of the social and institutional locations that these objects and holdings help to constitute.

Nussbaum's understanding of property does not include the relationship between thingness and placeness that is at the heart of both my approach to property and my perspective on ethical materialism. I believe that the placeness of property represents an extremely important part of the landscape of a developmental theory of democracy and social justice. In any case, if the analysis I have developed in these pages is even close to the mark, then placeness is an unavoidable and necessary part of any discussion of property that touches on issues of moral personality and citizenship. Of course, this also means that property-related locations of authority and labor must be part of the discussion, and at this point the developmental potential of placeness appears alongside the very checkered history of its association with paternalistic and exclusionary forms of guardianship. In fact, there is an important sense in which the struggle of Indian women for a measure of propertied independence has also been a struggle against the patriarchal placeness of the traditional Indian family estate.

Now, it would be wrong to think that the placeness of property is always precariously situated on the knife-edge of paternalistic guardianship and the goods of democracy and social justice. Things are rather more complicated than this, and some of the complicating factors can actually ease our concerns about placeness. For one thing, as I have stressed in earlier discussions of placeness, the explicit and direct connection to authority within placeness needs to be considered and judged in relation to the pronounced tendency within modern thingness to obfuscate and mystify authority. In addition, as I suggested in the previous chapter, the plurality of locations of late modern property can itself check tendencies towards the concentration of property-based authority. Finally, we have seen that there are property locations such as libraries that are crucial to human development and serve important civic purposes but are not, or at least need not be, deeply implicated in the problem of paternalistic guardianship. Nevertheless, a democratic theory of property must account for the dangers of both thingness and placeness.

The fact that these dangers are ongoing makes it impossible to have neat solutions to the age-old puzzle of how to harmonize property and democracy. However, we can chart some theoretical paths that are likely to avoid most if not all of the dangers of thingness and placeness. In the remaining pages of this book, I want to sketch some of the coordinates of these paths. Or to express things somewhat more optimistically, I want to try to show how we might be able to combine the best of thingness with the best of placeness—to be sure, more in the sense of creative tension than synthesis, but still in a hermeneutically meaningful and practical manner.

The Thingness and Placeness of Stakeholding

At several points in this inquiry I have linked my approach to property to a defense of the old ideal of citizen stakeholding. For some, the virtues of this ideal are its simplicity and its ability to cut through and reduce the complexity of the relationship between property and democracy. By contrast, the virtues of stakeholding that are central to my defense of it have more to do with its complexity and malleability. The grammar of "stakeholding" moves in many different directions. It moves between thingness and placeness and between separation from and connection to other citizens. A stake can be something claimed, possessed, or owned apart from society, but it can also be a stake in a community or an institution. Paradoxically, these grammatical possibilities can be simultaneous, as is often the case when we speak of "stakes in society." Like Lockean "fences" and Arendtian "boundaries," stakeholding can face both inwardly and outwardly. And like Arendt's "table" around which citizens gather, stakeholding can be a way of constituting independence within a context of interdependence. Stakeholding provides *dominium* in support of negative liberty and non-domination, but its grammar is also about psychological investment in, and responsible engagement with, the institution or community in which someone is a stakeholder. Stakeholding is about claiming or receiving a fair share of something valuable from the community or institution, but also about contributing to and participating in the community or institution. Stakeholding is about assets—labor, knowledge, skills, or economic resources—that a stakeholder brings to a community or institution, but also about how the assets of a community or institution become partly one's own by virtue of being a member of the institution or community.

"Stakeholding," in brief, has a very rich and richly complex grammar of citizenship.

A Point of Departure

It may be helpful to consider the richness and complexity of stakeholding in relation to Bruce Ackerman and Anne Alstott's proposal for a "stakeholder society."

The basic idea of their proposal is that each citizen receives a stake in the form of a lump sum of money upon reaching adulthood. (The amount that they suggested when they first put forward their proposal in 1999 was $80,000.) This stake is a matter of right, and while the stakeholders have a responsibility to pay back their stake when they die if it is financially possible to do so, there are very few restrictions on the use of the stake itself. As Ackerman and Alstott describe it, the stakeholders "may use their money for any purpose they choose: to start a business or pay for more education, to buy a house or raise a family or save for the future. But they must take responsibility for their choices. Their triumphs and blunders are their own."[2]

Ackerman and Alstott clearly believe that the simplicity of their proposal is a virtue. And the proposal is nothing if not simple: simple in its basic design, simple to administer, simple to understand in terms of its normative framework of freedom of choice and equal opportunity, simple as a solution to the problem of unearned and undeserved intergenerational class privilege, simple as a way of linking rights and responsibilities, and even simple as a political project of revitalizing the "old republican tradition" of property and citizenship while purging it of its "exclusionary purposes."[3]

Simplicity is often a virtue in political theory, but it is seldom a virtue in matters pertaining to the relationship between property and democracy. Even when we limit ourselves to the effect of Ackerman and Alstott's proposal on social welfare programs, there would be many gaps that would have to be filled in order to come up with a system that is in keeping with their own progressive, left liberal commitments. Whether for technical economic reasons or because of normative preferences that have been established through the political process, there are forms of social welfare that must be directly provided rather than being treated as part of a bundle of possible goods to be purchased by stakeholders. Ackerman and Alstott concede as much when they argue that there would be good reasons to supplement their stake with mandatory old-age pensions and unemployment insurance. But there are other forms of social insurance—most notably, health insurance—that get but tenuous support within their system. Moreover, there are many programs and services—for instance, parental leave programs for the care of young children, job training, and a variety of counseling and caregiving services—that do not fit well into the Ackerman and Alstott model of stakeholding. This is not to say that simplified, monetized stakeholding such as theirs should never be part of the mix of policy options in a democracy. Although there is little basis for thinking that one lump sum of money or one super-voucher could provide an adequate replacement for all but a few existing social welfare programs, a more targeted use of the Ackerman and Alstott model in the form of stakes for specific in-kind benefits such as education or housing makes some sense.[4]

In terms of how stakeholding is conceptualized, the biggest problem with Ackerman and Alstott's proposal is that it does not take into account the placeness of property. Their basic understanding of stakeholding is about as close as one gets to a pure form of modern thingness. Not only is it a completely monetized form of stakeholding, it is also organized around the idea of proprietary control over the possession and disposition of an asset or a bundle of assets. As a result, the stakes are not really *in* society in any deep, constitutive sense. The stake is neither embedded in particular institutional or communal locations nor defined by the ends and purposes of such locations. The stake is essentially a fungible, placeless instrument for whatever life plans the stakeholder—the subject of possession—chooses to follow.

Ackerman and Alstott would have us believe that their proposal represents a way of realizing the Jeffersonian vision of expanding freedom and opportunity within a property-owning democracy.[5] But while their proposal builds on broadly Jeffersonian ideas of individual rights, propertied independence, and economic opportunity, there is little of the republican vocabulary of virtue and corruption within which Jefferson often expressed his views of property. It is hard to imagine anything like what Jefferson said in homage to the virtuous independence of the yeoman farmer being said about Ackerman and Alstott's stakeholders. It would indeed seem more than a little ridiculous to hear these stakeholders described as "the chosen people of God, if ever he had a chosen people, whose breasts he has made his peculiar deposit for substantial and genuine virtue." Nor would we expect it to be said that "corruption of morals" in stakeholders such as Ackerman and Alstott's is unknown. If anything, we would expect these stakeholders to be lumped together with those who lacked the capacity for virtuous independence because they depended for their subsistence on the vagaries of commerce—the "casualties and caprices of customers," as Jefferson put it.[6]

I do not want to push this contrast too far; Jefferson was clearly guilty of hyperbole, and we are dealing with vastly different historical and intellectual contexts. The point is simply that Ackerman and Alstott's stakeholding society does not have anything like the rich moral and civic vocabulary that enabled Jefferson to talk about propertied independence in relation to the inhabitation and cultivation of land, the virtues of agricultural life, and the corruptive influence of commercial practices and beliefs.

As we have seen, a weakening of the connection between propertied independence and embedded moral and civic ends and responsibilities is part of the price that has to be paid to uphold the oppositionist Lockean principle that property should not be converted into exclusive rights of political authority. But Ackerman and Alstott go much farther down this path than is necessary, or advisable. They are apt to protest that a moral and civic culture *would* grow up around their system of stakeholding, a culture in which citizens take responsibility for their choices about how to use their stake and have "an obligation to contribute to a fair starting point for all."[7] They even write of the growth of a stakeholder culture in which citizens share stories about successful stakeholding experiences. I have no doubt that some of what they predict about the culture of stakeholding would come true. But the fact remains that Ackerman and Alstott's stakes are only loosely connected to moral and civic ends and responsibilities. It all depends on what plan of life the stakeholder chooses to follow.

The stories that will be told by Ackerman and Alstott's stakeholders are as likely to resemble the stories that poker players tell about wild games as stories about the realization of Jeffersonian freedom and opportunity. While the "citizen-players" in their proposed system are "fronted" their original sum, what happens afterward is a bit of gamble. There will be different strategies, of course. Some "citizen-players" will be risk-averse while others will take chances. But with so much riding on the game in terms of social justice and democracy, we need to know how we go about distinguishing reckless from responsible investments of the original sum. And it is simply impossible to do this with any degree of precision and accuracy within Ackerman and Alstott's system. Even if we could trace the economic losses of stakeholders to reckless and irresponsible gambling strategies, it would be very difficult to have this reflected in social welfare policies. But the basic problem is that a losing strategy for the use of one's stake could be the result of structural factors that were beyond the control of the stakeholder—things like unfavorable market forces and trends, and structural disadvantages such as entrenched forms of racism and sexism. Ackerman and Alstott try to compensate for some of these structural factors with their supplementary social insurance programs. But these programs are meant only to supplement the original stake.[8] Moreover, Ackerman and Alstott's normative justification for their proposal glosses over the problem of structural factors by emphasizing the idea that the stakeholders "must take responsibility for their choices." And at this point, we see that their proposal evokes a tradition of republican virtue that is very different from what they write about. I have in mind the tradition of commercial republicanism in which economic success and market position are equated with moral and civic virtue. In its most cruel and unfair expressions, this tradition holds individuals completely responsible for the economic circumstances of their lives. Obviously, Ackerman and Alstott do not support such a form of commercial republicanism. But their normative framework of individual choice and responsibility could easily be employed on behalf of it, and in any event, could serve to reinforce the liberal capitalist tendency towards a merely formal equality of opportunity. Not only does their framework open up the possibility of masking structural disadvantages with misplaced and exaggerated rhetoric of individual responsibility, it also does not account for issues of property and democracy stemming from corporate power and influence.

In sum, there is too much riding on the original stake in Ackerman and Alstott's proprietary model of stakeholding. Or to put it in Rawlsian terms, too much rides on the luck of the market 'and the luck of being born with economic and cultural advantages. But this is also a case of too much riding on a very narrow understanding of property. Never mind the neglect of placeness. Given the reduction of stakeholding to the possession and ownership of a lump sum of money, the Ackerman and Alstott model could even be said to be based on a very narrow view of modern thingness. Money represents the purest form of the economistic view of property. It is the universal form of economic value. It is the perfectly fungible property value x that is the measure of all things exchanged and exchangeable.

Yet I am not entirely unsympathetic to the desire to ground a proprietary form of stakeholding in a monetized form of thingness. The scope that such a form of stakeholding gives to freedom of choice provides some protection against the danger of tying the formative dimension of stakeholding to an exclusionary or hierarchical distribution of civic capacities. In addition, it has the virtue of being based on a common standard of proprietary control. True, giving every stakeholder the same amount of money does not account for the different needs of different stakeholders. To take an obvious example, a stake of $80,000 means one thing to a poor stakeholder who has several family members with special (and expensive) medical needs, and quite another to a stakeholder from a wealthy family who has no such burdens of caregiving. But monetized stakes do at least avoid invidious distinctions between different kinds and types of proprietary control. Precisely because a proprietary form of stakeholding places a premium on control of an asset or collection of assets, there is the danger of measuring the value of a stakeholding (and stakeholder!) in terms of the nature and degree of the control. Drawing on the history of propertied independence, we can see several possible hierarchical relationships pertaining to supposedly higher and lower forms of proprietary control: between real and personal property, between fee simple ownership and encumbered forms of ownership, between ownership and leasing, and between management and employees. Compared to these kinds of alternatives, the monetized stakeholding within the Ackerman and Alstott model is certainly preferable. But as we have seen, the costs of such an unencumbered, fungible form of stakeholding are very high.

Ackerman and Alstott show us the limits of democratic stakeholding within the framework of modern thingness. On the one hand, their proposal disproves the corollary of the disintegration thesis that holds that thing ownership is too fragmented and too mobile in the late modern era to provide the kind of independence that it once did. According to Ronald Terchek, "the mythic benefits attributed to private property ownership, particularly agrarian property, no longer make sense in a postindustrial world, and we ought not dwell too long on private property as the relevant stake in contemporary democracy."[9] But this leaves out the possibility developed by Ackerman and Alstott, the possibility of a government program—a late modern "agrarian law," as it were—in which assets are bundled together in the form of monetized stakes for citizens. On the other hand, the tradition of propertied stakeholding is also about psychological investment in, and engagement with, the civic ideals and ends of the stakeholding community. As Terchek expresses this aspect of stakeholding in republican thought, "patriotic citizens have normative or ideological investments in the vitality of the republic." Such normative and ideological investments are possible in the Ackerman and Alstott system, but they are not in any way an organic outgrowth of the stakeholding system. There is no deeper and certainly no structural connection between property and engagement with the goods of the republic. A lump sum of $80,000 dollars is not usually, and certainly not consistently, formative in these ways. Indeed, it is not clear what the civic ends of the Ackerman and Alstott model of stakeholding would be since these ends would be defined almost entirely in terms of the disparate choices of disparate individuals with disparate approaches to the poker game of life.

Fortunately, the choice that faces us is not a stark one of either monetized, proprietary stakeholding or no property-based stakeholding at all. Property is not only about proprietary thingness, and even in the late modern era, the grammar of "stakeholding" is complex and capacious enough to allow for a variety of contexts of property-based stakeholding.

From Proprietary to Habitational Stakeholding

The fundamental problem with the Ackerman and Alstott model is that it is very difficult to imbue their monetized stake with any of the "use values" that arise in connection with the moral and civic ends of particular institutions and particular communal and civic practices. It is these use values that make it possible to situate propertied independence within a moral and civic context of interdependence. It is also these use values that create the conditions for a formative psychological investment that extends beyond a mere interest in protecting or increasing one's stake to a broader "normative and ideological" investment in the shared goods of the stakeholding community.

But lo and behold! We have been led back to a broadly Aristotelian perspective on instrumental and internal goods. In terms of stakeholding, this means two things. First, the assets that are the foundation of a proprietary model of stakeholding are understood in the Aristotelian view as instrumental goods that are conditioned by the institutional, communal, and civic practices they serve. Second, an Aristotelian perspective links stakeholding to the inhabitation of communal locations and civic spaces. In other words, under the idea of the placeness of property, it becomes possible to have *habitational* as well as proprietary modes of stakeholding. While proprietary stakeholding is grounded in a right to control assets, habitational stakeholding revolves around the right to be respected and supported as an inhabitant of a property location. In one very big way, this represents a departure from the Aristotelian understanding of property locations. Habitational stakeholding as I understand it is not limited to those with the most authority in the property location. Rather, in keeping with norms of democratic equality and basic human dignity, the core meaning of habitational stakeholding covers all the inhabitants of a property location. This means that it covers both adult citizens (regardless of gender, of course) and future or potential citizens such as children and guest workers. This does not mean that every inhabitant has exactly the same rights and responsibilities, but it does mean that they all are equal in deserving respect and support as stakeholders.

No doubt, some will wonder how I can get from inhabitation to the kinds of independence and autonomy that are ordinarily associated with stakeholding. The problem, though, is that much modern Western thinking about stakeholding has been held captive by a picture of independence as a function of the degree of control over assets. There is some truth to this picture, of course. Proprietary control is associated with *dominium* in the form of power and resources, and this means having power and resources that support independence. But this picture is also a selective and in some respects arbitrary rendering of the conceptual universe of propertied independence.

Consider once again the example of the community land trust. Recall that a community land trust combines communal ownership of land (usually through a non-profit corporation) with long-term renewable leases for the use of buildings and other "improvements" of the land. Who are the stakeholders in such an arrangement? If we were to make proprietary control of assets the norm, we would have to say that the non-profit corporation is the stakeholder. But this is not quite right, or more precisely, there is an important sense in which the leaseholders are the primary stakeholders. True, the non-profit community might be seen as a stakeholder in terms of its role in trying to secure funding for community land trusts. And there is also a sense in which the non-profit community has both financial and psychological stakes in the effort to support those who lease the land. But in the end, the primary stakeholders—the ones who are developing independent stakes within the community—are those who lease and inhabit portions of the common land—the very people who in the proprietary model would be assumed to be dependent because they have less control of assets!

Here then is a very different model of stakeholding than that put forward by Ackerman and Alstott, a very different basis for a late modern agrarian law! The terms of the community land trust establish a web of independence and interdependence. The leases ensure that the leaseholders have their own stakes, and their own *dominium*, but these stakes are also clearly within their community. And the communal and civic aspects are often reinforced by specific terms of the lease arrangement pertaining to responsibilities for environmental stewardship and participation in the governance of the non-profit community.

The example of the community land trust problematizes the conventional proprietary model of stakeholding. But it also shows how proprietary and habitational stakeholding can complement each other. There are many ways in which proprietary control of assets might be related to habitational stakeholding and placeness. This means also that one or the other type of stakeholding might be emphasized in any given institutional context. There are bound to be forms of investment in highly mobile, intangible, and fragmented thing ownership that will not lend themselves all that well to habitational stakeholding. By the same token, forms of real property (as with the community land trust) will often be a better fit for habitational stakeholding. On the other hand, we must avoid the trap of privileging certain kinds of thing ownership. Again, the crucial question is how property functions as an instrument for moral and civic purposes.

Habitational stakeholding is not simply an offshoot of proprietary thingness. For one thing, there are forms of economic entitlement that function mainly to reinforce and support already existing locations of property. It may be that social welfare entitlements create their own habitational stakes, but many—for instance, old-age pensions and health insurance programs—are designed primarily to support goods like nurturance, health, caregiving, and the physical conditions of independence that are grounded in household and family life. Alternatively, there are circumstances where proprietary control becomes an instrument for the fuller realization of habitational ends and purposes. This is the case, for instance, when workers realize the ends of workplace democracy through ownership and control of the assets of their company, or when members of a community such as a farming community establish cooperative forms of ownership and control. And moving even farther away from proprietary stakeholding, there are instances of habitational stakeholding that do not—or at least should not—involve any kind of proprietary control over assets or resources. This is the point of the concept of "the commons." Although we associate the commons with resources, assets, or instrumentalities that are "held" collectively by the community, this does not mean that the commons is defined by the nature or type of proprietary control. Sometimes a commons is public property in a proprietary sense (as with public parks and public streets) and sometimes it is not (as with some natural resources but also ideas, theories, and literature in the public domain in the United States). Either way, the idea is that all members of the community have a collective stake in a commons, and because of this it is either freely available to everyone or available at a nominal price that is charged in an even-handed manner.[10] And beyond this, a commons has to do with the fact that we have stakes in the well-being of the earth as one of the species that inhabit it.

The task of systematically sorting through these combinations of proprietary and habitational forms of stakeholding is one for a different inquiry. In any case, the policy details are best left to the deliberative processes of democratic politics. So I will confine myself to five points concerning the general theoretical framework of stakeholding.

First, recognition of the habitational dimension of stakeholding changes the way in which we discuss and justify the proprietary control of assets. I would argue that it creates the presumption that the design and implementation of legal, public, and institutional policy in the area of property will include responsibilities for policymakers to define and serve the interests of the inhabitants of the relevant property locations.

Second, the "interests" of the inhabitants of property locations include responsibilities as well as rights and entitlements.[11] There is of course a general obligation for individuals to uphold the rules and norms of the various stakeholding systems in which they participate. But there are also specific responsibilities that apply to the acquisition, use, or care of particular stakes in particular locations of stakeholding—for instance, being a good steward of a commons, respecting the stakes of other members of a stakeholding community, being truthful in applying for stakes that are granted on the basis of need, and making good faith efforts to avoid becoming an unnecessary burden on the stakeholding community. The connection between rights and responsibilities exists in both the proprietary and the habitational modes of stakeholding. But it is especially pronounced in the habitational mode because in this mode the stake itself is defined and deeply conditioned by the moral and civic ends it is meant to serve. As always, there is danger here as well. That is to say, habitational stakeholding can, in the absence of adequate guarantees of equal rights and equal respect for the dignity of stakeholders, place too high and too exclusionary a premium on the capacity of stakeholders to serve the ends of their stakeholding community or institution. When this happens, we are faced once again with the kind of relational hierarchy that gives rise to the problem of republican paternalism. I will have more to say about this later.

Third, stakeholding interests are defined as much in functional terms as in terms of the institutional or physical boundaries of inhabitation. The boundaries of inhabitation certainly matter in this regard. For instance, it makes sense to give workers in a company more of a stake in its governance than far-flung consumers. Even so, consumers have certain stakes in things like the safety of the products they buy.

Fourth, recognition of the habitational mode of stakeholding opens up the possibility of a variety of overlapping stakeholding locations. These locations range from households to the earth itself, with a multitude of locations in between. This takes us well beyond the one-size-fits-all model of proprietary stakeholding proposed by Ackerman and Alstott. But emphasis also needs to be placed on the fact that we are dealing with *overlapping* locations of stakeholding. There is no neat institutional topography with clearly demarcated boundaries between stakeholding locations. Thus, when we inhabit our households, workplaces, markets, schools, or libraries, we also always inhabit planet Earth, and we always have a stake in the sustainability of the environment it provides for us. By the same token, there will be overlapping purposes. To supplement the goods and capabilities of household stakeholding with some forms of social welfare will also serve some civic purposes in supporting the life and liberty of citizens. For example, to provide homeless members of the political community with access to housing is to recognize and support their habitational rights and needs as citizens as well as their human rights and needs.

Fifth, then, there is an important sphere of stakeholding that is specifically concerned with the capabilities and goods of democratic citizenship. This is what I have been calling the civic infrastructure. In a conceptual and normative universe dominated by dichotomies of private versus public and the market versus the state, the civic infrastructure has often been pushed aside and neglected. Yet the civic infrastructure is one of the most important elements of a democratic theory of property.

The Civic Infrastructure

In general, the civic infrastructure has to do with property-related locations that protect, encourage, and develop important civic capabilities and virtues. This means that the civic infrastructure is closely related to, but also conceptually distinguishable from, two other concepts that are part of the theory of a democratic commonwealth. One of these is the concept of civil society, while the other is the concept of the commons.

The standard way of conceptualizing civil society in the literature is in terms of an institutional topography that separates it from the capitalist market on the one hand and the state on the other.[12] The assumption seems to be that property belongs in the sphere of the market. But this assumption becomes untenable once property is understood as a formative location of citizenship as well as an object of acquisition and exchange; indeed, the placeness of property blurs many of the lines between the market, civil society, and the state. The property-related locations of the civic infrastructure overlap with and also support the voluntary associations that are celebrated by students of civil society as sources of trust and social capital. At the same time, though, the civic infrastructure reveals a layer of support for democracy that is far more institutionalized than the associational life of civil society. And this of course is due in large part to the institutional structure that is created by proprietary and habitational stakeholding.

As we have already seen, some of the stakes in a democratic commonwealth will be stakes that are part of the commons. But there will be many other civic stakes that will not take this form. In a late modern liberal democracy, there will be (one hopes) many different locations and purposes of stakeholding. The key theoretical point is always the use value of different kinds and arrangements of property in relation to the capabilities and virtues of democratic citizenship.

I have in mind capabilities and virtues that are internal civic goods in that they are integral to either the common civic good of democratic public liberty or the civic practices that surround it. There are many such civic capabilities and virtues. They include, but are not necessarily limited to, the following: civility; a willingness to participate in practices of self-government; respect for democratic forms of authority; vigilance in holding those in power accountable; critical thinking and strong evaluation about social and political issues; respect for the norms of equal and inclusive citizenship; a willingness to explore connections between personal grievances and public issues; respect for the history and traditions of democratic liberty; a capacity to appreciate civic projects and civic celebrations; a willingness to pay attention to politics in both its domestic and global dimensions; an independence of civic belief and judgment; and the capacities for dialogue, deliberation, and collaborative decision-making.

There are two initial points that I want to make about these capabilities and virtues. First, they should not be seen as being part of a perfectionist order of moral ends and goods. The capabilities and virtues in the above list are not always in harmony with one another, let alone with other categories of ends and goods in a rank order of human well-being. In any case, no one could possibly develop all of these capabilities, and we should not expect them to. What we are talking about is simply institutional and public support and encouragement for an important cluster of human capabilities and virtues. To go much beyond this—to go further in the direction of perfectionism—would be to go down the path of invidious distinctions between citizens. And we know that this path leads to a relational hierarchy of first- and second-class citizens. Such a relational hierarchy violates the fundamental democratic norm of equal respect for all the stakeholders in a given property location.

Second, the capabilities and virtues of democratic citizenship are implicated in a wide variety of property locations. Which is also to say that there is an important formative, civic dimension to many, and arguably, all locations of property in a democratic community. Clearly, as the primary property-related mode of inhabitation, the family household plays an extremely important role in either developing or discouraging the cultivation of democratic capabilities and virtues. And there are other property-related locations and practices that play an important role as well—for instance, neighborhood associations, and churches and other religious organizations.

The question arises, then, as to what distinguishes the civic infrastructure from other spheres of stakeholding? There are essentially two distinguishing characteristics of the civic infrastructure. The first has to do with the fact that it involves locations in which civic identity (past, present, or future) is specifically and centrally implicated in the practices and purposes of stakeholding. It is about *civic* stakeholding. So when stakeholders gather in the locations of the civic infrastructure, they do so fundamentally (if not exclusively) as citizens rather than as family members, personal friends, lovers, companions, neighbors, religious adherents, members of a bowling league, artists, or in any other social role that is not primarily civic in nature.[13]

The second distinguishing characteristic has to do with the civic dimension of the property instruments and holdings in a location of civic stakeholding. This is partly just another way of saying that we are dealing with property locations that serve civic purposes. The crucial point in this regard is that the assets—the economic goods and services—of the property location are developed in furtherance of the internal goods of democratic citizenship. This might be done directly in the sense of assets that directly promote these internal goods. This is the case, for example, with public schools, libraries, museums, the news media, public parks, and civic centers. But the furtherance of internal civic goods might also take the indirect form of providing external goods that promote the development of citizens. Here, the crucial question is whether the external goods are offered to citizens in general as opposed to more personal and private forms of provision. In the context of late modern capitalism, both levels of provision are apt to involve the market system. But at the civic level, we are talking about firms, companies, and businesses whose market activities are geared (at least ultimately) to the provision of products and services for citizens (or citizen-consumers) in general. By contrast, at the personal and private level, we are dealing with provision for particular organizations or institutions by members of those organizations and institutions, as for instance, with household provision by a family member or provision of a private association by a member of the association. Provision at the personal and private level certainly has civic implications, but it does not rise to the level of activity within the civic infrastructure.

Clearly, in an era of global economic interdependence, civic provision will often involve provision through a transnational market. As a result, identification and oversight of the rights and responsibilities of stakeholders will increasingly require international collaboration. Yet this momentous shift to a global context does not obviate the fact that firms and companies continue to produce and provide economic goods and services for citizens in different political communities. And this is the dispositive consideration in terms of the theory of the civic infrastructure.

As Berle and Means recognized back in the 1930s, the "quasi-public" civic dimension of modern economic organizations like the business corporation gives rise to civic responsibilities to the communities in which these organizations operate.[14] At a minimum, there are responsibilities to support the health, safety, and other stakeholding interests of the workers who inhabit economic organizations; responsibilities to uphold rules of fair competition; responsibilities to adhere to standards of consumer protection and safety; and responsibilities of environmental stewardship. The question of when and how much these responsibilities should be internalized as costs of the firms and companies themselves is a technical one that is well beyond the scope of this inquiry. But a democratic theory of stakeholding provides some support for the proposition that the civic responsibilities of businesses should be internalized whenever possible in order to give concrete institutional expression to the relationship between property rights and property responsibilities.

Now, it would certainly make things a lot easier if the distinction between direct and indirect support for internal civic goods was neatly correlated with the difference between direct support through the government and indirect support through the "private" market. But here too a degree of messiness is in order. There are several reasons for this. First, both direct and indirect support might sometimes come from groups in civil society, for instance, non-profit organizations and voluntary associations that provide services to various kinds of groups in need.

Second, there is no simple formula for answering the question of when the government should be involved in providing direct support for internal goods, or for that matter, external goods. This is always a complex matter of determining the importance of the good in relation to norms of democracy and social justice, how well or badly either the market or civil society does in providing this good and meeting the relevant normative requirements, and how much economic efficiency should be traded off to support the relevant norms of democracy and social justice. In approaching these kinds of issues, the question of where proprietary control lies in each particular instance is less important than the question of which kind of proprietary control has the most use value in the achievement of valuable civic ends.

Third, there are cases when market organizations and institutions provide—or should provide—direct support for internal civic goods. The most notable example of this is probably the mass media. For very good reasons having to do with the danger of government control of information, the mass media in liberal democracies are privately owned for the most part. Nevertheless, the mass media are directly involved in several internal civic goods by virtue of their role in providing citizens with access to news and information about matters of public concern. In the United States, the civic dimension of the media is given constitutional support and protection through the first amendment. But because the stakes are so high, and because there are property responsibilities attached to the first amendment rights of media companies, there are also justifications for efforts to check and regulate concentrations and combinations of private media power. Certainly also citizens have good reasons to complain loudly about the corruption of the news that results from market-driven forms of sensationalism and "infotainment." And the combination of these problems of concentrated private media power and commercial corruption of civic purposes and responsibilities provides ample justification for two other items on the progressive policy agenda: publicly funded forms of media and public policies that create and protect spaces for civic dialogue in the media and on the internet.

Finally, the vision of a democratic commonwealth of stakeholder-citizens points toward the goal of expanding the opportunities for community and worker involvement in both the ownership and control of property locations in the market. The presumption is that property is a "general right" of and for democratic citizens, not a "special right" that is reserved only for select individuals or groups of citizens on the basis of special abilities or achievements.[15] In this respect, stakeholding rights are fundamental along with other basic civil liberties and political rights, and clearly the fundamental rights of citizens to be respected and supported as stakeholders are not confined (as they are in much of contemporary liberalism) to the use and ownership of *personal* belongings and possessions. So just as we design public policies to support civil liberties such as freedom of expression and political rights like the right to vote, the agenda of public policy debate should also include public policies that would help to include more citizens in the rights and responsibilities associated with the ownership and control of economic assets. I have in mind policies to promote things like community land trusts, community-based cooperatives, workplace democracy, and employee ownership of firms.

So far I have described the civic infrastructure in ways that emphasize its formative role in cultivating civic capabilities and virtues. This puts a positive-libertarian gloss on the civic infrastructure, which I want it to have. But there are also important defensive purposes associated with the civic infrastructure and democratic stakeholding. The case of concentrated private media power alluded to above is but one example of the ongoing problem of the threat to democracy and democratic goods that is posed by concentrated economic power. Indeed, this threat is especially pronounced in a global economy that is dominated by multinational corporations for whom civic responsibility is an increasingly marginal consideration. But we must also account for the threat to democracy that lurks within the formative aspects of the civic infrastructure. Because the civic infrastructure is built around the institutionalization of property and property-related structures of authority, it will have distributive conditions and consequences that may endanger the terms of equal and inclusive citizenship. A privileged position of authority within a location of civic stakeholding could become the basis for claiming a privileged capacity to rule over other citizens.

Things like economic democracy and expansive property rights have defensive functions in checking these tendencies toward concentrated economic power and republican paternalism. And one hopes that the existence of multiple locations of stakeholding will also help to check these tendencies. But in the end, we must look beyond property to develop a democratic ethic of equal rights. Such an ethic, I now wish to argue, represents a common estate of liberty that provides essential support for the goods of a democratic commonwealth. It is also the source of much of the messiness of democracy.

The Common Estate of Democratic Rights

This brings us back to the possibilities and problems of a neoclassical republican corrective to the communal republican critique of rights. Recall that in the neoclassical republican understanding, rights represent a form of *dominium* that can secure and promote a jurisdiction of independent citizenship. As I suggested in chapter 4, this can become the basis for a redescription of rights in terms of the placeness of democratic citizens being within their rightful jurisdiction. It is this placeness of democratic citizens being within their rights that I hope to capture with the idea of a common estate of democratic rights. This common estate includes fundamental rights of stakeholding along with basic civil liberties and political rights.

By securing a status of being "in authority" to adult members of the political community, a common estate of democratic rights provides protection against the superintendence of authoritative virtue by paternalistic and exclusionary foes of democracy. Rather than running away from property as communal republicans do with their critique of the relationship between rights and property (the R/P thesis), the idea of a common estate of rights builds on the intertextuality of rights and property. Both are forms of *dominium*, and both can provide democratic citizens with stakes in their community, or rather, their commonwealth. Moreover, if "the commons" of a democratic community has to do with those civic resources, assets, and instrumentalities that are held in common and available to all because of their importance in sustaining the ends and purposes of democracy, then it makes good sense to think of democratic rights as part of the commons.

I suspect most contemporary civic republicans would agree that merely getting to the point of having democratic rights viewed as a common estate would be a tremendous advance beyond individualistic and economistic forms of liberalism. Yet this common estate of democratic rights and civic assets must always be defensive and oppositionist as well as formative. And the reason is the same regardless of whether rights and property are identified with positive liberty, non-domination, or (as in my perspective) with both positive liberty and non-domination as a negative condition of positive liberty. The primary issue at stake has to do with the conditions of civic equality that are necessary to sustain a democratic form of public liberty, and this issue has considerably less to do with how exactly we conceptualize public liberty than with how external goods like rights and property are constituted in relation to structures and processes of power, authority, and labor.

The neopopulist Harry Boyte has defined "the commons" in terms of "the collective goods and resources over which human communities serve as guardians and caretakers."[16] This is perfectly valid, as far as it goes. But at this

stage in our inquiry, we know that we have to account for the sometimes problematic relationship between the guardianship of communal resources and
the guardianship of citizens. We also know that history provides us with many
examples of paternalistic and exclusionary forms of the quest for a civic-
minded guardianship of the common good.

In confronting the problem of paternalistic and exclusionary guardianship,
democratic rights to equal public liberty must sometimes have priority over
property. The common estate of rightful and equal citizen jurisdiction carries
with it the possibility of democratic rights being asserted against the kinds of
second-class citizenship that are created by both ancient placeness and modern thingness. To paraphrase Michael Walzer, property must not be allowed to
usurp or displace the power of collective decision-making in a democratic
community.[17]

As was discussed in chapter 6, in these instances, the estate of equal rights
functions as a form of property substitution, meaning that the rights themselves provide an alternative foundation for civic participation than that provided by property. Of course, in a democracy, the relationship between different kinds of rights is both complex and dynamic. And property rights are a
case in point, for in addition to the logic of property substitution there is the
logic of democratic stakeholding in which marginalized citizens challenge
their would-be civic guardians with the rights and the *dominium* that attach
to their propertied stakes in the community.

It might seem that despite my insistence on the priority of the good I have
wound up with a theory that is based on the priority of the right. This is not
the case, however. Rather, I am merely saying that a common estate of rights
is more closely linked to the internal civic goods of democracy than is recognized or appreciated by most contemporary civic republicans, and certainly
most communal republicans. To see what I mean, we need to get away from
the kind of dualistic perspective on instrumental and internal goods that often
accompanies post-socialist political theory. The truth is that even internal
goods have instrumental aspects. For example, the good of collaborative
decision-making is both an intrinsically valuable part of democratic liberty
and an instrument for its realization. By the same token, many of the internal
goods of democratic liberty serve as instruments for the realization of other
internal goods such as justice. This is the case, for example, with the good of
respect for the norms of equal and inclusive citizenship.

But this is not just a matter of analytic congruence. It is also about how
instrumental and internal goods condition each other in the lived experience of citizens. We have seen how this works with regard to the placeness
of property. But the same dialectical process of mutual conditioning goes on
with rights.

The idea of the placeness of rights is deeply at odds with the conceptual and normative polarities that inform the communal republican critique of rights. The grammar of the phrase, "being within one's rights," contains not only the possibility of the property-like fences of separation that communal republicans deplore, but also the possibility of a moral or civic location or standing within the community, as in "being within one's rights *as a citizen*." And with this we move well beyond the communal republican framework of unencumbered, disengaged, rights-bearing individuals versus situated and virtuously engaged citizens.

Even more unsettling for communal republicans is the possibility that fundamental democratic rights cannot be completely subsumed under the category of instrumental goods. Consider the following question: Why should we not think of rights, or at least certain fundamental rights, as good in themselves? True, there is an important sense in which, for example, a fundamental right to participate in politics is only an instrument, a means, for the end of participation. However, it is also part of the grammar of such fundamental rights that they can be valued, and even cherished, for their own sake, that is, apart from any particular use to which the rights are put by particular people who exercise them. This, for example, is what happens when we defend someone's right of free speech even when we find the content of that speech abhorrent. Yet as communal republicans formulate their defense of internal goods (the IG thesis) in relation to rights, such a defense of free speech is itself a potential or even actual form of corruption. For what it involves is the conversion of the *right* of free speech as an instrumental good into an end in itself. And to use Barber's words, that would mean making a "hedonist-individualist concept" an end in itself.

Consider also the goods of oppositionist democratic agency: dissent, protest, and resistance to oppression and injustice. Again, these goods are necessarily instrumental in nature. But in a flourishing democracy they come to be seen as integral to democratic liberty, necessary conditions of this liberty even if not moral or civic ends in themselves.

This transvaluation of democratic rights so that they come to be seen as integral to the good of democracy is not simply a sign of a second-best "patriotic liberal regime." To the contrary, it is a property of democracy that is rooted in the lived experience of democratic citizens.

Communal republicans might respond to this with the rejoinder that such a defense of rights is itself informed by a background understanding of the intrinsic good of human freedom. This seems incontrovertible, and in a certain analytic sense, I think it is. But to leave the matter here is to render the priority of the good as a pristine and almost formal truth without any meaningful hermeneutic or phenomenological connection to the alternative grammatical possibilities outlined above.[18] With good reason, revisionist liberal virtue theorists press the point that it is quite possible for an ethic of rights to be partly constitutive of the good.[19] In other words, it is quite possible to affirm the priority of the good in the larger order of things without reducing all rights simply and unqualifiedly to the status of instrumental goods. For example, Thomas Spragens turns to Kantian moral philosophy in search of a justification for fundamental rights. Of course, Kant is also an important source of deontological liberal thinking about rights. But where deontological liberals draw on Kant's understanding of a rational individual will that obligates itself to obey a moral law that it constructs for itself, Spragens draws on Kant's teleological understanding of the imperative of treating individuals as "ends-in-themselves."[20] Without fundamental "human rights," Spragens goes on to say, citizens cannot be treated with the equal respect they deserve as ends-in-themselves. In this way, Spragens is able to treat fundamental "human rights" as an integral feature of the good of liberalism.

Thus, the internal goods of democracy can be defined at least partly in the idiom of rights, with fundamental rights being a constitutive as well as instrumental dimension of their goodness. Support for this view comes from a thinker who is often cited with approval by communal republicans: Alexis de Tocqueville. What I have in mind is Tocqueville's argument in *Democracy in America* on behalf of the close and even symbiotic relationship between virtue and right. "After the general idea of virtue," Tocqueville wrote, "I know of no higher principle than that of right; or rather these two ideas are united in one. The idea of right is simply that of virtue introduced into the political world. It was the idea of right that enabled men to define anarchy and tyranny, and taught them how to be independent without arrogance and to obey without servility."[21]

Yet the persistence of the problem of republican paternalism means that we must also account for the transgressive aspects of democratic liberty and the need to challenge claims of virtuous superintendence. That is to say, we must account for the moment of oppositionist agency in which the discourse of rights is used to counter the claims of virtue that model republican citizens and leaders put forward on their own behalf. And with this, we come back to the tension between rights and virtue.

It seems that such a tension is itself one of the properties of democracy, and that Tocqueville's synthesis of rights and virtue will never, or more to the point, *should* never be brought to completion. No doubt civic republican partisans will be quick to point out that the history of republicanism also contains examples of the virtue of "the many" being asserted against the rights and privileges of "the few." But the deeper theoretical issue has to do with how rights are associated with being *in* authority rather than being *an* authority in matters of moral or civic virtue. This is the grain of truth in the communal republican critique of rights. That is to say, communal republicans are justified in worrying that rights discourse carries with it a tendency away from goods like civic identification, shared self-government, and even civility. This tendency is hardly confined to the intertextuality of rights and property or the problem of a commercial republic. Rather, it is rooted in the very grammar of rights discourse. To claim a right is to claim an immunity from other people or authorities, or alternatively, a power or privilege to act without interference or encumbrance. To be sure, there are forms of rights discourse—in property law, for instance!—in which rights are inextricably connected to duties. But it seems undeniable that rights often establish arms-length relationships with other citizens by virtue of the zones of jurisdiction and protection that they create, and that with these arms-length relationships (to quote Skinner) rights will sometimes become "trumps" that defeat "calls of social duty."[22] Civic republicans would undoubtedly remind us that this is especially true of liberal rights discourse. But it is also the case that within liberal discourse the idea of rights as trumps applies especially to those fundamental civil liberties such as freedom of speech that do not have correlative duties attached to them to any substantial degree. And I trust that civic republicans and other post-socialists would be leery of efforts to cast such unencumbered civil liberties aside.

This is not the place for a detailed exploration of the grammar of rights.[23] It is enough for my present purposes that we acknowledge that rights discourse contains the potential for what, from the point of view of much post-socialist virtue theory, appears as socially and civically irresponsible freedom.

At the risk of oversimplification, it can be said that contemporary civic republicans have developed two responses to the risk of social and civic irresponsibility within a liberal ethic of rights. The first one emerges from more radical expressions of the communal republican critique of rights, for instance, those put forward by Sullivan, Beiner, Barber, and Sandel in *Liberalism and the Limits of Justice*. This response seeks to minimize the role of rights and focuses on the cultivation of habits of virtuous citizenship as an alternative to the reliance on instrumentalist and individualist concepts such as rights and property. In essence, my argument against this approach is that it fails to account for the vital role of fundamental civil and political rights in securing the civic goods of democracy and that it therefore leaves civic republican citizens at the mercy of the problem of republican paternalism. The second response is a more moderate one that seeks to integrate rights into the project of civic recovery and renewal. This response is evinced in Taylor's idea of a "patriotic liberal regime" as well as in neoclassical republican efforts to bolster virtuous non-domination through the *dominium* of rights. This more moderate approach is also articulated by Sandel in *Democracy's Discontent*, where "respect" for fundamental rights like free speech and religious freedom is described as "a way of cultivating civic virtue or of encouraging among citizens certain worthy practices or beliefs or qualities of character."[24]

The moderate approach has the advantage of getting closer to a dialectical relationship between rights and internal goods. But it fails to account for the complexity of the relationship between democratic rights and civic virtue. One of the implications of the preceding discussion is that rights have some de-formative implications and consequences that cannot and should not be avoided in a democracy. The tendency towards socially irresponsible freedom is not to be "solved" simply by connecting rights to responsibilities and the cultivation of habits of responsible citizenship. For one thing, the transgressive aspects of rights such as civil liberties have deep roots in their grammar. But more important than this, there are some good reasons of democratic theory for the tension between rights and prevailing norms of social and civic responsibility. To try to define the common estate of rights as an attunement to models of virtuous citizenship can only go so far before it takes us back to republican paternalism. My point is not that we must accept overtly anti-social consequences of the type that some libertarian conservatives and liberals say is the price of (negative) liberty. Rather, I have in mind the transgressive aspects of rights discourse in relation to prevailing views of authoritative virtue—the moments of existential opposition to mainstream views of virtue and the common good, the disjunctive and disruptive dimensions of democratic rights talk, and the abrasive shouting of the dissenter and the protester. Simply put, democracy needs some uppity citizens, citizens who are not deferential to the paternalistic and exclusionary practices of those who would be their "virtuous" guardians.

We see, then, that the two instrumental goods that communal republicans complain the loudest about—rights and property—are the two goods that are most important for preserving and protecting the goods of democracy against the danger of paternalistic republican virtue. But then again stakeholding is defined by its virtues as well as its rights. So ironically property shows us that the challenge of addressing the problem of republican paternalism is partly a matter of defending democratic virtue against republican virtue. But it is also a matter of defending democratic virtue against republican rights, for as we have seen, the problem of republican paternalism has a neo-roman form in which being within one's rights as a citizen is defined in part as jurisdiction over those deemed to lack the capacity for civic independence. Virtue in this situation is the virtue of democratic opposition to the rights of masters and master-proprietors.

So we come full circle back to a politics of virtue; or rather, we have moved dialectically and progressively from a post-socialist, republican politics of civic virtue to a democratic politics of civic virtue, rights, and stakeholding.

A Concluding Confession

In the course of this inquiry, I have tried to develop a theoretical perspective on the properties of democracy that is practical in the sense that it accounts for the complexity of the understandings and conditions within the horizon of modern democracy. I believe that the vision of a democratic common-wealth that is supported by a civic infrastructure and a common estate of rights meets this requirement of hermeneutic practicality. Yet in bringing this inquiry to a close I must confess that I am not optimistic about the near-term prospects of political success for such a property-based vision of democracy.

In terms of property itself, the biggest reasons for my pessimism have to do with the hegemony of modern thingness and the economistic view of property as the institutional framework for economic value. But even if we could break free of the dominance of these ways of conceptualizing property, there would still be other obstacles to any attempt to connect left-leaning aspirations for social justice to a stakeholding democracy. Some of these obstacles have to do with threats to democracy in the late modern era while others have to do with an ideological context that works against leftist and left liberal perspectives on property and political economy.

As an American citizen, I am especially concerned about the threats to American democracy in the current era. In combination with increasing economic inequality and the restrictions on civil liberty that have accompanied the "war on terrorism," the apparent resurgence of militaristic imperialism poses a serious threat to the common estate of fundamental democratic rights. But the problems are not just with American democracy; they are global in nature. I have in mind things like the increasing commercialization of political discourse and civic life around the world; the difficulty of maintaining even basic democratic norms of accountability and responsiveness in the face of the predominately corporate form of globalization; the ongoing and indeed increasing danger of environmental devastation; the spread of technocratic models of management and institutional "governance"; and the increasingly placeless nature of civic life. These and related global trends are apt to put tremendous strains on the civic infrastructures of democratic communities around the world. The civic purposes of civic infrastructures will often be in danger of being corrupted by commercialism and a market model of civic life. How long will it be before advertisements in public schools become the norm rather than the American exception to the rule? In addition, it will likely become more and more difficult to support and sustain identification with locations of citizenship, let alone their actual inhabitation.

This perhaps paints too bleak a picture. Certainly, there are important movements of democratic civic activism around the world that seek to check these trends. But in the Western world of liberal democracy that I inhabit, there are also ideological obstacles to the furtherance of a property-based approach to social justice and democratic citizenship. Simply put, the hegemony of modern thingness and economism is associated with the dominance of conservative and centrist perspectives on property and political economy. I trust that it is clear by now that I am by no means an unreconstructed or radical leftist. I am too liberal, too tolerant of capitalism, and probably too much of a late modern environmentalist to qualify for such labels. Moreover, my interest in developing propertied stakes in society is apt to strike many leftists as a quintessentially bourgeois project. Nevertheless, as a liberal with social democratic leanings, my ideological commitments are decidedly left of center, especially with regard to matters of distributive justice and economic and workplace democracy.

Like many on the left, I am concerned that our commitments and our arguments about social and public policy are less and less likely to be heard these days, and less and less likely to be taken seriously when they are heard. As I see it, part of the problem is that leftists and left liberals have, in effect, ceded too much of the conceptual terrain of property and political economy to conservative defenders of free-market capitalism. Certainly, in America, the dominance of free-market conservatism on the right and the preoccupation of the left with post-materialist modes of cultural politics have left little room for theories of ethical materialism and democratic stakeholding. Faced with conservative proposals for a market-based "ownership society," liberals and other left-leaning progressives seem incapable of putting forward an alternative democratic vision, preferring instead simplistic attacks on capitalist materialism, and all the while hypocritically resting on the political-economic reforms and theories of previous generations of left liberals and progressives.

The reluctance of many on the left to be engaged with issues of property and political economy in a sustained manner would be more justifiable if there were no alternatives on the left to a failed collectivism. But there are such alternatives, and there always have been. It is almost as if the left remains caught in the same Trumanesque, Cold War framework of totalitarian collectivism versus capitalist freedom that it once ridiculed, the difference being that the left no longer has the courage of any convictions (whether collectivist or otherwise) concerning a more just or more democratic regime of property. This puts things too baldly, no doubt. Still, it is significant that a large portion of the left has thrown out the baby of property as a category of theoretical reconstruction along with the bath water of a politically and environmentally bankrupt collectivism and a vulgar philosophical materialism.

Yet it is also true that there are enormous obstacles to the efforts of leftists and left liberals to reclaim issues of property and political economy. Some of these obstacles—for instance, the seemingly relentless commercialization of the cultural and political life of late modern capitalism—are the same that face democracy in general. But there are other obstacles that are more specific to the left. I have in mind such things as the following: the erosion of the industrial working class and traditional "workerist" forms of progressivism in the wake of the shift to a post-industrial economy based on services and information technologies; the constraints on union organizing and bargaining as a result of global competition and the international mobility of capital; the difficulty of building and sustaining progressive, left-of-center political coalitions in an era of "new social movements" and non-labor forms of protest politics (e.g., coalitions among different groups seeking recognition in the politics of identity or between environmentalists and more traditional "workerist" and "welfarist" progressives); demographic and fiscal pressures that will make it increasingly difficult to sustain current levels of public spending for even basic forms of social welfare such as old age pensions and (outside of the United States) national health care programs; and a corporate and consumerist media culture that, among other things, sensationalizes and trivializes political discourse and provides citizens with an increasingly narrow range of views concerning issues of social justice and political economy.[25]

And yet it is also true that left-leaning progressives are the victims of their success in opposing the illegitimate translation of private property and wealth into political power and authority. The left helped to create modes of oppositionist agency and culture that simultaneously support democracy and hinder left-leaning movements. As the oppositionist progressive promise is realized, citizens feel free, and to varying degrees, are in fact free to pursue interests and forms of self-expression that once were disallowed by the masters of property. But this also seems to mean that over the long run there is a greater chance of citizens defining their freedom as disengagement from the kinds of issues of property and political economy that have to be addressed if the injustices and inequalities of capitalism are to be tackled. In the meantime, the relentless forces of capitalist marketing step in to take advantage of the possibilities for selling commodities on the basis of how they help us to lead lives free of the worries of property-related forms of authority and control.

As I indicated at previous points in this inquiry, my belief in the tragic qualities of democracy is not meant to be a message of hopelessness and despair. Although I am not optimistic, I am hopeful that the ideas of ethical materialism, placeness, and democratic stakeholding that I have outlined in these pages can play a role in the development of a new kind of progressivism in which issues of economic justice are once again joined to democratic theory. There is also something hopeful about the global context of progressive politics. As Martha Nussbaum discovered in India, there are many cultural settings in which issues of property not only still matter, but also are framed outside the narrow framework of economistic Western thingness. So there is reason also to hope that all will benefit from a global interchange about matters of property and political economy.

In the meantime, though, there is the ongoing existential challenge of going against the political and ideological mainstream. And so those of us who wish to reclaim issues of property and political economy for progressive purposes of justice and democracy must push on, Sisyphus-like, trying to change institutions so that they recognize the rights of inhabitation of those within them. In this struggle, there is at least the consolation of knowing that, these days, it is not those of us on the left side of the spectrum, but the conservative and centrist defenders of a market model of political economy who are doing the greatest damage to our fundamental property rights and the civic responsibilities that accompany them.

Notes

1. Martha C. Nussbaum, *Women and Human Development* (Cambridge: Cambridge University Press, 2000), 156.

2. Bruce Ackerman and Anne Alstott, *The Stakeholder Society* (New Haven, CT: Yale University Press, 1999), 5.

3. Ackerman and Alstott, 11.

4. For an analysis of the issues associated with the question of direct public provision versus transfer payments as well as an argument about the advantages of in-kind transfers over cash transfers, see Liam Murphy and Thomas Nagel, *The Myth of Ownership: Taxes and Justice* (Oxford: Oxford University Press, 2002), 90–93.

5. Ackerman and Alstott, *The Stakeholder Society,* 44 and 76.

6. Thomas Jefferson, *Notes on the State of Virginia,* in *The Portable Thomas Jefferson,* ed. Merrill D. Petersen (New York: Viking Press, 1975), Query XIX, 217.

7. Ackerman and Alstott, 5.

8. Otherwise, of course, the goal of moving past existing models of social welfare would be defeated.

9. Ronald J. Terchek, *Republican Paradoxes and Liberal Anxieties: Retrieving Neglected Fragments of Political Theory* (Lanham, MD: Rowman and Littlefield, 1997), 81.

10. I have benefited greatly from Lawrence Lessig's analysis of the concept of commons in *The Future of Ideas: The Fate of the Commons in a Connected World* (New York: Random House, 2001), 12–13, 20–23, and *passim.*

11. In this respect, something like what the law of landlord-tenant relations calls an "implied warranty of habitability" inheres in all forms of stakeholding, not just in relation to a landlord's obligation to keep his or her property in a habitable condition.

12. See, for example, Benjamin R. Barber, *A Place for Us: How to Make Society Civil and Democracy Strong* (New York: Hill and Wang, 1998); Jean Bethke Elshtain, *De-*

mocracy on Trial (New York: Basic Books, 1995); Robert K. Fullinwider, ed., *Civil Society, Democracy, and Civic Renewal* (Lanham, MD: Rowman and Littlefield, 1999); Robert D. Putnam, *Bowling Alone: The Collapse and Revival of American Community* (New York: Touchstone, 2000); Michael Walzer, ed., *Toward a Global Civil Society* (Providence, RI: Berghahn, 1995); and Alan Wolfe, *Whose Keeper? Social Science and Moral Obligation* (Berkeley: University of California Press, 1989).

13. In this respect, the civic infrastructure overlaps with Jurgen Habermas's "public sphere" of "private people coming together as a public" in contexts of public opinion and public dialogue and debate. However, the two are by no means coterminous. For one thing, Habermas distinguishes his public sphere from the private sphere of property and market exchange, whereas the civic infrastructure comprises property-related civic locations. In addition, while the civic infrastructure includes spaces of public dialogue and debate, it is by no means limited to them. On balance, Habermas's public sphere seems closer to the contemporary understanding of civil society than to the civic infrastructure. See Jurgen Habermas, *The Structural Transformation of the Public Sphere: An Inquiry into the Category of Bourgeois Society*, trans. Thomas Burger (Cambridge, MA: MIT Press, 1989), especially 27–31.

14. See the discussion of their reformulation of corporate property rights and responsibilities in chapter 6.

15. The distinction between "general" and "special" property rights is central to Jeremy Waldron's will theory of property. See Waldron, *The Right to Private Property* (Oxford: Clarendon Press, 1988), 106–15.

16. Harry C. Boyte, *Commonwealth: A Return to Citizen Politics* (New York: Free Press, 1989), 15.

17. Michael Walzer, *Spheres of Justice: A Defense of Pluralism and Equality* (New York: Basic Books, 1983), 300.

18. There is something of a grammatical sleight of hand here as well. What I have in mind is the readiness of civic republicans and other virtue theorists to evoke the notion of rights as a means to something else, while failing to recognize that one could just as easily say that virtue is merely an instrumental good because it is an instrument for realizing the good life.

19. See especially Thomas A. Spragens, Jr., *Reason and Democracy* (Durham, NC: Duke University Press, 1990), 215–20.

20. Spragens, 156–58.

21. Alexis de Tocqueville, *Democracy in America*, vol. 1 (New York: Vintage Books, 1945), 254.

22. Quentin Skinner, "On Justice, the Common Good, and the Priority of Liberty," in *Dimensions of Radical Democracy: Pluralism, Citizenship, Community*, ed. Chantal Mouffe (London: Verso, 1992), 215.

23. But see Richard Flathman, *The Practice of Rights* (London: Cambridge University Press, 1976).

24. Michael J. Sandel, *Democracy's Discontent: America in Search of a Public Philosophy* (Cambridge, MA: The Belknap Press, 1996), 290.

25. On the particular problems faced by socialists and social democrats, see Brad Rose and George Ross, "Socialism's Past, New Social Democracy, and Socialism's

Futures," *Social Science History* 18 (1994): 439–69. Also see the discussion of Swedish social democracy in David C. Korten, *When Corporations Rule the World,* 2nd ed. (San Francisco, CA: Kumarian Press, Inc. and Berrett-Koehler Publishers, Inc., 2001), 98–102. For a discussion of the resulting tensions within identity politics, see Nancy Fraser, *Justice Interruptus: Critical Reflections on the "Postsocialist" Condition* (New York: Routledge, 1997), especially chapter 1.

Bibliography

Ackerman, Bruce A. *Private Property and the Constitution.* New Haven, CT: Yale University Press, 1977.

Ackerman, Bruce and Anne Alstott, *The Stakeholder Society.* New Haven, CT: Yale University Press, 1999.

Adams, John. *Defence of the Constitutions.* In *The Works of John Adams, Second President of the United States,* vol. IV, ed. Charles Francis Adams. Boston: Little, Brown, and Co., 1853.

Alexander, Gregory S. *Commodity and Propriety: Competing Visions of Property in American Legal Thought 1776–1970.* Chicago: University of Chicago Press, 1997.

Allen, Anita L. and Milton C. Regan, Jr., eds. *Debating Democracy's Discontent: Essays on American Politics, Law, and Public Philosophy.* Oxford: Oxford University Press, 1998.

Almond, Gabriel and Sidney Verba. *The Civic Culture.* Boston: Little, Brown, and Company, 1965.

Appleby, Joyce. *Capitalism and a New Social Order: The Republican Vision of the 1970's.* New York: New York University Press, 1984.

———. *Liberalism and Republicanism in the Historical Imagination.* Cambridge, MA: Harvard University Press, 1992.

Arendt, Hannah. *Between Past and Future.* New York: Penguin Books, 1954.

———. *The Human Condition.* Chicago: University of Chicago Press, 1958.

———. *On Revolution.* New York: Viking Press, 1963.

———. *The Origins of Totalitarianism,* 3rd ed. New York: Harcourt Brace Jovanovich, 1973.

Aristotle. *Politics,* edited and translated by Ernest Barker. London: Oxford University Press, 1975.

Ashcraft, Richard. *Revolutionary Politics and Locke's Two Treatises of Government.* Princeton, NJ: Princeton University Press, 1986.

Bailyn, Bernard. *The Ideological Origins of the American Revolution.* Cambridge, MA: Belknap Press, 1967.

Banning, Lance. *The Jeffersonian Persuasion: Evolution of a Party Ideology.* Ithaca, NY: Cornell University Press, 1978.

———. *The Sacred Fire of Liberty: James Madison and the Founding of the Federal Republic.* Ithaca, NY: Cornell University Press, 1995.

Barber, Benjamin R. *Strong Democracy: Participatory Politics for a New Age.* Berkeley, CA: University of California Press, 1984.

———. "Liberal Democracy and the Costs of Consent." In *Liberalism and the Moral Life,* edited by Nancy Rosenblum. Cambridge, MA: Harvard University Press, 1989.

———. *A Passion for Democracy: American Essays.* Princeton, NJ: Princeton University Press, 1998.

———. *A Place for Us: How to Make Society Civil and Democracy Strong.* New York: Hill and Wang, 1998.

Beiner, Ronald. *What's the Matter with Liberalism?* Berkeley, CA: University of California Press, 1992.

———. *Philosophy in a Time of Lost Spirit.* Toronto: University of Toronto Press, 1997.

———. "Introduction: The Quest for a Post-Liberal Philosophy." In *Debating Democracy's Discontent: Essays on American Politics, Law, and Public Philosophy,* edited by Anita L. Allen and Milton C. Regan, Jr. Oxford: Oxford University Press, 1998.

———. *Liberalism, Nationalism, Citizenship: Essays on the Problem of Political Community.* Vancouver: UBC Press, 2003.

Bellah, Robert N. "Citizenship, Diversity, and the Search for the Common Good." In *"The Constitution of the People": Reflections on Citizens and Civil Society,* edited by Robert E. Calvert. Lawrence, KS: University Press of Kansas, 1991.

Bellah, Robert N., Richard Madsen, William M. Sullivan, Ann Swidler, and Steven M. Tipton. *The Good Society.* New York: Alfred A. Knopf, 1991.

———. *Habits of the Heart: Individualism and Commitment in American Life.* 2nd ed. Berkeley, CA: University of California Press, 1996.

Benhabib, Seyla. *Situating the Self: Gender, Community, and Postmodernism in Contemporary Ethics.* New York: Routledge, 1992.

———. *The Reluctant Modernism of Hannah Arendt.* Thousand Oaks, CA: Sage Publications, 1996.

Berle Jr., Adolf and Gardiner C. Means, *The Modern Corporation and Private Property.* New York: Commerce Clearing House, Inc., 1932.

Bloch, Ruth H. "The Gendered Meanings of Virtue." *Signs* 13 (1987): 37–58.

Booth, William J. "The New Household Economy." *American Political Science Review* 85 (1991): 113–29.

Boyte, Harry C. *Commonwealth: A Return to Citizen Politics.* New York: Free Press, 1989.

Burtt, Shelly. *Virtue Transformed: Political Argument in England, 1688–1740.* Cambridge: Cambridge University Press, 1992.

Canovan, Margaret. *Hannah Arendt: A Reinterpretation of Her Thought*. Cambridge: Cambridge University Press, 1992.

Cohen, Morris R. "Property and Sovereignty." In *Readings in Jurisprudence and Legal Philosophy*, edited by Morris R. Cohen and Felix S. Cohen. New York: Prentice-Hall, 1951.

Cohler, Anne M. *Montesquieu's Comparative Politics and the Spirit of American Constitutionalism*. Lawrence, KS: University Press of Kansas, 1988.

Connelly, William E. *Politics and Ambiguity*. Madison, WI: University of Wisconsin Press, 1987.

Dagger, Richard. *Civic Virtues: Rights, Citizenship, and Republican Liberalism*. New York: Oxford University Press, 1997.

Dahl, Robert A. *Democracy and Its Critics*. New Haven, CT: Yale University Press, 1989.

Damico, Alfonso J. "The Democratic Consequences of Liberalism." In *Liberals on Liberalism*, edited by Alfonso J. Damico. Totowa, NJ: Rowman and Littlefield, 1986.

Dietz, Mary G. "Citizenship with a Feminist Face: The Problem with Maternal Thinking." *Political Theory* 13 (1985): 19–37.

———. "Patriotism." In *Political Innovation and Conceptual Change*, edited by Terence Ball, James Farr, and Russell Hanson. Cambridge: Cambridge University Press, 1989.

Diggens, John P. *The Lost Soul of American Politics: Virtue, Self-Interest, and the Foundations of Liberalism*. Chicago: University of Chicago Press, 1984.

Douglass, Frederick. "What to the Slave Is the Fourth of July?: An Address Delivered in Rochester, New York, on 5 July 1852." In *The Frederick Douglass Papers*, vol. 2 of *Series One: Speeches, Debates, Interviews*, edited by John W. Blassingame. New Haven, CT: Yale University Press, 1982.

Dunn, John. *The Political Thought of John Locke: An Historical Account of the Argument of the 'Two Treatises of Government'*. Cambridge: Cambridge University Press, 1969.

———. *Locke*. Oxford: Oxford University Press, 1984.

Elshtain, Jean Bethke. *Public Man, Private Woman: Women in Social and Political Thought*. Princeton, NJ: Princeton University Press, 1981.

———. "Antigone's Daughters." *Democracy* 2 (1982): 46–59.

———. "The Communitarian Individual." In *New Communitarian Thinking: Persons, Virtues, Institutions, and Families*, edited by Amitai Etzioni. Charlottesville, VA: University Press of Virginia, 1995.

———. *Democracy on Trial*. New York: Basic Books, 1995.

Epstein, Richard. *Takings: Private Property and the Power of Eminent Domain*. Cambridge, MA: Harvard University Press, 1985.

Fink, Leon. *Workingmen's Democracy: The Knights of Labor and American Politics*. Urbana, IL: University of Illinois Press, 1983.

———. "The New Labor History and the Powers of Historical Pessimism." *The Journal of American History* 75 (1988): 114–40.

Flathman, Richard E. *The Practice of Rights*. London: Cambridge University Press, 1976.

———. *The Practice of Political Authority: Authority and the Authoritative*. Chicago: University of Chicago Press, 1980.

———. *Towards a Liberalism* . . . Ithaca, NY: Cornell University Press, 1989.

———. "Citizenship and Authority: A Chastened View of Citizenship." In *Theorizing Citizenship*, edited by Ronald Beiner. Albany, NY: State University Press of New York, 1995.

Foner, Eric. *Tom Paine and Revolutionary America*. New York: Oxford University Press, 1976.

Forbath, William E. "The Ambiguities of Free Labor: Labor and Law in the Gilded Age." *Wisconsin Law Review* (1985): 777–815.

Fowler, Robert Booth. *The Dance with Community: The Contemporary Debate in American Political Thought*. Lawrence, KS: University Press of Kansas, 1991.

Fox, Russell Arben. "Confucianism and Communitarianism in a Liberal Democratic World." In *Border Crossings: Toward a Comparative Political Theory*, edited by Fred Dallmayr. Lanham, MD: Lexington Books, 1999.

Fraser, Nancy. *Justice Interruptus: Critical Reflections on the "Postsocialist" Condition*. New York: Routledge, 1997.

Friedman, Milton. *Capitalism and Freedom*. Chicago: University of Chicago Press, 1962.

Friedman, Richard B. "On the Concept of Authority in Political Philosophy." In *Concepts in Social and Political Philosophy*, edited by Richard E. Flathman. New York: Macmillan, 1973.

Fullinwider, Robert K., ed. *Civil Society, Democracy, and Civic Renewal*. Lanham, MD: Rowman and Littlefield, 1999.

Gadamer, Hans-Georg. *Truth and Method*, 2nd ed. New York: Crossroad, 1989.

Galston, William A. *Liberal Purposes: Goods, Virtues, and Diversity in the Liberal State*. Cambridge: Cambridge University Press, 1991.

———. *Liberalism and Pluralism: The Implications of Value Pluralism for Political Theory and Practice*. Cambridge: Cambridge University Press, 2002.

Galston, William A. and Peter Levine. "America's Civic Condition: A Glance at the Evidence." In *Community Works*, edited by E. J. Dionne. Washington: Brookings, 1998.

Giddens, Anthony. *Beyond Left and Right: The Future of Radical Politics*. Stanford, CA: Stanford University Press, 1994.

———. *The Third Way: The Renewal of Social Democracy*. Malden, MA: Polity Press, 1998.

Gill, Emily R. "Goods, Virtues, and the Constitution of the Self." In *Liberals on Liberalism*, edited by Alfonso J. Damico. Totowa, NJ: Rowman and Littlefield, 1986.

Goodwyn, Lawrence. *The Populist Moment: A Short History of the Agrarian Revolt in America*. Oxford: Oxford University Press, 1978.

Gordon, Thomas and John Trenchard. *Cato's Letters*. In *The English Libertarian Heritage*, edited by David L. Jacobsen. Indianapolis, IN: Bobbs-Merrill Company, 1965.

Gould, Carol C. *Rethinking Democracy: Freedom and Social Cooperation in Politics, Economy, and Society*. Cambridge: Cambridge University Press, 1990.

———. "Feminism and Democratic Community Revisited." In *Democratic Community*. Vol. XXXV of *Nomos*, edited by John Chapman and Ian Shapiro. New York: New York University Press, 1993.

Green, Judith M. *Deep Democracy: Community, Diversity, and Transformation*. Lanham, MD: Rowman and Littlefield, 1999.

Grey, Thomas C. "The Disintegration of Property." In *Property*, vol. XXII of *Nomos*, edited by Roland Pennock and John Chapman. New York: New York University Press, 1980.

Gundersen, Joan R. "Independence, Citizenship, and the American Revolution." *Signs* 13 (1987): 59–77.

Gutmann, Amy. "Communitarian Critics of Liberalism." *Philosophy and Public Affairs* 14 (1985): 308–22.

———. *Identity in Democracy*. Princeton, NJ: Princeton University Press, 2003.

Haar, Charles M. and Lance Liebman. *Property and Law*. Boston: Little, Brown, and Company, 1977.

Habermas, Jurgen. *The Philosophical Discourse of Modernity: Twelve Lectures*, translated by Frederick Lawrence. Cambridge, MA: MIT Press, 1987.

———. *The Structural Transformation of the Public Sphere: An Inquiry into a Category of Bourgeois Society*, translated by Thomas Burger. Cambridge, MA: MIT Press, 1989.

———. *Between Facts and Norms: Contributions to a Discourse Theory of Law and Democracy*, translated by William Roeg. Cambridge, MA: MIT Press, 1996.

Hardt, Michael and Antonio Negri. *Empire*. Cambridge, MA: Harvard University Press, 2000.

Harrington, James. *The Commonwealth of Oceana*. In *The Political Works of James Harrington*, edited by J. G. A. Pocock. Cambridge: Cambridge University Press, 1977.

———. *A System of Politics Delineated in Short and Easy Aphorisms. Published from the Author's Own Manuscript*. In *The Political Works of James Harrington*, edited by J. G. A. Pocock. Cambridge: Cambridge University Press, 1977.

Hattam, Victoria C. *Labor Visions and State Power: The Origins of Business Unionism in the United States*. Princeton, NJ: Princeton University Press, 1993.

Heidegger, Martin. "Building Dwelling Thinking." In *Martin Heidegger: Basic Writings*, edited by David Farrell Krell. New York: Harper and Row, 1977.

Herzog, Don. "Some Questions for Republicans." *Political Theory* 14 (1986): 473–93.

Hirsch, H. N. "The Threnody of Liberalism: Constitutional Liberty and the Renewal of Community." *Political Theory* 14 (1986): 423–49.

Hirschman, Albert O. *The Passions and the Interests: Political Arguments for Capitalism Before Its Triumph*. Princeton, NJ: Princeton University Press, 1977.

Hobbes, Thomas. *Leviathan*. London: Penguin Books, 1968.

Hobhouse, L. T. "The Historical Evolution of Property, in Fact and Idea." In *Property: Its Duties and Rights*. London: Macmillan and Co., 1913.

Hofstadter, Richard. *The Progressive Historians: Turner, Beard, Parrington*. New York: Vintage Books, 1970.

Honig, Bonnie. *Political Theory and the Displacement of Politics*. Ithaca, NY: Cornell University Press, 1993.

Honohan, Iseult. *Civic Republicanism*. London: Routledge, 2002.

Hont, Istvan. "Free Trade and the Economic Limits to National Politics: Neo-Machiavellian Political Economy Reconsidered." In *The Economic Limits to Politics*, edited by John Dunn. Cambridge: Cambridge University Press, 1990.

Hont, Istvan and Michael Ignatieff. "Needs and Justice in the *Wealth of Nations*: An Introductory Essay," in *Wealth and Virtue: The Shaping of Political Economy in the Scottish Enlightenment*, edited by Istvan Hont and Michael Ignatieff. Cambridge: Cambridge University Press, 1983.

Houston, Alan Craig. *Algernon Sydney and the Republican Heritage in England and America*. Princeton, NJ: Princeton University Press, 1991.

Hudson, William E. *American Democracy in Peril*, 3rd ed. New York: Chatham House Publishers, 2001.

Ignatieff, Michael. "The Myth of Citizenship." In *Theorizing Citizenship*, edited by Ronald Beiner. Albany, NY: State University of New York Press, 1995.

Issac, Jeffrey C. "Republicanism vs. Liberalism? A Reconsideration." *History of Political Thought* 9 (1988): 349–77.

Jefferson, Thomas. *Notes on the State of Virginia*. In *The Portable Thomas Jefferson*, edited by Merrill D. Petersen. New York: Viking Press, 1975.

Jones, Gareth Stedman. *Languages of Class: Studies in English Working Class History 1832–1982*. Cambridge: Cambridge University Press, 1983.

Kateb, George. *Hannah Arendt: Politics, Conscience, Evil*. Totowa, NJ: Rowman and Littlefield Publishers, 1984.

Kazin, Michael. *The Populist Persuasion: An American History*. New York: Basic Books, 1995.

Kemmis, Daniel. *Community and the Politics of Place*. Norman, OK: University of Oklahoma Press, 1990.

———. *The Good City and the Good Life: Renewing the Sense of Community*. Boston: Houghton Mifflin Company, 1995.

Kerber, Linda. "Making Republicanism Useful." *The Yale Law Journal* 97 (1988): 1663–72.

Kloppenberg, James T. "The Virtues of Liberalism: Christianity, Republicanism, and Ethics in Early American Discourse." *The Journal of American History* 74 (1987): 9–33.

Korten, David C. *When Corporations Rule the World*, 2nd ed. San Francisco: Kumarian Press, Inc. and Berrett-Koehler Publishers, Inc., 2001.

Kramnick, Isaac. *Republicanism and Bourgeois Radicalism: Political Ideology in Late Eighteenth-Century England and America*. Ithaca, NY: Cornell University Press, 1990.

Kraut, Richard. *Aristotle on the Human Good*. Princeton, NJ: Princeton University Press, 1989.

Kundera, Milan. *The Unbearable Lightness of Being*. New York: Harper and Row, 1984.

Kymlicka, Will. *Liberalism, Community, and Culture*. Oxford: Oxford University Press, 1989.

———. "Liberal Individualism and Liberal Neutrality." *Ethics* 99 (1989): 883–905.

———. *Contemporary Political Philosophy: An Introduction*, 2nd ed. Oxford: Oxford University Press, 2002.

Lasch, Christopher. *The True and Only Heaven: Progress and Its Critics*. New York: W. W. Norton and Company, 1991.

Lessig, Lawrence. *The Future of Ideas: The Fate of the Commons in a Connected World*. New York: Random House, 2001.

Locke, John. *Two Treatises of Government*, ed. Peter Laslett, 2nd ed. Cambridge: Cambridge University Press, 1967.

Macedo, Stephen. *Liberal Virtues: Citizenship, Virtue, and Community in Liberal Constitutionalism*. Oxford: Clarendon Press, 1990.

MacIntyre, Alasdair. *After Virtue: A Study in Moral Theory*, 2nd ed. Notre Dame, IN: University of Notre Dame Press, 1984.

———. *Dependent Rational Animals: Why Human Beings Need the Virtues*. La Salle, IL: Open Court Publishing, 1999.

MacPherson, C. B. *The Political Theory of Possessive Individualism: Hobbes to Locke*. Oxford: At the Clarendon Press, 1962.

———. *Democratic Theory: Essays in Retrieval*. London: Oxford University Press, 1973.

Madison, James. *Notes of the Debates in the Federal Convention*. New York: W. W. Norton and Company, 1966.

Mansbridge, Jane. *Beyond Adversary Democracy*. Chicago: University of Chicago Press, 1983.

Marx, Karl. "On the Jewish Question." In *The Marx-Engels Reader*, edited by Robert C. Tucker. New York: W. W. Norton and Company, 1972.

———. "Theses on Feuerbach." In *The Marx-Engels Reader*, edited by Robert C. Tucker. New York: W. W. Norton and Company, 1972.

McCoy, Drew R. *The Elusive Republic: Political Economy in Jeffersonian America*. Chapel Hill, NC: University of North Carolina Press, 1980.

McDonald, Forrest. *Novus Ordo Seclorum: The Intellectual Origins of the Constitution*. Lawrence, KS: University of Kansas Press, 1985.

McWilliams, Wilson Carey. "On Equality and the Moral Foundation of Community." In *The Moral Foundation of the American Republic*, edited by Robert H. Horwitz. Charlottesville, VA: University of Virginia Press, 1986.

Michelman, Frank I. "Property as a Constitutional Right." *Washington and Lee Law Review* 39 (1981): 1097–14.

———. "The Supreme Court, 1985 Term—Foreword: Traces of Self-Government." *Harvard Law Review* 100 (1986): 4–77.

———. "Possession vs. Distribution in the Constitutional Idea of Property." *Iowa Law Review* 72 (1987): 1319–50.

———. "Law's Republic." *The Yale Law Journal* 97 (1988): 1493–537.

Miller, David. *Citizenship and National Identity*. Malden, MA: Polity Press, 2000.

Minogue, Kenneth R. "The Concept of Property and Its Contemporary Significance." In *Property*, vol. XXII of *Nomos*, edited by J. Roland Pennock and John W. Chapman. New York: New York University Press, 1980.

Montesquieu. *The Spirit of the Laws*, edited by Anne M Cohler, Basia Carolyn Miller, and Harold Samuel Stone. Cambridge: Cambridge University Press, 1989.

Montgomery, David. *Citizen Worker*. Cambridge: Cambridge University Press, 1993.

Mouffe, Chantal. *The Democratic Paradox*. London: Verso, 2000.

Murphy, Liam and Thomas Nagel. *The Myth of Ownership: Taxes and Justice*. Oxford: Oxford University Press, 2002.

Nash, Gary B. *Red, White, & Black: The Peoples of Early North America*. 3rd ed. Englewood Cliffs, NJ: Prentice Hall, 1992.

Nedelsky, Jennifer. *Private Property and the Limits of American Constitutionalism.* Chicago: University of Chicago Press, 1990.

Norberg-Hodge, Helena. *Ancient Futures: Learning from Ladakh.* San Francisco: Sierra Club Books, 1991.

Norton, David L. *Democracy and Moral Development: A Politics of Virtue.* Berkeley, CA: University of California Press, 1991.

Novak, Michael. "How to Make a Republic Work: The Originality of the Commercial Republicans." In *"The Constitution of the People": Reflections on Citizens and Civil Society,* edited by Robert E. Calvert. Lawrence, KS: University Press of Kansas, 1991.

Nussbaum, Martha C. and Amartya Sen, eds. *The Quality of Life.* Oxford: Clarendon Press, 1993.

———. "Non-Relative Values: An Aristotelian Approach." In *The Quality of Life,* edited by Martha C. Nussbaum and Amartya Sen. Oxford: Clarendon Press, 1993.

———. *Women and Human Development.* Cambridge: Cambridge University Press, 2000.

———. "The Future of Feminist Liberalism." In *Social and Political Philosophy: Classical Western Texts in Feminist and Multicultural Perspectives,* edited by James P. Sterba, 3rd ed. Belmont, KY: Wadsworth, 2003.

Nussbaum, Martha C. "Aristotelian Social Democracy." In *Liberalism and the Good,* edited by R. Bruce Douglass, Gerald M. Mara, and Henry S. Richardson. New York: Routledge, 1990.

Okin, Susan Moller. *Justice, Gender, and the Family.* New York: Basic Books, 1989.

Oldfield, Adrian. *Citizenship and Community: Civic Republicanism and the Modern World.* London: Routledge, 1990.

Pangle, Thomas L. *The Ennobling of Democracy: The Challenge of the Postmodern Age.* Baltimore: John Hopkins University Press, 1992.

Peterson, Tom. "Community Land Trusts: An Introduction." *Planning Commissioners Journal* (1996): 10–12.

Pettit, Philip. *Republicanism: A Theory of Freedom and Government.* Oxford: Oxford University Press, 1997.

———. "Reworking Sandel's Republicanism." In *Debating Democracy's Discontent: Essays on American Politics, Law, and Public Philosophy,* edited by Anita L. Allen and Milton C. Regan, Jr. Oxford, Oxford University Press, 1998.

Pitkin, Hanna F. "Justice: On Relating Private and Public." *Political Theory* 9 (1981): 327–52.

———. *Fortune Is a Woman: Gender and Politics in the Thought of Niccolo Machiavelli.* Berkeley, CA: University of California Press, 1984.

Pocock, J. G. A. The *Machiavellian Moment: Florentine Political Thought and the Atlantic Republican Tradition.* Princeton, NJ: Princeton University Press, 1975.

———. "Historical Introduction." In *The Political Works of James Harrington,* edited by J. G. A. Pocock. Cambridge: Cambridge University Press, 1977.

———. *Virtue, Commerce, and History: Essays on Political Thought and History, Chiefly in the Eighteenth Century.* Cambridge: Cambridge University Press, 1985.

Pollock, Sir Frederick and Frederic William Maitland. *The History of English Law Before the Time of Edward I,* vol. 1, 2nd ed. Cambridge: University Press, 1898.

Putnam, Robert. *Bowling Alone.* New York: Touchstone, 2000.

Radin, Margaret Jane. *Reinterpreting Property.* Chicago: University of Chicago Press, 1993.

Rahe, Paul A. *New Modes and Orders in Early Modern Political Thought,* vol. 2 of *Republics Ancient and Modern.* Chapel Hill, NC: The University of North Carolina Press, 1994.

Rawls, John. *A Theory of Justice.* Cambridge, MA: Belknap Press, 1971.

———. *Political Liberalism.* New York: Columbia University Press, 1993.

———. *Justice as Fairness: A Restatement,* edited by Erin Kelly. Cambridge, MA: Belknap Press, 2001.

Ricoeur, Paul. *Freud and Philosophy,* translated by Denis Savage. New Haven, CT: Yale University Press, 1970.

Robertson, John. "The Scottish Enlightenment at the Limits of the Civic Tradition." In *Wealth and Virtue: The Shaping of Political Economy in the Scottish Enlightenment,* edited by Istvan Hont and Michael Ignatieff. Cambridge: Cambridge University Press, 1983.

Rock, Howard B. *Artisans of the Republic: The Tradesmen of New York City in the Age of Jefferson.* New York: New York University Press, 1984.

Rose, Brad and George Ross. "Socialism's Past, New Social Democracy, and Socialism's Futures." *Social Science History* 18 (1994): 439–69.

Ryan, Alan. *Property.* Minneapolis: University of Minnesota Press, 1987.

Sale, Kirkpatrick. *Dwellers in the Land: The Bioregional Vision,* 2nd ed. Athens, GA: University of Georgia Press, 2000.

Sandel, Michael J. "The Procedural Republic and the Unencumbered Self." *Political Theory* 12 (1984): 81–96.

———. "Introduction." In *Liberalism and Its Critics,* edited by Michael J. Sandel. New York: New York University Press, 1984.

———. *Democracy's Discontent: America in Search of a Public Philosophy.* Cambridge, MA: Belknap Press, 1996.

———. *Liberalism and the Limits of Justice,* 2nd ed. Cambridge: Cambridge University Press, 1998.

Scalia, Laura J. "The Many Faces of Locke in America's Early Nineteenth-Century Democratic Philosophy." *Political Research Quarterly* 49 (1996): 807–35.

Schlatter, Richard. *Private Property: The History of an Idea.* New Brunswick, NJ: Rutgers University Press, 1951.

Schudson, Michael. *The Good Citizen: A History of American Civic Life.* Cambridge, MA: Harvard University Press, 1998.

Schumacher, E. F. *Small Is Beautiful.* New York: Harper and Row, 1973.

Selznick, Phillip. *The Communitarian Persuasion.* Washington, DC: Woodrow Wilson Center Press, 2002.

Sen, Amartya. *Freedom as Development.* New York: Anchor Books, 1999.

Shapiro, Ian. *Democratic Justice.* New Haven, CT: Yale University Press, 1999.

Singer, Joseph William. *Entitlement: The Paradoxes of Property.* New Haven, CT: Yale University Press, 2000.

Sinopoli, Richard. *The Foundations of American Citizenship: Liberalism, the Constitution, and Civic Virtue.* New York: Oxford University Press, 1993.

Skinner, Quentin. *The Renaissance*, vol. 1 of *The Foundations of Modern Political Thought*. Cambridge: Cambridge University Press, 1978.

———. "The Idea of Negative Liberty: Philosophical and Historical Perspectives." In *Philosophy in History*, edited by Richard Rorty, J. B. Schneewind, and Quentin Skinner. Cambridge: Cambridge University Press, 1984.

———. "On Justice, the Common Good, and the Priority of Liberty." In *Dimensions of Radical Democracy: Pluralism, Citizenship, Community*, edited by Chantal Mouffe. London: Verso, 1992.

———. *Liberty before Liberalism*. Cambridge: Cambridge University Press, 1997.

Skocpol, Theda and Fiorina, Morris. "Making Sense of the Civic Engagement Debate." In *Civic Engagement in American Democracy*, edited by Theda Skocpol and Morris Fiorina. Washington, DC: Brookings Institution Press, 1999.

Smith, Adam. *An Inquiry into the Nature and Causes of the Wealth of Nations*, edited by Edwin Cannan. Chicago: University of Chicago Press, 1976.

Smith, Rogers M. *Civic Ideals: Conflicting Visions of Citizenship in U.S. History*. New Haven, CT: Yale University Press, 1997.

Soto, Hernando de. *The Mystery of Capital: Why Capitalism Triumphs in the West and Fails Everywhere Else*. New York: Basic Books, 2000.

Spragens, Jr., Thomas. *Reason and Democracy*. Durham, NC: Duke University Press, 1990.

———. "Communitarian Liberalism." In *New Communitarian Thinking: Persons, Virtue, Institutions, and Communities*, edited by Amitai Etzioni. Charlottesville, VA: University Press of Virginia, 1995.

———. *Civic Liberalism: Reflections on Our Democratic Ideals*. Lanham, MD: Rowman and Littlefield Publishers, Inc., 1999.

Stanton, Elizabeth Cady. "Address to the Legislature of New York on Women's Rights." In *Elizabeth Cady Stanton/Susan B. Anthony: Correspondence, Writings, Speeches*, edited by Ellen Carol DuBois. New York: Schocken Books, 1981.

———. "Home Life." In *Elizabeth Cady Stanton/Susan B. Anthony: Correspondence, Writings, Speeches*, edited by Ellen Carol DuBois. New York: Schocken Books, 1981.

Sullivan, William M. *Reconstructing Public Philosophy*. Berkeley, CA: University of California Press, 1986.

———. "Bringing the Good Back In." In *Liberalism and the Good*, edited by R. Bruce Douglass, Gerald M. Mara, and Henry S. Richardson. New York: Routledge, 1990.

Sunstein, Cass R. "Beyond the Republican Revival." *The Yale Law Journal* 97 (1988): 1539–90.

———. *The Partial Constitution*. Cambridge, MA: Harvard University Press, 1993.

Taylor, Charles. "Philosophy and Its History." In *Philosophy in History: Essays on the Historiography of Philosophy*, edited by Richard Rorty, J. B. Schneewind, and Quentin Skinner. Cambridge: Cambridge University Press, 1984.

———. "Introduction." In *Philosophical Papers*. Cambridge: Cambridge University Press, 1985.

———. *Human Agency and Language*, vol. 1 of *Philosophical Papers*. Cambridge: Cambridge University Press, 1985.

——. *Philosophy and the Human Sciences*, vol. 2 of *Philosophical Papers*. Cambridge: Cambridge University Press, 1985.

——. "Cross Purposes: The Liberal Communitarian Debate." In *Liberalism and the Moral Life*, edited by Nancy L. Rosenblum. Cambridge, MA: Harvard University Press, 1989.

——. *Sources of the Self: The Making of Modern Identity*. Cambridge, MA: Harvard University Press, 1989.

——. *The Ethics of Authenticity*. Cambridge, MA: Harvard University Press, 1991.

——. "The Politics of Recognition." In *Multiculturalism and "The Politics of Recognition,"* edited by Amy Gutmann. Princeton, NJ: Princeton University Press, 1992.

——. *Philosophical Arguments*. Cambridge, MA: Harvard University Press, 1995.

——. *Modern Social Imaginaries*. Durham, NC: Duke University Press, 2004.

Tercheck, Ronald J. *Republican Paradoxes and Liberal Anxieties: Retrieving Neglected Fragments of Political Theory*. Lanham, MD: Rowman and Littlefield, 1997.

Tocqueville, Alexis de. *Democracy in America*. New York: Vintage Books, 1945.

Tronto, Joan C. *Moral Boundaries: Political Arguments for an Ethic of Care*. New York: Routledge, 1993.

Tully, James. *A Discourse on Property: John Locke and his Adversaries*. Cambridge: Cambridge University Press, 1980.

Villa, Dana R. *Arendt and Heidegger: The Fate of the Political*. Princeton, NJ: Princeton University Press, 1996.

Viroli, Maurizio. *Republicanism*. New York: Hill and Wang, 2002.

Waldron, Jeremy. *The Right to Private Property*. Oxford: Clarendon Press, 1988.

——. "Homelessness and the Issue of Freedom." *UCLA Law Review* 39 (1991): 295–324.

Walzer, Michael. *Spheres of Justice*. New York: Basic Books. 1983.

——. "Socialism Then and Now." *The New Republic*, Nov. 6, 1989.

——. "The Communitarian Critique of Liberalism." In *New Communitarian Thinking: Persons, Virtues, Institutions, and Families*, edited by Amitai Etzioni. Charlottesville, VA: University Press of Virginia, 1995.

——, ed. *Toward a Global Civil Society*. Providence, RI: Berghahn, 1995.

Warren, Mark. "Democratic Theory and Self-Transformation." *American Political Science Review* 86 (1992): 8–23.

West, Cornel. *Race Matters*. Boston: Beacon Press, 1993.

Wharton, Leslie. *Polity and the Public Good: Conflicting Theories of Republican Government in the New Nation*. Ann Arbor, MI: UMI Research Press, 1980.

Wilentz, Sean. *Chants Democratic: New York City and the Rise of the American Working Class, 1788–1850*. New York: Oxford University Press, 1984.

Wolfe, Alan. *Whose Keeper? Social Science and Moral Obligation*. Berkeley, CA: University of California Press, 1989.

Wood, Gordon S. *The Creation of the American Republic, 1776–1787*. New York: W. W. Norton and Company, 1969.

——. *The Radicalism of the American Revolution*. New York: Vintage Books, 1991.

Worden, Blair. "Harrington and 'The Commonwealth of Oceana.'" In *Republicanism, Liberty, and Commercial Society, 1649–1776*, edited by David Wootton. Stanford, CA: Stanford University Press, 1994.

Young, Iris Marion. *Justice and the Politics of Difference*. Princeton, NJ: Princeton University Press, 1980.

Zuckert, Michael P. *Natural Rights and the New Republicanism*. Princeton, NJ: Princeton University Press, 1994.

Index

materialism, 90, 96; defined, 29; property and, 29, 32, 71, 94, 97, 104, 265; independence and, 95, 123; relationship between instrumental (external) and internal goods and, 97, 113–14, 119, 126, 183, 213–214, 221, 264–65, 272, 277, 282; sources of, 29, 32, 34. *See also* Aristotle

equality. *See* democratic equality

exchange value, 154, 244, 255, 264

external (instrumental) goods, 7, 32, 36n10, 96–98, 105, 108, 110–11, 113–14, 122, 141, 147, 150–51, 162, 168, 178, 213–14, 221, 278–79, 281. *See also* rights

feudalism, 22–23, 161, 195, 203–4, 207–8, 220

Fink, Leon, 218

Flathman, Richard, 38n26, 210

Forbath, William, 218

formative contexts and conditions of civic virtue, 28, 30, 48, 567, 59, 64–65, 87, 109, 116, 120, 122–23, 125, 131–32, 182, 248, 265, 272, 276–77; civic republicans' neglect of distributive dimension of, 179, 183, 185n15, 193, 211–12; in classical republicanism (*see* distributive conditions and consequences of civic virtue; republican paternalism, problem of)

fortuna, 141, 172

freedom (liberty), 5, 7, 8, 15, 25, 45–46, 50–51; civic republican views of (*see* civic republicanism); civic virtue and, 2, 13–14, 43, 47–51, 56, 63, 103, 105, 109, 125, 146–47, 159, 168, 183, 199; classical republicanism and, 2, 43, 51, 63, 123–24, 133–34, 140–41, 146–47, 159–60; combinations of classical republican and Lockean liberal forms of, 170–72, 174–76, 200–2, 217–19; communal republican perspective on, 32, 48–53, 105–7, 110–12; democracy

(collective self-government) and, 42–43, 46, 48–50, 52, 212, 282; democratic theory and, 13–15; empowerment and, 49–51, 169, 206; ethical materialism and, 29, 95; Harrington's view of (*see* Harrington, James); independence (masterlessness) and, 106, 112–13, 203, 214; internal goods and, 109, 114, 276–77, 282; Iroquois spirit of liberty (as non-domination), 215; liberalism and, 1, 53, 110–13, 159, 206–8, 219–21, 226n49; Locke's proprietary liberty and oppositionist moment, 198, 200, 204–6; Montesquieu's view of (*see* Montesquieu); modern critique of capitalism and, 207–9; negative liberty, 67, 110, 112, 124, 133, 145, 183, 201, 206, 211, 266, 286; neoclassical republican perspective on, 32, 45–46, 50–51, 105, 107, 109, 112–13, 133–34, 144–45; non-domination and, 32, 45–46, 50–51, 109, 113, 124, 140, 168–70, 211, 266, 281; non-domination as negative condition of positive liberty, 67n11, 124, 140, 211, 281; oppositionist moment and democratic form of, 23, 211, 214–15; perfectionism and, 52–53; positive liberty, 32, 46, 48–53, 57n11, 124, 140, 162, 168–70, 174, 194, 206, 211, 223n3, 281; post-socialist perspective on (*see* post-socialist political theory); problems with proprietary model of, 7, 105, 107, 110, 133, 183, 198–99; property and, 5, 16, 25, 110–13, 122, 168, 170, 281, 110, 144, 147, 159–60, 163, 175, 240, 281–82; public (republican) liberty, 2, 9, 12–13, 46, 48, 63, 105–6, 109–10, 112–14, 123–24, 134, 143–47, 159, 163, 165, 174–76, 199, 203, 212, 240, 254, 276, 281–82; relational hierarchy (republican paternalism)

320

Index

21, 26–28, 30, 34, 93, 114, 170, 172,
175, 183, 199–200, 217, 219–21,
227n56, 235, 237–38, 280–83,
285–86; rights of inhabitation, 34,
121, 216, 244, 257–58, 272, 275, 290;
rights of ownership (proprietary
control), 34, 39n41, 121, 198, 230–31,
237, 244; stakeholding and, 39n48,
266, 270–74, 277, 282, 286; true
wealth, 151–55, 174, 245–46, 251–52
(*see also* Aristotle); thingness of (*see*
thingness of property); welfare state
and, 220, 222
property substitution. *See* rights
proprietary stakeholding: civic
infrastructure and, 276; contrasted
with habitational stakeholding,
29–30, 270, 272, 274; relationship to
habitational stakeholding, 273–74;
responsibilities of, 256–57, 274–75;
rights of ownership and proprietary
control and, 221, 244, 268, 270–71,
279 (*see also* property; thingness of
property); thingness of property and,
29, 221, 268, 270–71

race: as a distributive context of
republican paternalism, 165, 179;
racism in republican tradition, 87,
158, 167, 179
Radin, Margaret Jane, 28, 258–59n10,
259n13
Rahe, Paul, 187n41
Rawls, John, 18, 72–74, 79–80, 116–18,
125–26, 137n37, 220–21, 227n56,
231, 239, 270
relational hierarchy, 124, 166, 172, 184,
200, 205, 218, 275, 277
republican paternalism, problem of:
Aristotle and, 98, 128, 139, 141, 147,
155, 155–59; as problem of
interaction of formative and
distributive contexts, 122–23, 125,
130, 133, 138n60, 185n15, 211–12;
commercial republicanism and, 139,

144–45, 161; defined, 10; democratic
equality and, 63, 103, 124–25, 131,
133–34, 143, 194, 211, 282; early
modern classical republicanism and,
63, 124, 143, 171, 180, 210, 212;
Harrington and, 161, 163, 165–66,
171; Montesquieu and, 33, 174–75,
177; placeness of property and, 32,
63, 105, 122, 133, 139, 155–59, 184,
209, 216, 252–54; relational hierarchy
and (*see* relational hierarchy); rights
and, 133, 171, 210, 280, 284, 286. *See
also* civic republicanism; freedom;
guardianship; masters' vision of civic
virtue; problem of a commercial
republic
republican tradition in America, 106,
146, 179, 185n15, 252
rights (equal rights, natural rights):
absence of in Aristotle's thought,
147, 162; authority and, 112, 172,
216, 281, 284–86; classical
republicanism and, 159–60, 171–72,
201; commons and, 281; common
estate of, 281–82, 286–87;
communal republican critique of
(*see* communal republicanism); de-
emphasized in Harrington, 162,
170–72; deontological liberalism
and, 66, 117, 128, 131; external
goods and, 108, 11, 114, 182–83,
221, 283–84, 286, 291n18; formal
equality and, 24; fundamental
rights, 280–81, 283–85, 287; general
versus special rights, 28, 217;
human rights, 275, 284; importance
of for democratic equality (*see*
democratic equality); importance of
in liberalism (*see* liberalism);
internal goods (virtue) and, 214,
282–84, 286; jurisdiction (equal
jurisdiction) and, 113, 133–34, 181,
194, 210–11, 281–82, 285–86; Locke
and, 160, 171, 201; masters' vision
and (*see* masters' vision of civic

virtue); neoclassical republican perspective on (*see* neoclassical republicanism); neo-roman perspective on, 133–34; oppositionist agency and, 34, 147, 205–6, 209, 211, 221–22, 225n22, 284, 286; oppositionist self and, 181, 211; placeness of, 133–34, 281, 283; positive liberty and, 223n3; producer republicanism and, 218–19; property substitution and, 209–10, 282; republican paternalism and (*see* republican paternalism); transgressive aspects of, 284–86; Whig opposition thought and, 171–72

rights/property thesis (R/P thesis). *See* problem of a commercial republic

Roosevelt, Franklin, 207

Rousseau, Jean-Jacques, 83

Ryan, Alan, 25, 148–49

Sale, Kirkpatrick, 89

Sandel, Michael: analytic approach to property, 117–18; civic republican project and, 43; communal republican hermeneutics of identity and, 54, 117–18; communal republicanism of, 45, 47, 49; communitarian view of civil society, 45; critique of possessive individualism in Rawls, 116–17, 125–26, 132; critique of unencumbered self, 32, 43, 49, 115, 117–19, 128; empowerment and, 45, 49, 131; hermeneutics of avoidance and, 54, 116, 185n10; neglect of authority, 115, 127–28, 183; neglect of property, 73–74, 81, 89, 117; perspective on justice, 77, 120; perspective on rights, 106, 117, 128, 285–86; placeness of property and, 118, 127; political economy of citizenship and, 45, 81, 106; positive liberty and, 49–51; post-socialist

collectivism and, 132–33; republican paternalism and, 32, 122, 127, 129, 131; situated self and, 32, 42, 54, 115, 117–19, 128, 137n33, 138n60, 180; theory of guardianship, 32, 36n10, 89, 104, 118, 125–33, 180, 183

Selznick, Phillip, 77, 89, 226n53

Singer, Joseph William, 27–28, 39n41, 235, 259n14

Sinopoli, Richard, 51–52

situated self, 9, 32, 54, 57–58, 72, 86; civic republican critique of liberalism and, 62, 105–8; communal republican hermeneutics and, 54, 57–59, 62, 104, 113, 121, 149; communitarian-liberal debate and, 1–2, 12, 18, 115–16, 137n40; placeness of property and, 9, 105, 115, 121, 132. *See also* Sandel, Michael

Skinner, Quentin: civic humanism and, 46–47, 184n2; interpretation of classical republicanism, 140–41; neoclassical republicanism and, 46, 50–51, 112; perspective on freedom as non-domination, 133–34; perspective on history, 143; republican paternalism and, 134; rights/property thesis and, 112, 285

slavery: American republicanism and, 166; Arendt's analysis of, 240, 242, 253; Aristotle's view of, 98, 108, 150, 155–56; civic humanism and, 166; Douglass and modern opposition to, 205; early modern classical republicanism and, 10, 134, 166–67, 188n59, 188n60; Harrington and, 163–64, 166–69; importance of in Roman understanding of freedom, 133–34, 188n61; Locke and, 200; Montesquieu and, 166; neo-roman views of, 134, 168

Smith, Adam, 173, 204–5, 238

social democracy, 65

Spragens, Thomas, 17, 185n6, 220, 284

About the Author

Erik J. Olsen holds a Ph.D. in political science from the University of Wisconsin–Madison. He is associate professor of political science at Seattle University, where he has received two awards for distinguished teaching. He is co-author, along with Sandra Shane-Dubow and Alice P. Brown, of *Sentencing Reform: History, Content, and Effect*. His current research focuses on the legacy of slavery in the development of modern liberal thinking about freedom, property, and race. When time permits, he plays jazz piano and writes songs. He lives in Seattle with his wife, Saroja Reddy, and their daughter, Rekha.